D1567270

Speeches that Shaped the Modern World

Speeches that Shaped the Modern World

Alan J Whiticker

NEW
HOLLAND

Dedication

For my teachers—especially Peter Connelly, Bob Mitchell, Norbert Egan and Terry Keogh—
who instilled and fostered a love of history in their students … of whom I was just one.

Contents

CONTENTS

7

Acknowledgements

There are many people whom I would like to thank for their assistance in the writing and publishing of this book: Fiona Schultz, Lliane Clarke, Karl Roper and all the team at New Holland; my wife Karen and family for their patience and support in meeting yet another deadline.

Introduction:
The Power of Persuasion

Rhetoric ... is the artificer of a persuasion which creates belief
about the just and unjust, but gives no instruction about them...
(Socrates, quoted in Plato's Gorgias).

Speeches That Shaped the Modern World is not meant to be a definitive list of the 'greatest' speeches of all time—that has been already done by other authors. This collection takes recurring themes such as politics and diplomacy, war and peace, freedom and justice, civil rights and human rights, and puts them into a historical context from 1901 to the more recent past. These themes ring out across the decades but what they have in common is the rhetoric—the power of persuasion.

Although the philosopher and mathematician Aristotle studied the use of language as a tool of persuasion (in *The Rhetoric*, he believed that rhetoric was neither good nor bad, but an art form), Plato argued that 'the rhetorician need not know the truth about things; he only has to discover some way of persuading the ignorant that he has more knowledge than those who know ...' Whether that course of action is 'just or unjust' depends on the character of the speaker and the context of the speech.

An example of the power of speech to move the masses is arguably the greatest speech in the history of mankind—Jesus Christ's 'Sermon on the Mount'. Even if one disregards the religious context of the speech (or even the nature of God) and views Jesus purely as a teacher—or civil rights leader—his words have moved millions during the past two thousand years. These simple words, written and recorded in the gospels, changed the world:

And seeing the multitudes, (Jesus) went up into a mountain: and when he was set, his disciples came unto him:
  And he opened his mouth, and taught them, saying:
  'Blessed are the poor in spirit: for theirs is the kingdom of heaven.
  Blessed are they that mourn: for they shall be comforted.
  Blessed are the meek: for they shall inherit the earth.
  Blessed are they which do hunger and thirst after righteousness: for they shall be filled.
  Blessed are the merciful: for they shall obtain mercy.
  Blessed are the pure in heart: for they shall see God.
  Blessed are the peacemakers: for they shall be called the children of God.

Blessed are they which are persecuted for righteousness' sake: for theirs is the kingdom of heaven. Blessed are ye, when men shall revile you, and persecute you, and shall say all manner of evil against you falsely, for my sake.'

A more contemporary example is Abraham Lincoln's Gettysburg Addresss. Dedicating a National Cemetery on November 19, 1863 on the former battlefield of Gettysburg, Pennsylvania, Lincoln took out his handwritten notes and delivered a speech that lasted barely two minutes:

'Four score and seven years ago our fathers brought forth on this continent, a new nation, conceived in liberty, and dedicated to the proposition that all men are created equal.

Now we are engaged in a great civil war, testing whether that nation, or any nation so conceived and so dedicated, can long endure. We are met on a great battlefield of that war. We have come to dedicate a portion of that field, as a final resting place for those who here gave their lives that that nation might live. It is altogether fitting and proper that we should do this.

But in a larger sense, we cannot dedicate—we cannot consecrate—we cannot hallow—this ground. The brave men, living and dead, who struggled here, have consecrated it, far above our poor power to add or detract. The world will little note, nor long remember, what we say here, but it can never forget what they did here. It is for us the living, rather, to be dedicated here to the unfinished work which they who fought here have thus far so nobly advanced. It is rather for us to be here dedicated to the great task remaining before us—that from these honored dead we take increased devotion to that cause for which they gave the last full measure of devotion—that we here highly resolve that these dead shall not have died in vain—that this nation, under God, shall have a new birth of freedom—and that government of the people, by the people, for the people, shall not perish from the earth.'

These 275 words did not initially resonate with Lincoln's audience but once published in newspapers and journals, over time they (especially the final sentence, 'government of the people, by the people, for the people') have come to define a nation of people. Although Lincoln's Gettysburg Address belongs to a world now long gone, it resonated with the public via the mass media and as such, it can be viewed as the starting point of this book.

This collection of speeches reflect not only the historic events of one of the most cataclysmic centuries known to humanity, they also represent a fair share of the century's heroes and villains, martyrs and monsters. In this book the speeches of Josef Stalin, Mahatma Gandhi, Adolf Hitler, Nelson Mandela, Joseph McCarthy, the Kennedy family, Fidel Castro and Pope John Paul II, are presented side-by-side.

Selecting the speeches that shaped a century of human endeavour is no easy task, not least because any list was always going to be dominated by Americans and men. If modern rhetoric is an art from (although Socrates would disagree) then it is an American art form. The 'public address' is such an important part of American political life that any list of important speeches is dominated by United States politicians. However, these are balanced by the views of civil rights leaders, peace activists, women and voices from other nations—15 countries are represented here—to provide equilibrium of social conscience and political views.

Although there are only 11 speeches by women they are among the most powerful and influential of the last 100 years. Emmeline Pankhurst, Emma Goldman, Margaret Sanger, Golda Meir, Indira Ghandi, Queen Elizabeth II and the indefatigable Arundhati Roy— speak on everything from women's suffrage to human rights.

Some speeches, such as Winston Churchill's 'Our Finest Hour', John F Kennedy's 'Cuban Missile Crisis' and Martin Luther King's 'I Have a Dream'—which was voted the most important speech of last century—were obvious choices. This book would have been much the lesser had they not been included just because they are so well-known.

Several speeches have become icons of modern history, such as Lou Gehrig's 'Farewell to Baseball', Neil Armstrong's 'One Small Step' and Douglas MacArthur's 'Old Soldiers Never Die'.

Some, such as Soviet leader Nikita Khrushchev's denouncement of Stalin, German Cardinal Clement von Galen's criticism of Hitler and George S. Patton's D-Day address to his troops, are relatively unknown. Others still—Teddy Roosevelt's 'The Man with the Muck-rake', Dwight D Eisenhower's 'Cross of Iron' and Lyndon B Johnson's 'Let Us Continue'—take on a new poignancy and power because of the passage of time.

In this book I have provided an historical context for each speech and a biographical background of each speaker. I have however, wherever possible, avoided offering my own critique of the merits of each speech. Let the words speak for themselves … they are, after all, the *Speeches That Shaped the Modern World*.

The Old World
1901-1919

The Duke of
Cornwall and York
'The Opening of
the Australian Federal Parliament'
Exhibition Building, Melbourne, 9 May 1901.

An illustration of The Duke of Cornwall and Kent at the Inauguration Ceremony
of the Commonwealth of Australia in Sydney's Centennial Park in 1901.

On January 1, 1901, a new nation came into being. The Commonwealth of Australia, a member nation of the British Empire, was proclaimed at a ceremony in Sydney's Centennial Park attended by Governor General Lord Hopetoun, the country's newly appointed Prime Minister Edmund Barton, and the members of his Executive Council.

Australia's road to federation—the union of the six British colonies on the continent under one constitution, one flag and one federal government—had started much earlier. In 1891 the First National Australasian Convention in Sydney, New South Wales had drafted a federal constitution. In 1898 referendums in favour of federation were held in New South Wales, Victoria, Tasmania and South Australia while Western Australia (1899) and Queensland (1900) soon followed suit. On July 9, 1900 the Commonwealth of Australia Constitution Act was passed by the British Parliament and received Royal assent from Queen Victoria.

Queen Victoria did not live to see the formation of the first Australian Parliament—she died on 22 January 1901, and was succeeded by her son, King Edward VII. The Australian Parliament met in Melbourne's Exhibition Building on 9 May, 1901, for the first sitting of the nation's newly-elected federal representatives. Australia's First Parliament House was not opened for another 26 years in Canberra (in the Australian Capital Territory) on 9 May, 1927. Sixty one years after that, on the same date during Australia's Bicentenary, the country's new Parliament House building was opened by Queen Elizabeth II.

At exactly 12 o'clock, on 9 May, 1901, the Duke of Cornwall and York (who, 35 years later, was crowned King George V after his brother Edward abdicated the throne) accompanied by the Duchess of Cornwall and York (later the Queen Mother), entered the Exhibition Building. They were alongside their Excellencies the Governor-General, the Earl of Hopetoun, and the Countess of Hopetoun. The orchestra played the National Anthem, not surprisingly, England's 'God Save the King.'

After the Clerk of the Parliaments read the Proclamation to the Senate, the clerk of the House of Representatives read the same Proclamation to the members of that chamber. The Proclamation stated:

'Whereas, by the Commonwealth of Australia Constitution Act, it is amongst other things enacted that the Governor-General may appoint such times for holding the sessions of the Parliament as he thinks fit; and whereas, by the said Act, it is further enacted that the Parliament shall sit at Melbourne until it meets at the seat of Government; and whereas, it is expedient now to appoint the time for holding the first session of the Parliament of the Commonwealth: Now, therefore, I, John Adrian Lewis, Earl of Hopetoun, the Governor-General aforesaid, in exercise of the power conferred by the said Act, do by this my Proclamation appoint Thursday, the ninth day of May instant, as the day for the said Parliament to assemble ...

THE DUKE OF CORNWALL AND YORK

His Royal Highness the Duke of Cornwall and York then motioned to the Usher of the Black Rod to inform the House of Representatives that he, authorised by virtue of His Majesty's commission, desired the immediate attendance of the Members of the House of Representatives. Several minutes later the Members, headed by the Prime Minister Edmund Barton, entered the main hall of the building.

The Hundredth Psalm was then sung with accompaniment by the orchestra. Following a short prayer, the Clerk of Parliaments read His Majesty the King's Commission to His Royal Highness the Duke of Cornwall and York to open the Australian Parliament. The following message from His Majesty, King George V, was delivered by His Royal Highness the Duke of Cornwall and York who advanced to the edge of the dais, placed his hat on his head and read the following speech.

'Gentlemen of the Senate and Gentlemen of the House of Representatives...

My beloved and deeply-lamented grandmother, Queen Victoria, had desired to mark the importance of the opening of this the first Parliament of the Commonwealth of Australia, and to manifest her special interest in all that concerns the welfare of her loyal subjects in Australia, by granting to me a special commission to open the first session. That commission had been duly signed before the sad event which has plunged the whole Empire into mourning, and the King, my dear father, fully sharing her late Majesty's wishes, decided to give effect to them, although His Majesty stated, on the occasion of his opening his first Parliament, that a separation from his son at such a time could not be otherwise than deeply painful to him.

'His Majesty has watched with the deepest interest the social and material progress made by His people in Australia.'

His Majesty has been pleased to consent to this separation, moved by his sense of the loyalty and devotion which prompted the generous aid afforded by all the colonies in the South African War, both in its earlier and more recent stages, and of the splendid bravery of the colonial troops. It is also His Majesty's wish to acknowledge the readiness with which the ships of the Special Australasian Squadron were placed at his disposal for service in China, and the valuable assistance rendered there by the Naval Contingents of the several colonies.

His Majesty further desired in this way to testify to his heartfelt gratitude for the warm sympathy extended by every part of his dominions to himself and his family in the irreparable loss they have sustained by the death of his beloved mother.

His Majesty has watched with the deepest interest the social and material progress made by His people in Australia, and has seen with thankfulness and heartfelt satisfaction the completion of that political union of which this Parliament is the embodiment.

The King is satisfied that the wisdom and patriotism which have characterised the exercise of the wide powers of self-government hitherto enjoyed by the colonies will continue to be displayed in the exercise of the still wider powers with which the united Commonwealth has been endowed. His Majesty feels assured that the enjoyment of these powers will, if possible, enhance that loyalty and devotion to his throne and Empire of which the people of Australia have already given such signal proofs.

It is His Majesty's earnest prayer that this union so happily achieved may, under God's blessing, prove an instrument for still further promoting the welfare and advancement of his subjects in Australia, and for the strengthening and consolidation of his Empire.

Gentlemen of the Senate and Gentlemen of the House of Representatives. It affords me much pleasure to convey to you this message from His Majesty. I now, in his name, and on his behalf, declare this Parliament open.'

And so, in a bloodless recognition of constitutional power, the Commonwealth of Australia was born. Never far from 'Mother England' Australia followed her into both World Wars during the next fifty years, after which it aligned itself more closely with the United States (Vietnam, Iraq and the 'War on Terrorism') whilst searching for its own identity amongst its Asian and Islander neighbours in the South Pacific. Interestingly, when given the chance to become an independent republic in a 1999 referendum (thereby having an Australian as head of state), the majority of Australians opted to stay a member of the British Commonwealth.

THE DUKE OF CORNWALL AND YORK

Mary Church Terrell

'Being Colored in the Nation's Capital'

Speech to United Women's Club, Washington, DC, 10 October 1906.

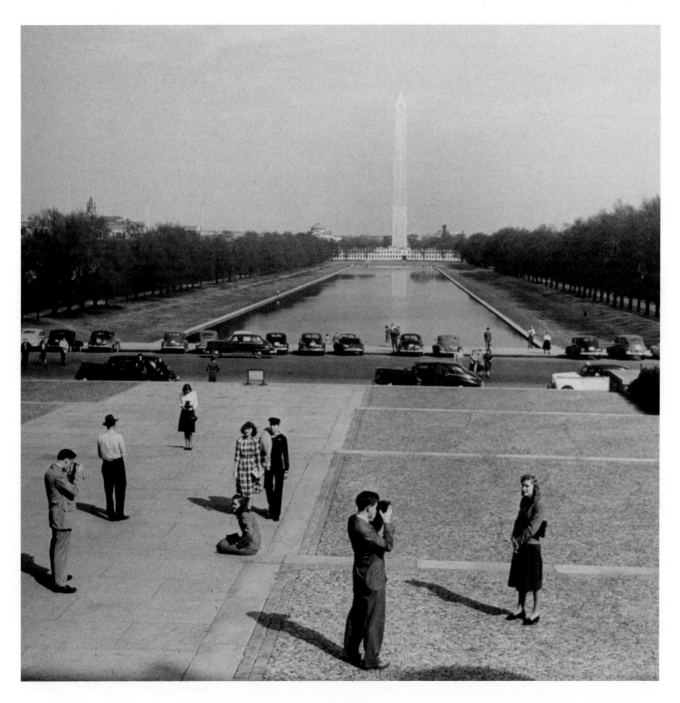

The Washington Monument, Washington DC, in the late-1940s.

The life of Mary Church Terrell (1863-1954) bridged an expanse of history from the emancipation of the slaves in the American Civil War (1861-65) to the US Supreme Court decision to end segregation in schools (*Brown v Board of Education*, 1954).

Terrell spent her life at the forefront of the fight for civil rights. In 1884 she was the first African-American woman to earn a college degree and later studied education in Europe for two years. A high school teacher and principal, she became the first black woman in America to be appointed to an Education Board (District of Columbia).

As the first president of the National Association of Colored Women, Mary Church Terrell spoke out in support of women's suffrage and an end to racial segregation. In October 1906, Terrell addressed the United Women's Club in Washington DC about the discrimination faced by black women because of both their race and their gender. Terrell's speech is considered to be one of the most influential speeches on race in the 20th century.

' Washington DC has been called 'The Colored Man's Paradise'. Whether this sobriquet was given to the national capital in bitter irony by a member of the handicapped race, as he reviewed some of his own persecutions and rebuffs, or whether it was given immediately after the war by an ex-slaveholder who for the first time in his life saw colored people walking about like free men, minus the overseer and his whip, history saith not. It is certain that it would be difficult to find a worse misnomer for Washington than 'The Colored Man's Paradise' if so prosaic a consideration as veracity is to determine the appropriateness of a name.

For fifteen years I have resided in Washington, and while it was far from being a paradise for colored people when I first touched these shores, it has been doing its level best ever since to make conditions for us intolerable. As a colored woman I might enter Washington any night, a stranger in a strange land, and walk miles without finding a place to lay my head. Unless I happened to know colored people who live here or ran across a chance acquaintance who could recommend a colored boarding-house to me, I should be obliged to spend the entire night wandering about. Indians, Chinamen, Filipinos, Japanese and representatives of any other dark race can find hotel accommodations, if they can pay for them. The colored man alone is thrust out of the hotels of the national capital like a leper...

'If I try to enter many of the numerous vocations in which my white sisters are allowed to engage, the door is shut in my face.'

As a colored woman I cannot visit the tomb of the Father of this Country, which owes its very existence to the love of freedom in the human heart and which stands for equal opportunity to all, without being forced to sit in the Jim Crow section of an electric car which starts from the

MARY CHURCH TERRELL

21

'With the exception of the Catholic University, there is not a single white college in the national capital to which colored people are admitted, no matter how great their ability ...'

very heart of the city—midway between the Capitol and the White House. If I refuse thus to be humiliated, I am cast into jail and forced to pay a fine for violating the Virginia laws...

As a colored woman I may enter more than one white church in Washington without receiving that welcome which as a human being I have a right to expect in the sanctuary of God. Sometimes the color blindness of the usher takes on that peculiar form which prevents a dark face from making any impression whatsoever upon his retina, so that it is impossible for him to see colored people at all. If he is not so afflicted, after keeping a colored man or woman waiting a long time, he will ungraciously show these dusky Christians who have had the temerity to thrust themselves into a temple where only the fair of face are expected to worship God to a seat in the rear, which is named in honor of a certain personage, well known in this country, and commonly called Jim Crow.

Unless I am willing to engage in a few menial occupations, in which the pay for my services would be very poor, there is no way for me to earn an honest living, if I am not a trained nurse or a dressmaker or can secure a position as a teacher in the public schools, which is exceedingly difficult to do. It matters not what my intellectual attainments may be or how great is the need of the services of a competent person, if I try to enter many of the numerous vocations in which my white sisters are allowed to engage, the door is shut in my face.

From one Washington theater I am excluded altogether ... [After explaining that] in some of the theaters colored nurses were allowed to sit with the white children for whom they cared, the ticket seller told me that in Washington it was very poor policy to employ colored nurses, for they were excluded from many places where white girls would be allowed to take children for pleasure.

If I possess artistic talent, there is not a single art school of repute which will admit me. A few years ago a colored woman who possessed great talent submitted some drawings to the Corcoran Art School, of Washington, which were accepted by the committee of awards, who sent her a ticket entitling her to a course in this school. But when the committee discovered that the young woman was colored, they declined to admit her, and told her that if they had suspected that her drawings had been made by a colored woman, they would not have examined them at all...

With the exception of the Catholic University, there is not a single white college in the national capital to which colored people are admitted, no matter how great their ability, how lofty their ambition, how unexceptionable their character or how great their thirst for knowledge may be. A few years ago the Columbian Law School [in Washington] admitted colored students, but in deference to the Southern white students the authorities have decided to exclude them altogether...

I might go on citing instance after instance to show the variety of ways in which our people are sacrificed on the altar of prejudice in the capital of the United States and how almost insurmountable are the obstacles which block our paths to success. Early in life many a colored youth is so appalled by the helplessness and the hopelessness of his situation in this country that, in a sort of stoical despair he resigns himself to his fate. 'What is the good of our trying to acquire an education? We can't all be preachers, teachers, doctors and lawyers. Besides those professions, there is almost nothing for colored people to do but engage in the most menial occupations, and we do not need an education for that.' More than once such remarks, uttered by young men and women in our public schools who possess brilliant intellects, have wrung my heart.

It is impossible for any white person in the United States, no matter how sympathetic and broadminded, to realize what life would mean to him if his incentive to effort were suddenly snatched away. To the lack of incentive to effort, which is the awful shadow under which we live, may be traced the wreck and ruin of scores of colored youth. And surely nowhere in the world do oppression and persecution based solely on the color of the skin appear more hateful and hideous than in the capital of the United States, because the chasm between the principles upon which this Government was founded, in which it still professes to believe, and those which are daily practiced under the protection of the flag, yawns so wide and deep.'

'The chasm between the principles upon which this Government was founded ... and those which are daily practiced under the protection of the flag, yawns ... wide and deep.'

The fact that Church Terrell's speech was delivered in the national capital—the centre of American democracy—contrasted the ideals of the country's founding fathers with the realities experienced by many of the city's minorities. Martin Luther King exposed the same paradox 57 years later when he delivered his famous 'I Have a Dream' speech on the steps of the Lincoln Memorial (see Revolution, 1960-69).

In 1953, a year before her death at 91, Mary Church Terrell led a campaign to end the segregation of public facilities in Washington, DC.

Theodore Roosevelt
'The Man with the Muck-Rake'

Laying the cornerstone of the House of Representatives, Washington DC, 1906.

Theodore Roosevelt in 1906.

Theodore 'Teddy' Roosevelt (1858-1919) became the twenty-sixth President of the United States in September 1901 upon the assassination of President William McKinley. He was re-elected for a second term in 1904.

Roosevelt was leader of the New York legislature at the age of 26, and came back from the Cuban War in 1898 as a hero after raising a volunteer army known as 'Roosevelt's Roughriders'. Elected Republican Vice-President in 1900 he was a popular, idiosyncratic public speaker. In 1900 he used a West African proverb that became the motto of his political career: 'Speak quietly but carry a big stick.'

In this famous speech delivered at the laying of the cornerstone of the House of Representatives in Washington DC in 1906, Roosevelt established a new idiom—the muck-raking journalist—when he cleverly compared the political and journalistic 'mudslinging' of his time with a character from John Bunyon's *The Pilgrim's Progress* of 1684. It was a trend that would dominate the mass media during the entire twentieth century and beyond.

'Over a century ago Washington laid the cornerstone of the Capitol in what was then little more than a tract of wooded wilderness here beside the Potomac. We now find it necessary to provide great additional buildings for the business of the government. This growth in the need for the housing of the government is but a proof and example of the way in which the nation has grown and the sphere of action of the National Government has grown. We now administer the affairs of a nation in which the extraordinary growth of population has been outstripped by the growth of wealth and the growth in complex interests.

The material problems that face us today are not such as they were in Washington's time, but the underlying facts of human nature are the same now as they were then. Under altered external form we war with the same tendencies toward evil that were evident in Washington's time, and are helped by the same tendencies for good.

'Hysterical sensationalism is the very poorest weapon wherewith to fight for lasting righteousness.'

It is about some of these that I wish to say a word to-day. In Bunyan's *Pilgrim's Progress* you may recall the description of the 'man with the muck-rake', the man who could look no way but downward, with the muck-rake in his hand; who was offered a celestial crown for his muck-rake, but who would neither look up nor regard the crown he was offered, but continued to rake to himself the filth of the floor.

In *Pilgrim's Progress,* the 'man with the muck-rake' is set forth as the example of him whose vision is fixed on carnal instead of on spiritual things. Yet he also typifies the man who in this life consistently refuses to see aught that is lofty, and fixes his eyes with solemn intentness only on that which is vile and debasing. Now, it is very necessary that we should not flinch from seeing what is vile and debasing. There is filth on the floor and it must be scraped up with the muck-rake; and there are times and places where this service is the most needed of all the services that can be performed. But the man who never does anything else, who never thinks or speaks or writes, save of his feats with the muck-rake, speedily becomes, not a help to society, not an incitement to good, but one of the most potent forces for evil.

'There is nothing more distressing to every good patriot, to every good American, than the hard, scoffing spirit which treats the allegation of dishonesty in a public man as a cause for laughter.'

There are, in the body politic, economic and social, many and grave evils, and there is urgent necessity for the sternest war upon them. There should be relentless exposure of and attack upon every evil man whether politician or business man, every evil practice, whether in politics, in business, or in social life. I hail as a benefactor every writer or speaker, every man who, on the platform, or in book, magazine, or newspaper, with merciless severity makes such attack, provided always that he in his turn remembers that the attack is of use only if it is absolutely truthful. The liar is no whit better than the thief, and if his mendacity takes the form of slander, he may be worse than most thieves. It puts a premium upon knavery untruthfully to attack an honest man, or even with hysterical exaggeration to assail a bad man with untruth. An epidemic of indiscriminate assault upon character does not good, but very great harm. The soul of every scoundrel is gladdened whenever an honest man is assailed, or even when a scoundrel is untruthfully assailed.

Now, it is easy to twist out of shape what I have just said, easy to affect to misunderstand it, and, if it is slurred over in repetition, not difficult really to misunderstand it. Some persons are sincerely incapable of understanding that to denounce mud-slinging does not mean the endorsement of whitewashing; and both the interested individuals who need whitewashing, and those others who practice mud-slinging, like to encourage such confusion of ideas. One of the chief counts against those who make indiscriminate assault upon men in business or men in public life, is that they invite a reaction which is sure to tell powerfully in favor of the unscrupulous scoundrel who really ought to be attacked, who ought to be exposed, who ought, if possible, to be put in the penitentiary. If Aristides is praised overmuch as just, people get tired of hearing it; and over censure of the unjust finally and from similar reasons results in their favor.

Any excess is almost sure to invite a reaction; and, unfortunately, the reaction, instead of taking the form of punishment of those guilty of the excess, is very apt to take the form either of punishment of the unoffending or of giving immunity, and even strength, to offenders. The effort to make financial or political profit out of the destruction of character can only result in public calamity.

Gross and reckless assaults on character, whether on the stump or in newspaper, magazine, or book, create a morbid and vicious public sentiment, and at the same time act as a profound deterrent to able men of normal sensitiveness and tend to prevent them from entering the public service at any price.

As an instance in point, I may mention that one serious difficulty encountered in getting the right type of men to dig the Panama Canal is the certainty that they will be exposed, both without, and, I am sorry to say, sometimes within, Congress, to utterly reckless assaults on their character and capacity.

At the risk of repetition let me say again that my plea is not for immunity from the most unsparing exposure of the politician who betrays his trust, or the big business man who makes or spends his fortune in illegitimate or corrupt ways. There should be a resolute effort to hunt every such man out of the position he has disgraced. Expose the crime, and hunt down the criminal; but remember that even in the case of crime, if it is attacked in sensational, lurid, and untruthful fashion, the attack may do more damage to the public mind than the crime itself. It is because I feel that there should be no rest in the endless war against the forces of evil that I ask that the war be conducted with sanity as well as with resolution.

The men with the muck-rakes are often indispensable to the well-being of society; but only if they know when to stop raking the muck, and to look upward to the celestial crown above them, to the crown of worthy endeavor.

There are beautiful things above and roundabout them; and if they gradually grow to feel that the whole world is nothing but muck, their power of usefulness is gone. If the whole picture is painted black there remains no hue whereby to single out the rascals for distinction from their fellows. Such painting finally induces a kind of moral color-blindness; and people affected by it come to the conclusion that no man is really black, and no man is really white, but they are all gray. In other words, they neither believe in the truth of the attack, nor in the honesty of the man who is attacked; they grow as suspicious of the accusation as of the offense; it becomes well-nigh hopeless to stir them either to wrath against wrong-doing or to enthusiasm for what is right; and such a mental attitude in the public gives hope to every knave, and is the despair of honest men.

To assail the great and admitted evils of our political and industrial life with such crude and sweeping generalizations as to include decent men in the general condemnation means the searing of the public conscience. There results a general attitude either of cynical belief in and indifference to public corruption or else of a distrustful inability to discriminate between the good and the bad. Either attitude is fraught with untold damage to the country as a whole. The fool who has not sense to discriminate between what is good and what is bad is well-nigh as dangerous as the man who does discriminate and yet chooses the bad. There is nothing more distressing to every good patriot, to every good American, than the hard, scoffing spirit which treats the allegation of dishonesty in a public man as a cause for laughter.

'Gross and reckless assaults on character, whether on the stump or in newspaper, magazine, or book, create a morbid and vicious public sentiment.'

THEODORE ROOSEVELT

27

Such laughter is worse than the crackling of thorns under a pot, for it denotes not merely the vacant mind, but the heart in which high emotions have been choked before they could grow to fruition.

'The liar is no whit better than the thief, and if his mendacity takes the form of slander, he may be worse than most thieves.'

There is any amount of good in the world, and there never was a time when loftier and more disinterested work for the betterment of mankind was being done than now. The forces that tend for evil are great and terrible, but the forces of truth and love and courage and honesty and generosity and sympathy are also stronger than ever before. It is a foolish and timid, no less than a wicked, thing to blink the fact that the forces of evil are strong, but it is even worse to fail to take into account the strength of the forces that tell for good.

Hysterical sensationalism is the very poorest weapon wherewith to fight for lasting righteousness. The men who with stern sobriety and truth assail the many evils of our time, whether in the public press or in magazines, or in books, are the leaders and allies of all engaged in the work for social and political betterment. But if they give good reason for distrust of what they say, if they chill the ardor of those who demand truth as a primary virtue, they thereby betray the good cause, and play into the hands of the very men against whom they are nominally at war ...'

'Teddy' Roosevelt won the Nobel Peace prize in 1906 for helping to negotiate an end to the Russo-Japanese War (1904-05) but was not afraid to exercise an 'expansionist' foreign policy during his career. He invaded Panama in order to protect the building of the Panama Canal and intervened in the Philippines, but he was also a vigorous reformer of government social policy and introduced the 'Square Deal' reform. Roosevelt stood as a Progressive Party candidate at the 1912 presidential election but was defeated by Democratic nominee Woodrow Wilson. Roosevelt was a supporter of United States intervention in World War I long before it acted in 1917. He passed away in 1919.

Emmeline Pankhurst
'Freedom or Death'

Fundraising Speech, Hartford, Connecticut, United States, 13 November 1913.

Emmeline Pankhurst in the Battery area of New York, after her release from Ellis Island Immigration Station in 1913.

Emmeline Pankhurst (1857-1928) is arguably the most famous representative of the struggle for Votes for Women. The English barrister drafted the first women's suffrage bill in Britain and founded the Women's Franchise League in 1899.

Pankhurst took the fight for women's suffrage to a new level. Public demonstrations and rallies often resulted in police violence and the arrest of her and her followers. Under arrest, Pankhurst and her fellow suffragettes staged hunger and thirst strikes and had to be force-fed by the police—usually through a funnel thrust down their throats. The police released the women until they were nursed back to health and re-arrested them. The cycle—known as the 'cat and mouse game'—would start all over again. The damage to the women's health was 'astounding', and Pankhurst would often speak at rallies from a stretcher.

In November 1913 Pankhurst made her third 'fundraising' tour of the United States, where her tactics had received widespread publicity since the turn of the century.

‘I do not come here as an advocate, because whatever position the suffrage movement may occupy in the United States of America, in England it has passed beyond the realm of advocacy and it has entered into the sphere of practical politics. It has become the subject of revolution and civil war, and so tonight I am not here to advocate women's suffrage. American suffragists can do that very well for themselves. I am here as a soldier who has temporarily left the field of battle in order to explain—it seems strange it should have to be explained—what civil war is like when civil war is waged by women. I am not only here as a soldier temporarily absent from the field of battle; I am here—and that, I think, is the strangest part of my coming—I am here as a person who, according to the law courts of my country, it has been decided, is of no value to the community at all; and I am adjudged because of my life to be a dangerous person, under sentence of penal servitude in a convict prison. So you see there is some special interest in hearing so unusual a person address you. I dare say, in the minds of many of you— you will perhaps forgive me this personal touch—that I do not look either very like a soldier or very like a convict, and yet I am both.

'I am here as a soldier who has temporarily left the field of battle in order to explain ... what civil war is like when civil war is waged by women.'

It would take too long to trace the course of militant methods as adopted by women, because it is about eight years since the word militant was first used to describe what we were doing; it is about eight years since the first militant action was taken by women. It was not militant at all, except that it provoked militancy on the part of those who were opposed to it. When women asked questions in political meetings and failed to get answers, they were not doing anything militant. To ask questions at political meetings is an acknowledged right of all people who attend public meetings; certainly in my country, men have always done it, and I hope they do it in America, because it seems to me that if you allow people to enter your legislatures without asking them any questions as to what they arc going to do when they get there you are not exercising your citizen rights and your citizen duties as you ought.

At any rate in Great Britain it is a custom, a time-honoured one, to ask questions of candidates for Parliament, and ask questions of members of the government. No man was ever put out of a public meeting for asking a question until Votes for Women came on to the political horizon. The first people who were put out of a political meeting for asking questions were women; they were brutally ill-used; they found themselves in jail before twenty-four hours had expired. But instead of the newspapers, which are largely inspired by the politicians, putting militancy, and the reproach of militancy, if reproach there is, on the people who had assaulted the women, they actually said it was the women who were militant and very much to blame.

It was not the speakers on the platform who would not answer them who were to blame, or the ushers at the meeting; it was the poor women who had had their bruises and their knocks and scratches, and who were put into prison for doing precisely nothing but holding a protest meeting in the street after it was all over.

'We will put the enemy in the position where they will have to choose between giving us freedom or giving us death.'

However, we were called militant for doing that, and we were quite willing to accept the name, because militancy for us is time-honoured; you have the church militant and in the sense of spiritual militancy we were very militant indeed. We were determined to press this question of the enfranchisement of the women to the point where we were no longer to be ignored by the politicians as had been the case for about fifty years, during which time women had patiently used every means open to them to win their political enfranchisement.

Experience will show you that if you really want to get anything done, it is not so much a matter of whether you alienate sympathy; sympathy is a very unsatisfactory thing if it is not practical sympathy. It does not matter to the practical suffragist whether she alienates sympathy that was never of any use to her. What she wants is to get something practical done, and whether it is done out of sympathy or whether it is done out of fear, or whether it is done because you want to be comfortable again and not be worried in this way, doesn't particularly matter so long as you get it. We had enough of sympathy for fifty years; it never brought us anything; and we would rather have an angry man going to the government and saying, my business is interfered with and I won't submit to its being interfered with any longer because you won't give women the vote, than to have a gentleman come on to our platforms year in and year out and talk about his ardent sympathy with woman suffrage.

'Put them in prison,' they said, 'that will stop it.' But it didn't stop it. They put women in prison for long terms of imprisonment, for making a nuisance of themselves—that was the

EMMELINE PANKHURST

expression when they took petitions in their hands to the door of the House of Commons; and they thought that sending them to prison, giving them a day's imprisonment, would cause them to all settle down again and there would be no further trouble. But it didn't happen so at all: instead of the women giving it up, more women did it, and more and more and more women did it until there were three hundred women at a time, who had not broken a single law, only 'made a nuisance of themselves' as the politicians say.

The whole argument with the anti-suffragists, or even the critical suffragist man, is this: that you can govern human beings without their consent. They have said to us, 'Government rests upon force; the women haven't force, so they must submit.' Well, we are showing them that government does not rest upon force at all; it rests upon consent. As long as women consent to be unjustly governed, they can be; but directly women say: 'We withhold our consent, we will not be governed any longer so long as that government is unjust,' not by the forces of civil war can you govern the very weakest woman. You can kill that woman, but she escapes you then; you cannot govern her. And that is, I think, a most valuable demonstration we have been making to the world.

Now, I want to say to you who think women cannot succeed, we have brought the government of England to this position, that it has to face this alternative; either women are to be killed or women are to have the vote. I ask American men in this meeting, what would you say if in your State you were faced with that alternative, that you must either kill them or give them their citizenship—women, many of whom you respect, women whom you know have lived useful lives, women whom you know, even if you do not know them personally, are animated with the highest motives, women who are in pursuit of liberty and the power to do useful public service? Well, there is only one answer to that alternative; there is only one way out of it, unless you are prepared to put back civilization two or three generations; you must give those women the vote. Now that is the outcome of our civil war.

You won your freedom in America when you had the Revolution, by bloodshed, by sacrificing human life. You won the Civil War by the sacrifice of human life when you decided to emancipate the negro. You have left it to the women in your land, the men of all civilised countries have left it to women, to work out their own salvation. That is the way in which we women of England are doing. Human life for us is sacrificed, but we say if any life is to be sacrificed it shall be ours; we won't do it ourselves, but we will put the enemy in the position where they will have to choose between giving us freedom or giving us death.'

'… they actually said it was the women who were militant and very much to blame … the poor women who had their bruises and their knocks and scratches, and who were put into prison for doing precisely nothing but holding a protest meeting in the street.'

Emmeline Pankhurst was detained on Ellis Island Immigration Station, New York during this tour, which was not unusual for her. She was arrested several times during her life—for conspiracy in 1912 and for inciting violence under the 'Cat and Mouse' Act in 1913. (She was arrested twelve times during 1914.) Her call was 'freedom or death' and some took Pankhurst at her word. In June 1913, suffragette Emily Davidson threw herself in front of King George V's horse, Anmer, as it competed in the English Derby. The 40 year old Miss Davidson lingered on for six days before she died—the women's movement's first heroine and martyr.

'We had enough of sympathy for fifty years; it never brought us anything; and we would rather have an angry man going to the government ... because you won't give women the vote, than to have a gentleman come on to our platforms and talk about his ardent sympathy for women's suffrage.'

Despite New Zealand granting women the vote in 1889 (the first country to do so) and Australian women achieving suffrage in 1902, World War I put the issue of 'Votes for Women' in England and the United States on hold for four years. In England, women over the age of thirty were finally granted the vote in 1918 with full suffrage achieved in 1928. In 1920 the Nineteenth Amendment to the US Constitution was passed giving American women the right to vote, one year after Pankhurst had returned to America and settled in Canada after remarrying.

Historians now credit the work of suffragists Millicent Fawcett (England) and Carrie Chapman Catt (USA) as the driving force which led to women achieving the right to vote in the two largest democracies in the world at the time. However, it was Emmeline Pankhurst who put the movement—through her own example and sacrifice—on the world stage.

Patrick Pearse
'Ireland Unfree Shall Never Be At Peace'

Glasnevin Cemetery, Dublin, 1 August 1915.

Patrick Pearse in 1916.

Padraic Henry Pearse (1879-16) graduated from the King's Inn Law School in Dublin before gaining his BA in linguistics. A foundation member of the Irish Volunteers militia, Pearse was committed to the establishment of an Irish republic after centuries of unrest over British occupation of Ireland. However, the outbreak of World War I further delayed the implementation of legislation that would have restored the Dublin parliament. The Irish Republican Brotherhood (the forerunner of the Irish Republican Army) saw England's preoccupation with the war as its opportunity to press—by force if necessary—for independence.

Pearse had already travelled to America in 1914 to raise money for weapons and ammunition to force the British out of Ireland and campaigned for the use of force against the British. He gave this speech at the funeral of Jeremiah O'Donovan Rossa at Glasnevin Cemetery in Dublin in August 1915 and used the opportunity to agitate for Irish rebellion. O'Rossa was one of the old Fenian Republicans, who had been imprisoned in England and had died in exile in America after a long illness. In front of thousands of mourners, Pearse's speech became a rallying cry for armed resistance in Northern Ireland, which culminated in the failed Easter Uprising of 1916.

'It has seemed right, before we turn away from this place in which we have laid the mortal remains of O'Donovan Rossa, that one among us should, in the name of all, speak the praise of that valiant man, and endeavour to formulate the thought and the hope that are in us as we stand around his grave. And if there is anything that makes it fitting that I, rather than some other, I rather than one of the grey-haired men who were young with him and shared in his labour and in his suffering, should speak here, it is perhaps that I may be taken as speaking on behalf of a new generation that has been rebaptized in the Fenian faith, and that has accepted the responsibility of carrying out the Fenian programme. I propose to you then that, here by the grave of this unrepentant Fenian, we renew our baptismal vows; that, here by the grave of this unconquered and unconquerable man, we ask of God, each one for himself, such unshakable purpose, such high and gallant courage, such unbreakable strength of soul as belonged to O'Donovan Rossa.

'Life springs from death; and from the graves of patriot men and women spring living nations.'

Deliberately here we avow ourselves, as he avowed himself in the dock, Irishmen of one allegiance only. We of the Irish Volunteers, and you others who are associated with us in today's task and duty, are bound together and must stand together henceforth in brotherly union for the achievement of the freedom of Ireland. And we know only one definition of freedom: it is

PATRICK PEARSE

'Deliberately here we avow ourselves, Irishmen of one allegiance only. We of the Irish Volunteers are bound together and must stand together henceforth in brotherly union for the achievement of the freedom of Ireland.'

Tone's definition, it is Mitchel's definition, it is Rossa's definition. Let no man blaspheme the cause that the dead generations of Ireland served by giving it any other name and definition than their name and their definition.

We stand at Rossa's grave not in sadness but rather in exaltation of spirit that it has been given to us to come thus into so close a communion with that brave and splendid Gael. Splendid and holy causes are served by men who are themselves splendid and holy. O'Donovan Rossa was splendid in the proud manhood of him, splendid in the heroic grace of him, splendid in the Gaelic strength and clarity and truth of him. And all that splendour and pride and strength was compatible with a humility and a simplicity of devotion to Ireland, to all that was olden and beautiful and Gaelic in Ireland, the holiness and simplicity of patriotism of a Michael O'Cleary or of an Eoghan O'Growney. The clear true eyes of this man almost alone in his day visioned Ireland as we of today would surely have her: not free merely but Gaelic as well; not Gaelic merely, but free as well.

In a closer spiritual communion with him now than ever before or perhaps ever again, in a spiritual communion with those of his day, living and dead, who suffered with him in English prisons, in communion of spirit too with our own dear comrades who suffer in English prisons today, and speaking on their behalf as well as our own, we pledge to Ireland our love, and we pledge to English rule in Ireland our hate. This is a place of peace, sacred to the dead, where men should speak with all charity and with all restraint; but I hold it a Christian thing, as O'Donovan Rossa held it, to hate evil, to hate untruth, to hate oppression, and, hating them, to strive to overthrow them.

Our foes are strong and wise and wary but, strong and wise and wary as they are, they cannot undo the miracles of God who ripens in the hearts of young men the seeds sown by the young men of a former generation. And the seeds sown by the young men of (18)65 and '67 are coming to their miraculous ripening today. Rulers and Defenders of Realms had need to be wary if they would guard against such processes. Life springs from death; and from the graves of patriot men and women spring living nations. The Defenders of this Realm have worked well in secret and in the open. They think that they have pacified Ireland. They think that they have purchased half of us and intimidated the other half. They think that they have foreseen everything, think that they have provided against everything; but the fools, the fools, the fools! They have left us our Fenian dead, and while Ireland holds these graves, Ireland unfree shall never be at peace.'

Although many rebels questioned whether the Irish Brotherhood was ready for armed battle with the British, a major uprising began on 23 April (Easter Sunday) in 1916. Pearse was a teacher and poet, and although he described himself as 'commandant-general' he did not have a military background. Only 1700 rebels took part, mainly in Dublin itself. The following day, on the steps of the captured general Post Office, Pearse proclaimed the Irish Republic. But the uprising was routed by 20 000 British troops and with Dublin ablaze and many innocent civilians killed, the rebels surrendered. Those who signed the republican proclamation as part of the provisional government—Thomas J Clarke, Sean MacDiarmada, Thomas MacDonagh, Eamonn Ceannt, James Connolly, Joseph Plunkett and Padraic Pearse—were among 16 rebels executed on 3 May, 1916.

From the dock during his trial, Pearse foretold of the century of bitter struggle for Irish independence: 'You cannot conquer Ireland. You cannot extinguish the Irish passion for freedom. If our deed has not been sufficient to win freedom, then our children will win it by a better deed.'

Woodrow Wilson

'War Message'

Address to Extraordinary Session of US Congress, Washington DC, 2 April 1917.

Woodrow Wilson addresses a joint session of the US Congress
to announce an official break in relations with Germany, in 1917.

Thomas Woodrow Wilson (1856-24) was a lawyer, Princeton University Professor and Democratic Governor of New Jersey before elected President of the United States of America in 1912. This was a time when war clouds were gathering in Europe. For three years America stayed out of the conflict and Wilson was re-elected in 1916 on the slogan: 'He kept us out of the War'. However, within three months of his inauguration he reversed America's isolationist stance, despite his personal commitment to peace and neutrality. In this speech, Wilson cites submarine attacks in the Atlantic, which led to the sinking of the commercial liner *Lusitania* in 1915, and declares Germany's sponsorship of Mexico's bid for lost territory in Texas as reasons for entering the war.

'I have called the Congress into extraordinary session because there are serious, very serious, choices of policy to be made, and made immediately, which it was neither right nor constitutionally permissible that I should assume the responsibility of making ...

With a profound sense of the solemn and even tragic character of the step I am taking and of the grave responsibilities which it involves, but in unhesitating obedience to what I deem my constitutional duty, I advise that the Congress declare the recent course of the Imperial German Government to be in fact nothing less than war against the government and people of the United States; that it formally accept the status of belligerent which has thus been thrust upon it, and that it take immediate steps not only to put the country in a more thorough state of defense but also to exert all its power and employ all its resources to bring the Government of the German Empire to terms and end the war.

What this will involve is clear. It will involve the utmost practicable cooperation in counsel and action with the governments now at war with Germany, and, as incident to that, the extension to those governments of the most liberal financial credit, in order that our resources may so far as possible be added to theirs.

It will involve the organization and mobilization of all the material resources of the country to supply the materials of war and serve the incidental needs of the Nation in the most abundant and yet the most economical and efficient way possible. It will involve the immediate full equipment of the navy in all respects but particularly in supplying it with the best means of dealing with the enemy's submarines. It will involve the immediate addition to the armed forces of the United States already provided for by law in case of war at least five hundred thousand men, who should, in my opinion, be chosen upon the principle of universal lia-

'It is a fearful thing to lead this great peaceful people into war, into the most terrible and disastrous of all wars, civilization itself seeming to be in the balance.'

bility to service, and also the authorization of subsequent additional increments of equal force so soon as they may be needed and can be handled in training.

It will involve also, of course, the granting of adequate credits to the Government, sustained, I hope, so far as they can equitably be sustained by the present generation, by well conceived taxation. I say sustained so far as may be equitable by taxation because it seems to me that it would be most unwise to base the credits which will now be necessary entirely on money borrowed. It is our duty, I most respectfully urge, to protect our people so far as we may against the very serious hardships and evils which would be likely to arise out of the inflation which would be produced by vast loans.

'We desire no conquest, no dominion. We seek no indemnities for ourselves, no material compensation for the sacrifices we shall freely make. We are but one of the champions of the rights of mankind.'

In carrying out the measures by which these things are to be accomplished we should keep constantly in mind the wisdom of interfering as little as possible in our own preparation and in the equipment of our own military forces with the duty—for it will be a very practical duty—of supplying the nations already at war with Germany with the materials which they can obtain only from us or by our assistance. They are in the field and we should help them in every way to be effective there.

I shall take the liberty of suggesting, through the several executive departments of the Government, for the consideration of your committees, measures for the accomplishment of the several objects I have mentioned. I hope that it will be your pleasure to deal with them as having been framed after very careful thought by the branch of the Government upon which the responsibility of conducting the war and safeguarding the Nation will most directly fall.

While we do these things, these deeply momentous things, let us be very clear, and make very clear to all the world what our motives and our objects are. My own thought has not been driven from its habitual and normal course by the unhappy events of the last two months, and I do not believe that the thought of the Nation has been altered or clouded by them. I have exactly the same things in mind now that I had in mind when I addressed the Senate on the twenty-second of January last, the same that I had in mind when I addressed the Congress on the third of February and on the twenty-sixth of February.

Our object now, as then, is to vindicate the principles of peace and justice in the life of the world as against selfish and autocratic power and to set up amongst the really free and self-governed peoples of the world such a concert of purpose and of action as will henceforth insure the observance of those principles. Neutrality is no longer feasible or desirable where the peace of the world is involved and the freedom of its peoples, and the menace to that peace and freedom lies in the existence of autocratic governments backed by organized force which is controlled wholly by their will, not by the will of their people. We have seen the last of neutrality in such circumstances. We are at the beginning of an age in which it will be insisted that the same standards of conduct and of responsibility for wrong done shall be observed among nations and their governments that are observed among the individual citizens of civilized states.

We have no quarrel with the German people. We have no feeling towards them but one of sympathy and friendship. It was not upon their impulse that their government acted in entering this war. It was not with their previous knowledge or approval. It was a war determined upon as wars used to be determined upon in the old, unhappy days when peoples were nowhere consulted by their rulers and wars were provoked and waged in the interest of dynasties or of little groups of ambitious men who were accustomed to use their fellow men as pawns and tools.

Self-governed nations do not fill their neighbor states with spies or set the course of intrigue to bring about some critical posture of affairs which will give them an opportunity to strike and make conquest. Such designs can be successfully worked out only under cover and where no one has the right to ask questions. Cunningly contrived plans of deception or aggression, carried, it may be, from generation to generation, can be worked out and kept from the light only within the privacy of courts or behind the carefully guarded confidences of a narrow and privileged class. They are happily impossible where public opinion commands and insists upon full information concerning all the nation's affairs.

A steadfast concert for peace can never be maintained except by a partnership of democratic nations. No autocratic government could be trusted to keep faith within it or observe its covenants. It must be a league of honor, a partnership of opinion. Intrigue would eat its vitals away; the plottings of inner circles who could plan what they would and render account to no one would be a corruption seated at its very heart. Only free peoples can hold their purpose and their honor steady to a common end and prefer the interests of mankind to any narrow interest of their own.

'We are glad, now that we see the facts with no veil of false pretense about them to fight thus for the ultimate peace of the world and for the liberation of its peoples, the German peoples included.'

Does not every American feel that assurance has been added to our hope for the future peace of the world by the wonderful and heartening things that have been happening within the last few weeks in Russia? Russia was known by those who knew it best to have been always in fact democratic at heart, in all the vital habits of her thought, in all the intimate relationships of her people that spoke their natural instinct, their habitual attitude towards life. The autocracy that crowned the summit of her political structure, long as it had stood and terrible as was the reality of its power, was not in fact Russian in origin, character, or purpose; and now it has been shaken off and the great, generous Russian people have been added in all their naive majesty and might to the forces that are fighting for freedom in the world, for justice, and for peace. Here is a fit partner for a League of Honor.

One of the things that has served to convince us that the Prussian, autocracy was not and could never be our friend is that from the very outset of the present war it has filled our unsuspecting communities and even our offices of government with spies and set criminal intrigues everywhere afoot against our national unity of counsel, our peace within and without, our industries and our commerce. Indeed it is now evident that its spies were here even before the war began; and it is unhappily not a matter of conjecture but a fact proved in our courts of justice that the intrigues which have more than once come perilously near to disturbing the peace and dislocating the industries of the country have been carried on at the instigation, with the support, and even under the personal direction of official agents of the Imperial Government accredited to the Government of the United States. Even in checking these things and trying to extirpate them we have sought to put the most generous interpretation possible upon them because we knew that their source lay, not in any hostile feeling or purpose of the German people towards us (who were, no doubt, as ignorant of them as we ourselves were), but only in the selfish designs of a Government that did what it pleased and told its people nothing. But they have played their part in serving to convince us at last that that Government entertains no real friendship for us and means to act against our peace and security at its convenience. That it means to stir up enemies against us at our very doors the intercepted note to the German Minister at Mexico City is eloquent evidence.

'We have no quarrel with the German people. We have no feeling towards them but one of sympathy and friendship.'

We are accepting this challenge of hostile purpose because we know that in such a Government, following such methods, we can never have a friend; and that in the presence of its organized power, always lying in wait to accomplish we know not what purpose, there can be no assured security for the democratic Governments of the world. We are now about to accept gauge of battle with this natural foe to liberty and shall, if necessary, spend the whole force of the nation to check and nullify its pretensions and its power. We are glad, now that we see the facts with no veil of false pretense about them to fight thus for the ultimate peace of the world and for the liberation of its peoples, the German peoples included: for the rights of nations great and small and the privilege of men everywhere to choose their way of life and of obedience. The world must be made safe for democracy. Its peace must be planted upon the tested foundations of political liberty. We have no selfish ends to serve.

We desire no conquest, no dominion. We seek no indemnities for ourselves, no material compensation for the sacrifices we shall freely make. We are but one of the champions of the rights of mankind. We shall be satisfied when those rights have been made as secure as the faith and the freedom of nations can make them. Just because we fight without rancor and without selfish object, seeking nothing for ourselves but what we shall wish to share with all free peoples, we shall, I feel confident, conduct our operations as belligerents without passion and ourselves observe with proud punctilio the principles of right and of fair play we profess to be fighting for.

I have said nothing of the Governments allied with the Imperial Government of Germany because they have not made war upon us or challenged us to defend our right and our honor. The

Austro-Hungarian Government has, indeed, avowed its unqualified endorsement and acceptance of the reckless and lawless submarine warfare adopted now without disguise by the Imperial German Government, and it has therefore not been possible for this Government to receive Count Tarnowski, the Ambassador recently accredited to this Government by the Imperial and Royal Government of Austria-Hungary; but that Government has not actually engaged in warfare against citizens of the United States on the seas, and I take the liberty, for the present at least, of postponing a discussion of our relations with the authorities at Vienna. We enter this war only where we are clearly forced into it because there are no other means of defending our rights....

It is a distressing and oppressive duty, Gentlemen of the Congress, which I have performed in thus addressing you. There are, it may be many months of fiery trial and sacrifice ahead of us. It is a fearful thing to lead this great peaceful people into war, into the most terrible and disastrous of all wars, civilization itself seeming to be in the balance.

But the right is more precious than peace, and we shall fight for the things which we have always carried nearest our hearts—for democracy, for the right of those who submit to authority to have a voice in their own Governments, for the rights and liberties of small nations, for a universal dominion of right by such a concert of free peoples as shall bring peace and safety to all nations and make the world itself at last free. To such a task we can dedicate our lives and our fortunes, every thing that we are and everything that we have, with the pride of those who know that the day has come when America is privileged to spend her blood and her might for the principles that gave her birth and happiness and the peace which she has treasured. God helping her, she can do no other.'

'Neutrality is no longer feasible or desirable where the peace of the world is involved.'

Despite his personal misgivings, Woodrow Wilson asked for a declaration of war and received thunderous applause from Congress. That night, as he reflected on the historic day, he remarked, 'My message today was a message of death for our young men. How strange it seems to applaud that.' Wilson then laid his head down and wept.

In January 1918, ten months before the end of World War I, Wilson appeared before a joint session of Congress and outlined possible peace terms to end World War I. The Fourteen Points outlined in his speech served as both the basis for peace and the establishment of a 'League of Nations' to promote post-war understanding and peaceful relations. But the war dragged on until the end of 1918, until Germany's allies collapsed or surrendered and English, French and American forces were poised to invade Germany itself.

In August, the Chancellor of Germany, Prince Max of Baden, appealed for an armistice based upon Wilson's Fourteen Points but by the time the war ended—at 11am on 11 November—nearly 40 million people had perished. As for Wilson's idealism, his 'Fourteen Points' were but a memory when the victors met in Versailles, France in 1919, and punished Germany under the guise of a peace treaty. While England and France listened politely to Wilson, they were intent on exacting reparations from Germany.

Wilson was forced to compromise heavily to bring his dream of a 'League of Nations' into a reality. Despite winning the Nobel Peace Prize in 1919, the Republican-dominated US Congress rejected the 'Treaty of Versailles' that Wilson presented to it. Despite his best efforts the US President had lost the confidence of the Congress and suffered a complete physical and mental breakdown. The President who had lost the support of his own country had outlined his personal dream of future international security based upon an idealism for which the world was not yet ready. Woodrow Wilson died a broken man in 1924.

Emma Goldman
'Address to the Jury'

Address to the jury of the United States District Court in the City of New York, 9 July 1917.

Emma Goldman, shortly before she was deported to the Soviet Union in 1919.

Emma Goldman (1869-1940) was born in Lithuania (Russia) and immigrated to the United States as a teenager in 1885. Although living in New York, Goldman was drawn to the anarchism movement after the Haymarket Square tragedy in Chicago in 1886. A bomb had been thrown into a crowd of police during a workers' rally for the eight-hour day. Four anarchists were put on trial for the crime and after being convicted on the slimmest of evidence, eventually hanged to become forever known as the Haymarket Martyrs. At the trial the judge declared; 'Not because you caused the Haymarket bomb, but because you are Anarchists, you are on trial.'

Emma Goldman followed the event intensely and decided to become a revolutionary on the day of the hangings. An anarchist, feminist and labour activist, she was arrested in 1893 for inciting an unemployed mob to take bread 'by force' in New York and was jailed for a year. Her anarchist views directly led to the attempted assassination of strike suppressor Henry Clay Finch in 1892 by her colleague Alexander Berkman. Anarchism was also widely blamed for inciting the assassination of President William McKinley in 1901.

Goldman was jailed for a second time for distributing birth control literature but after the outbreak of World War I in 1914 she set up 'No Conscription' leagues and spoke against the war at rallies. In March 1917, when America finally entered the war, Goldman and Alexander Berkman were arrested for conspiring to obstruct the draft. At their trial, Goldman addressed the jury to argue her cause.

'Never can a new idea move within the law. It matters not whether that idea pertains to political and social changes or to any other domain of human thought and expression—to science, literature, music; in fact, everything that makes for freedom and joy and beauty must refuse to move within the law. How can it be otherwise? The law is stationary, fixed, mechanical, 'a chariot wheel' which grinds all alike without regard to time, place and condition, without ever taking into account cause and effect, without ever going into the complexity of the human soul.

'We are but the atoms in the incessant human struggle towards the light that shines in the darkness—the ideal of economic, political and spiritual liberation of mankind!'

Progress knows nothing of fixity. It cannot be pressed into a definite mould. It cannot bow to the dictum, 'I have ruled' or 'I am the regulating finger of God'. Progress is ever renewing, ever becoming, ever changing—never is it within the law.

If that be crime, we are criminals even like Jesus, Socrates, Gallileo, Bruno, John Brown and scores of others. We are in good company, among those whom Havelock Ellis, the greatest living psychologist, describes as the political criminals recognized by the whole civilized world, except America, as men and women who out of deep love for humanity, out of a passionate reverence for liberty and an all-absorbing devotion to an ideal are ready to pay for their faith even with their blood. We cannot do otherwise if we are to be true to ourselves—we know that the political criminal is the precursor of human progress—the political criminal of today must needs be the hero, the martyr and the saint of the new age.

But, says the Prosecuting Attorney, the press and the unthinking rabble, in high and low station, 'that is a dangerous doctrine and unpatriotic at this time'. No doubt it is. But are we to be held responsible for something which is as unchangeable and unalienable as the very stars hanging in the heavens unto time and all eternity?

Gentlemen of the jury, we respect your patriotism. We would not, if we could, have you change its meaning for yourself. But may there not be different kinds of patriotism as there are different kinds of liberty? I for one cannot believe that love of one's country must needs consist in blindness to its social faults, to deafness to its social discords, of inarticulation to its social wrongs. Neither can I believe that the mere accident of birth in a certain country or the mere scrap of a citizen's paper constitutes the love of country.

I know many people—I am one of them—who were not born here, nor have they applied for citizenship, and who yet love America with deeper passion and greater intensity that many natives whose patriotism manifests itself by pulling, kicking, and insulting those who do not rise when the national anthem is played. Our patriotism is that of the man who loves a woman with open eyes. He is enchanted by her beauty, yet he sees her faults. So we, too, who know America, love her beauty, her richness, her great possibilities; we love her mountains, her canyons, her forests, her Niagara, and her deserts—above all do we love the people that have produced her wealth, her artists who have created beauty, her great apostles who dream and work for liberty—but with the same passionate emotion we hate her superficiality, her cant, her corruption, her mad, unscrupulous worship at the alter of the Golden Calf.

We say that if America has entered the war to make the world safe for democracy, she must first make democracy safe in America. How else is the world to take America seriously, when democracy at home is daily being outraged, free speech suppressed, peaceable assemblies broken up by overbearing and brutal gangsters in uniform; when free press is curtailed and every independent opinion gagged. Verily, poor as we are in democracy, how can we give of it to the world? We further say that a democracy conceived in the military servitude of the masses, in

'... even if we were convicted and found guilty and the penalty were that we be placed against a wall and shot dead, I should nevertheless cry out with the great Luther: 'Here I am and here I stand and I cannot do otherwise.'

EMMA GOLDMAN

47

their economic enslavement, and nurtured in their tears and blood, is not democracy at all. It is despotism—the cumulative result of a chain of abuses which, according to the dangerous document, the Declaration of Independence, the people have the right to overthrow.

The District Attorney has dragged in our Manifesto, and he has emphasized the passage, 'Resist conscription'. Gentlemen of the jury, please remember that that is not the charge against us. But admitting that the Manifesto contains the expression, 'resist conscription', may I ask you, is there only one kind of resistance? Is there only the resistance which means the gun, the bayonet, the bomb or flying machine? Is there not another kind of resistance? May not the people simply fold their hands and declare, 'We will not fight when we do not believe in the necessity of war'? May not the people who believe in the repeal of the Conscription Law, because it is unconstitutional, express their opposition in word and by pen, in meetings and in other ways? What right has the District Attorney to interpret that particular passage to suit himself? Moreover, gentlemen of the jury, I insist that the indictment against us does not refer to conscription. We are charged with a conspiracy against registration. And in no way or manner has the prosecution proven that we are guilty of conspiracy or that we have committed an overt act.

'Whatever your verdict, gentlemen, it cannot possibly affect the rising tide of discontent in this country against war which, despite all boasts, is a war for conquest and military power.'

Gentlemen of the jury, you are not called upon to accept our views, to approve of them or to justify them. You are not even called upon to decide whether our views are within or against the law. You are called upon to decide whether the prosecution has proven that the defendants Emma Goldman and Alexander Berkman have conspired to urge people not to register. And whether their speeches and writings represent overt acts.

Whatever your verdict, gentlemen, it cannot possibly affect the rising tide of discontent in this country against war which, despite all boasts, is a war for conquest and military power. Neither can it affect the ever increasing opposition to conscription which is a military and industrial yoke placed upon the necks of the American people. Least of all will your verdict affect those to whom human life is sacred, and who will not become a party to the world slaughter. Your verdict can only add to the opinion of the world as to whether or not justice and liberty are a living force in this country or a mere shadow of the past.

Your verdict may, of course, affect us temporarily, in a physical sense—it can have no effect whatever upon our spirit. For even if we were convicted and found guilty and the penalty were that we be placed against a wall and shot dead, I should nevertheless cry out with the great Luther: 'Here I am and here I stand and I cannot do otherwise.'

And gentlemen, in conclusion let me tell you that my co-defendant, Mr. Berkman, was right when he said the eyes of America are upon you. They are upon you not because of sympathy for us or agreement with Anarchism. They are upon you because it must be decided sooner or later whether we are justified in telling people that we will give them democracy in Europe, when we have no democracy here? Shall free speech and free assemblage, shall criticism and opinion—which even the espionage bill did not include—be destroyed? Shall it be a shadow of the past, the great historic American past? Shall it be trampled underfoot by any detective, or policeman, anyone who decides upon it? Or shall free speech and free press and free assemblage continue to be the heritage of the American people?

Gentlemen of the jury, whatever your verdict will be, as far as we are concerned, nothing will be changed. I have held ideas all my life. I have publicly held my ideas for twenty-seven years. Nothing on earth would ever make me change my ideas except one thing; and that is, if you will prove to me that our position is wrong, untenable, or lacking in historic fact. But never would I change my ideas because I am found guilty. I may remind you of two great Americans, undoubtedly not unknown to you, gentlemen of the jury; Ralph Waldo Emerson and Henry David Thoreau. When Thoreau was placed in prison for refusing to pay taxes, he was visited by Ralph Waldo Emerson and Emerson said: 'David, what are you doing in jail?' and Thoreau replied: 'Ralph, what are you doing outside, when honest people are in jail for their ideals?'. Gentlemen of the jury, I do not wish to influence you. I do not wish to appeal to your passions. I do not wish to influence you by the fact that I am a woman. I have no such desires and no such designs. I take it that you are sincere enough and honest enough and brave enough to render a verdict according to your convictions, beyond the shadow of a reasonable doubt.

> 'A democracy conceived in the military servitude of the masses, in their economic enslavement, and nurtured in their tears and blood, is not democracy at all. It is despotism.'

Please forget that we are Anarchists. Forget that it is claimed that we propagated violence. Forget that something appeared in Mother Earth when I was thousands of miles away, three years ago. Forget all that, and merely consider the evidence. Have we been engaged in a conspiracy? Has that conspiracy been proven? Have we committed overt acts? Have those overt acts been proven? We for the defense say they have not been proven. And therefore your verdict must be not guilty.

But whatever your decision, the struggle must go on. We are but the atoms in the incessant human struggle towards the light that shines in the darkness—the ideal of economic, political and spiritual liberation of mankind!'

Emma Goldman, also known as 'Red Emma', was jailed for two years along with her co-accused Alexander Berkman. Stripped of her American citizenship, Goldman was deported to the Soviet Union in 1919. Disillusioned by the bureaucracy and political persecution in Russia after the October Revolution of 1918, she reassessed her earlier philosophies about social and political revolution—especially the maxim that the ends justified the means—and moved to England in 1921 where she married in order to remain in that country. With a British passport she was allowed to travel to

France and Canada on lecture tours and was even allowed back into the United States in 1934. She was later described by FBI head Edgar Hoover as 'one of the most dangerous women in America'.

Emma Goldman become an important figure in the sexual politics of her time and was jailed for distributing literature supporting a woman's right to practice birth control. She argued that massive social transformation was needed to bring about political change but also to rid the word of the repressive social conditions against women. After going to Spain to support the Civil War, she passed away in 1940 and was buried in Chicago near the graves of the Haymarket Martyrs.

Vladimir Ilyich Lenin

'Constructing the Socialist Order'

Address to the First Congress of the Communist International, 2 March 1919.

Lenin (centre) walks through Red Square in Moscow with a group of military comrades in 1919.

Vladimir Ilyich Lenin (originally Ulyanov) was born in Simbirski, Russia in 1870 and studied law at Kazan State University. A Marxist revolutionary, Lenin was exiled to Serbia from 1897 to 1900. He became the leader of the Social Democratic Workers' Party and, after the overthrow of Tsar Nicholas in March 1917, returned to St Petersberg from Zurich and urged his followers to seize control from the provisional government led by Alexander Kerensky. Lenin marshalled the Bolshevik forces and captured government buildings, the Winter Palace in St Petersberg and finally all of Moscow.

Lenin headed the Russian Communist Party (formerly the Social Democratic Workers Party) but the Bolsheviks performed poorly in the election of a constituent assembly and had to seize power by force. The Bolsheviks executed the Tsar's family and sought peace with Germany, giving up sovereignty to 1.3 million square miles of land in the Treaty of Brest Litovsk.

News of the Russian Revolution reverberated all over the world and resonated with workers in England, France, Germany and America. In March 1919, Lenin addressed the First Congress of the Communist International, advocating the Soviet system's 'dictatorship of the proletariat'.

❮ On behalf of the Central Committee of the Russian Communist Party I declare the First Congress of the Communist International open. First I would ask all present to rise in tribute to the finest representatives of the Third International: Karl Liebknecht and Rosa Luxemburg.

Comrades, our gathering has great historic significance. It testifies to the collapse of all the illusions cherished by bourgeois democrats. Not only in Russia, but in the most developed capitalist countries of Europe, in Germany for example, civil war is a fact.

The bourgeois are terror-stricken at the growing workers' revolutionary movement. This is understandable if we take into account that the development of events since the imperialist war inevitably favors the workers' revolutionary movement, and that the world revolution is beginning and growing in intensity everywhere.

'The imperialist war inevitably favours the workers' revolutionary movement, and that the world revolution is beginning and growing in intensity everywhere.'

The people are aware of the greatness and significance of the struggle now going on. All that is needed is to find the practical form to enable the proletariat to establish its rule. Such a form is the Soviet system with the dictatorship of the proletariat. Dictatorship of the proletariat—until now these words were Latin to the masses. Thanks to the spread of the Soviets throughout the world this Latin has been translated into all modern languages; a practical form of dictatorship has been found by the working people. The mass of workers now understand it thanks to Soviet power in Russia, thanks to the Spartacus League in Germany and to similar organizations in other countries, such as, for example, the Shop Stewards Committees of Britain. All this shows that a revolutionary form of the dictatorship of the proletariat has been found, that the proletariat is now able to exercise its rule.

Comrades, I think that after the events in Russia and the January struggle in Germany, it is especially important to note that in other countries, too, the latest form of the workers' movement is asserting itself and getting the upper hand. Today, for example, I read in an anti-socialist newspaper a report to the effect that the British government had received a dedication from the Birmingham Workers' Council and had expressed its readiness to recognize the Councils as economic bodies. The Soviet system has triumphed not only in backward Russia, but also in the most developed country of Europe—in Germany, and in Britain, the oldest capitalist country.

'Even though the bourgeoisie are still raging, even though they may kill thousands more workers, victory will be ours, the victory of the worldwide Communist revolution is assured.'

Even though the bourgeoisie are still raging, even though they may kill thousands more workers, victory will be ours, the victory of the worldwide Communist revolution is assured.

Comrades, I extend hearty greetings to you on behalf of the Central Committee of the Russian Communist Party. I move that we elect a presidium. Let us have nominations.'

In 1922, after the end of the Russian Civil War between the Bosheviks (Reds) and the anti-Bolsheviks (Whites), the Union of Soviet Socialist Republics was formed. In April 1922, Josef Stalin was elected General Secretary of the Communist Party. The following month Lenin suffered the first of several strokes that would eventually claim his life in January 1924. Although he warned the Party in his final will and testament to remove Josef Stalin from power, Stalin survived Lenin's criticism from the grave and out-manoeuvred—and gradually purged—the Communist Party of his political rivals, including Trotsky. In 1924 the Soviet Union adopted a constitution based on the dictatorship of the proletariat and the public ownership of land and all means of production. The revolution was complete.

Between the Wars
1920-1939

Clarence S Darrow
'Against the Death Penalty'

Closing Argument to the Jury, Chicago Criminal Court, Dearborn Street, 1924.

Clarence Darrow in 1925.

Clarence S Darrow (1857-38) was a famous Chicago lawyer and advocate for the defence in criminal cases. In 1922 two youths, Nathan Leopold and Richard Loeb, members of prominent Chicago families, confessed to mutilating and then murdering local boy Bobby Frank. Darrow took on the 'Leopold and Loeb' case, which was described at the time as 'the most sensational murder trial of the century'. Darrow, at that time, could boast that he had never seen a client executed.

Even though the defendants fully confessed in court, the trial lasted for months on the sole question of whether the youths should be executed or imprisoned. In his closing argument, Darrow virtually admitted that he loathed both the case and his clients, but delivered a stinging plea against the use of the death penalty.

'There are causes for this terrible crime. There are causes, as I have said, for everything that happens in the world. War is a part of it; education is a part of it; birth is a part of it; money is a part of it—all these conspired to compass the destruction of these two poor boys.

Has the court any right to consider anything but these two boys? The State says that Your Honor has a right to consider the welfare of the community, as you have. If the welfare of the community would be benefited by taking these lives, well and good! I think it would work evil that no one could measure. Has Your Honor a right to consider the families of these two defendants? I have been sorry, and I am sorry for the bereavement of Mr and Mrs Frank, for those broken ties that cannot be healed. All I can hope and wish is that some good may come from it all. But as compared with the families of Leopold and Loeb, the Franks are to be envied—and every one knows it.

I do not know how much salvage there is in these two boys. I hate to say it in their presence, but what is there to look forward to? I do not know but what Your Honor would be merciful if you tied a rope around their necks and let them die; merciful to them, but not merciful to civilization, and not merciful to those who would be left behind. To spend the balance of their days in prison is mighty little to look forward to, if anything. Is it anything?

They may have the hope that as the years roll around they might be released. I do not know. I do not know. I will be honest with this court, as I have tried to be from the beginning. I know that these boys are not fit to be at large. I believe they will not be until they pass through the next stage of life, at forty-five or fifty. Whether they will then, I cannot tell. I am sure of this; that I will not be here to help them. So far as I am concerned, it is over ...

But there are others to consider. Here are these two families, who have led honest lives, who will bear the name that they

'You may hang these boys; you may hang them by the neck until they are dead. But in doing it you will turn your face toward the past.'

CLARENCE S DARROW

57

bear, and future generations must carry it on. Here is Leopold's father—and this boy was the pride of his life. He watched him, he cared for him, he worked for him; the boy was brilliant and accomplished, he educated him, and he thought that fame and position awaited him, as it should have awaited. It is a hard thing for a father to see his life's hopes crumble into dust.

Should he be considered? Should his brothers be considered? Will it do society any good or make your life safer, or any human being's life safer, if it should be handed down from generation to generation, that this boy, their kin, died upon the scaffold?

And Loeb's the same. Here are the faithful uncle and brother, who have watched here day by day, while Dickie's father and his mother are too ill to stand this terrific strain, and shall be waiting for a message which means more to them than it can mean to you or me. Shall these be taken into account in this general bereavement?

'You may save [these boys] and make it easier for every child that sometime may stand where these boys stand. I am pleading for the future; I am pleading for a time when hatred and cruelty will not control the hearts of men.'

Have they any rights? Is there any reason, Your Honor, why their proud names and all the future generations that bear them shall have this bar sinister written across them? How many boys and girls, how many unborn children will feel it? It is bad enough as it is, God knows. It is bad enough, however it is. But it's not yet death on the scaffold. It's not that. And I ask Your Honor, in addition to all that I have said, to save two honorable families from a disgrace that never ends, and which could be of no avail to help any human being that lives.

Now, I must say a word more and then I will leave this with you where I should have left it long ago. None of us are unmindful of the public; courts are not, and juries are not. We placed our fate in the hands of a trained court, thinking that he would be more mindful and considerate than a jury. I cannot say how people feel. I have stood here for three months as one might stand at the ocean trying to sweep back the tide. I hope the seas are subsiding and the wind is falling, and I believe they are, but I wish to make no false pretense to this court.

The easy thing and the popular thing to do is to hang my clients. I know it. Men and women who do not think will applaud. The cruel and thoughtless will approve. It will be easy today; but in Chicago, and reaching out over the length and breadth of the land, more and more fathers and mothers, the humane, the kind and the hopeful, who are gaining an understanding and asking questions not only about these poor boys, but about their own—these will join in no acclaim at the death of my clients. These would ask that the shedding of blood be stopped, and that the normal feelings of man resume their sway. And as the days and the months and the years go on, they will ask it more and more.

But, Your Honor, what they shall ask may not count. I know the easy way. I know Your Honor stands between the future and the past. I know the future is with me, and what I stand for here; not merely for the lives of these two unfortunate lads, but for all boys and all girls; for all of the young, and as far as possible, for all of the old. I am pleading for life, understanding, charity, kindness, and the infinite mercy that considers all. I am pleading that we overcome cruelty with kindness and hatred with love. I know the future is on my side. Your Honor stands between the past and the future. You may hang these boys; you may hang them by the neck until they are dead. But in doing it you will turn your face toward the past. In doing it you are making it harder for every other boy, who in ignorance and darkness must grope his way through the mazes which only childhood knows. In doing it you will make it harder for unborn children. You may save them and make it easier for every child that sometime may stand where these boys stand. You will make it easier for every human being with an aspiration and a vision and a hope and a fate. I am pleading for the future; I am pleading for a time when hatred and cruelty will not control the hearts of men. When we can learn by reason and judgment and understanding and faith that all life is worth saving, and that mercy is the highest attribute of man ... (Darrow then apologises for the length of his speech in the final paragraph).'

'The easy thing and the popular thing to do is to hang my clients. I know it. Men and women who do not think will applaud. The cruel and thoughtless will approve.'

Darrow successfully saved the pair of young murderers from execution (both were imprisoned, with Leopold dying after a razor attack in jail in 1936 and Loeb released in 1958). What made Darrow's speech so memorable, even to those members of the press who questioned his sincerity and speculated on the size of the fee paid to him, was its persuasive argument against the use of the death penalty for any crime. Darrow was forever immortalised the following year when he represented schoolteacher John T. Scopes who was charged with teaching Darwin's theory of evolution in a 'bible belt' school. The infamous 'Scopes-Monkey' Trial was the basis for the play (and film, with Spencer Tracy starring as Darrow) *Inherit the Wind*.

CLARENCE S DARROW

Margaret Sanger

'The Children's Era'

Address to The Birth Control League, New York, March 1925.

Margaret Sanger at a Birth Control Conference in New York, 1925.

Margaret H. Sanger (1883-1966) was the founder of the American birth control movement and fought for the revision of archaic rules which prohibited the publication of facts about contraception. Sanger's mother died at the age of 49 after 18 pregnancies (seven children died). As a practising nurse in New York's impoverished lower East Side, Sanger learnt first hand about the relationship between high infant and maternal mortality rates and poverty. Of most concern was the methods used by some women to induce abortion.

Sanger resolved to seek out the 'root of the evil'—the lack of education about birth control. In 1914 she began publishing material about contraception and opened the first American birth control clinic in Brooklyn. Sanger also argued—controversially for the time—that birth control would 'fulfill a critical psychological need by enabling women to fully enjoy sexual relations free from the fear of pregnancy'. Opposition to Sanger was strong and many of her speeches were greeted with shouts of abuse. She fled to England under an alias in 1914 to escape prosecution, and spent 30 days in the workhouse in 1917 for 'maintaining a public nuisance'. Her greatest opposition came from the Catholic Church.

Sanger founded the American Birth Control League in 1921, serving as its president for seven years, and offered women an alternative that the Church could not—the ability to control their own lives. In March 1925, Sanger addressed a Birth Control League conference in New York.

‘My subject is 'The Children's Era'. The Children's Era! This makes me think of Ellen Key's book—The Century of the Child. Ellen Key hoped that this twentieth century was to be the century of the child. The twentieth century, she said, would see this old world of ours converted into a beautiful garden of children. Well, we have already lived through a quarter of this twentieth century. What steps have we taken toward making it the century of the child? So far, very, very few.

Why does the Children's Era still remain a dream of the dim and the distant future? Why has so little been accomplished? In spite of all our acknowledged love of children, all our generosity, all our good-will, all the enormous spending of millions on philanthropy and charities, all our warm-hearted sentiment, all our incessant activity and social consciousness? Why?

Before you can cultivate a garden, you must know something about gardening. You have got to give your seeds a proper soil in which to grow. You have got to give them sunlight and fresh air. You have got to give them space and the opportunity (if they are to lift their flowers to the sun), to strike their roots deep into that soil. And always—do not forget this—you have got to fight weeds. You cannot have a garden, if you let weeds overrun it. So, if we want to make this world a garden for children, we must first of all learn the lesson of the gardener.

So far we have not been gardeners. We have only been a sort of silly reception committee, a reception committee at the Grand Central Station of life. Trainload after trainload of children are coming in, day and night—nameless refugees arriving out of the Nowhere into the Here. Trainload after trainload—many unwelcome, unwanted, unprepared for, unknown, without baggage, without passports, most of them without pedigrees. These unlimited hordes of refugees arrive in such numbers that the reception committee is thrown into a panic—a panic of activity. The reception committee arouses itself heroically, establishes emergency measures: milk stations, maternity centers, settlement houses, playgrounds, orphanages, welfare leagues, and every conceivable kind of charitable effort. But still trainloads of children keep on coming—human weed crop up that spread so fast in this sinister struggle for existence, that the overworked committee becomes exhausted, inefficient, and can think of no way out.

When we protest against this immeasurable, meaningless waste of motherhood and child-life; when we protest against the ever-mounting cost to the world of asylums, prisons, homes for the feeble-minded, and such institutions for the unfit, when we protest against the disorder and chaos and tragedy of modern life, when we point out the biological corruption that is destroying the very heart of American life, we are told that we are making merely an "emotional" appeal. When we point to the one immediate practical way toward order and beauty in society, the only way to lay the foundations of a society composed of happy children, happy women, and happy men, they call this idea indecent and immoral.

'There can be no hope for the future of civilization, no certainty of racial salvation, until every woman can decide for herself whether she will or will not become a mother, and when and how many children she cares to bring into the world.'

It is not enough to clean up the filth and disorder of our overcrowded cities. It is not enough to stop the evil of Child Labor—even if we could! It is not enough to decrease the rate of infantile mortality. It is not enough to open playgrounds, and build more public schools in which we can standardize the mind of the young. It is not enough to throw millions upon millions of dollars into charities and philanthropies. Don't deceive ourselves that by so doing we are making the world 'Safe for Children'.

Those of you who have followed the sessions of this Conference must, I am sure, agree with me that the first real step towards the creation of a Children's Era must lie in providing the conditions of healthy life for children not only before birth but even more imperatively before conception. Human society must protect its children—yes, but prenatal care is most essential! The child-to-be, as yet not called into being, has rights no less imperative.

We have learned in the preceding sessions of this Conference that, if we wish to produce strong and sturdy children, the embryo must grow in a chemically healthy medium. The blood stream of the mother must be chemically normal. Worry, strain, shock, unhappiness, enforced maternity, may all poison the blood of the enslaved mother. This chemically poisoned blood may produce a defective baby—a child foredoomed to idiocy, or feeble-mindedness, crime, or failure.

Do I exaggerate? Am I taking a rare exception and making it a general rule? Our opponents declare that children are conceived in love, and that every new-born baby converts its parents to love and unselfishness. My answer is to point to the asylums, the hospitals, the ever-growing institutions for the unfit. Look into the family history of those who are feeble-minded; or behind the bars of jails and prisons. Trace the family histories; find out the conditions under which they were conceived and born, before you attempt to persuade us that reckless breeding has nothing to do with these grave questions.

'We want to free women from enslavery and unwilling motherhood. We are fighting for the emancipation for the mothers of the world, of the children of the world, and the children to be.'

There is only one way out. We have got to fight for the health and happiness of the Unborn Child. And to do that in a practical, tangible way, we have got to free women from enforced, enslaved maternity. There can be no hope for the future of civilization, no certainty of racial salvation, until every woman can decide for herself whether she will or will not become a mother, and when and how many children she cares to bring into the world. That is the first step.

I would like to suggest Civil Service examinations for parenthood! Prospective parents after such an examination would be given a parenthood license, proving that they are physically and mentally fit to be the fathers and mothers of the next generation.

This is an interesting idea—but then arises the questions: 'Who is to decide?', 'Would there be a jury, like a play jury?' Would a Republican administration give parenthood permits only to Republicans—or perhaps only to Democrats? The more you think of governmental interference, the less it works out. Take this plan of civil service examination for parenthood. It suggests Prohibition: there might even be bootlegging in babies!

No, I doubt the advisability of governmental sanction. The problem of bringing children into the world ought to be decided by those most seriously involved—those who run the greatest risks; in the last analysis—by the mother and the child. If there is going to be any Civil Service examination, let it be conducted by the Unborn Child, the Child-to-be.

Just try for a moment to picture the possibilities of such an examination. When you want a cook or housemaid, you go to an employment bureau. You have to answer questions. You have to exchange references. You have to persuade the talented cook that you conduct a proper well-run household. Children ought to have at least the same privilege as cooks.

Sometimes in idle moments I like to think it would be a very good scheme to have a bureau of the Child-to-be. At such a bureau of the unborn, the wise child might be able to find out a few things about its father—and its mother. Just think for a moment of this bureau where prospective parents might apply for a baby. Think of the questions they would be asked by the agent of the unborn or by the baby itself.

First: "Mr. Father, a baby is an expensive luxury. Can you really afford one?"

MARGARET SANGER

63

"Have you paid for your last baby yet?"

"How many children have you already? Six? You must have your hands full. Can you take care of so many?"

"Do you look upon children as a reward—or a penalty?"

"How are your ductless glands—well balanced?"

"Can you provide a happy home for one! A sunny nursery? Proper food?"

"What's that you say? Ten children already? Two dark rooms in the slums?"

"No, thank you! I don't care to be born at all if I cannot be well-born. Good-bye!"

And if we could organize a society for the prevention of cruelty to unborn children, we would make it a law that children should be brought into the world only when they were welcome, invited, and wanted; that they would arrive with a clean bill of health and heritage; that they would possess healthy, happy, well-mated, and mature parents.

And there would be certain conditions of circumstances which would preclude parenthood. These conditions, the presence of which would make parenthood a crime, are the following:

1. Transmissible disease
2. Temporary disease
3. Subnormal children already in the family
4. Space out between births
5. Twenty-three years as a minimum age for parents
6. Economic circumstances adequate
7. Spiritual harmony between parents.

In conclusion, let me repeat: we are not trying to establish a dictatorship over parents. We want to free women from enslavery and unwilling motherhood. We are fighting for the emancipation for the mothers of the world, of the children of the world, and the children to be. We want to create a real Century of the Child—usher in a Children's Era. We can do this by handling the terrific gift of life in bodies fit and perfect as can be fashioned. Help us to make this Conference, which has aroused so much interest, the turning point toward this era. Only so can you help in the creation of the future.'

Margaret Sanger had many of her writings labelled lewd, even pornographic. She was charged with nine counts of violating the postal act regarding the distribution of 'vulgar' material and travelled to England to escape prosecution. Lies were spread about her teachings regarding 'planned parenthood' and much was misrepresented in the press in order to discredit her.

In 1927 Margaret Sanger organised the first World Population Conference in Geneva, Switzerland, and was the first president of the

International Planned Parenthood Federation. Jailed eight times during her adult life, one of the compromises she had to make was to secure her message among the upper and middle classes, thereby missing her target audience—the poor and uneducated.

In the late 1950s, with donations from her supporters, she funded the development of the birth control pill based on the research of the Worcester Foundation, at a time when the transference of birth control information was still a criminal act in some American states.

Franklin D Roosevelt

'The Only Thing We Have To Fear is Fear Itself'

Inaugural Presidential Address, Washington DC, 4 March 1933.

President Franklin D Roosevelt (centre) gives his inaugural address in 1933.

Franklin Delano Roosevelt (1882-1945) rose from being governor of New York in 1928 to President of the United States in 1932, despite being stricken with polio in 1921, which left him partially paralysed in the legs and necessitated the use of a wheelchair in later years. 'FDR' as he was known, was elected President in November 1932 at a time when America, and the world, was beset by economic depression after the Wall Street crash of October 1929. In this speech, Roosevelt outlines his plan for a 'New Deal' and economic recovery.

'This is a day of national consecration, and I am certain that on this day my fellow Americans expect that, on my induction into the presidency, I will address them with a candor and a decision which the present situation of our people impels.

This is pre-eminently the time to speak to truth—the whole truth, frankly and boldly. Nor need we shrink from honestly facing conditions in our country today. This great nation will endure as it has endured, will revive and will prosper. So, first of all, let me assert my firm belief that the only thing we have to fear is fear itself—nameless, unreasoning, unjustified terror, which paralyzes needed efforts to convert retreat into advance.

In every dark hour of our national life a leadership of frankness and vigor has met with that understanding and support of the people themselves which is essential to victory. I am convinced that you will again give that support to leadership in these critical days.

In such a spirit on my part and yours, we face our common difficulties. They concern, thank God, only material things. Values have shrunk to fantastic levels; taxes have risen; our ability to pay has fallen; government of all kinds is faced by serious curtailment of income; the means of exchange are frozen in the currents of trade; the withered leaves of industrial enterprise lie on every side; farmers find no markets for their produce; the savings of many years, in thousands of families, are gone.

> 'Let me assert my firm belief that the only thing we have to fear is fear itself—nameless, unreasoning, unjustified terror, which paralyzes needed efforts to convert retreat into advance.'

More important, a host of unemployed citizens face the grim problem of existence, and an equally great number toil with little return. Only a foolish optimist can deny the dark realities of the moment.

And, yet our distress comes from no failure of substance. We are stricken by no plague of locusts. Compared with the perils which our forefathers conquered, because they believed and were not afraid, we have still much to be thankful for. Nature still offers her bounty, and human efforts have multiplied it. Plenty is at our doorstep, but a generous use of it languishes in the very sight of the supply.

Primarily, this is because the rulers of the exchange of mankind's goods have failed through their own stubbornness and their own incompetence, have admitted their failure and have abdicated. Practices of the unscrupulous money-changers stand indicted in the court of public opinion, rejected by the hearts and minds of men.

True, they have tried, but their efforts have been cast in the pattern of an outworn tradition. Faced by the failure of credit, they have proposed only the lending of more money. Stripped of the lure of profit by which to induce our people to follow their false leadership, they have resorted to exhortations, pleading tearfully for restored confidence. They know only the rules of a generation of self-seekers. They have no vision, and when there is no vision, the people perish.

Yes, the money-changers have fled from their high seats in the temple of our civilization. We may now restore that temple to the ancient truths!

'I am prepared under my constitutional duty to recommend the measures that a stricken nation in the midst of a stricken world may require.'

The measure of the restoration lies in the extent to which we apply social values more noble than mere monetary profit. Happiness lies not in the mere possession of money; it lies in the joy of achievement, in the thrill of creative effort. The joy and moral stimulation of work no longer must be forgotten in the mad chase of evanescent profits.

These dark days will be worth all they cost us if they teach us that our true destiny is not to be ministered unto but to minister to ourselves and to our fellow men. Recognition of the falsity of material wealth as the standard of success goes hand in hand with the abandonment of the false belief that public office and high political position are to be valued only by the standards of pride of place and personal profit. There must be an end to a conduct in banking and in business which too often has given to a sacred trust the likeness of callous and selfish wrongdoing.

Small wonder that confidence languishes, for it thrives only on honesty, on honor, on the sacredness of obligations, on faithful protection, and on unselfish performance. Without them it cannot live.

Restoration calls, however, not for changes in ethics alone. This nation asks for action, and action now! Our greatest primary task is to put people to work.

This is no unsolvable problem if we face it wisely and courageously. It can be accomplished, in part, by direct recruiting by the Government itself, treating the task as we would treat the emergency of a war, but at the same time, through this employment, accomplishing greatly needed projects to stimulate and reorganize the use of our natural resources.

Hand in hand with that, we must frankly recognize the overbalance of population in our industrial centers and, by engaging on a national scale in a redistribution, endeavor to provide a better use of the land for those best fitted for the land. Yes, the task can be helped by definite efforts to raise the values of agricultural products and with this the power to purchase the output of our cities. It can be helped by preventing realistically the tragedy of the growing loss, through foreclosure, of our small homes and our farms. It can be helped by insistence that the Federal, State, and local governments act forthwith on the demand that their cost be drastically reduced. It can be helped by the unifying of relief activities, which today are often scattered, uneconomical, and unequal. It can be helped by national planning for and supervision of all forms of transportation and of communications and other utilities that have a definite public character.

There are many ways in which it can be helped, but it can never be helped merely by talking about it! We must act, we must act quickly. Finally, in our progress toward a resumption of work, we require two safeguards against a return of the evils of the old order: There must be a strict supervision of all banking and credits and investments; there must be an end to speculation with other people's money. And there must be provision for an adequate but sound currency.

There are the lines of attack. I shall presently urge upon a new Congress, in special session, detailed measures for their fulfillment, and I shall seek the immediate assistance of the 48 States!

Through this program of action, we address ourselves to putting our own national house in order and making income balance outgo. Our international trade relations, though vastly important, are in point of time and necessity secondary to the establishment of a sound national economy! I favor, as a practical policy, putting of first things first. I shall spare no effort to restore world trade by international economic readjustment, but the emergency at home cannot wait on that accomplishment.

'Happiness lies not in the mere possession of money; it lies in the joy of achievement, in the thrill of creative effort.'

The basic thought that guides these specific means of national recovery is not narrowly nationalistic. It is the insistence, as a first consideration, upon the interdependence of the various elements in all parts of the United States; a recognition of the old and permanently important manifestation of the American spirit of the pioneer. It is the way to recovery. It is the immediate way. It is the strongest assurance that the recovery will endure!

In the field of world policy, I would dedicate this Nation to the policy of the good neighbor; the neighbor who resolutely respects himself and, because he does so, respects the rights of others; the neighbor who respects his obligations and respects the sanctity of his agreements in and with a world of neighbors.

If I read the temper of our people correctly, we now realize as we have never realized before our interdependence on each other; that we can not merely take but we must give as well; that if we are to go forward, we must move as a trained and loyal army willing to sacrifice for the good of a common discipline, because without such discipline no progress is made, no leadership becomes effective. We are, I know, ready and willing to submit our lives and property to such discipline, because it makes possible a leadership which aims at a larger good. This, I propose to offer, pledging that the larger purposes will bind upon us—bind upon us all—as a sacred obligation with a unity of duty hitherto evoked only in times of armed strife.

FRANKLIN D ROOSEVELT

With this pledge taken, I assume unhesitatingly the leadership of this great army of our people dedicated to a disciplined attack upon our common problems. Action in this image, and to this end, is feasible under the form of government which we have inherited from our ancestors. Our Constitution is so simple and practical that it is possible always to meet extraordinary needs by changes in emphasis and arrangement without loss of essential form. That is why our constitutional system has proved itself the most superbly enduring political mechanism the modern world has ever seen. It has met every stress of vast expansion of territory, of foreign wars, of bitter internal strife, and of world relations.

'We require safeguards against a return of the evils of the old order—there must be a strict supervision of all banking and credits and investments; there must be an end to speculation with other people's money.'

And, it is to be hoped that the normal balance of executive and legislative authority may be wholly adequate to meet the unprecedented task before us. But it may be that an unprecedented demand and need for undelayed action may call for temporary departure from that normal balance of public procedure.

I am prepared under my constitutional duty to recommend the measures that a stricken nation in the midst of a stricken world may require. These measures, or such other measures as the Congress may build out of its experience and wisdom, I shall seek, within my constitutional authority, to bring to speedy adoption.

But, in the event that the Congress shall fail to take one of these two courses, and in the event that the national emergency is still critical, I shall not evade the clear course of duty that will then confront me. I shall ask the Congress for the one remaining instrument to meet the crisis—broad executive power to wage a war against the emergency as great as the power that would be given to me if we were in fact invaded by a foreign foe!

For the trust reposed in me, I will return the courage and the devotion that befit the time. I can do no less.

We face the arduous days that lie before us in the warm courage of the national unity; with the clear consciousness of seeking old and precious moral values; with the clean satisfaction that comes from the stern performance of duty by old and young alike. We aim at the assurance of a rounded, a permanent national life. We do not distrust the future of essential democracy.

The people of the United States have not failed. In their need they have registered a mandate that they want direct, vigorous action. They have asked for discipline and direction under leadership. They have made me the present instrument of their wishes. In the spirit of the gift, I take it.

In this dedication of a nation, we humbly ask the blessing of God. May He protect each and every one of us! May He guide me in the days to come.'

Franklin D. Roosevelt's 'bold, persistent' leadership sought to make government and its institutions responsible for the economic well-being of the American people. (It was once facetiously reported that he ordered 'a grilled millionaire' for breakfast each morning). FDR created government agencies, closed banks and even took on the Supreme Court in order to facilitate economic recovery. But although he held more power than any other US President before or since, he never lost the common touch with the people.

Roosevelt used a powerful new communication medium—radio—to speak to the American people in a series of historic speeches he called 'fireside' chats. He served four consecutive terms as President (1933-45)—a feat unprecedented in the history of the country and one not allowable today because of constitutional amendment. It was a situation borne out of the incredible events of that time—the Depression, the conflict in Europe, the unprovoked attack on Pearl Harbour by Japanese forces and finally, World War II itself.

For Roosevelt's part, he proved an inspirational war-time commander-in-chief despite being confined to a wheelchair in later life. Winning the war became his number one priority, even in the face of criticism of the internment of 112 000 Japanese-Americans, the failure of his government to articulate an adequate response to Hitler's treatment of the Jews in Europe and the apparent appeasement of Russian leader Josef Stalin at the Yalta Conference in 1945. However, Roosevelt was fated never to see victory; he succumbed to a cerebral haemorrhage, aged 63, on 12 April, 1945.

The irony remains: would the American people have elected a partially crippled man to the White House if television had been in operation during the 1930s?

King Edward VIII

'Abdication Speech'

Radio broadcast, London, England, 11 December 1936.

King Edward VIII at his desk in January 1936.

Edward VIII (1894-1972) became King of the United Kingdom upon the death of his father, George V, on 20 January 1936. In his early forties and a bachelor, Edward was both popular and good-looking but quickly made known his desire to marry an American woman, Wallis Warfield (Spencer) Simpson, whom he had known since 1931. When King Edward sought the approval of his family, the Church of England, Prime Minister Stanley Baldwin and his government in order to marry her, he met with complete opposition. Simpson had been married twice before, her second divorce was still pending and her ability to provide an heir was questionable (Simpson was already forty, and childless).

On 10 December, King Edward VIII submitted his abdication and became the only British monarch to voluntarily resign his station. The decision was endorsed by Parliament on 11 December, and on that day Edward publicly announced his decision via radio to a breathless, world-wide audience.

'At long last I am able to say a few words of my own. I have never wanted to withhold anything, but until now it has not been constitutionally possible for me to speak.

A few hours ago I discharged my last duty as King and Emperor, and now that I have been succeeded by my brother, the Duke of York, my first words must be to declare my allegiance to him. This I do with all my heart.

You all know the reasons which have impelled me to renounce the throne. But I want you to understand that in making up my mind I did not forget the country or the empire, which, as Prince of Wales and lately as King, I have for twenty-five years tried to serve.

But you must believe me when I tell you that I have found it impossible to carry the heavy burden of responsibility and to discharge my duties as King as I would wish to do without the help and support of the woman I love.

And I want you to know that the decision I have made has been mine and mine alone. This was a thing I had to judge entirely for myself. The other person most nearly concerned has tried up to the last to persuade me to take a different course.

I have made this, the most serious decision of my life, only upon the single thought of what would, in the end, be best for all.

This decision has been made less difficult to me by the sure knowledge that my brother, with his long training in the public affairs of this country and with his fine qualities, will be able to take my place forthwith without interruption or injury to the life and progress of the empire. And he has one matchless blessing, enjoyed by so many of you, and not bestowed on me—a happy home with his wife and children.

During these hard days I have been comforted by Her Majesty, my mother, and by my family. The ministers of the crown, and in particular, Mr Baldwin, the Prime Minister, have always treated me with full consideration. There has never been any constitutional difference between me and them, and between me and Parliament. Bred in the constitutional tradition by my father, I should never have allowed any such issue to arise.

Ever since I was Prince of Wales, and later on when I occupied the throne, I have been treated with the greatest kindness by all classes of the people wherever I have lived or journeyed throughout the empire. For that I am very grateful.

I now quit altogether public affairs and I lay down my burden. It may be some time before I return to my native land, but I shall always follow the fortunes of the British race and empire with profound interest, and if at any time in the future I can be found of service to His Majesty in a private station, I shall not fail.

And now, we all have a new King. I wish him and you, his people, happiness and prosperity with all my heart. God bless you all! God save the King!'

Edward's younger brother, George VI, took the throne and immediately gave Edward the title Duke of Windsor. The Duke and Mrs Simpson (who was given the title Duchess of Windsor) were married in France on 3 June, 1937 and lived in Paris. An apparent personal appeasement of Hitler's Nazi regime (the Windsors met the German Chancellor in 1937 and found him 'charming') made them something of an embarrassment when World War II broke out. Edward and Wallis were sent to the Commonwealth outposts of Bermuda and the Bahamas to serve out the conflict, with the former monarch serving as Governor. The family of King George VI, especially his wife Mary (the Queen Mother) and daughter Elizabeth (later Queen Elizabeth II) never forgave Edward for abdicating and exposing his brother George to the throne. They indirectly blamed Edward for the premature death of George VI—a quiet, shy man with a nervous stutter—from cancer in 1953, aged 57.

Edward died in Paris on 28 May, 1972, forever estranged from his family and former subjects. His wife, the former Mrs Simpson, died there also, on April 24, 1986, a virtual recluse. She was afforded one concession by the Royal family and was buried beside her late husband in Windsor Castle.

Almost 67 years after King Edward VIII's abdication, the British Parliament and the Church of England avoided another potential constitutional crisis and allowed Charles, Prince of Wales and heir to the throne, to marry fellow divorcee Camilla Parker-Bowles in April 2005.

Josef V Stalin

'Election Speech'

A Meeting of the Voters of the Stalin Electoral District,
Bolshoi Theatre, Moscow, 11 December 1937.

Josef Stalin in 1937.

Under Stalin's leadership, millions of Russian peasants were either executed or sent to forced labour camps and their properties confiscated by the state. Conservative figures put the loss of life from the resulting 1931-32 famine at 10 million people. In this 'impromptu' address to members of his own electorate in December 1937, the hypocrisy behind the façade of 'elections'—as Stalin gives 'advice' to his 'electors'—is patently clear.

'First of all, I would like to express my thanks to the electors for the confidence they have shown me.

I have been nominated as candidate, and the Election Commission of the Stalin District of the Soviet capital has registered my candidature. This, comrades, is an expression of great confidence. Permit me to convey to you my profound Bolshevik gratitude for this confidence that you have shown the Bolshevik Party of which I am a member, and me personally as a representative of that Party.

'The electors, the people, must demand that their deputies should remain equal to their tasks; that in their work they should not sink to the level of political philistines; that in their posts they should remain political figures of the Lenin type.'

I know what confidence means. It naturally lays upon me new and additional duties and, consequently, new and additional responsibilities. Well, it is not customary among us Bolsheviks to refuse responsibilities. I accept them willingly.

For my part, I would like to assure you, comrades, that you may safely rely on Comrade Stalin. You may take it for granted that Comrade Stalin will be able to discharge his duty to the people, to the working class, to the peasantry and to the intelligentsia.

Further, comrades, I would like to congratulate you on the occasion of the forthcoming national holiday, the day of the elections to the Supreme Soviet of the Soviet Union. The forthcoming elections are not merely elections, comrades, they are really a national holiday of our workers, our peasants and our intelligentsia. Never in the history of the world have there been such really free and really democratic elections—never! History knows no other example like it. The point is not that our elections will be universal, equal, secret and direct, although that fact in itself is of great importance. The point is that our universal elections will be carried out as the freest elections and the most democratic compared with elections in any other country in the world.

Universal elections exist and are also held in some capitalist countries, so-called democratic countries. But in what atmosphere are elections held there? In an atmosphere of class conflicts, in an atmosphere of class enmity, in an atmosphere of pressure brought to bear on the electors by the capitalists, landlords, bankers and other capitalist sharks. Such elections, even if they are universal, equal, secret and direct, cannot be called altogether free and altogether democratic elections.

Here, in our country, on the contrary, elections are held in an entirely different atmosphere. Here there are no capitalists and no landlords and, consequently, no pressure is exerted by propertied classes on non-propertied classes. Here elections are held in an atmosphere of collaboration between the workers, the peasants and the intelligentsia, in an atmosphere of mutual confidence between them, in an atmosphere, I would, say, of mutual friendship; because there are no capitalists in our country, no landlords, no exploitation, and nobody, in fact, to bring pressure to bear on people in order to distort their will.

That is why our elections are the only really free and really democratic elections in the whole world …

Further, comrades, I would like to give you some advice, the advice of a candidate to his electors. If you take capitalist countries you will find that peculiar, I would say, rather strange relations exist there between deputies and voters. As long as the elections are in progress, the deputies flirt with the electors, fawn on them, swear fidelity and make heaps of promises of every kind. It looks as though the deputies are completely dependent on the electors. As soon as the elections are over, and the candidates have become deputies, relations undergo a radical change. Instead of the deputies being dependent on the electors, they become entirely independent. For four or five years, that is, until the next elections, the deputy feels quite free, independent of the people, of his electors. He may pass from one camp to another, he may turn from the right road to the wrong, he may even become entangled in machinations of a not altogether savoury character, he may turn as many somersaults as he likes—he is independent.

'Never in the history of the world have there been such really free and really democratic elections—never!'

Can such relations be regarded as normal? By no means, comrades. This circumstance was taken into consideration by our Constitution and it made it a law that electors have the right to recall their deputies before the expiration of their term of office if they begin to play tricks, if they turn off the road, or if they forget that they are dependent on the people, on the electors.

This is a wonderful law, comrades. A deputy should know that he is the servant of the people, their emissary in the Supreme Soviet, and that he must follow the line laid down in the mandate given him by the people. If he turns off the road, the electors are entitled to demand new elections, and as to the deputy who turned off the road, they have the right to send him packing. This is a wonderful law. My advice, the advice of a candidate to his electors, is that they remember this electors' right, the right to recall deputies before the expiration of their term of office, that they keep an eye on their deputies, control them and, if they should take it into their heads to turn off the right road, to get rid of them and demand new elections. The

JOSEF V STALIN

77

Government is obliged to appoint new elections. My advice is to remember this law and to take advantage of it should need arise.

And, lastly, one more piece of advice from a candidate to his electors. What, in general, must one demand of one's deputies, selecting from all possible demands the most elementary?

The electors, the people, must demand that their deputies should remain equal to their tasks; that in their work they should not sink to the level of political philistines; that in their posts they should remain political figures of the Lenin type; that as public figures they should be as clear and definite as Lenin was that they should be as fearless in battle and as merciless towards the enemies of the people as Lenin was that they should be free from all panic, from any semblance of panic, when things begin, to get complicated and some danger or other looms on the horizon; that they should be as free from all semblance of panic as Lenin was that they should be as wise and deliberate in deciding complex problems requiring a comprehensive orientation and a comprehensive weighing of all pros and cons as Lenin was that they should be as upright and honest as Lenin was that they should love their people as Lenin did.

'Here elections are held in an atmosphere of collaboration between the workers, the peasants and the intelligentsia, in an atmosphere of mutual confidence between them ...'

Can we say that all the candidates are public figures precisely of this kind? I would not say so. There are all sorts of people in the world, there are all sorts of public figures in the world. There are people of whom you cannot say what they are, whether they are good or bad, courageous or timid, for the people heart and soul, or for the enemies of the people. There are such people and there are such public figures. They are also to be found among us, the Bolsheviks. You know yourselves, comrades, there are black sheep in every family. Of people of this indefinite type, people who resemble political philistines rather than political figures, people of this vague, uncertain type, the great Russian writer, Gogol, rather aptly said: 'Vague sort of people,' says he, 'neither one thing nor the other, you can't make head or tail of them, they are neither Bogdan in town nor Seliphan in the country.' There are also some rather apt popular sayings about such indefinite people and public figures: 'A middling sort of man—neither fish nor flesh', 'neither a candle for god nor a poker for the devil'.

I cannot say with absolute certainty that among the candidates (I beg their pardon, of course) and among our public figures there are no people who resemble political philistines more than anything else, who in character and make up resemble people of the type referred to in the popular saying: 'Neither a candle for god nor a poker for the devil.' I would like you, comrades, to exercise systematic influence on your deputies, to impress upon them that they must constantly keep before them the great image of the great Lenin and imitate Lenin in all things.

The functions of the electors do not end with the elections. They continue during the whole term of the given Supreme Soviet. I have already mentioned the law which empowers the electors to recall their deputies before the expiration of their term of office if they should turn off the right road. Hence, it is the duty and right of the electors to keep their deputies constantly under their control and to impress upon them that they must under no circumstances sink to the level of political philistines, impress upon them that they must be like the great Lenin. Such, comrades, is my second piece of advice to you, the advice of a candidate to his electors.'

Josef Stalin (1879-1953) was born Iosif Vissarionovich Dzhugashvili in Gori, Georgia (he adopted the name 'Stalin'—which literally means 'man of steel'—during his political career). Expelled from the Tiflis Orthodox Theological Seminary for spreading Marxist ideology he joined the Social Democratic Workers' Party, was arrested several times and twice exiled to Siberia during the period 1902-13. After playing a major role in the October 1917 Revolution, Stalin emerged as a leading Bolshevik figure during the Russian Civil War (1918-20). He became a member of the Communist Party Politburo and was appointed General Secretary of the Party in 1922—a position he held until his death forty years later.

After securing the undisputed leadership of the Party following Lenin's death in 1924, Stalin denounced his main rival, Trotsky, and allied himself with Nikolay Bukharin. After attacking the 'united opposition' of Zinoviev, Kamenov and Trotsky, Stalin removed Bukharin from the Politburo. During the next decade Stalin's agents murdered political opponents (Kirov) and paraded rivals in 'show trials' before executing them (Zinoviev, Kamenov, Bukharin and Rykov among others). In June 1937 he began a purge of the army, and tried and executed many of his top generals.

In 1928 Stalin began the first of his 'five year plans' requiring the forced collectivism of all agriculture and the industrialisation of the Soviet economy. When the kulak class of land-owners resisted, millions of peasants were executed or sent to forced labour camps and their properties confiscated. But Stalin's position in power—and the propagation of his 'cult of personality'—were so entrenched there was no way of deposing him.

Nothing could match Stalin's hypocrisy in signing a 'non-aggression' pact with Germany in August 1939. This treaty, which stated that the Soviet Union would not intervene if Hitler attacked neighbouring Poland from the East, was the precursor to World War II. After the start of the war in September 1939, Soviet troops occupied Lithuania, Latvia and Estonia while Romania succeeded Bessarabia and North Bukovian to the USSR. In April 1941 the Soviets signed a similar agreement with Japan but these 'non-aggression' pacts bought only momentary peace for the Russians. In June 1941 Germany launched a surprise attack on the Russian border and by mid-July the Nazis had pushed 450 miles inland to Smolensk.

Adolf Hitler

'The Jewish Question'

The Reichstag, Berlin, 30 January 1939.

Adolf Hitler in 1939.

In this speech marking the sixth anniversary of his ascension to power, Adolf Hitler (1889-1945) reveals the paranoia and obsession that drove him to become one of the most evil dictators of the twentieth century. The tactic of playing on people's insecurities—especially about the economy, nationalism and the shame of losing World War I, as Hitler did—was not unusual in politics, but Hitler directed this fear at one ethnic minority. Here, the German Fuehrer shows his unbridled hatred of the Jewry of Europe … a contempt that led to World War II, the death of over 50 million people and the systematic murder of an estimated 6 million people during the Holocaust. Hitler delivered this speech on the eve of Britain's entry into World War II.

‘When on the evening of 30 January 1933, six years ago today, beneath the light of their torches the tens of thousands of National Socialist fighters passed through the Brandenberger Tor to express to me the newly nominated Chancellor of the Reich, their feelings of overflowing joy and their confession of loyalty as my followers, countless anxious eyes both here in Berlin and throughout Germany gazed at the beginning of a development the issue of which it appeared impossible to discern or to foresee. Some 13 million German voters, men and women then stood beside me. An imposing number, but yet only a little more than a third of the sum of the votes cast. It was true that the remaining twenty million were divided and split up between thirty five other parties and groups.

The one thing which united the opponents of National Socialism was their common hatred of the young movement, a hatred born of their guilty consciences and worse intentions. As is still does today in other parts of the world, this united the priests of the Centre Party and Communist atheists, the Socialist out to abolish private property and capitalists whose interests were bound up with the stock exchange, Conservatives who wished to destroy the State and Republicans whose aim was to destroy the Reich. During the long battle of National Socialism for the leadership of the country they had all come together in defense of their interests and made common cause with Jewry. The bishop politicians of the various Churches extended their hands in benediction over this union. And against this splitting up of the nation, united only in negation stood that third of German men and women, with their faith, those who had undertaken to raise anew the German people and Reich in the face of world internal and external opposition.

The whole picture of the greatness of the collapse of Germany at that time begins gradually to grow dim, but one thing even today is not forgotten. It seemed that only a miracle could save Germany at the twelfth hour. And we National Socialists believed in this miracle. Over the belief in this miracle our foes made merry. The thought that one should wish to redeem the

ADOLF HITLER

81

nation from a ruin which now lasted a decade and a half simply through the force of a new idea appeared to those who were not National Socialists as the delusion of visionaries [phantasterei]; to the Jews and other enemies of the State it appeared as the last insignificant spasm of force within the national resistance, and when that was exhausted one might hope to be able finally to annihilate not only Germany but Europe.

A Germany sinking in Bolshevist chaos would at that time have hurled the whole West into a crisis of unimaginable gravity. Only the most limited of islanders could persuade themselves into believing that the Red plague would of its own accord have cried a halt before the sacredness of a democratic idea at the frontiers of States who had shown no interest in its advance. The rescue of Europe began at one end of the continent with Mussolini and Fascism. National Socialism continued this rescue in another part of Europe, and at the present moment we are witnessing in still a third country the same drama of a brave triumph over the Jewish international attempt to destroy European civilization. The six years which now lie behind us are filled with the most stupendous events in the whole of our German history. On 30 January 1933 I entered the Wilhelmstrasse filled with profound anxiety for the future of my people. Today after six years I am able to speak before the Reichstag of Greater Germany. We are indeed perhaps better able than other generations to realize the full meaning of those pious words "What a change by the grace of God" ...

'... at the present moment we are witnessing in still a third country the same drama of a brave triumph over the Jewish international attempt to destroy European civilization.'

The German nation has no feeling of hatred towards England, America or France; all it wants is peace and quiet. But the other nations are continually being stirred up to hatred for Germany and the German people by Jewish and non-Jewish agitators. And so, should warmongers achieve what they are aiming at, our own people would be landed in a situation for which they would be psychologically quite unprepared and which they would thus fail to grasp. I therefore consider it necessary that from now on our propaganda and our press should always make a point of answering these attacks, and above all bring them to the notice of the German people. The German nation must know who the men are who want to bring about war by hook or crook. It is my conviction that these people are mistaken in their calculations, for when once National Socialist propaganda is devoted to the answering of the attacks, we shall succeed just as we succeeded inside Germany herself in overcoming, through the convincing power of our propaganda, the Jewish world-enemy. The nations will in a short time realize that National Socialist Germany wants no enmity with other nations; that all the assertions as to our intended attacks on other nations are lies, lies born of morbid hysteria, or of a mania for self-preservation on the part of certain politicians; but that in certain States these lies are being used by unscrupulous profiteers to salvage their own finances. That, above all, international Jewry may hope in this way to satisfy its thirst for revenge and gain, but that on the other hand this is the grossest defamation which can be brought to bear on a great and peace loving nation. Never, for instance, have German soldiers fought on American soil, unless it was in the cause of American independence and freedom; but American soldiers were brought to Europe to help strangle a great nation which was fighting for its freedom. Germany did not attack America, but America attacked Germany and as the Committee of Investigation of the American House of Representatives concluded: from purely capitalist motives, without any other cause. There is but one thing that everyone should realize: these attempts cannot influence Germany in the slightest as to the way in which she settles her Jewish problem. On the contrary, in connection with the Jewish question I have this to say: it is a shameful spectacle to see how the whole democratic world is oozing sympathy for the poor tormented Jewish people, but remains hard-hearted and obdurate when it comes to helping them—which is surely, in view of its attitude, an obvious duty. The arguments that are brought up as an excuse for not helping them actually speak for us Germans and Italians.

For this is what they say:

1. 'We', that is the democracies, 'are not in a position to take in the Jews'. Yet in these empires there are not 10 people to the square kilometre. While Germany, with her 135 inhabitants to the square kilometre, is supposed to have room for them!
2. They assure us: We cannot take them unless Germany is prepared to allow them a certain amount of capital to bring with them as immigrants.

For hundreds of years Germany was good enough to receive these elements, although they possessed nothing except infectious political and physical diseases. What they possess today, they have by a very large extent gained at the cost of the less astute German nation by the most reprehensible manipulations.

Today we are merely paying this people what it deserves. When the German nation was, thanks to the inflation instigated and carried through by Jews, deprived of the entire savings which it had accumulated in years of honest work, when the rest of the world took away the German nation's foreign investments, when we were divested of the whole of our colonial possessions, these philanthropic considerations evidently carried little noticeable weight with democratic statesmen.

Today I can only assure these gentlemen that, thanks to the brutal education with which the democracies favoured us for fifteen years, we are completely hardened to all attacks of sentiment. After more than 800 000 children of the nation had died of hunger and undernourishment at the close of the War, we witnessed almost one million head of milking cows being driven away from us in accordance with the cruel paragraphs of a dictate which the humane democratic apostles of the world forced upon us as a peace treaty. We witnessed over one million German prisoners of war being retained in confinement for no reason at all for a whole year after the War was ended. We witnessed over one and a half million Germans being torn away from all that they possessed in the territories lying on our frontiers, and being whipped out with practically only what they wore on their backs. We had to endure having millions of our fellow countrymen torn from us without their consent, and without their being afforded the slightest possibility of existence. I could supplement these examples with dozens of the most cruel kind. For this reason we ask to be spared all sentimental talk.

The German nation does not wish its interests to be determined and controlled by any foreign nation. France to the French, England to the English, America to the Americans, and Germany to the Germans. We are resolved to prevent the settlement in our country of a strange people which was capable of snatching for itself all the leading positions in the land, and to oust it. For it is our will to educate our own nation for these leading positions. We have hundreds of thousands of very intelligent children of peasants and of the working classes. We shall have them educated—in fact we have already begun—and we wish that one day they, and not the representatives of an alien race, may hold the leading positions in the State together with our educated classes. Above all, German culture, as its name alone shows, is German and not Jewish, and therefore its management and care will be entrusted to members of our own nation.

'Today I will once more be a prophet: If the international Jewish financiers in and outside Europe should succeed in plunging the nations once more into a world war, then the result will not be the Bolshevization of the earth, and thus the victory of Jewry, but the annihilation of the Jewish race in Europe!'

If the rest of the world cries out with a hypocritical mien against this barbaric expulsion from Germany of such an irreplaceable and culturally eminently valuable element, we can only be astonished at the conclusions they draw from this situation. For how thankful they must be that we are releasing these precious apostles of culture, and placing them at the disposal of the rest of the world. In accordance with their own declarations they cannot find a single reason to excuse themselves for refusing to receive this most valuable race in their own countries. Nor can I see a reason why the members of this race should be imposed upon the German nation, while in the States, which are so enthusiastic about these 'splendid people', their settlement should suddenly be refused with every imaginable excuse. I think that the sooner this problem is solved the better; for Europe cannot settle down until the Jewish question is cleared up. It may very well be possible that sooner or later an agreement on this problem may be reached in Europe, even between those nations which otherwise do not so easily come together.

The world has sufficient space for settlements, but we must once and for all get rid of the opinion that the Jewish race was only created by God for the purpose of being in a certain percentage a parasite living on the body and the productive work of other nations. The Jewish race will have to adapt itself to sound constructive activity as other nations do, or sooner or later it will succumb to a crisis of an inconceivable magnitude.

One thing I should like to say on this day which may be memorable for others as well as for us Germans. In the course of my life I have very often been a prophet, and have usually been ridiculed for it. During the time of my struggle for power it was in the first instance the Jewish race which only received my prophecies with laughter when I said that I would one day take over the leadership of the State, and with it that of the whole nation, and that I would then among many other things settle the Jewish problem. Their laughter was uproarious, but I think that for some time now they have been laughing on the other side of their face. Today I will once more be a prophet: If the international Jewish financiers in and outside Europe should succeed in plunging the nations once more into a world war, then the result will not be the Bolshevization of the earth, and thus the victory of Jewry, but the annihilation of the Jewish race in Europe!

For the time when the non-Jewish nations had no propaganda is at an end. National Socialist Germany and Fascist Italy have institutions which enable them when necessary to enlighten the world about the nature of a question of which many nations are instinctively conscious, but which then have not yet clearly thought out. At the moment the Jews in certain countries may be fomenting hatred under the protection of the press, of the film, of wireless propaganda, of the theatre, of literature, etc., all of which they control. If this nation should once more succeed in inciting the millions which compose the nations into a conflict which is utterly senseless and only serves Jewish interests, then there will be revealed the effectiveness of an enlightenment which has completely routed the Jews of Germany in the space of a few years. The nations are no longer willing to die on the battlefield so that this unstable international race may profiteer from a war or satisfy its Old Testament vengeance. The Jewish watchword 'Workers of the world unite' will be conquered by a higher realization, namely 'Workers of all classes and of all nations, recognize your common enemy!'

Born illegitimately in Braunau, Austria, Hitler enlisted in World War I where he achieved the modest rank of corporal. When the war ended in 1918, Hitler felt betrayed by the conditions set out in the Treaty of Versailles and found a platform for venting his anger and frustration against the federal government in one of the minor, post-war political parties—the National Socialist German Workers' Party (abbreviated to Nazi).

Hitler was appointed Chancellor in January 1933 when President Paul von Hindenberg was wrongly advised that the 'little corporal' could be more closely controlled inside the German Parliament. Hitler's followers burned the Reichstag to the ground that year—an act he blamed on the Communist Party—and after calling a general election and seizing power, he crushed rivals inside his own party in June 1934.

When von Hindenberg died in August, Hitler was named sole ruler of Germany and opposition parties were outlawed. In 1938 he created 'Greater

Germany' by annexing Austria and then engineered events to present to an appeasing Britain and France an excuse to reclaim the German-populated borderland (Sudetenland) of neighbouring Czechoslovakia. On 1 September, 1939 German troops marched into Poland and started World War II (1939-45).

Hitler's megalomania ended with a self-inflicted gunshot wound—surrounded by his new wife, Eva Braun, his children and closest allies who calmly followed his lead—as Russian troops surrounded his Berlin bunker on 30 April 1945.

Lou Gehrig
'Farewell to Baseball'

Yankee Stadium, New York, 4 July 1939.

Lou Gehrig in the New York Yankee dugout in 1939.

Ludwig H. Gehrig (1903-1940) is considered the greatest first base-man in the history of baseball and has become an important part of the legend of the New York Yankees and the mythology of the game itself. A prodigious talent at Columbia University, 'Columbia Lou' as he was first known, came to the Yankees in 1923. Between May 1925 and May 1939 Gehrig played in 2130 consecutive games—setting a major league record which earned him the nickname the 'Iron Horse'. Gehrig had a career batting average of .340 (which means he safely got onto base 340 times out of every 1000 times he came up to bat) and hit 493 home runs (including four in one game) during his career. In early 1939, he inexplicably lost form. His batting average fell to .143 that year and he looked uncharacteristically clumsy in the outfield. On 2 May he voluntarily took himself out of the Yankees line-up when manager Joe McCarthy didn't have the heart to sit him out.

Gehrig was diagnosed with amyotrophic lateral sclerosis—a rare disease that causes spinal paralysis—that was to tragically cut short his life. On 4 July, 1939 he stood before 61 808 fans at Yankee Stadium and confirmed newspaper speculation about his career and health.

'Fans, for the past two weeks you have been reading about a bad break I got. Yet today I consider myself the luckiest man on the face of the earth. I have been in ballparks for seventeen years and have never received anything but kindness and encouragement from you fans.

Look at these grand men. Which of you wouldn't consider it the highlight of his career to associate with them for even one day? Sure, I'm lucky. Who wouldn't consider it an honor to have known Jacob Ruppert—also the builder of baseball's greatest empire, Ed Barrow—to have spent the next nine years with that wonderful little fellow Miller Huggins—then to have spent the next nine years with that outstanding leader, that smart student of psychology—the best manager in baseball today, Joe McCarthy!

Sure, I'm lucky. When the New York Giants, a team you would give your right arm to beat, and vice versa, sends you a gift, that's something! When everybody down to the groundskeepers and those boys in white coats remember you with trophies, that's something.

When you have a wonderful mother-in-law who takes sides with you in squabbles against her own daughter, that's something. When you have a father and mother who work all their lives so that you can have an education and build your body, it's a blessing! When you have a wife who has been a tower of strength and shown more courage than you dreamed existed, that's the finest I know. So I close in saying that I might have had a tough break—but I have an awful lot to live for!'

Lou Gehrig earned a new nickname—the 'Pride of the Yankees'—and immediately retired from the game to fight his disease. (Gehrig remained captain of the team and continued to carry the team line-up out to the umpires until even that task became too difficult for him). The Yankees took the extraordinary step of retiring his playing number (number 4, this first time that had been done) and the five-year waiting period for admission into the newly established Hall of Fame was waived for 1939—Gehrig was the sole admission in the Hall's first year.

Gehrig died in Riverdale, New York, aged just 38, in 1941. His story was given the full Hollywood treatment in *The Pride of the Yankees* starring Gary Cooper, which was released in 1942. Lou Gehrig's courage and humility belonged to a time now long gone in life and sport. Amyotrophic lateral sclerosis is now often referred to as 'Lou Gehrig's' disease, a victim of which is famous scientist and author of *A Brief History of Time*, Steven Hawkings.

Neville Chamberlain
'A Hint of War'

Speech to the House of Commons, 1 September 1939.

Neville Chamberlain announces the declaration of war in a BBC studio, 3 September 1939.

During the 1930s British Prime Minister Neville Chamberlain (1869-40) endeavoured to appease the nations of Germany and Italy to prevent another war in Europe. As a result, Britain stood by as Hitler's troops annexed Austria and threatened to wage war to 'liberate' the Sudeten Germans in neighbouring Czechoslovakia.

In 1938 Chamberlain was twice snubbed by Hitler before meeting him in Munich in September and securing an understanding from Germany that it could occupy the Sudetenland as long as it respected the sovereignty of its Czech neighbour. Arriving at Croydon Airport on 30 September 1938 Neville Chamberlain stood on the tarmac and spoke to the waiting media.

'I have in my hand a piece of paper, signed by Mr. Hitler, in which he assures us that there will be no war in Europe.'

The British Prime Minister was waving a statement that read:

'We, the German Fuehrer and Chancellor, and the British Prime Minister, have had a further meeting today and are agreed in recognizing that the question of Anglo-German relations is of the first importance for two countries and for Europe.

We regard the agreement signed last night and the Anglo-German Naval Agreement as symbolic of the desire of our two peoples never to go to war with one another again.

We are resolved that the method of consultation shall be the method adopted to deal with any other questions that may concern our two countries, and we are determined to continue our efforts to remove possible sources of difference, and thus to contribute to assure the peace of Europe.'

Chamberlain then went to the Prime Minister's residence at 10 Downing Street and declared:

'My good friends, this is the second time in our history that there has come from Germany to Downing Street peace with honour. I believe it is peace for our time. We thank you from the bottom of our hearts. And now I recommend you to go home and sleep quietly in your beds.'

Neville Chamberlain's 'peace for our time' declaration proved prophetically short-lived. Within six months German troops marched into Prague. By 1939 it was clear to most international observers that Hitler was on the path to war and any further attempts to negotiate with Germany were fruitless. In August 1939 Hitler signed a 'non-aggression' pact with his sworn enemy, Josef Stalin, which guaranteed that Russia would not come to

Poland's defence if attacked from the East. The Nazis then staged a fake raid on a German radio outpost along the German-Polish border as an excuse to invade Poland.

Just hours after Hitler's troops had invaded Poland, Prime Minister Neville Chamberlain gave this speech to the House of Commons on 1 September 1939.

'I do not propose to say many words tonight. The time has come when action rather than speech is required. Eighteen months ago in this House I prayed that the responsibility might not fall upon me to ask this country to accept the awful arbitrament of war. I fear that I may not be able to avoid that responsibility.

But, at any rate, I cannot wish for conditions in which such a burden should fall upon me in which I should feel clearer than I do today as to where my duty lies.

No man can say that the Government could have done more to try to keep open the way for an honourable and equitable settlement of the dispute between Germany and Poland. Nor have we neglected any means of making it crystal clear to the German Government that if they insisted on using force again in the manner in which they had used it in the past we were resolved to oppose them by force.

> 'I prayed that the responsibility might not fall upon me to ask this country to accept the awful arbitrament of war. I fear that I may not be able to avoid that responsibility.'

Now that all the relevant documents are being made public we shall stand at the bar of history knowing that the responsibility for this terrible catastrophe lies on the shoulders of one man, the German Chancellor, who has not hesitated to plunge the world into misery in order to serve his own senseless ambitions.

Only last night the Polish Ambassador did see the German Foreign Secretary, Herr von Ribbentrop. Once again he expressed to him what, indeed, the Polish Government had already said publicly, that they were willing to negotiate with Germany about their disputes on an equal basis.

What was the reply of the German Government? The reply was that without another word the German troops crossed the Polish frontier this morning at dawn and are since reported to be bombing open towns. In these circumstances there is only one course open to us.

His Majesty's Ambassador in Berlin and the French Ambassador have been instructed to hand to the German Government the following document:

"Early this morning the German Chancellor issued a proclamation to the German Army which indicated that he was about to attack Poland. Information which has reached His Majesty's Government in the United Kingdom and the French Government indicates that attacks upon Polish towns are proceeding. In these circumstances it appears to the

Governments of the United Kingdom and France that by their action the German Government have created conditions, namely, an aggressive act of force against Poland threatening the independence of Poland, which call for the implementation by the Government of the United Kingdom and France of the undertaking to Poland to come to her assistance. I am accordingly to inform your Excellency that unless the German Government are prepared to give His Majesty's Government satisfactory assurances that the German Government have suspended all aggressive action against Poland and are prepared promptly to withdraw their forces from Polish territory, His Majesty's Government in the United Kingdom will without hesitation fulfil their obligations to Poland."

If a reply to this last warning is unfavourable, and I do not suggest that it is likely to be otherwise, His Majesty's Ambassador is instructed to ask for his passports. In that case we are ready.

Yesterday, we took further steps towards the completion of our defensive preparation. This morning we ordered complete mobilization of the whole of the Royal Navy, Army and Royal Air Force. We have also taken a number of other measures, both at home and abroad, which the House will not perhaps expect me to specify in detail. Briefly, they represent the final steps in accordance with pre-arranged plans. These last can be put into force rapidly, and are of such a nature that they can be deferred until war seems inevitable. Steps have also been taken under the powers conferred by the House last week to safeguard the position in regard to stocks of commodities of various kinds.

'We shall enter [the war] with a clear conscience, with the support of the Dominions and the British Empire, and the moral approval of the greater part of the world.'

The thoughts of many of us must at this moment inevitably be turning back to 1914, and to a comparison of our position now with that which existed then. How do we stand this time? The answer is that all three Services are ready, and that the situation in all directions is far more favourable and reassuring than in 1914, while behind the fighting services we have built up a vast organization of Civil Defence under our scheme of Air Raid Precautions.

As regards the immediate manpower requirements, the Royal Navy, the Army and the Air Force are in the fortunate position of having almost as many men as they can conveniently handle at this moment. There are, however, certain categories of service in which men are immediately required, both for Military and Civil Defence. These will be announced in detail through the press and the BBC.

The main and most satisfactory point to observe is that there is today no need to make an appeal in a general way for recruits such as was issued by Lord Kitchener 25 years ago. That appeal has been anticipated by many months, and the men are already available. So much for the immediate present. Now we must look to the future. It is essential in the face of the tremendous task which confronts us, more especially in view of our past experiences in this matter, to organize our manpower this time upon as methodical, equitable and economical a basis as possible.

NEVILLE CHAMBERLAIN

We, therefore, propose immediately to introduce legislation directed to that end. A Bill will be laid before you which for all practical purposes will amount to an expansion of the Military Training Act. Under its operation all fit men between the ages of 18 and 41 will be rendered liable to military service if and when called upon. It is not intended at the outset that any considerable number of men other than those already liable shall be called up, and steps will be taken to ensure that the manpower essentially required by industry shall not be taken away.

'How do we stand this time? The answer is that all three Services are ready, and that the situation in all directions is far more favourable and reassuring than in 1914.'

There is one other allusion which I should like to make before I end my speech, and that is to record my satisfaction of His Majesty's Government, that throughout these last days of crisis Signor Mussolini also has been doing his best to reach a solution. It now only remains for us to set our teeth and to enter upon this struggle, which we ourselves earnestly endeavoured to avoid, with determination to see it through to the end.

We shall enter it with a clear conscience, with the support of the Dominions and the British Empire, and the moral approval of the greater part of the world.

We have no quarrel with the German people, except that they allow themselves to be governed by a Nazi Government. As long as that Government exists and pursues the methods it has so persistently followed during the last two years, there will be no peace in Europe. We shall merely pass from one crisis to another, and see one country after another attacked by methods which have now become familiar to us in their sickening technique.

We are resolved that these methods must come to an end. If out of the struggle we again re-establish in the world the rules of good faith and the renunciation of force, why, then even the sacrifices that will be entailed upon us will find their fullest justification.'

Just two days later on 3 September, Neville Chamberlain announced that a state of war existed between England and Germany. Chamberlain remained Prime Minister until May 1940 when criticism of his wartime leadership in the face of Hitler's invasion of Norway and Denmark saw him condemned by the hoots and jeers of his own supporters in the House of Commons. Announcing his resignation, he was replaced on 10 May 1940 by Winston Churchill. Neville Chamberlain died suddenly from stomach cancer later that same year.

War, Peace
and Freedom
1940-1949

Winston Churchill
'Our Finest Hour'

House of Commons, London, 18 June 1940.

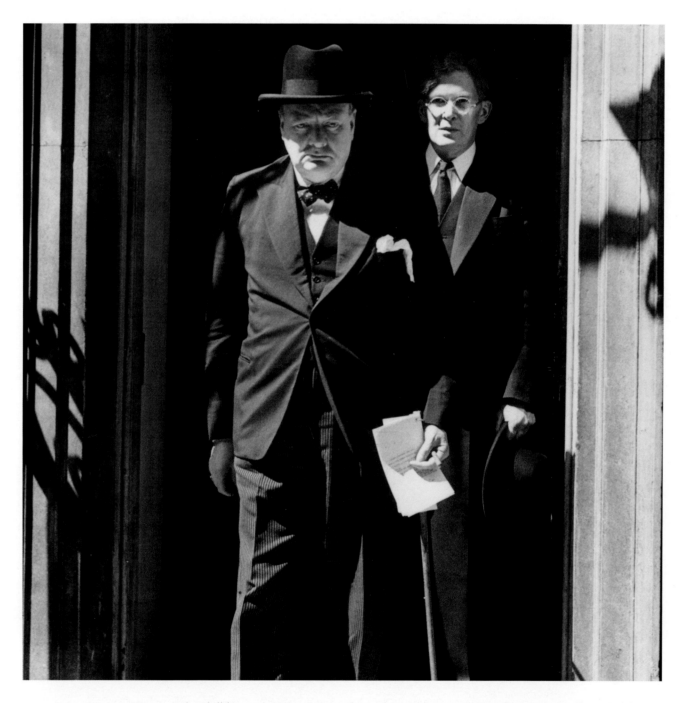

Prime Minister Winston Churchill leaves the Prime Minister's London residence at 10 Downing Street in June 1940.

Winston Leonard Spencer Churchill (1875-1965) is regarded as one of the most important statesmen of the twentieth century. The son of an aristocratic and politically influential father—Lord Randolph Churchill, seventh Duke of Marlborough—Winston appeared destined for high office from an early age.

The sound of World War II for a generation of people was Churchill's voice crackling over the radio across the Commonwealth. But the journey to his iconic status was by no means predictable. In 1900 he was elected to parliament as the Conservative MP for Oldham but his opposition to party leader Neville Chamberlain's policies saw him join the Liberal Party in 1904. Appointed Home Secretary in 1910, Churchill's political career suffered a major setback with his handling of the failed Dardanelles invasion at Gallipoli in 1915. Left out of the Conservative-Liberal coalition government, he resigned his seat and joined the army (serving in France) before returning to parliament as an independent member. However, Churchill's support of the Conservatives saw him serve in both Lloyd George and Stanley Baldwin's governments.

During the late 1930s Churchill again found himself an 'outcast' as a vocal opponent to Prime Minister Neville Chamberlain's seeming appeasement of Hitler during Germany's military build-up. When war broke out in September 1939 Chamberlain appointed Churchill First Lord of the Admiralty. After Chamberlain's resignation, Churchill was asked to lead the coalition government on 10 May 1940.

At the time of his appointment, Germany had begun massive attacks against Holland, Belgium, Luxembourg, and France and were experiencing stunning victories on all fronts. By the end of May, Holland, Luxembourg and Belgium had capitulated and the following month France fell. Britain now stood alone against the seemingly unstoppable German military juggernaut. As an island, the country's greatest threat was from the air—the Royal Air Force's 640 aircraft pitted against the German Luftwaffe's 2600. In this famous speech to the House of Commons, Prime Minister Winston Churchill inspired the nation to fight from the corner, and win.

❛The disastrous military events which have happened during the past fortnight have not come to me with any sense of surprise. Indeed, I indicated a fortnight ago as clearly as I could to the House that the worst possibilities were open; and I made it perfectly clear then that whatever happened in France would make no difference to the resolve of Britain and the British Empire to fight on, if necessary for years, if necessary alone. This brings me, naturally, to the great question of invasion from the air, and of the impending struggle between the British and German Air Forces. It seems quite clear that no invasion on a scale beyond the capacity of our land forces to crush speedily is likely to take place from the air until our Air Force has been definitely overpowered. In the meantime, there may be raids by parachute troops and attempted descents of airborne soldiers. But the great question is: Can we break Hitler's air weapon?

Now, of course, it is a very great pity that we have not got an Air Force at least equal to that of the most powerful enemy within striking distance of these shores. But we have a very powerful Air Force which has proved itself far superior in quality, both in men and in many types of machine, to what we have met so far in the numerous and fierce air battles which have been fought with the Germans. In France, where we were at a considerable disadvantage and lost many machines on the ground when they were standing round the aerodromes, we were accustomed to inflict in the air losses of as much as two and two-and-a-half to one. In the fighting over Dunkirk, which was a sort of no-man's-land, we undoubtedly beat the German Air Force, and gained the mastery of the local air, inflicting here a loss of three or four to one day after day. Anyone who looks at the photographs which were published a week or so ago of the re-embarkation, showing the masses of troops assembled on the beach and forming an ideal target for hours at a time, must realize that this re-embarkation would not have been possible unless the enemy had resigned all hope of recovering air superiority at that time and at that place.

'I see great reason for intense vigilance and exertion, but none whatever for panic or despair.'

In the defence of this Island the advantages to the defenders will be much greater than they were in the fighting around Dunkirk. We hope to improve on the rate of three or four to one which was realized at Dunkirk; and in addition all our injured machines and their crews which get down safely—and, surprisingly, a very great many injured machines and men do get down safely in modern air fighting—all of these will fall, in an attack upon these Islands, on friendly soil and live to fight another day; whereas all the injured enemy machines and their complements will be total losses as far as the war is concerned.

During the great battle in France, we gave very powerful and continuous aid to the French Army, both by fighters and bombers; but in spite of every kind of pressure we never would allow the entire metropolitan fighter strength of the Air Force to be consumed. This decision was painful, but it was also right, because the fortunes of the battle in France could not have been decisively affected even if we had thrown in our entire fighter force. That battle was lost by the unfortunate strategical opening, by the extraordinary and unforseen power of the armoured columns, and by the great preponderance of the German Army in numbers. Our fighter Air Force might easily have been exhausted as a mere accident in that great struggle, and then we should have found ourselves at the present time in a very serious plight. But as it is, I am happy to inform the House that our fighter strength is stronger at the present time relatively to the Germans, who have suffered terrible losses, than it has ever been; and consequently we believe ourselves possessed of the capacity to continue the war in the air under better conditions than we have ever experienced before. I look forward confidently to the exploits of our fighter pilots—these splendid men, this brilliant youth—who will have the glory of saving their native land, their island home, and all they love, from the most deadly of all attacks.

There remains, of course, the danger of bombing attacks, which will certainly be made very soon upon us by the bomber forces of the enemy. It is true that the German bomber force is superior in numbers to ours; but we have a very large bomber force also, which we shall use to strike at military targets in Germany without intermission. I do not at all underrate the severity of the ordeal which lies before us; but I believe our countrymen will show themselves capable of standing up to it, like the brave men of Barcelona, and will be able to stand up to it, and carry on in spite of it, at least as well as any other people in the world. Much will depend upon this; every man and every woman will have the chance to show the finest qualities of their race, and render the highest service to their cause. For all of us, at this time, whatever our sphere, our station, our occupation or our duties, it will be a help to remember the famous lines:

"He nothing common did or mean,
Upon that memorable scene."

I have thought it right upon this occasion to give the House and the country some indication of the solid, practical grounds upon which we base our inflexible resolve to continue the war. There are a good many people who say, "Never mind. Win or lose, sink or swim, better die than submit to tyranny—and such a tyranny." And I do not dissociate myself from them. But I can assure them that our professional advisers of the three Services unitedly advise that we should carry on the war, and that there are good and reasonable hopes of final victory. We have fully informed and consulted all the self-governing Dominions, and I have received from their Prime Ministers—Mr. Mackenzie King of Canada, Mr. Menzies of Australia, Mr. Fraser of New Zealand, and General Smuts of South Africa—I have received from all these eminent men, who all have Governments behind them elected on wide franchises, who are all there because they represent the will of their people, messages couched in the most moving terms in which they endorse our decision to fight on, and declare themselves ready to share our fortunes and to persevere to the end. That is what we are going to do.

We may now ask ourselves: In what way has our position worsened since the beginning of the war? It has worsened by the fact that the Germans have conquered a large part of the coast line of Western Europe, and many small countries have been overrun by them. This aggravates the possibilities of air attack and adds to our naval preoccupations. It in no way diminishes, but

'Let us brace ourselves to our duties, and bear ourselves that if the British Empire and its Commonwealth last for a thousand years, men will still say, "This was their finest hour."'

on the contrary definitely increases, the power of our long-distance blockade. Similarly, the entrance of Italy into the war increases the power of our long-distance blockade. We have stopped the worst leak by that. We do not know whether military resistance will come to an end in France or not, but should it do so, then of course the Germans will be able to concentrate their forces, both military and industrial, upon us. But for the reasons I have given to the House these will not be found so easy to apply. If invasion has become more imminent, as no doubt it has, we, being relieved from the task of maintaining a large army in France, have far larger and more efficient forces to meet it.

'If we fail, then the whole world, including all that we have known and cared for, will sink into the abyss of a new Dark Age made more sinister by the lights of perverted science.'

If Hitler can bring under his despotic control the industries of the countries he has conquered, this will add greatly to his already vast armament output. On the other hand, this will not happen immediately, and we are now assured of immense, continuous and increasing support in supplies and munitions of all kinds from the United States; and especially of aeroplanes and pilots from the Dominions and across the oceans coming from regions which are beyond the reach of enemy bombers.

I do not see how any of these factors can operate to our detriment on balance before the winter comes; and the winter will impose a strain upon the Nazi regime, with almost all Europe writhing and starving under its cruel heel, which, for all their ruthlessness, will run them very hard. We must not forget that from the moment when we declared war on the 3rd September it was always possible for Germany to turn all her Air Force upon this country, together with any other devices of invasion she might conceive, and that France could have done little or nothing to prevent her doing so. We have, therefore, lived under this danger, in principle and in a slightly modified form, during all these months. In the meanwhile, however, we have enormously improved our methods of defence, and we have learned what we had no right to assume at the beginning, namely, that the individual aircraft and the individual British pilot have a sure and definite superiority. Therefore, in casting up this dread balance sheet and contemplating our dangers with a disillusioned eye, I see great reason for intense vigilance and exertion, but none whatever for panic or despair.

We do not yet know what will happen in France or whether the French resistance will be prolonged, both in France and in the French Empire overseas. The French Government will be throwing away great opportunities and casting adrift their future if they do not continue the war in accordance with their treaty obligations, from which we have not felt able to release them. The House will have read the historic declaration in which, at the desire of many Frenchmen— and of our own hearts—we have proclaimed our willingness at the darkest hour in French history to conclude a union of common citizenship in this struggle. However matters may go in France or with the French Government, or other French Governments, we in this Island and in the British Empire will never lose our sense of comradeship with the French people. If we are now called upon to endure what they have been suffering, we shall emulate their courage, and if final victory rewards our toils they shall share the gains, aye, and freedom shall be restored to all. We abate nothing of our just demands; not one jot or tittle do we recede. Czechs, Poles, Norwegians, Dutch, Belgians have joined their causes to our own. All these shall be restored.

What General Weygand called the Battle of France is over. I expect that the Battle of Britain is about to begin. Upon this battle depends the survival of Christian civilization? Upon it depends our own British life, and the long continuity of our institutions and our Empire. The whole fury and might of the enemy must very soon be turned on us.

Hitler knows that he will have to break us in this Island or lose the war. If we can stand up to him, all Europe may be free and the life of the world may move forward into broad, sunlit uplands. But if we fail, then the whole world, including the United States, including all that we have known and cared for, will sink into the abyss of a new Dark Age made more sinister, and perhaps more protracted, by the lights of perverted science.

Let us therefore brace ourselves to our duties, and so bear ourselves that if the British Empire and its Commonwealth last for a thousand years, men will still say, 'This was their finest hour.'

Under Churchill's leadership, England weathered the 'Battle of Britain' during that summer before the RAF successfully repelled the German air attack by the end of October 1940. ('Never before had so few done so much for so many', Churchill famously stated). The British Prime Minister worked tirelessly during the next five years to bring a successful end to the war; he travelled over 150 000 miles, took a hands-on approach in devising military strategy, attended meetings with Roosevelt and Stalin at Yalta and inspired England, occupied Europe and the world with the sound of his voice in constant radio broadcasts (it was later revealed after his death that Churchill often utilised the services of a 'voice actor' for some radio broadcasts). It was Churchill who announced the unconditional surrender of German troops on 8 May 1945.

With Japanese forces in retreat in the Pacific, Churchill blundered politically when he dissolved the parliamentary coalition and sent the country to the polls. Tired and weary after the war, and looking to a new and brighter future, the people of Great Britain voted out his caretaker government in June 1945 in favour of Labour's Clement Atlee, who had served in Churchill's coalition cabinet as Deputy Prime Minister during the war.

Charles Lindbergh
'Neutrality and War'

Radio Broadcast on the United States Mutual Radio Network,
13 October, 1939.

Charles Lindbergh gives a radio address in 1939.

Charles A Lindbergh (1902-1974), the son of a United States Congressman, became an instant hero to millions in May 1927 when he was the first to fly an aeroplane non-stop across the Atlantic Ocean. After a gruelling 33-hour flight from New York, the quietly-spoken, handsome young man landed his small plane, the Spirit of St Louis, in Paris. Tragically, the kidnapping and subsequent murder of his infant son in 1932 (German born carpenter Bruno Richard Hauptmann was executed for the crime but there are many who still believe his innocence) and Lindbergh's anti-war stance (misrepresented as 'pro-Nazi' sympathies) changed the direction of his life.

In 1939, as Europe plunged into World War II and America wavered over its level of involvement, Charles Lindbergh spoke out against President Franklin Roosevelt's indirect military support of England and France and gave a voice to those Americans who wanted to keep their country out of war.

Two of Charles Lindbergh's most persuasive neutrality speeches were broadcast to the United States public over the Mutual Radio Network. This was the second of these, broadcast in October 1939.

❛Tonight, I speak again to the people of this country who are opposed to the United States entering the war which is now going on in Europe. We are faced with the need of deciding on a policy of American neutrality. The future of our nation and of our civilization rests upon the wisdom and foresight we use. Much as peace is to be desired, we should realize that behind a successful policy of neutrality must stand a policy of war. It is essential to define clearly those principles and circumstances for which a nation will fight. Let us give no one the impression that America's love for peace means that she is afraid of war, of that we are not fully capable and willing to defend all that is vital to us. National life and influence depend upon national strength, both in character and in arms. A neutrality built on pacifism alone will eventually fail.

Before we can intelligently enact regulations for the control of our armaments, our credit, and our ships, we must draw a sharp dividing line between neutrality and war; there must be no gradual encroachment on the defenses of our nation. Up to this line we may adjust our affairs to gain the advantages of peace, but beyond it must lie all the armed might of America, coiled in readiness to spring if once this bond is cut. Let us make clear to all countries where this line lies. It must be both within our intent and our capabilities. There must be no question of trading or bluff in this hemisphere. Let us give no promises we cannot keep make no meaningless assurances to an Ethiopia, a Czechoslovakia, or a Poland. The policy we decide upon should be as clear cut as our shorelines, and as easily defended as our continent.

This western hemisphere is our domain. It is our right to trade freely within it. From Alaska to Labrador, from the Hawaiian Islands to Bermuda, from Canada to South America, we must allow no invading army to set foot. These are the outposts of the United States. They form the essential outline of our geographical defense. We must be ready to wage war with all the resources of our nation if they are ever seriously threatened. Their defense is the mission of our army, our navy, and our air corps the minimum requirement of our military strength. Around these places should lie our line between neutrality and war. Let there be no compromise about our right to defend or trade within this area. If it is challenged by any nation, the answer must be war. Our policy of neutrality should have this as its foundation.

'When the time came to pay us back, these [European] countries simply refused to do so. They seized all the German colonies and carved up Europe to suit their fancy. These were the 'fruits of war'. They took our money and they took our soldiers.'

We must protect our sister American nations from foreign invasion, both for their welfare and our own. But, in turn, they have a duty to us. They should not place us in the position of having to defend them in America while they engage in wars abroad. Can we rightfully permit any country in America to give bases to foreign warships, or to send its army abroad to fight while it remains secure in our protection at home? We desire the utmost friendship with the people of Canada. If their country is ever attacked, our Navy will be defending their seas, our soldiers will fight on their battlefields, our fliers will die in their skies. But have they the right to draw this hemisphere into a European war simply because they prefer the Crown of England to American independence?

Sooner or later we must demand the freedom of this continent and its surrounding islands from the dictates of European power. American history clearly indicates this need. As long as European powers maintain their influence in our hemisphere, we are likely to find ourselves involved in their troubles. And they will loose no opportunity to involve us.

Our congress is now assembled to decide upon the best policy for this country to maintain during the war which is going on in Europe. The legislation under discussion involves three major issues - the embargo of arms, the restriction of shipping, and the allowance of credit. The action we take in regard to these issues will be an important indication to ourselves, and to the nations of Europe, whether or not we are likely to enter the conflict eventually as we did in the last war. The entire world is watching us. The action we take in America may either stop or precipitate this war.

Let us take up these issues, one at a time, and examine them. First, the embargo of arms: It is argued that the repeal of this embargo would assist democracy in Europe, that it would let us make a profit for ourselves from the sale of munitions abroad, and, at the same time, help to build up our own arms industry.

I do not believe that repealing the arms embargo would assist democracy in Europe—because I do not believe this is a war for democracy. This is a war over the balance of power in Europe a war brought about by the desire for strength on the part of Germany and the fear of strength on the part of England and France. The [more] munitions the armies obtain, the longer the war goes on, and the more devastated Europe becomes, the less hope there is for democracy. That is a lesson we should have learned from participation in the last war. If democratic principles had been applied in Europe after that war, if the 'democracies' of Europe had been willing to make some sacrifice to help democracy in Europe while it was fighting for its life, if England and France had offered a hand to the struggling republic of Germany, there would be no war today.

If we repeal the arms embargo with the idea of assisting one of the warring sides to overcome the other, then why mislead ourselves by talk of neutrality? Those who advance this argument should admit openly that repeal is a step toward war. The next step would the extension of credit, and the next step would be the sending of American troops.

To those who argue that we could make a profit and build up our own industry by selling munitions abroad, I reply that we in America have not yet reached a point where we wish to capitilize on the destruction and death of war. I do not believe that the material welfare of this country need, or that our spiritual welfare could withstand, such a policy. If our industry depends upon a commerce of arms for its strength, then our industrial system should be changed.

It is impossible for me to understand how America can contribute civilization and humanity by sending offensive instruments of destruction to European battlefields. This would not only implicate us in the war, but it would make us partly responsible for its devastation. The fallacy of helping to defend a political ideology, even though it be somewhat similar to our own, was clearly demonstrated to us in the last war. Through our help that war was won, but neither the democracy nor the justice for which we fought grew in the peace that followed our victory.

Our bond with Europe is a bond of race and not of political ideology. We had to fight a European army to establish democracy in this country. It is the European race we must preserve; political progress will follow. Racial strength is vital politics, a luxury. If the white race is ever seriously threatened, it may then be time for us to take our part in its protection, to fight side by side with the English, French, and Germans, but not with one against the other for our mutual destruction.

'Let us not dissipate our strength in these wars of politics and possession.'

Let us not dissipate our strength, or help Europe to dissipate hers, in these wars of politics and possession. For the benefit of western civilization, we should continue our embargo on offensive armaments. As far as purely defensive arms are concerned, I, for one, am in favor of supplying European countries with as much as we can spare of the material that falls within this category. There are technicians who will argue that offensive and defensive arms cannot be separated completely. That is true, but it is no more difficult to make a list of defensive weapons than it is to separate munitions of war from semi-manufactured articles, and we are faced with that problem today. No one says that we should sell opium because it is difficult to make a list of narcotics. I would as soon see our country traffic in opium as in bombs. There are certain

'I do not believe this is a war for democracy. This is a war over the balance of power in Europe ... the desire for strength on the part of Germany and the fear of strength on the part of England and France.'

borderline cases, but there are plenty of clear cut examples: for instance, the bombing plane and the anti-aircraft cannon. I do not want to see American bombers dropping bombs which will kill and mutilate European children, even if they are not flown by American pilots. But I am perfectly willing to see American anti-aircraft guns shooting American shells at invading bombers over any European country. And I believe that most of you who are listening tonight will agree with me.

The second major issue for which we must create a policy concerns the restrictions to be placed on our shipping. Naval blockades have long been accepted as an element of warfare. They began on the surface of the sea, followed the submarine beneath it, and now reach up into the sky with aircraft. The laws and customs which were developed during the surface era were not satisfactory to the submarine. Now, aircraft bring up new and unknown factors for consideration. It is simple enough for a battleship to identify the merchantman she captures. It is a more difficult problem for a submarine if that merchantman may carry cannon; it is safer to fire a torpedo than to come up and ask. For bombing planes flying at high altitudes and through conditions of poor visibility, identification of a surface vessel will be more difficult still.

In modern naval blockades and warfare, torpedoes will be fired and bombs dropped on probabilities rather than on certainties of identification. The only safe course for neutral shipping at this time is to stay away from the warring countries and dangerous waters of Europe.

The third issue to be decided relates to the extension of credit. Here again we may draw from our experience in the last war. After that war was over, we found ourselves in the position of having financed a large portion of European countries. And when the time came to pay us back, these countries simply refused to do so. They not only refused to pay the wartime loans we made, but they refused to pay back what we loaned them after the war was over. As is so frequently the case, we found that loaning money eventually created animosity instead of gratitude. European countries felt insulted when we asked to be repaid. They called us 'Uncle Shylock'. They were horror struck at the idea of turning over to us any of their islands in America to compensate for their debts, or for our help in winning their war. They seized all the German colonies and carved up Europe to suit their fancy. These were the 'fruits of war'. They took our money and they took our soldiers. But there was not the offer of one Caribbean island in return for the debts they 'could not afford to pay'.

The extension of credit to a belligerent country is a long step toward war, and it would leave us close to the edge. If American industry loans money to a belligerent country, many interests will feel that it is more important for that country to win than for our own to avoid the war. It is unfortunate but true that there are interests in America who would rather lose American lives than their own dollars. We should give them no opportunity.

I believe that we should adopt as our program of American neutrality—as our contribution to western civilization—the following policy:

1. An embargo on offensive weapons and munitions.
2. The unrestricted sale of purely defensive armaments.
3. The prohibition of American shipping from the belligerent countries of Europe and their danger zones.
4. The refusal of credit to belligerent nations or their agents.

Whether or not this program is adopted depends upon the support of those of us who believe in it. The United States of America is a democracy. The policy of our country is still controlled by our people. It is time for us to take action. There has never been a greater test for the democratic principle of government.'

The former hero of a nation was publicly denounced by President Roosevelt for his stance. He resigned his Army Air Corps officer's commission but when he tried to re-enlist after the Japanese attack on Pearl Harbour in December 1941, his request was refused. Lindbergh worked as at technical advisor and test pilot for the Ford Motor Company and the United Aircraft Corporation during the war. Although he remained in the private sector after the war, President Eisenhower restored Lindbergh's commission and appointed him a brigadier general in the air force. Lindbergh's book, *Spirit of St Louis*, won the Pulitzer Prize in 1954. Charles Lindbergh, who spoke out about conservation issues in latter life, died of cancer in 1974.

Cardinal Clement von Galen
'Against Aktion T4'

Sermon at Münster Cathedral, Germany, 3 August 1941.

Cardinal Clement von Galen is congratulated on his elevation to Cardinal in 1946.

Clement August von Galen (1878-1946) was the Catholic Bishop of Münster during the rise to power of the Nazi Party in the 1930s and was an outspoken opponent of the German government and its policies. He attacked the Gestapo for their raids on Jesuit houses in Münster and stated from the pulpit that no German citizen had any defence against the Nazis' power now 'they had replaced the courts and were above the law'.

The Nazi program to eliminate 'life unworthy of life', code-named 'Aktion T4', began in October 1939. It first focused on newborn and very young children, where midwives and doctors were required to register children up to age three who showed symptoms of mental retardation or physical deformity. On Hitler's orders, certain medical staff were granted the authority to name those who 'according to human judgment, are incurable … (and) can, upon a most careful diagnosis of their condition of sickness, be accorded a mercy death.'

The Nazi euthanasia program expanded to include older disabled children and adults and was eventually taken over by the SS. Six 'killing centres' were established, including a well-known psychiatric clinic at Hadamar. A former prison at Brandenburg was converted into a killing centre where the first experimental gassings took place. The gas chambers were disguised as shower rooms, but were sealed chambers connected by pipes to cylinders of carbon monoxide. Each killing centre also included a crematorium where the bodies were taken for disposal (families were then informed the cause of death was purely medical, such as heart failure or pneumonia). This later became the blueprint for the extermination of Jewish people.

In 1941 the chaplain of a mental asylum briefed von Galen about the Nazi removal of patients to concentration camps for extermination because they were no longer 'productive'. On a Sunday in 1941, in Münster Cathedral, Cardinal Clement von Galen risked his life by openly condemning the Nazi euthanasia program.

❝ Fellow Christians! In the pastoral letter of the German bishops of June 26 1941, which was read out in all the Catholic churches in Germany on July 6 1941, it states among other things: It is true that there are definite commandments in Catholic moral doctrine which are no longer applicable if their fulfilment involves too many difficulties.

However, there are sacred obligations of conscience from which no one has the power to release us and which we must fulfil even if it costs us our lives. Never under any circumstances may a human being kill an innocent person apart from war and legitimate self-defence. On July 6, I already had cause to add to the pastoral letter the following explanation: for some months we have been hearing reports that, on the orders of Berlin, patients from mental asylums who have been ill for a long time and may appear incurable, are being compulsorily removed. Then, after a short time, the relatives are regularly informed that the corpse has been burnt and the ashes can be delivered. There is a general suspicion verging on certainty, that these numerous unexpected deaths of mentally ill people do not occur of themselves but are deliberately brought about, that the doctrine is being followed, according to which one may destroy so-called "worthless life," that is, kill innocent people if one considers that their lives are of no further value for the nation and the state.

I am reliably informed that lists are also being drawn up in the asylums of the province of Westphalia as well of those patients who are to be taken away as so-called "unproductive national comrades" and shortly to be killed. The first transport left the Marienthal institution near Münster during this past week.

German men and women, section 211 of the Reich Penal Code is still valid. It states: "He who deliberately kills another person will be punished by death for murder if the killing is premeditated."

Those patients who are destined to be killed are transported away from home to a distant asylum presumably in order to protect those who deliberately kill those poor people, members of our families, from this legal punishment. Some illness is then given as the cause of death. Since the corpse has been burnt straight away, the relatives and also the criminal police are unable to establish whether the illness really occurred and what the cause of death was.

'Who will be able to trust his doctor any more? He may report his patient as "unproductive" and receive instructions to kill him. It is impossible to imagine the degree of moral depravity, that would then spread if this dreadful doctrine is tolerated.'

However, I have been assured that the Reich Interior Ministry and the office of the Reich Doctors' Leader, Dr. Conti, make no bones about the fact that in reality a large number of mentally ill people in Germany have been deliberately killed and more will be killed in the future.

The Penal Code lays down in section 139: "He who receives credible information concerning the intention to commit a crime against life and neglects to alert the authorities or the person who is threatened in time ... will be punished."

When I learned of the intention to transport patients from Marienthal in order to kill them, I brought a formal charge at the State Court in Münster and with the Police President in Münster by means of a registered letter which read as follows: "According to information which I have received, in the course of this week a large number of patients from the Marienthal Provincial Asylum near Münster are to be transported to the Eichberg asylum as so-called "unproductive national comrades" and will then soon be deliberately killed, as is generally believed has occurred with such transports from other asylums. Since such an action is not only contrary to the moral laws of God and Nature but also is punishable with death as murder under section 211 of the Penal Code, I hereby bring a charge in accordance with my duty under section 139 of the Penal Code, and request you to provide immediate protection for the national comrades threatened in this way by taking action against those agencies who are intending their removal and murder, and that you inform me of the steps that have been taken."

I have received no news concerning intervention by the Prosecutor's Office or by the police ... Thus we must assume that the poor helpless patients will soon be killed.

For what reason? Not because they have committed a crime worthy of death. Not because they attacked their nurses or orderlies so that the latter had no other choice but to use legitimate force to defend their lives against their attackers. Those are cases where, in addition to the killing of an armed enemy in a just war, the use of force to the point of killing is allowed and is often required.

'None of our lives will be safe any more. No police force will protect us and no court will investigate our murder and give the murderer the punishment he deserves.'

No, it is not for such reasons that these unfortunate patients must die but rather because, in the opinion of some department, on the testimony of some commission, they have become "worthless life" because according to this testimony they are "unproductive national comrades." The argument goes: they can no longer produce commodities, they are like an old machine that no longer works, they are like an old horse which has become incurably lame, they are like a cow which no longer gives milk.

What does one do with such an old machine? It is thrown on the scrap heap. What does one do with a lame horse, with such an unproductive cow?

No, I do not want to continue the comparison to the end—however fearful the justification for it and the symbolic force of it are. We are not dealing with machines, horses and cows whose only function is to serve mankind, to produce goods for man. One may smash them, one may slaughter them as soon as they no longer fulfil this function.

No, we are dealing with human beings, our fellow human beings, our brothers and sisters. With poor people, sick people, if you like unproductive people.

But have they for that reason forfeited the right to life?

Have you, have I the right to live only so long as we are productive, so long as we are recognized by others as productive?

If you establish and apply the principle that you can kill "unproductive" fellow human beings then woe betide us all when we become old and frail! If one is allowed to kill the unproductive people then woe betide the invalids who have used up, sacrificed and lost their health and strength in the productive process. If one is allowed forcibly to remove one's unproductive fellow human beings then woe betide loyal soldiers who return to the homeland seriously disabled, as cripples, as invalids. If it is once accepted that people have the right to kill "unproductive" fellow humans—and even if initially it only affects the poor defenceless mentally ill—then as a matter of principle murder is permitted for all unproductive people, in other words for the incurably sick,

CARDINAL CLEMENT VON GALEN

113

the people who have become invalids through labour and war, for us all when we become old, frail and therefore unproductive.

Then, it is only necessary for some secret edict to order that the method developed for the mentally ill should be extended to other "unproductive" people ... to those suffering from incurable lung disease, to the elderly who are frail or invalids, to the severely disabled soldiers. Then none of our lives will be safe any more. Some commission can put us on the list of the "unproductive," who in their opinion have become worthless life. And no police force will protect us and no court will investigate our murder and give the murderer the punishment he deserves.

Who will be able to trust his doctor any more? He may report his patient as "unproductive" and receive instructions to kill him. It is impossible to imagine the degree of moral depravity, of general mistrust that would then spread even through families if this dreadful doctrine is tolerated, accepted and followed.

Woe to mankind, woe to our German nation if God's Holy Commandment "Thou shalt not kill," which God proclaimed on Mount Sinai amidst thunder and lightning, which God our Creator inscribed in the conscience of mankind from the very beginning, is not only broken, but if this transgression is actually tolerated and permitted to go unpunished.'

As a result of this sermon, Hitler momentarily suspended 'Aktion T4', however, the program quietly continued but without the gassings—drugs and starvation were used instead—and doctors were encouraged to decide in favour of death whenever euthanasia was considered. A report published in 2005 stated that 200 000 mentally ill and handicapped German citizens were put to death under this program.

Although the Nazis left Bishop von Galen 'unharmed' to avoid making him into a martyr, persecution of priests continued with the arrest and then execution of three parish priests who had distributed von Galen's sermon. Hundreds of clergy were arrested, arraigned before Nazi courts and interned in concentration camps (in Dachau alone, 2770 priests, mainly Polish, were interned and some 4000 priests were put to death in concentration camps during the war). Ironically, the Cathedral in Münster was destroyed by allied bombs in October 1943.

In 1946 Pope Pius XII announced that Bishop von Galen would be one of thirty new cardinals ordained in Rome and the man who had defied Hitler, was warmly greeted by crowds outside St Peters. The following month, on 22 March, Cardinal von Galen died from a burst appendix upon his return to Germany. Calls for his beatification—the first step on road to sainthood—began in 1956 and were finally answered by Pope John Paul II in 2004.

Hideki Tojo
'The Hegemony of East Asia'

Commemoration rally, Tokyo, Japan, 29 November 1941.

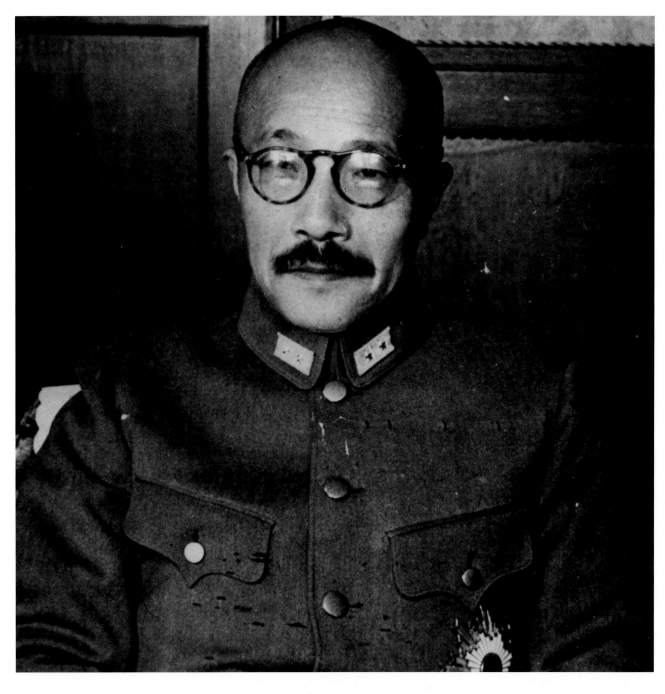

Hideki Tojo in 1942.

Japanese General and Prime Minister Hideki Tojo (1885-1945) ordered the surprise attack on the US Naval base in Pearl Harbor on 7 December 1941, but many analysts view this little-known speech, delivered a week before, as an indication of his intent. Under Tojo, Japanese foreign policy became inexorably linked with expansion, invasion and occupation. After military successes in China during the 1930s, where Japan set up a puppet government in Manchukuo and captured Peking, Japan invaded Burma and Indochina (Vietnam). Thailand and British interests in Singapore were the next logical threat but the US freeze of oil imports severely threatened Japan's plans for extending its control in East Asia. An attack on the US Naval base in Pearl Harbour, Hawaii was planned in 1940 and finally approved in September 1941 after Tojo was named Prime Minister.

On 29 November 1941 the US State Department received a Japanese message protesting the alleged flight of an American airplane over the island of Formosa on November 20, claiming this was a violation of Japanese territory and requesting that the matter 'be brought to the attention of the United States authorities concerned.' On November 24, an unidentified airplane had carried out a reconnaissance of Guam. The same afternoon, the State Department instructed American diplomatic and consular offices at Saigon, Bangkok and Singapore to report 'all movements of military or naval units' to the American Consul at Manila so that they could be transmitted to Admiral Hart, the Commander in Chief of the US Asiatic Fleet.

Overshadowing the events of the day, however, was an Associated Press report of this speech made by Premier Tojo in Tokyo in commemoration of the first anniversary of the Joint Declaration by the Governments of Japan and Manchukuo and the Wang Ching-wei regime in Japanese-occupied China.

'It is certainly the most fortunate lot of the three powers to have the privilege of collaborating together under this banner for cutting open the thorny way, and one year has already gone by since we started this honorable work together, and if it is not the greatest task of the present century what else can it be.

However, if we look around we find that there are still many countries who are indulging in actions hostile to us. In fact they are trying to throw obstacles in the way of the construction of the East Asia co-prosperity sphere and are trying to enjoy the dream of exploitation of East Asia at the cost of the 1000 million populace of the East Asiatic peoples to satisfy their greed of possession.

The fact that [Chinese Nationalist leader] Chiang Kai-shek is dancing to the tune of Britain, America, and communism at the expense of able-bodied and promising young men in his futile resistance against Japan is only due to the desire of Britain and the United States to fish in the troubled waters of East Asia by pitting the East Asiatic peoples against each other and to grasp the hegemony of East Asia. This is a stock in trade of Britain and the United States. For the honor and pride of mankind we must purge this sort of practice from East Asia with a vengeance.'

Extracts from Premier Tojo's speech were carried in American newspapers on November 30 under the headline, 'Japan Threatens to Purge Asia of US And Britain' (1). November 29 was also the date fixed by Tojo as the final deadline for his US Ambassadors to obtain a written agreement from the United States about the Japanese protest or else things would 'automatically' begin to happen. That day, US State Secretary Hull telephoned President Roosevelt at Warm Springs and after discussing the Japanese Prime Minister's 'bellicose statement', the US President was prompted to return to Washington DC because of the extreme acuteness of the situation. The president's press secretary offered a brief statement to this effect which was also reported in newspapers.

United States' intelligence had cracked the Japanese diplomatic code and was already listening to messages between Tokyo and its US Ambassadors. On November 28 (Japan time), Tojo cabled his ambassador and stated that he did not wish for Ambassador Nomura 'to give the impression that the negotiations are broken off.'

This message was available in Washington on Sunday 30 November (Washington time). Late that evening US Ambassador Kurusu informed Bureau Chief Yamamoto in Tokyo that arrangements had been made for the two Ambassadors to meet with Secretary Hull on Monday, 1 December. Kurusu reported that President Roosevelt was returning to Washington the next day because of Premier Tojo's speech. When Yamamoto urged the Ambassador to continue negotiations, Kurusu said that both the Premier and the Foreign Minister would need 'to change the tone of their speeches.'

At 1:28pm on Sunday afternoon, 30 November, the US State Department also received, through Ambassador Winant in London, the following message from British Prime Minister Churchill for President Roosevelt:

'It seems to me that one important method remains unused in averting war between Japan and our two countries, namely a plain declaration, secret or public as may be thought best, that any further act of aggression by Japan will lead immediately to the gravest consequence. I realize your constitutional difficulties but it would be tragic if Japan drifted into war by encroachment without having before her fairly and squarely the dire character of a further aggressive step. I beg you to consider whether, at the moment which you judge right which may be very near, you should not say that "any further Japanese aggression would compel you to place the gravest issues before Congress", or words to that effect. We would, of course, make a similar declaration or share in a joint declaration, and in any ease arrangements are being made to synchronize our action with yours. Forgive me, my dear friend, for presuming to press such a course upon you, but I am convinced that it might make all the difference and prevent a melancholy extension of the war.'

One of the purposes of the British Ambassador's call was to hand Secretary Hull the following memorandum:

MOST SECRET

There are important indications that Japan is about to attack Thailand and this attack will include a sea-borne expedition to seize strategic points in the Kra isthmus.

We have plans for the rapid movement of a force from Malaya to hold a line across the Kra isthmus in the neighborhood of Singora. Time is the essence of this plan, particularly at this season of the year when the Kra isthmus is water logged. Consequently great tactical advantage lies with the side which gets there first.

R.A.F. are reconnoitring an arc of 180 miles from Tedta Bharu for three days commencing November 29th and our Commander in Chief, Far East has requested Commander in Chief, Asiatic Fleet at Manila to undertake air reconnaissance …

Thus US attention was diverted away from its naval base at Pearl Harbor. While negotiations continued between Japan and the US, Japan launched an unprovoked attack that catapulted America into World War II. Wake Island, Singapore, the Philippines, the Solomons, Sumatra, Java, Timor, Burma and most of New Guinea came under Japanese Imperialist control in 1942 before the Battle of Midway turned the tide of the Pacific War in the Allies' favour.

Arrested in 1945, Hideki Tojo attempted to commit suicide by shooting himself in the chest but survived and was later hanged as a war criminal by the US in 1948.

Mohandas K Gandhi

'Quit India'

Address to All India Congress Committee, Bombay, 8 August 1942.

Mohandas Gandhi leads a non-violent protest against government monopoly on salt production in 1930.

Mohandas Gandhi proved in his lifetime that non-violent defiance of unjust laws could change the world. He used this effectively both against the British and in an attempt to broker peace between Muslim and Hindu factions in his own country. It was a message as old as the time of Jesus and one subsequently used in protest movements throughout the world.

'Mahatma' (which means 'Great Soul') Gandhi's belief in the injustice of British colonialism in India saw him imprisoned several times, where he used fasting as an act of defiance and protest. In 1931 Gandhi was released from prison and, after brokering a truce between the National Congress and the British, travelled to London to attend the Round Table Conference on Indian constitutional reform. Returning to India, his pattern of civil disobedience and arrest continued but he also threatened to fast 'unto death' to placate warring religious factions. Finally Britain allowed Indian Congress ministers to hold office in provincial legislatures in 1937.

After the outbreak of World War II in September 1939, Gandhi stepped up his campaign for Indian home rule, arguing that an independent India could best serve Britain in her fight against fascism. In August 1942 Gandhi outlined his plan of action to the All India Congress Committee in Bombay, which was the formal vehicle being used to communicate with Britain. The following extract is part of the concluding portion of Gandhi's speech which was delivered in English.

'I have taken such an inordinately long time over pouring out what was agitating my soul, to those whom I had just now the privilege of serving. I have been called their leader or, in the military language, their commander. But I do not look at my position in that light. I have no weapon but love to wield my authority over anyone. I do sport a stick which you can break into bits without the slightest exertion. It is simply my staff with the help of which I walk. Such a cripple is not elated, when he has been called upon to bear the greatest burden. You can share that burden only when I appear before you not as your commander but as a humble servant. And he who serves best is the chief among equals.

I want to declare to the world. Although I may forfeit the regard of many friends in the West and I must bow my head low; but even for their friendship or love I must not suppress the voice of conscience—promoting my inner basic nature today. There is something within me impelling me to cry out my agony. I have known humanity. I have studied something of psychology. Such a man knows exactly what it is. I do not mind how you describe it. That voice within tells me, 'You have to stand against the whole world although you may have to stand alone. You have to stare in the face the whole world although the world may look at you with bloodshot eyes. Do not fear. Trust the little voice residing within your heart. It says : "Forsake friends, wife and all; but testify to that for which you have lived and for which you have to die. I want to live my full span of life. And for me I put my span of life at 120 years. By that time India will be free, the world will be free."

Let me tell you that I do not regard England or for that matter America as free countries. They are free after their own fashion, free to hold in bondage coloured races of the earth. Are England and America fighting for the liberty of these races today? If not, do not ask me to wait until after the war. You shall not limit my concept of freedom.

Unconsciously from its very foundations long ago, this Congress has been building on non-violence known as constitutional methods. I trust the whole of India today to launch upon a non-violent struggle. I trust, because of my nature to rely upon the innate goodness of human nature which perceives the truth and prevails during the crisis as if by instinct. But even if I am deceived in this I shall not swerve. I shall not flinch. From its very inception the Congress based its policy on peaceful methods, included Swaraj and the subsequent generations added non-violence. When Dadabhai entered the British Parliament, Salisbury dubbed him as a black man; but the English people defeated Salisbury and Dadabhai went to the Parliament by their vote. India was delirious with joy. These things however India has outgrown.

It is, however, with all these things as the background that I want Englishmen, Europeans and all the United Nations to examine in their hearts what crime has India committed in demanding Independence. I ask, is it right for you to distrust such an organization with all its background, tradition and record of over half a century and misrepresent its endeavours before all the world by every means at your command? Is it right that by hook or by crook, aided by the foreign press, aided by the President of the USA, or even by the Generalissimo of China [Chiang Kai-shek] who has yet to win his laurels, you should present India's struggle in shocking caricature? I have met the Generalissimo. I have known him through Madame Shek who was my interpreter; and though he seemed inscrutable to me, not so Madame Shek; and he allowed me to read his mind through her. There is a chorus of disapproval and righteous protest all over the world against us. They say we are erring, the move is inopportune. I used to have great regard for British diplomacy which has enabled them to hold the Empire so long. Now it stinks in my nostrils, and others have studied that diplomacy and are putting it into practice. They may succeed in getting, through these methods, world opinion on their side for a time; but India will speak against that world opinion. She will raise her voice against all the organized propaganda. I will speak against it. Even if all the United Nations opposed me, even if the whole of India forsakes me, I will say, "You are wrong. India will wrench with non-violence her liberty from unwilling hands."

'And even when India is met with such angry opposition, she says, "We won't hit below the belt, we have learnt sufficient gentlemanliness. We are pledged to non-violence."'

I will go ahead not for India's sake alone, but for the sake of the world. Even if my eyes close before there is freedom, non-violence will not end. They will be dealing a mortal blow to China and to Russia if they oppose the freedom of non-violent India which is pleading with bended knees for the fulfilment of debt along overdue. Does a creditor ever go to debtor like that? And even when India is met with such angry opposition, she says, "We won't hit below the belt, we have learnt sufficient gentlemanliness. We are pledged to non-violence." I have been the author of the non-embarrassment policy of the Congress and yet today you find me

MOHANDAS K GANDHI

121

talking this strong language. I say it is consistent with our honour. If a man holds me by the neck and wants to drawn me, may I not struggle to free myself directly? There is no inconsistency in our position today.

There are representatives of the foreign press assembled here today. Through them I wish to say to the world that the United Powers who somehow or other say that they have need for India, have the opportunity now to declare India free and prove their bona fides. If they miss it, they will be missing the opportunity of their lifetime, and history will record that they did not discharge their obligations to India in time, and lost the battle. I want the blessings of the whole world so that I may succeed with them. I do not want the United Powers to go beyond their obvious limitations. I do not want them to accept non-violence and disarm today. There is a fundamental difference between fascism and this imperialism which I am fighting. Do the British get from India which they hold in bondage? Think what difference it would make if India was to participate as a free ally. That freedom, if it is to come, must come today. It will have no taste left in it today if you who have the power to help cannot exercise it. If you can exercise it, under the glow of freedom what seems impossible, today, will become possible tomorrow.

> 'Think what difference it would make if India was to participate as a free ally. That freedom, if it is to come, must come today.'

If India feels that freedom, she will command that freedom for China. The road for running to Russia's help will be open. The Englishmen did not die in Malaya or on Burma soil. What shall enable us to retrieve the situation? Where shall I go, and where shall I take the forty crores of India? How is this vast mass of humanity to be aglow in the cause of world deliverance, unless and until it has touched and felt freedom. Today they have no touch of life left. It has been crushed out of them. It lustre is to be put into their eyes, freedom has to come not tomorrow, but today.'

Mohandas Karamchand Gandhi was born in 1869 in Poorbandar, West India. The son of the chief minister of the province and his fourth wife, a deeply religious Hindu, Gandhi was unable to find suitable work as a barrister and so accepted a contract to work in Natal, South Africa. There he came face to face with institutionalised racial discrimination and for the next 20 years opposed legislation that sought to deprive Indians and other minorities of their rights. Gandhi's non-violent defiance of unfair laws focused attention on his civil activities for the first time and his establishment of a volunteer Ambulance Corps during the Boer War (1899-1902) won him the English War Medal.

Returning to India in 1914, Gandhi became an advocate for 'home rule'— the complete withdrawal of English Imperial interests. He became the dominant figure of the National Congress movement but never wavered from his policies of non-violent, non co-operation in achieving Indian independence despite the threat of arrest and jail.

In the 1920s, with Hindu and Muslim members of the National Congress unable to find common ground, warring factions aligned to the two religious groups led to bloodshed. Unable to reason with either side Gandhi undertook a three-week fast that not only restored the non-violent aims of the 'home rule' campaign but also promoted his personal act of spiritual cleansing.

'I will go ahead not for India's sake alone, but for the sake of the world. Even if my eyes close before there is freedom, non-violence will not end.'

Gandhi famously described a British proposal for a new constitution after the war as 'a post-dated cheque on a crashing bank.' In 1942 he was jailed for civil disobedience designed to 'obstruct the war effort' and was not released until 1944. Gandhi then negotiated with the British Cabinet Mission in India which ultimately recommended a new constitutional structure for home rule in India.

However, divisions between Muslim and Hindu factions within the National Congress ultimately led to the formation of separate nations, India and Pakistan, and the dream of a country united in its freedom was lost. Britain effectively relinquished 163 years of empirial rule in India on 15 August, 1947—an act Gandhi described as 'the noblest act of the British nation.'

The final months of Gandhi's life were spent shaming the instigators of community and religious violence by fasting. Just as his fasting looked set to avert the country from plummeting into complete anarchy, Mohandas Gandhi was assassinated in Delhi on 30 January, 1948 by Hindu fanatic Nathuram Godse while walking in a garden with his grandchildren.

General George S Patton
'D-Day Address'

Enniskillen Manor Grounds, England, 17 May 1944.

General Patton in 1944.

George Smith Patton Jnr (1885-1945) was one of the most outspoken, complicated and ultimately controversial American generals in military history. Educated at West Point, he competed in the modern pentathlon during the 1912 Stockholm Olympics—an event originally open only to military personnel—but lost his chance for a medal when he used his favoured .38 revolver for the pistol shooting event instead of the smaller .22 calibre pistol. In World War I Patton became the first member of the newly formed US Tank Corps and saw tanks as the future of modern warfare. In World War II, Patton played an important role in the Allied invasion of North Africa (1942) and led the US 7th Army's sweep of Sicily before being put in charge of the US 3rd Army in preparation of the liberation of France.

Three weeks before the D-Day invasion of Normandy—the straight-talking General gave his US troops a pep-talk at Enniskillen Manor Grounds, England where they were preparing for the liberation of France.

❛Men, this stuff some sources sling around about America wanting to stay out of the war and not wanting to fight is a lot of baloney! Americans love to fight, traditionally. All real Americans love the sting and clash of battle. America loves a winner. America will not tolerate a loser. Americans despise a coward; Americans play to win. That's why America has never lost and never will lose a war.

You are not all going to die. Only two percent of you, right here today, would be killed in a major battle.

Death must not be feared. Death, in time, comes to all of us. And every man is scared in his first action. If he says he's not, he's a goddamn liar. Some men are cowards, yes, but they fight just the same, or get the hell slammed out of them.

The real hero is the man who fights even though he's scared. Some get over their fright in a minute, under fire; others take an hour; for some it takes days; but a real man will never let the fear of death overpower his honor, his sense of duty, to his country and to his manhood.

'When you're sitting around the fireside with your grandson on your knee and he asks you what you did in the war, you won't have to shift him to the other knee, cough, and say, "I shovelled shit in Louisiana".'

All through your Army careers, you've been bitching about what you call "chicken-shit drills". That, like everything else in the Army, has a definite purpose. That purpose is instant obedience to orders and to create and maintain constant alertness! This must be bred into every soldier. A man must be alert all the time if he expects to stay alive. If not, some German son-of-a-bitch will sneak up behind him with a sock full of shit! There are four hundred neatly marked graves somewhere in Sicily, all because one man went to sleep on his job—but they are German graves, because we caught the bastards asleep!

'A man must be alert all the time if he expects to stay alive. If not, some German son-of-a-bitch will sneak up behind him with a sock full of shit!'

An Army is a team; lives, sleeps, fights, and eats as a team. This individual hero stuff is a lot of horse shit! The bilious bastards who write that kind of stuff for the Saturday Evening Post don't know any more about real fighting under fire than they know about fucking! Every single man in the Army plays a vital role. Every man has his job to do and must do it. What if every truck driver decided that he didn't like the whine of a shell overhead, turned yellow and jumped headlong into a ditch? What if every man thought, "They won't miss me, just one in millions?" Where in Hell would we be now? Where would our country, our loved ones, our homes, even the world, be?

No, thank God, Americans don't think like that. Every man does his job, serves the whole. Ordnance men supply and maintain the guns and vast machinery of this war, to keep us rolling. Quartermasters bring up clothes and food, for where we're going, there isn't a hell of a lot to steal. Every last man on K.P. has a job to do, even the guy who boils the water to keep us from getting the G.I. shits!

Remember, men, you don't know I'm here. No mention of that is to be made in any letters. The USA is supposed to be wondering what the hell has happened to me. I'm not supposed to be commanding this Army, I'm not supposed even to be in England. Let the first bastards to find out be the goddamn Germans. I want them to look up and howl, "Ach, it's the goddamn Third Army and that son-of-a-bitch Patton again!"

We want to get this thing over and get the hell out of here, and get at those purple-pissin' Japs! The shortest road home is through Berlin and Tokyo! We'll win this war, but we'll win it only by showing the enemy we have more guts than they have or ever will have!

There's one great thing you men can say when it's all over and you're home once more. You can thank God that twenty years from now, when you're sitting around the fireside with your grandson on your knee and he asks you what you did in the war, you won't have to shift him to the other knee, cough, and say, "I shovelled shit in Louisiana".'

This speech was never meant to be published and a request to Patton's widow after the War to have an audio recording of Patton's address published was politely refused. Mrs Patton took the position that the speech was made by the General only for the men who were going to fight and die with him— it was not a speech for posterity, and somewhat embarrassed by the frank language, not one for public consumption.

George Patton's single-mindedness, and lack of political and personal tact, often brought him into conflict with military hierarchy but there was no denying his brilliance as a tactician (Patton also had a strong moral character; when his Third Army liberated the Buchenwald concentration camp he made local Germans tour the camp—a policy adopted by other generals). On 9 December 1945 he was fatally injured in a car accident in occupied Germany and died 12 days later. Patton was buried in Hamm, Germany alongside his men who had died in the Battle of the Bulge.

It is easy to see why Patton was regarded as a man of the people when you compare his rhetoric with the then Supreme Commander General Dwight D. 'Ike' Eisenhower's. Ike's actual D-Day order on 6 June was understated, dispassionate and historic—it was later broadcast to the world:

❦ Soldiers, Sailors, and Airmen of the Allied Expeditionary Force! You are about to embark upon the Great Crusade, toward which we have striven these many months. The eyes of liberty loving people everywhere march with you. In company with our brave Allies and brothers in arms on other fronts, you will bring about the destruction of the German war machine, the elimination of Nazi tyranny over the oppressed peoples of Europe, and security for ourselves in a free world.

Your task will not be an easy one. Your enemy is well trained, well equipped, and battle-hardened. He will fight savagely.

But this is the year 1944. Much has happened since the Nazi triumphs of 1940-41.

The United Nations have inflicted upon the Germans great defeat in open battle man to man. Our air offensive has seriously reduced their strength in the air and their capacity to wage war on the ground.

Our home fronts have given us an overwhelming superiority in weapons and munitions of war and placed at our disposal great reserves of trained fighting men.

The tide has turned.

The free men of the world are marching together to victory. I have full confidence in your courage, devotion to duty, and skill in battle.

We will accept nothing less than full victory.

Good luck, and let us all beseech the blessings of Almighty God upon this great and noble undertaking. ❞

Harry S Truman

'An Atomic Bomb Destroys Hiroshima'

Radio broadcast from the White House, Washington, 9 August 1945.

Harry S Truman talks to the nation in April 1945 after the death of President Roosevelt.

Harry S. Truman (1884-1972) was the 'accidental' president. Elected as a Democratic Senator in 1934 he was only named Vice-President in 1944, the year President Roosevelt stood for an unprecedented fourth term, and became the US's 33rd President upon Roosevelt's death the following year. As soon as he took office, President Truman was informed of the development of an atomic weapon that would be ready for testing in July 1945. On 1 June it was decided by an 'Interim Committee' that the bomb should be used against Japan as soon as possible; that it should be used against a military target; and that it should be used without prior warning.

It was estimated that an invasion of Japan (set down for 1 November, 1945) would cost the lives of between 500 000 and 1 million allied troops. Japan still had 5 million men under arms—2 million based at home—and had made plans for a 'house-to-house' defence of its homeland.

On 25 July, 1945, Truman recorded in his diary that:

'We have discovered the most terrible bomb in the history of the world. It may be the fire destruction prophesied in the Euphrates Valley Era, after Noah and his fabulous Ark. Anyway we 'think' we have found the way to cause a disintegration of the atom. An experiment in the New Mexico desert was startling—to put it mildly.'

When the Japanese Prime Minister ignored the terms of the Potsdam Proclamation for unconditional surrender on 26 June, Truman ordered the bomb be dropped on a 'purely military' target, so that 'military objectives and soldiers and sailors are the target and not women and children.' He again wrote in his diary:

'Even if the Japs are savages, ruthless, merciless and fanatic, we as the leader of the world for the common welfare cannot drop that terrible bomb on the old capital or the new ... the target will be a purely military one and we will issue a warning statement asking the Japs to surrender and save lives. I'm sure they will not do that, but we will have given them the chance. It is certainly a good thing for the world that Hitler's crowd or Stalin's did not discover this atomic bomb. It seems to be the most terrible thing ever discovered, but it can be made the most useful.'

However, the final bombing order issued by General Spaatz made no mention of targeting military objectives or sparing civilians with the cities themselves targetted. Hiroshima was destroyed on 6 August, 1945 and Nagasaki three days later.

In a radio speech to the nation on 9 August 1945, President Truman spoke about the post-war situation in Germany and briefly referred to the atomic bomb on Hiroshima, 'a military base', and not the bustling city it was.

‘The world will note that the first atomic bomb was dropped on Hiroshima, a military base. That was because we wished in this first attack to avoid, insofar as possible, the killing of civilians. But that attack is only a warning of things to come. If Japan does not surrender, bombs will have to be dropped on her war industries and, unfortunately, thousands of civilian lives will be lost. I urge Japanese civilians to leave industrial cities immediately, and save themselves from destruction.’

Truman did not mention the number of victims killed—conservative figures placed the death toll for both cities at 180 000 but a further 500 000 people died from the effects of the two bombs over the next ten years.

Truman always believed that he had made the correct choice to use the atomic bomb. 'I regarded (it) as a military weapon and never had any doubt it should be used,' he wrote. The argument that the atomic bomb saved American lives is a valid one; the planned 'Operation Overlord'—the systematic invasion of Japan itself—would have been long and costly. However there are those, including some scientists who worked on the development of the bomb, who believed that a demonstration of the bomb's power for the Japanese leadership may have brokered exactly the same peace terms and surrender.

Truman accepted the unconditional Japanese surrender—after almost four years of bloodshed in the Pacific—on 'VJ' (Victory over Japan) Day, 15 August 1945. On 2 September General MacArthur formally accepted the surrender of Japanese forces on the aircraft carrier *Missouri* in Tokyo Harbour.

Golda Meir

'The Struggle for a Jewish State'

Council of Jewish Federations, Chicago, 2 January 1948.

Golda Meir lands in New York in May 1948 to address the United Jewish Appeal Conference.

Israel's third Prime Minister, Golda Meir (1898-1978) was born in Kiev in Russia and emigrated with her family to Milwaukee, Wisconsin, US in 1906. In 1915 she joined the Labor Zionist Organization (Poalei Zion) and moved to Palestine with her husband Morris Myerson. A leading socialist Zionist during the 1930s, she was also an International Zionist representative and spent 1932 working in the United States. After the end of World War II, Golda adopted the Hebrew name 'Meir' (which means 'to burn brightly') and became president of the political bureau of the Jewish Agency as thousands of Palestinian Jews and European refugees agitated for the formation of an official Jewish State in the traditional Holy Land region.

In February 1947 Britain ceded control of occupied Palestine to the United Nations which passed the seemingly impossible resolution to partition Palestine into Jewish and Arab states. Britain was ordered to leave Palestine by August 1948 but could do little to prepare either Jewish or Arab communities for independence. By the end of 1947, Palestinian and resettled Jewry were fighting both Arab terrorist and British peace-keeping forces.

In January 1948, Golda Meir flew to the United States to raise funds for weapons that were urgently needed to defend the 700 000 Jews in Palestine being threatened by Arab attacks. She made an unscheduled appearance before the Council of Jewish Federations and gave this heartfelt speech that moved thousands of people to give moral and financial support to the fledgling nation os Israel.

'I have had the privilege of representing Palestine Jewry in this country and in other countries when the problems that we faced were those of building more kibbutzim, of bringing in more Jews in spite of political obstacles and Arab riots.

We always had faith that in the end we would win, that everything we were doing in the country led to the independence of the Jewish people and to a Jewish state.

Long before we had dared pronounce that word, we knew what was in store for us.

Today we have reached a point when the nations of the world have given us their decision—the establishment of a Jewish state in a part of Palestine. Now in Palestine we are fighting to make this resolution of the United Nations a reality, not because we wanted to fight. If we had the choice, we would have chosen peace to build in peace.

We have no alternative.

Friends, we have no alternative in Palestine. The Mufti and his men have declared war upon us. We have to fight for our lives, for our safety, and for what we have accomplished in Palestine, and perhaps above all, we must fight for Jewish honour and Jewish independence.

Without exaggeration, I can tell you that the Jewish community in Palestine is doing this well. Many of you have visited Palestine; all of you have read about our young people and have a notion as to what our youth is like. I have known this generation for the last twenty-seven years. I thought I knew them. I realize now that even I did not.

These young boys and girls, many in their teens, are bearing the burden of what is happening in the country with a spirit that no words can describe. You see these youngsters in open cars—not armoured cars—in convoys going from Tel Aviv to Jerusalem, knowing that every time they start out from Tel Aviv or from Jerusalem there are probably Arabs behind the orange groves or the hills, waiting to ambush the convoy.

These boys and girls have accepted the task of bringing Jews over these roads in safety as naturally as though they were going out to their daily work or to their classes in the university.

We must ask the Jews the world over to see us as the front line.

All we ask of Jews the world over, and mainly of the Jews in the United States, is to give us the possibility of going on with the struggle.

When trouble started, we asked young people from the age of seventeen to twenty-five who were not members of Haganah, to volunteer. Up to the day that I left home on Thursday morning, when the registration of this age group was still going on, over 20 000 young men and women had signed up. As of now we have about 9 000 people mobilized in the various parts of the country. We must triple this number within the next few days.

We have to maintain these men. No government sends its soldiers to the front and expects them to take along from their homes the most elementary requirements—blankets, bedding, clothing.

A people that is fighting for its very life knows how to supply the men they send to the front lines. We too must do the same.

Thirty-five of our boys, unable to go by car on the road to besieged Kfar Etzion to bring help, set out by foot through the hills; they knew the road, the Arab villages on that road, and the danger they would have to face. Some of the finest youngsters we have in the country were in that group, and they were all killed, every one of them. We have a description from an Arab of how they fought to the end for over seven hours against hundreds of Arabs. According to this Arab, the last boy killed, with no more ammunition left, died with a stone in his hand.

I want to say to you, friends, that the Jewish community in Palestine is going to fight to the very end. If we have arms to fight with, we will fight with those, and if not, we will fight with stones in our hands.

I want you to believe me when I say that I came on this special mission to the United States today not to save 700 000 Jews. During the last few years the Jewish people lost 6 million Jews, and it would be audacity on our part to worry the Jewish people throughout the world because a few hundred thousand more Jews were in danger. That is not the issue.

The issue is that if these 700 000 Jews in Palestine can remain alive, then the Jewish people as such is alive and Jewish independence is assured. If these 700 000 people are killed off, then for many centuries, we are through with this dream of a Jewish people and a Jewish homeland.

My friends, we are at war. There is no Jew in Palestine who does not believe that finally we will be victorious. That is the spirit of the country. And every Jew in the country also knows that within a few months a Jewish state in Palestine will be established.

We knew that the price we would have to pay would be the best of our people. There are over 300 killed by now. There will be more. There is no doubt that there will be more. But there is also no doubt that the spirit of our young people is such that no matter how many Arabs invade the country, their spirit will not falter. However, this valiant spirit alone cannot face rifles and machine guns. Rifles and machine guns without spirit are not worth very much, but spirit without arms can in time be broken with the body.

I have come to the United States, and I hope you will understand me if I say that it is not an easy matter for any of us to leave home at present—to my sorrow I am not in the front line. I am not with my daughter in the Negev or with other sons and daughters in the trenches. But I have a job to do.

'I have come here to try to impress Jews in the United States with the fact that within a very short period, a couple of weeks, we must have in cash between 25 and 30 million dollars.'

I have come here to try to impress Jews in the United States with the fact that within a very short period, a couple of weeks, we must have in cash between 25 and 30 million dollars. In the next two or three weeks we can establish ourselves. Of that we are convinced, and you must have faith; we are sure that we can carry on.

I said before that the Yishuv will give, is giving of its means. But please remember that even while shooting is going on, we must carry on so that our economy remains intact. Our factories must go on. Our settlements must not be broken up.

We know that this battle is being waged for those not yet in the country.

There are 30 000 Jews detained right next door to Palestine in Cyprus. I believe that within a very short period, within the next two or three months at most, these 30 000 will be with us, among them thousands of infants and young children. We must now think of preparing means of absorbing them. We know that within the very near future, hundreds of thousands more will be coming in. We must see that our economy is intact.

I want you to understand that there is no despair in the Yishuv. When you go to Tel Aviv now, you will find the city full of life; only the shooting that you hear on the outskirts of Tel Aviv and Jaffa reminds one that the situation in the country is not normal. But it would be a crime on my part not to describe the situation to you exactly as it is.

Merely with our ten fingers and merely with spirit and sacrifice, we cannot carry on this battle, and the only hinterland that we have is you. The Mufti has the Arab states—not all so enthusiastic about helping him but states with government budgets. The Egyptian government can vote a budget to aid our antagonists. The Syrian government can do the same.

We have no government. But we have millions of Jews in the Diaspora, and exactly as we have faith in our youngsters in Palestine I have faith in Jews in the United States; I believe that they will realize the peril of our situation and will do what they have to do.

I know that we are not asking for something easy. I myself have sometimes been active in various campaigns and fund collections, and I know that collecting at once a sum such as I ask is not simple.

But I have seen our people at home. I have seen them come from the offices to the clinics when we called the community to give their blood for a blood bank to treat the wounded. I have seen them lined up for hours, waiting so that some of their blood can be added to this bank.

It is blood plus money that is being given in Palestine.

We are not a better breed; we are not the best Jews of the Jewish people. It so happened that we are there and you are here. I am certain that if you were in Palestine and we were in the United States, you would be doing what we are doing there, and you would ask us here to do what you will have to do.

I want to close with paraphrasing one of the greatest speeches that was made during the Second World War—the words of Churchill. I am not exaggerating when I say that the Yishuv in Palestine will fight in the Negev and will fight in Galilee and will fight on the outskirts of Jerusalem until the very end.

You cannot decide whether we should fight or not. We will. The Jewish community in Palestine will raise no white flag for the Mufti. That decision is taken. Nobody can change it. You can only decide one thing: whether we shall be victorious in this fight or whether the Mufti will be victorious. That decision American Jews can make. It has to be made quickly within hours, within days.

And I beg of you—don't be too late. Don't be bitterly sorry three months from now for what you failed to do today. The time is now.

I have spoken to you without a grain of exaggeration. I have not tried to paint the picture in false colours. It consists of spirit and certainty of our victory on the one hand, and dire necessity for carrying on the battle on the other.

I want to thank you again for having given me the opportunity at a conference that I am certain has a full agenda to say these few words to you. I leave the platform without any doubt in my mind or my heart that the decision that will be taken by American Jewry will be the same as that which was taken by the Jewish community in Palestine, so that within a few months from now we will all be able to participate not only in the joy of resolving to establish a Jewish state, but in the joy of laying the cornerstone of the Jewish state.'

'The Jewish community in Palestine is going to fight to the very end. If we have arms to fight with, we will fight with those, and if not, we will fight with stones in our hands.'

The State of Israel was proclaimed on 14 May 1948 but the fight against Egypt, Transjordan, Iraq, Syria and Lebanon for ultimate survival began the next day. Thousands of Israeli and Arab soldiers died in the ensuing fighting with 600 000 Palestinian refugees fleeing their homeland—a problem that continues today. Foundation Prime Minister, David Ben-Gurion, later stated: 'Someday, when history will be written, it will be said that there was a Jewish woman who got the money which made the state possible.'

In 1966 Golda Meir became secretary general of the Israeli Workers Party (Mapai) and following its incorporation into the Israeli Labor Party, she was chosen as its secretary. Upon the death of Levi Eshkol in 1969 the respective party factions chose Meir as Prime Minister. Her first challenge as Israeli leader was during the victorious Six-Day War in June 1967 in which neighbouring Arab States of Egypt, Syria and Jordan attempted to exact revenge for territories lost in disputes in 1948 and 1956.

In 1972 Palestinian terrorists killed 11 Israeli athletes competing in the Munich Olympics. The following year, Israel was involved in another conflict—the 'Yom Kippur War'—in which Egyptian leader Anwar el-Sadat attempted to enforce the United Nations 'Resolution 242'—Israel's total withdrawal from territories taken in 1967. Although Meir was able to form a government following the end of the conflict in the December 1973 elections, she had lost the control of her cabinet and resigned as Prime Minister in April 1974.

Golda Meir died in Jerusalem on 8 December, 1978, aged 80.

The Cold War
1950-1959

Joseph R McCarthy
'Wheeling Speech'

Delivered in Wheeling and repeated to US Congress, 20 February 1950.

Senator Joe McCarthy during the Army-McCarthy US Congress hearings of 1954.

In the 1950s, US Wisconsin Republican Senator Joseph R McCarthy (1908-1957) did more than any other individual to turn post-war concerns about domestic security into national hysteria. His highly-publicised witch-hunts that threatened to expose anyone remotely suspected of being a subversive influence in government or public institutions, including Hollywood, created a new term in the English language—'McCarthyism'.

McCarthy had entered the Senate in 1946 and with his first term coming to an end he desperately searched for an issue to increase his national profile before re-election. As the mid-term Congressional election year got underway in 1946, Alger Hiss, a former State Department official suspected of espionage, was convicted of perjury. Following the Communist Party victory in China, the successful explosion of an A-bomb by the Soviet Union and the 'Alger Hiss' investigation, the Republican Party was on the attack in an atmosphere of growing paranoia about the spread of communism.

Democratic President Harry S Truman seemed to buckle to political pressure when he announced the establishment of a 'loyalty program' for all federal employees and asked the Justice Department to compile an official list of subversive organisations inside the US.

On February 9 1950, Senator McCarthy spoke at the Ohio County Women's Republican Club in Wheeling, West Virginia and attacked President Truman's foreign policy, stating that the State Department and its Secretary, Dean Acheson, were harbouring 'traitorous' communists.

According to press reports of the speech, McCarthy said that he had in his hand a list of 205 members of the Communist Party and members of a spy ring who were 'shaping the policy of the State Department.' When later challenged to produce his evidence, McCarthy maintained that he was actually referring to communist 'party loyalists' in the State Department.

In this moderated version of that 'Wheeling' speech, repeated in Congress on February 20, he reduced the number of alleged communists to 57. In fact, McCarthy had no such list at all, but the damage was done. Those he named and accused lost their jobs as they were branded communists, but their guilt was never proved.

❝ Tonight as we celebrate the 141st birthday of one of the great men in American history, I would like to be able to talk about what a glorious day today is in the history of the world. As we celebrate the birth of this man, who with his whole heart and soul hated war, I would like to be able to speak of peace in our time, of war being outlawed, and of worldwide disarmament.

These would be truly appropriate things to be able to mention as we celebrate the birthday of Abraham Lincoln.

Five years after a world war has been won, men's hearts should anticipate a long peace, and men's minds should be free from the heavy weight that comes with war. But this is not such a period—for this is not a period of peace. This is a time of the Cold War. This is a time when all the world is split into two vast, increasingly hostile armed camps—a time of a great armaments race. Today we can almost physically hear the mutterings and rumblings of an invigorated god of war. You can see it, feel it, and hear it all the way from the hills of Indochina, from the shores of Formosa right over into the very heart of Europe itself ...

'When [the Secretary of State] this pompous diplomat in striped pants, with a phony British accent, proclaimed to the American people that Christ on the Mount endorsed communism, high treason, and betrayal of a sacred trust, the blasphemy was so great that it awakened the dormant indignation of the American people.'

Today we are engaged in a final, all-out battle between communistic atheism and Christianity. The modern champions of communism have selected this as the time. And, ladies and gentlemen, the chips are down—they are truly down.

Lest there be any doubt that the time has been chosen, let us go directly to the leader of communism today—Joseph Stalin. Here is what he said—not back in 1928, not before the war, not during the war—but two years after the last war was ended: 'To think that the communist revolution can be carried out peacefully, within the framework of a Christian democracy, means one has either gone out of one's mind and lost all normal understanding, or has grossly and openly repudiated the communist revolution.'

And this is what was said by Lenin in 1919, which was also quoted with approval by Stalin in 1947: 'We are living', said Lenin, 'not merely in a state but in a system of states, and the existence of the Soviet Republic side by side with Christian states for a long time is unthinkable. One or the other must triumph in the end. And before that end supervenes, a series of frightful collisions between the Soviet Republic and the bourgeois states will be inevitable.'

Ladies and gentlemen, can there be anyone here tonight who is so blind as to say that the war is not on? Can there be anyone who fails to realize that the communist world has said, 'The time is now'—that this is the time for the showdown between the democratic Christian world and the communist atheistic world? Unless we face this fact, we shall pay the price that must be paid by those who wait too long.

Six years ago, at the time of the first conference to map out peace—Dumbarton Oaks—there was within the Soviet orbit 180 million people. Lined up on the anti-totalitarian side there were in the world at that time roughly 1.625 billion people. Today, only six years later, there are 800 million people under the absolute domination of Soviet Russia—an increase of over 400 percent. On our side, the figure has shrunk to around 500 million. In other words, in less than six years the odds have changed from 9 to 1 in our favor to 8 to 5 against us. This indicates the swiftness of the tempo of communist victories and American defeats in the Cold War. As one of our outstanding historical figures once said, "When a great democracy is destroyed, it will not be because of enemies from without but rather because of enemies from within." The truth of this statement is becoming terrifyingly clear as we see this country each day losing on every front.

At war's end we were physically the strongest nation on Earth and, at least potentially, the most powerful intellectually and morally. Ours could have been the honor of being a beacon in the desert of destruction, a shining, living proof that civilization was not yet ready to destroy itself. Unfortunately, we have failed miserably and tragically to arise to the opportunity.

The reason why we find ourselves in a position of impotency is not because our only powerful, potential enemy has sent men to invade our shores, but rather because of the traitorous actions of those who have been treated so well by this nation. It has not been the less fortunate or members of minority groups who have been selling this nation out, but rather those who have had all the benefits that the wealthiest nation on earth has had to offer—the finest homes, the finest college education, and the finest jobs in government we can give.

This is glaringly true in the State Department. There the bright young men who are born with silver spoons in their mouths are the ones who have been worst.

Now I know it is very easy for anyone to condemn a particular bureau or department in general terms. Therefore, I would like to cite one rather unusual case—the case of a man who has done much to shape our foreign policy.

When Chiang Kai-shek was fighting our war, the State Department had in China a young man named John S. Service. His task, obviously, was not to work for the communization of China. Strangely, however, he sent official reports back to the State Department urging that we torpedo our ally Chiang Kai-shek and stating, in effect, that communism was the best hope of China.

Later, this man—John Service—was picked up by the Federal Bureau of Investigation for turning over to the communists' secret State Department information. Strangely, however, he was never prosecuted. However, Joseph Grew, the undersecretary of state, who insisted on his prosecution, was forced to resign. Two days after, Grew's successor, Dean Acheson, took over as undersecretary of state, this man—John Service—who had been picked up by the FBI and who had previously urged that communism was the best hope of China, was not only reinstated in the State Department but promoted; and finally, under Acheson, placed in charge of all placements and promotions. Today, ladies and gentlemen, this man Service is on his way to represent the State Department and Acheson in Calcutta—by far and away the most important listening post in the Far East.

Now, let's see what happens when individuals with communist connections are forced out of the State Department. Gustave Duran, who was labeled as, I quote, "a notorious international communist," was made assistant Secretary of State in charge of Latin American affairs. He was taken into the State Department from his job as a lieutenant colonel in the Communist International Brigade. Finally, after intense congressional pressure and criticism, he resigned in

JOSEPH R McCARTHY

143

1946 from the State Department—and, ladies and gentlemen, where do you think he is now? He took over a high-salaried job as chief of Cultural Activities Section in the office of the assistant secretary-general of the United Nations.

This, ladies and gentlemen, gives you somewhat of a picture of the type of individuals who have been helping to shape our foreign policy. In my opinion the State Department, which is one of the most important government departments, is thoroughly infested with communists.

I have in my hand 57 cases of individuals who would appear to be either card-carrying members or certainly loyal to the Communist Party, but who nevertheless are still helping to shape our foreign policy.

One thing to remember in discussing the communists in our government is that we are not dealing with spies who get 30 pieces of silver to steal the blueprints of new weapons. We are dealing with a far more sinister type of activity because it permits the enemy to guide and shape our policy.

This brings us down to the case of one Alger Hiss, who is important not as an individual anymore but rather because he is so representative of a group in the State Department. It is unnecessary to go over the sordid events showing how he sold out the nation which had given him so much. Those are rather fresh in all of our minds. However, it should be remembered that the facts in regard to his connection with this international communist spy ring were made known to the then-Under Secretary of State Berle three days after Hitler and Stalin signed the Russo-German Alliance Pact. At that time one Whittaker Chambers—who was also part of the spy ring—apparently decided that with Russia on Hitler's side, he could no longer betray our nation to Russia. He gave Under Secretary of State Berle—and this is all a matter of record—practically all, if not more, of the facts upon which Hiss' conviction was based.

Under Secretary Berle promptly contacted Dean Acheson and received word in return that Acheson, and I quote, "could vouch for Hiss absolutely"—at which time the matter was dropped. And this, you understand, was at a time when Russia was an ally of Germany. This condition existed while Russia and Germany were invading and dismembering Poland, and while the communist groups here were screaming "warmonger" at the United States for their support of the Allied nations.

Again in 1943, the FBI had occasion to investigate the facts surrounding Hiss' contacts with the Russian spy ring. But even after that FBI report was submitted, nothing was done.

Then, late in 1948—on August 5—when the Un-American Activities Committee called Alger Hiss to give an accounting, President Truman at once issued a presidential directive ordering all government agencies to refuse to turn over any information whatsoever in regard to the communist activities of any government employee to a congressional committee.

Incidentally, even after Hiss was convicted, it is interesting to note that the president still labeled the expose of Hiss as a "red herring."

If time permitted, it might be well to go into detail about the fact that Hiss was Roosevelt's chief adviser at Yalta when Roosevelt was admittedly in ill health and tired physically and mentally ... and when, according to the Secretary of State, Hiss and Gromyko drafted the report on the conference.

According to the then-Secretary of State Stettinius, here are some of the things that Hiss helped to decide at Yalta: 1) the establishment of a European High Commission; 2) the treatment of Germany—this you will recall was the conference at which it was decided that we would occupy Berlin with Russia occupying an area completely encircling the city, which as you know, resulted in the Berlin airlift which cost 31 American lives; 3) the Polish question; 4) the relationship between UNRRA and the Soviet; 5) the rights of Americans on control commissions of Rumania, Bulgaria and Hungary; 6) Iran; 7) China—here's where we gave away Manchuria; 8) Turkish Straits question; 9) international trusteeships; 10) Korea.

Of the results of this conference, Arthur Bliss Lane of the State Department had this to say: "As I glanced over the document, I could not believe my eyes. To me, almost every line spoke of a surrender to Stalin."

'As one of our outstanding historical figures once said, "When a great democracy is destroyed, it will not be because of enemies from without but rather because of enemies from within".'

As you hear this story of high treason, I know that you are saying to yourself, "Well, why doesn't the Congress do something about it?" Actually, ladies and gentlemen, one of the important reasons for the graft, the corruption, the dishonesty, the disloyalty, the treason in high government positions—one of the most important reasons why this continues—is a lack of moral uprising on the part of the 140 million American people. In the light of history, however, this is not hard to explain.

It is the result of an emotional hangover and a temporary moral lapse which follows every war. It is the apathy to evil which people who have been subjected to the tremendous evils of war feel. As the people of the world see mass murder, the destruction of defenseless and innocent people, and all of the crime and lack of morals which go with war, they become numb and apathetic. It has always been thus after war. However, the morals of our people have not been destroyed. They still exist. This cloak of numbness and apathy has only needed a spark to rekindle them. Happily, this spark has finally been supplied.

As you know, very recently the Secretary of State proclaimed his loyalty to a man guilty of what has always been considered as the most abominable of all crimes—of being a traitor to the people who gave him a position of great trust.

The Secretary of State, in attempting to justify his continued devotion to the man who sold out the Christian world to the atheistic world, referred to Christ's Sermon on the Mount as a justification and reason therefore, and the reaction of the American people to this would have made the heart of Abraham Lincoln happy. When this pompous diplomat in striped pants, with a phony British accent, proclaimed to the American people that Christ on the Mount endorsed communism, high treason, and betrayal of a sacred trust, the blasphemy was so great that it awakened the dormant indignation of the American people. He has lighted the spark which is

JOSEPH R McCARTHY

145

resulting in a moral uprising and will end only when the whole sorry mess of twisted warped thinkers are swept from the national scene so that we may have a new birth of national honesty and decency in government.'

President Truman responded to these charges in a news conference the following month and stated that McCarthy's attacks were sabotaging the nation's bipartisan foreign policy agenda and were actually advancing the cause of communism. But with the outbreak of war in Korea in April that year the Republican Party finally had a weapon to attack the Democrats and 'Tail-gunner' Joe McCarthy had finally achieved national—and international—notoriety. 'McCarthyism' raged out of control for the next four years, even after Truman had been voted out of office.

Edward Murrow's CBS program in 1954 exposed McCarthy's fanaticism and saw his ratings in the Gallup polls drop substantially. When the Senator lost further 'face' against Army Chief Counsel Joseph Welch in the 'Senate-Army' hearings in June, his political career was over. McCarthy was condemned by his own party for his unsubstantiated allegations and later lost his seat in the Senate and died, a broken alcoholic, in 1957 aged just 49.

Margaret Chase Smith
'Declaration of Conscience'

Speech to the US Senate, 1 June 1950.

Margaret Chase Smith in 1950.

Margaret Madeline Chase (1897-1995) was the only woman elected to serve both houses of the United States Congress. After establishing the Maine chapter of the Business and Professional Women's Club in 1922 she married newspaper publisher Clyde Smith, who was elected to Congress in 1936. When Smith died suddenly, she succeeded him in the House of Representatives and began 33 years of Congressional service.

Although a Republican, she often opposed her party and voted with her conscience in the best interests of the people of Maine.

In 1948 Mrs Chase Smith was elected to the US Senate without the support of her party with the greatest majority total vote in the history of Maine—70 per cent—which she maintained in election victories in 1954, 1960 and 1966. In June 1950 she was one of the first elected representatives to speak out against Joseph McCarthy—a fellow Republican—and denounce the smear and bullying tactics used by the Senator in his anti-communist campaign.

ʻMr. President. I would like to speak briefly and simply about a serious national condition. It is a national feeling of fear and frustration that could result in national suicide and the end of everything that we Americans hold dear. It is a condition that comes from the lack of effective leadership in either the Legislative Branch or the Executive Branch of our Government.

That leadership is so lacking that serious and responsible proposals are being made that national advisory commissions be appointed to provide such critically needed leadership.

I speak as briefly as possible because too much harm has already been done with irresponsible words of bitterness and selfish political opportunism. I speak as briefly as possible because the issue is too great to be obscured by eloquence. I speak simply and briefly in the hope that my words will be taken to heart.

I speak as a Republican. I speak as a woman. I speak as a United States Senator. I speak as an American.

The United States Senate has long enjoyed worldwide respect as the greatest deliberative body in the world. But recently that deliberative character has too often been debased to the level of a forum of hate and character assassination sheltered by the shield of congressional immunity.

It is ironical that we Senators can in debate in the Senate directly or indirectly, by any form of words, impute to any American who is not a Senator any conduct or motive unworthy or unbecoming an American—and without that non-Senator American having any legal redress against us—yet if we say the same thing in the Senate about our colleagues we can be stopped on the grounds of being out of order.

It is strange that we can verbally attack anyone else without restraint and with full protection and yet we hold ourselves above the same type of criticism here on the Senate Floor. Surely the United States Senate is big enough to take self-criticism and self-appraisal. Surely we should be able to take the same kind of character attacks that we "dish out" to outsiders.

I think that it is high time for the United States Senate and its members to do some soul-searching—for us to weigh our consciences—on the manner in which we are performing our duty to the people of America—on the manner in which we are using or abusing our individual powers and privileges.

I think that it is high time that we remembered that we have sworn to uphold and defend the Constitution. I think that it is high time that we remembered that the Constitution, as amended, speaks not only of the freedom of speech but also of trial by jury instead of trial by accusation.

'I think that it is high time that we remembered that the Constitution, as amended, speaks not only of the freedom of speech but also of trial by jury instead of trial by accusation.'

Whether it be a criminal prosecution in court or a character prosecution in the Senate, there is little practical distinction when the life of a person has been ruined.

Those of us who shout the loudest about Americanism in making character assassinations are all too frequently those who, by our own words and acts, ignore some of the basic principles of Americanism:

The right to criticize;
The right to hold unpopular beliefs;
The right to protest;
The right of independent thought.

The exercise of these rights should not cost one single American citizen his reputation or his right to a livelihood nor should he be in danger of losing his reputation or livelihood merely because he happens to know someone who holds unpopular beliefs. Who of us doesn't? Otherwise none of us could call our souls our own. Otherwise thought control would have set in. The American people are sick and tired of being afraid to speak their minds lest they be politically smeared as "communists" or "fascists" by their opponents. Freedom of speech is not what it used to be in America. It has been so abused by some that it is not exercised by others.

The American people are sick and tired of seeing innocent people smeared and guilty people whitewashed. But there have been enough proved cases, such as the 'Amerasia' case, the Hiss case, the Coplon case, the Gold case, to cause the nationwide distrust and strong suspicion that there may be something to the unproved, sensational accusations.

As a Republican, I say to my colleagues on this side of the aisle that the Republican Party faces a challenge today that is not unlike the challenge that it faced back in Lincoln's day. The Republican Party so successfully met that challenge that it emerged from the Civil War as the

MARGARET CHASE SMITH

149

champion of a united nation—in addition to being a Party that unrelentingly fought loose spending and loose programs.

Today our country is being psychologically divided by the confusion and the suspicions that are bred in the United States Senate to spread like cancerous tentacles of "know nothing, suspect everything" attitudes. Today we have a Democratic Administration that has developed a mania for loose spending and loose programs. History is repeating itself—and the Republican Party again has the opportunity to emerge as the champion of unity and prudence.

The record of the present Democratic Administration has provided us with sufficient campaign issues without the necessity of resorting to political smears. America is rapidly losing its position as leader of the world simply because the Democratic Administration has pitifully failed to provide effective leadership.

The Democratic Administration has completely confused the American people by its daily contradictory grave warnings and optimistic assurances—that show the people that our Democratic Administration has no idea of where it is going.

'The nation sorely needs a Republican victory. But I don't want to see the Republican Party ride to political victory on the Four Horsemen of Calumny— Fear, Ignorance, Bigotry, and Smear.'

The Democratic Administration has greatly lost the confidence of the American people by its complacency to the threat of communism here at home and the leak of vital secrets to Russia though key officials of the Democratic Administration. There are enough proved cases to make this point without diluting our criticism with unproved charges.

Surely these are sufficient reasons to make it clear to the American people that it is time for a change and that a Republican victory is necessary to the security of this country. Surely it is clear that this nation will continue to suffer as long as it is governed by the present ineffective Democratic Administration.

Yet to displace it with a Republican regime embracing a philosophy that lacks political integrity or intellectual honesty would prove equally disastrous to this nation. The nation sorely needs a Republican victory. But I don't want to see the Republican Party ride to political victory on the Four Horsemen of Calumny—Fear, Ignorance, Bigotry, and Smear.

I doubt if the Republican Party could—simply because I don't believe the American people will uphold any political party that puts political exploitation above national interest. Surely we Republicans aren't that desperate for victory.

I don't want to see the Republican Party win that way. While it might be a fleeting victory for the Republican Party, it would be a more lasting defeat for the American people. Surely it would ultimately be suicide for the Republican Party and the two-party system that has protected our American liberties from the dictatorship of a one party system.

As members of the Minority Party, we do not have the primary authority to formulate the policy of our Government. But we do have the responsibility of rendering constructive criticism, of clarifying issues, of allaying fears by acting as responsible citizens.

As a woman, I wonder how the mothers, wives, sisters, and daughters feel about the way in which members of their families have been politically mangled in the Senate debate -- and I use the word "debate" advisedly.

As a United States Senator, I am not proud of the way in which the Senate has been made a publicity platform for irresponsible sensationalism. I am not proud of the reckless abandon in which unproved charges have been hurled from the side of the aisle. I am not proud of the obviously staged, undignified counter-charges that have been attempted in retaliation from the other side of the aisle.

I don't like the way the Senate has been made a rendezvous for vilification, for selfish political gain at the sacrifice of individual reputations and national unity. I am not proud of the way we smear outsiders from the Floor of the Senate and hide behind the cloak of congressional immunity and still place ourselves beyond criticism on the Floor of the Senate.

As an American, I am shocked at the way Republicans and Democrats alike are playing directly into the Communist design of "confuse, divide, and conquer." As an American, I don't want a Democratic Administration "whitewash" or "cover-up" any more than I want a Republican smear or witch hunt.

As an American, I condemn a Republican "Fascist" just as much I condemn a Democratic "Communist." I condemn a Democrat "Fascist" just as much as I condemn a Republican "Communist." They are equally dangerous to you and me and to our country. As an American, I want to see our nation recapture the strength and unity it once had when we fought the enemy instead of ourselves.

It is with these thoughts that I have drafted what I call a "Declaration of Conscience." I am gratified that Senator Tobey, Senator Aiken, Senator Morse, Senator Ives, Senator Thye, and Senator Hendrickson have concurred in that declaration and have authorized me to announce their concurrence.'

'Today our country is being psychologically divided by the confusion and the suspicions that are bred in the United States Senate to spread like cancerous tentacles of "know nothing, suspect everything" attitudes.'

Although she didn't mention her Republican colleague by name, Smith's 15-minute speech earned McCarthy's ire—and the admiration of her president, Harry S Truman. McCarthy removed Mrs Chase Smith as a member of the Permanent Subcommittee on Investigations, and gave her place to the junior senator from California—Richard M Nixon.

In 1964 Margaret Chase Smith became the first woman to be nominated by a major party as a Presidential candidate and received 27 nominating votes at the Republican National Convention. In 1973, after serving in the Senate for 24 years, Chase Smith lost her seat. After leaving the Senate,

Smith lectured at colleges and conducted public policy seminars. She wrote for newspapers and magazines and authored *Gallant Women* (biographies of twelve American women) and *Declaration of Conscience*, about her time serving the American people.

Chase Smith continued to champion women's rights and oppose bigotry and injustice long after she left office. She received innumerable awards during her lifetime and was one of the original inductees of the National Women's Hall of Fame (1973). She received more than 85 honorary degrees and was named 'Woman of the Year' by the Associated Press in 1948, 1949, 1950 and 1957. In 1989 she received the Presidential Medal of Freedom from President Bill Clinton. Margaret Chase Smith died in Skowhegan, Maine in 1995.

Douglas MacArthur

'Old Soldiers Never Die'

Address to US Congress, Washington DC, 20 April 1951.

Douglas MacArthur addresses a joint session of the US Congress.

Douglas MacArthur (1880-1964), the hero of the Pacific during World War II, fell spectacularly from grace during the Korean War. Despite being relieved of his command, he was given a hero's homecoming, and is today remembered as a modern military icon.

After serving in the Philippines and France in World War I, he became Commander in Chief of US army forces in the Pacific theatre of World War II. Forced to retreat from the Philippines in March 1942, he conducted the liberation of the southwest Pacific from his Australian base during the next three years. In September 1945, MacArthur formally accepted the Japanese surrender aboard the *USS Missouri* and as the head of occupied forces in Japan earned the unflattering empirical mantle of 'Viceroy of Japan' for his superior single-mindedness in doing things his own way. MacArthur was even considered as a Republican presidential candidate but his defeat in the Wisconsin primary in 1948 eroded his support base.

During World War II, Korea had been divided into two states along the invisible 38th Parallel, with Russia protecting the northern section and America the southern. Both sections held 'elections' in the late 1940s but North Korea had become dominated by communists and unification with the (southern-based) 'Republic of Korea' seemed as far as away as ever. In June 1950, 80 000 North Korean troops backed by Russian tanks launched a surprise invasion of South Korea. US President Harry S Truman immediately dispatched American troops based in Japan and was able to garner support from the United Nations to undertake a 'police action' under the control of General Douglas MacArthur to recapture Seoul.

After early success pushing North Korean troops back past the 38th Parallel, MacArthur rashly pressed on towards the northern capital Pyongyang. Sure that Russian and Chinese troops would not support the North Koreans, MacArthur bombed bridges on the Yula which prompted China's Chairman Mao to send 300 000 troops to support the North Koreans. United Nations forces were then forced to retreat.

The hero of World War II was determined to this conflict and openly criticised President Truman, his own military superiors and America's allies for their lack of support in the face of Chinese aggression. He made his intentions clear in the press—blockade the Chinese mainland, use atomic weapons to suppress the enemy and invade both China and Korea with the help of Chiang Kai-shek's Nationalist forces. When he independently invited the Chinese leadership to meet with him in April 1951, Truman removed MacArthur from his command.

On his return to the United States, General Douglas MacArthur was invited to address a joint session of Congress. He condemned America's 'blackmail of appeasement' and ended with one of the most-quoted epitaphs of the twentieth century—old soldiers never die; they just fade away.

'I stand on this rostrum with a sense of deep humility and great pride—humility in the wake of those great architects of our history who have stood here before me, pride in the reflection that this home of legislative debate represents human liberty in the purest form yet devised.

Here are centered the hopes and aspirations and faith of the entire human race.

I do not stand here as advocate for any partisan cause, for the issues are fundamental and reach quite beyond the realm of partisan considerations. They must be resolved on the highest plane of national interest, if our course is to prove sound and our future protected.

I trust, therefore, that you will do me the justice of receiving that which I have to say as solely expressing the considered viewpoint of a fellow American.

I address you with neither rancor nor bitterness in the fading twilight of life, with but one purpose in mind: To serve my country.

The issues are global, and so interlocked that to consider the problems of one sector oblivious to those of another is to court disaster for the whole. While Asia is commonly referred to as the gateway to Europe, it is no less true that Europe is the gateway to Asia, and the broad influence of the one cannot fail to have its impact upon the other.

> 'The Communist threat is a global one. Its successful advance in one sector threatens the destruction of every other sector.'

There are those who claim our strength is inadequate to protect on both fronts, that we cannot divide our effort. I can think of no greater expression of defeatism.

If a potential enemy can divide his strength on two fronts, it is for us to counter his efforts. The Communist threat is a global one. Its successful advance in one sector threatens the destruction of every other sector. You cannot appease or otherwise surrender to Communism in Asia without simultaneously undermining our efforts to halt its advance in Europe.

Beyond pointing out these general truisms, I shall confine my discussion to the general areas of Asia.

While I was not consulted prior to the President's decision to intervene in support of the Republic of Korea, that decision, from a military standpoint, proved a sound one. As I say, it proved a sound one, as we hurled back the invader and decimated his forces. Our victory was complete, and our objectives within reach, when Red China intervened with numerically superior ground forces.

This created a new war and an entirely new situation, a situation not contemplated when our forces were committed against the North Korean invaders; a situation which called for new

DOUGLAS MACARTHUR
155

decisions in the diplomatic sphere to permit the realistic adjustment of military strategy. Such decisions have not been forthcoming. While no man in his right mind would advocate sending our ground forces into continental China, and such was never given a thought, the new situation did urgently demand a drastic revision of strategic planning, if our political aim was to defeat this new enemy as we had defeated the old.

Apart from the military need, as I saw it, to neutralize the sanctuary protection given the enemy north of the Yalu, I felt that military necessity in the conduct of the war made necessary:

1. The intensification of our economic blockade against China.
2. The imposition of a naval blockade against the China coast.
3. Removal of restrictions on air reconnaissance of China's coastal area and of Manchuria.
4. Removal of restrictions on the forces of the Republic of China on Formosa, with logistical support to contribute to their effective operations against the Chinese mainland.

For entertaining these views, all professionally designed to support our forces committed to Korea and to bring hostilities to an end with the least possible delay and at a saving of countless American and Allied lives, I have been severely criticized in lay circles, principally abroad, despite my understanding that, from a military standpoint, the above views have been fully shared in the past by practically every military leader concerned with the Korean campaign, including our own Joint Chiefs of Staff.

'While no man in his right mind would advocate sending our ground forces into continental China, and such was never given a thought, the new situation did urgently demand a drastic revision of strategic planning.'

I called for reinforcements, but was informed that reinforcements were not available. I made clear that if not permitted to destroy the enemy built-up bases north of the Yalu, if not permitted to utilize the friendly Chinese force of some 600 000 men on Formosa, if not permitted to blockade the China coast to prevent the Chinese Reds from getting succor from without, and if there were to be no hope of major reinforcements, the position of the command from the military standpoint forbade victory.

We could hold in Korea by constant manoeuvre and at an approximate area where our supply-line advantages were in balance with the supply-line disadvantages of the enemy, but we could hope at best for only an indecisive campaign with its terrible and constant attrition upon our forces if the enemy utilized his full military potential.

I have constantly called for the new political decisions essential to a solution. Efforts have been made to distort my position. It has been said, in effect, that I was a warmonger. Nothing could be further from the truth.

I know war as few other men now living know it, and nothing to me is more revolting! I have long advocated its complete abolition, as its very destructiveness on both friend and foe has rendered it useless as a means of settling international disputes.

Indeed, on the second day of September, 1945, just following the surrender of the Japanese nation on the battleship Missouri, I formally cautioned as follows:

'Men since the beginning of time have sought peace. Various methods through the ages have been attempted to devise an international process to prevent or settle disputes between nations. From the very start, workable methods were found in so far as individual citizens were concerned, but the mechanics of an instrumentality of larger international scope have never been successful.

Military alliances, balances of power, leagues of nations, all in turn failed, leaving the only path to be by way of the crucible of war. The utter destructiveness of war now blocks out this alternative. We have had our last chance. If we will not devise some greater and more equitable system, our Armageddon will be at our door. The problem basically is theological and involves a spiritual recrudescence, an improvement of human character that will synchronize with our almost matchless advances in science, art, literature, and all material and cultural developments of the past two thousand years. It must be of the spirit if we are to save the flesh.

But once war is forced upon us, there is no other alternative than to apply every available means to bring it to a swift end. War's very object is victory, not prolonged indecision. In war, there is no substitute for victory.

There are some who, for varying reasons, would appease Red China. They are blind to history's clear lesson, for history teaches with unmistakable emphasis that appeasement but begets new and bloodier war. It points to no single instance where this end has justified that means, where appeasement has led to more than a sham peace. Like blackmail, it lays the basis for new and successively greater demands until, as in blackmail, violence becomes the only other alternative.

Why, my soldiers asked of me, surrender military advantages to an enemy in the field? I could not answer.

Some may say to avoid spread of the conflict into an all-out war with China. Others, to avoid Soviet intervention. Neither explanation seems valid, for China is already engaging with the maximum power it can commit, and the Soviet [Union] will not necessarily mesh its actions with our moves. Like a cobra, any new enemy will more likely strike whenever it feels that the relativity in military or other potential is in its favor on a world-wide basis.

The tragedy of Korea is further heightened by the fact that its military action is confined to its territorial limits. It condemns that nation, which it is our purpose to save, to suffer the devastating impact of full naval and air bombardment, while the enemy's sanctuaries are fully protected from such attack and devastation.

Of the nations of the world Korea alone, up to now, is the sole one which has risked its all against communism. The magnificence of the courage and fortitude of the Korean people defies description. They have chosen to risk death rather than slavery. Their last words to me were: "Don't scuttle the Pacific."

'It has been said, in effect, that I was a warmonger. Nothing could be further from the truth. I know war as few other men now living know it, and nothing to me is more revolting!'

DOUGLAS MACARTHUR

157

I have just left your fighting sons in Korea. They have met all tests there, and I can report to you without reservation that they are splendid in every way. It was my constant effort to preserve them and end this savage conflict honorably and with the least loss of time and a minimum sacrifice of life. Its growing bloodshed has caused me the deepest anguish and anxiety. Those gallant men will remain often in my thoughts and in my prayers always.

I am closing my 52 years of military service. When I joined the army, even before the turn of the century, it was the fulfillment of all of my boyish hopes and dreams.

'In war, there is no substitute for victory.'

The world has turned over many times since I took the oath on the plain at West Point, and the hopes and dreams have long since vanished, but I still remember the refrain of one of the most popular barracks ballads of that day which proclaimed most proudly that 'old soldiers never die; they just fade away.' And like the old soldier of that ballad, I now close my military career and just fade away, an old soldier who tried to do his duty as God gave him the light to see that duty. Good-bye.'

General MacArthur retired to private life when he was defeated by another war hero—Dwight D.Eisenhower—for the Republican nomination for the 1952 presidential race. MacArthur later worked on the boards of several companies before passing away in Washington DC on 5 April, 1964, aged 84.

Dwight D Eisenhower

'Cross of Iron'

Speech to the American Society of Newspaper Editors, 16 April 1953.

Dwight D Eisenhower in 1955.

Dwight D 'Ike' Eisenhower (1890-1969) was the Supreme Commander of Allied forces during World War II and was perceived by the American public and as a living hero. After first declining to run as a Democratic presidential nominee, 'Ike' accepted the Republican Party's nomination as presidential candidate in 1952. After winning the New Hampshire Republican primary without even campaigning, his presidential victory became a formality when he used a new communication medium—television—to sell his candidacy to the American public. Eisenhower's magnetism as a leader, running a campaign that addressed the issues of 'Communism, Corruption and Korea', overcame the potential scandal concerning his running mate, Richard M Nixon.

Eisenhower's presidency received an immediate boost when relations with Russia mellowed following the death of Soviet dictator Josef Stalin in March 1953. However Eisenhower's greatest fear remained that America would 'spend itself broke' in an arms race before a threat from Russia ever eventuated. In this speech of 1953, Eisenhower demonstrated the futility of a 'cold war' arms race. He compared William Jennings Bryan's phrase, a 'cross of gold'—first used in 1896 at the Democratic National Convention to criticise public monetary policy—to a 'cross of iron' to describe the expenditures of both the United States and the Soviet Union on armaments.

The following speech was broadcast over television and radio from the Statler Hotel in Washington.

❝ In this spring of 1953 the free world weighs one question above all others: the chance for a just peace for all peoples.

To weigh this chance is to summon instantly to mind another recent moment of great decision. It came with that yet more hopeful spring of 1945, bright with the promise of victory and of freedom. The hope of all just men in that moment too was a just and lasting peace.

The eight years that have passed have seen that hope waver, grow dim, and almost die. And the shadow of fear again has darkly lengthened across the world.

Today the hope of free men remains stubborn and brave, but it is sternly disciplined by experience. It shuns not only all crude counsel of despair but also the self-deceit of easy illusion. It weighs the chance for peace with sure, clear knowledge of what happened to the vain hope of 1945.

In that spring of victory the soldiers of the Western Allies met the soldiers of Russia in the center of Europe. They were triumphant comrades in arms. Their peoples shared the joyous prospect of building, in honor of their dead, the only fitting monument—an age of just peace.

All these war-weary peoples shared too this concrete, decent purpose: to guard vigilantly against the domination ever again of any part of the world by a single, unbridled aggressive power.

This common purpose lasted an instant and perished. The nations of the world divided to follow two distinct roads.

The United States and our valued friends, the other free nations, chose one road.

The leaders of the Soviet Union chose another.

The way chosen by the United States was plainly marked by a few clear precepts, which govern its conduct in world affairs.

First: No people on earth can be held, as a people, to be enemy, for all humanity shares the common hunger for peace and fellowship and justice.

Second: No nation's security and well-being can be lastingly achieved in isolation but only in effective cooperation with fellow-nations.

Third: Any nation's right to a form of government and an economic system of its own choosing is inalienable.

Fourth: Any nation's attempt to dictate to other nations their form of government is indefensible.

And fifth: A nation's hope of lasting peace cannot be firmly based upon any race in armaments but rather upon just relations and honest understanding with all other nations.

In the light of these principles the citizens of the United States defined the way they proposed to follow, through the aftermath of war, toward true peace.

This way was faithful to the spirit that inspired the United Nations: to prohibit strife, to relieve tensions, to banish fears. This way was to control and to reduce armaments. This way was to allow all nations to devote their energies and resources to the great and good tasks of healing the war's wounds, of clothing and feeding and housing the needy, of perfecting a just political life, of enjoying the fruits of their own free toil.

'The shadow of fear again has darkly lengthened across the world.'

The Soviet government held a vastly different vision of the future.

In the world of its design, security was to be found, not in mutual trust and mutual aid but in force: huge armies, subversion, rule of neighbor nations. The goal was power superiority at all costs. Security was to be sought by denying it to all others.

The result has been tragic for the world and, for the Soviet Union, it has also been ironic.

The amassing of the Soviet power alerted free nations to a new danger of aggression. It compelled them in self-defence to spend unprecedented money and energy for armaments. It forced them to develop weapons of war now capable of inflicting instant and terrible punishment upon any aggressor.

It instilled in the free nations—and let none doubt this—the unshakable conviction that, as long as there persists a threat to freedom, they must, at any cost, remain armed, strong, and ready for the risk of war. It inspired them—and let none doubt this—to attain a unity of purpose and will beyond the power of propaganda or pressure to break, now or ever.

DWIGHT D EISENHOWER

There remained, however, one thing essentially unchanged and unaffected by Soviet conduct: the readiness of the free nations to welcome sincerely any genuine evidence of peaceful purpose enabling all peoples again to resume their common quest of just peace.

> 'The world knows that an era ended with the death of Joseph Stalin.'

The free nations, most solemnly and repeatedly, have assured the Soviet Union that their firm association has never had any aggressive purpose whatsoever. Soviet leaders, however, have seemed to persuade themselves, or tried to persuade their people, otherwise.

And so it has come to pass that the Soviet Union itself has shared and suffered the very fears it has fostered in the rest of the world.

This has been the way of life forged by eight years of fear and force.

What can the world, or any nation in it, hope for if no turning is found on this dread road?

The worst to be feared and the best to be expected can be simply stated.

The worst is atomic war.

The best would be this: a life of perpetual fear and tension; a burden of arms draining the wealth and the labor of all peoples; a wasting of strength that defies the American system or the Soviet system or any system to achieve true abundance and happiness for the peoples of this earth.

Every gun that is made, every warship launched, every rocket fired signifies, in the final sense, a theft from those who hunger and are not fed, those who are cold and are not clothed.

This world in arms is not spending money alone.

It is spending the sweat of its laborers, the genius of its scientists, the hopes of its children.

The cost of one modern heavy bomber is this: a modern brick school in more than 30 cities.

It is two electric power plants, each serving a town of 60 000 population.

It is two fine, fully equipped hospitals.

It is some 50 miles of concrete highway.

We pay for a single fighter with a half million bushels of wheat.

We pay for a single destroyer with new homes that could have housed more than 8000 people.

This, I repeat, is the best way of life to be found on the road the world has been taking.

This is not a way of life at all, in any true sense. Under the cloud of threatening war, it is humanity hanging from a cross of iron.

These plain and cruel truths define the peril and point the hope that comes with this spring of 1953.

This is one of those times in the affairs of nations when the gravest choices must be made, if there is to be a turning toward a just and lasting peace.

It is a moment that calls upon the governments of the world to speak their intentions with simplicity and with honesty.

It calls upon them to answer the questions that stirs the hearts of all sane men: is there no other way the world may live? The world knows that an era ended with the death of Joseph

Stalin. The extraordinary 30-year span of his rule saw the Soviet Empire expand to reach from the Baltic Sea to the Sea of Japan, finally to dominate 800 million souls.

The Soviet system shaped by Stalin and his predecessors was born of one World War. It survived the stubborn and often amazing courage of a second World War. It has lived to threaten a third.

Now, a new leadership has assumed power in the Soviet Union. It links to the past, however strong, cannot bind it completely. Its future is, in great part, its own to make.

This new leadership confronts a free world aroused, as rarely in its history, by the will to stay free.

This free world knows, out of bitter wisdom of experience, that vigilance and sacrifice are the price of liberty.

It knows that the defence of Western Europe imperatively demands the unity of purpose and action made possible by the North Atlantic Treaty Organization, embracing a European Defense Community.

It knows that Western Germany deserves to be a free and equal partner in this community and that this, for Germany, is the only safe way to full, final unity.

It knows that aggression in Korea and in Southeast Asia are threats to the whole free community to be met by united action.

This is the kind of free world which the new Soviet leadership confront. It is a world that demands and expects the fullest respect of its rights and interests. It is a world that will always accord the same respect to all others.

So the new Soviet leadership now has a precious opportunity to awaken, with the rest of the world, to the point of peril reached and to help turn the tide of history.

Will it do this?

We do not yet know. Recent statements and gestures of Soviet leaders give some evidence that they may recognize this critical moment.

This we do know: a world that begins to witness the rebirth of trust among nations can find its way to a peace that is neither partial nor punitive.

The first great step along this way must be the conclusion of an honorable armistice in Korea. This means the immediate cessation of hostilities and the prompt initiation of political discussions leading to the holding of free elections in a united Korea.

It should mean, no less importantly, an end to the direct and indirect attacks upon the security of Indochina and Malaya. For any armistice in Korea that merely released aggressive armies to attack elsewhere would be fraud. We seek, throughout Asia as throughout the world, a peace that is true and total.

Out of this can grow a still wider task—the achieving of just political settlements for the other serious and specific issues between the free world and the Soviet Union.

None of these issues, great or small, is insoluble-given only the will to respect the rights of all nations.

Again we say: the United States is ready to assume its just part.

DWIGHT D EISENHOWER

We are ready not only to press forward with the present plans for closer unity of the nations of Western Europe by also, upon that foundation, to strive to foster a broader European community, conducive to the free movement of persons, of trade, and of ideas.

As progress in all these areas strengthens world trust, we could proceed concurrently with the next great work—the reduction of the burden of armaments now weighing upon the world. To this end we would welcome and enter into the most solemn agreements. These could properly include:

1. The limitation, by absolute numbers or by an agreed international ratio, of the sizes of the military and security forces of all nations.

2. A commitment by all nations to set an agreed limit upon that proportion of total production of certain strategic materials to be devoted to military purposes.

3. International control of atomic energy to promote its use for peaceful purposes only and to insure the prohibition of atomic weapons.

4. A limitation or prohibition of other categories of weapons of great destructiveness.

5. The enforcement of all these agreed limitations and prohibitions by adequate safeguards, including a practical system of inspection under the United Nations.

'Every gun that is made, every warship launched, every rocket fired signifies, in the final sense, a theft from those who hunger and are not fed, those who are cold and are not clothed.'

The peace we seek, founded upon decent trust and cooperative effort among nations, can be fortified, not by weapons of war but by wheat and by cotton, by milk and by wool, by meat and by timber and by rice. These are words that translate into every language on earth. These are needs that challenge this world in arms.

We are prepared to reaffirm, with the most concrete evidence, our readiness to help build a world in which all peoples can be productive and prosperous.

The monuments to this new kind of war would be these: roads and schools, hospitals and homes, food and health.

We are ready, in short, to dedicate our strength to serving the needs, rather than the fears, of the world.

We are ready, by these and all such actions, to make of the United Nations an institution that can effectively guard the peace and security of all peoples.

The test of truth is simple. There can be no persuasion but by deeds.

Is the new leadership of Soviet Union prepared to use its decisive influence in the Communist world, including control of the flow of arms, to bring not merely an expedient truce in Korea but genuine peace in Asia?

Is it prepared to allow other nations, including those of Eastern Europe, the free choice of their own forms of government?

Is it prepared to act in concert with others upon serious disarmament proposals to be made firmly effective by stringent U.N. control and inspection?

If not, where then is the concrete evidence of the Soviet Union's concern for peace?

The test is clear. There is, before all peoples, a precious chance to turn the black tide of events. If we failed to strive to seize this chance, the judgment of future ages would be harsh and just.

If we strive but fail and the world remains armed against itself, it at least need be divided no longer in its clear knowledge of who has condemned humankind to this fate.

The purpose of the United States, in stating these proposals, is simple and clear. These proposals spring, without ulterior purpose or political passion, from our calm conviction that the hunger for peace is in the hearts of all peoples—those of Russia and of China no less than of our own country.

They conform to our firm faith that God created men to enjoy, not destroy, the fruits of the earth and of their own toil.

They aspire to this: the lifting, from the backs and from the hearts of men, of their burden of arms and of fears, so that they may find before them a golden age of freedom and of peace.'

Despite an end to fighting in Korea in 1953, the Cold War atmosphere of the mid-1950s did little to slow the arms race. In December 1953 Eisenhower proposed the ideal of 'Atoms for Peace' to the United Nations—even going so far as suggesting that atomic materials be managed by a single international agency—but the brutal repression of rebellious eastern bloc countries Poland and Hungary (both in 1958) meant that the US felt that it had to be 'ready' for any conflict. Although he avoided a Third World War, Eisenhower warned America in his final address as president that 'security and liberty' must learn to prosper together. The arms race would continue for another three decades.

After eight years in the White House, Dwight D Eisenhower left Washington DC in 1961 and retired with his wife Mamie to their farm in Gettysburg, Pennsylvania, overlooking the famous Civil War battlefield. The former two-term US President died there on 28 March, 1969, aged 78.

Bertrand Russell

'Russell-Einstein Manifesto'

BBC Broadcast, London, 9 July 1955.

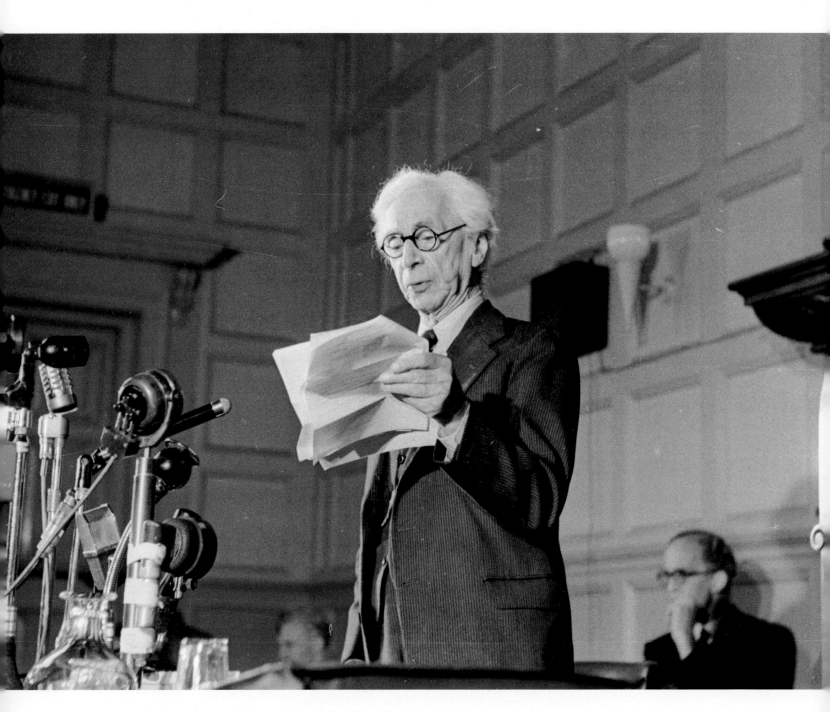

Bertrand Russell speaks at a peace meeting in 1955.

A long-standing collaboration between pacifist Bertrand Russell and atomic scientist Albert Einstein resulted in the publication of the 'Russell-Einstein' Manifesto in 1955. The two men came from very different backgrounds, yet their powerful union laid the foundations for the modern peace movement—especially the Campaign for Nuclear Disarmament.

Albert Einstein was born in Ulm, Germany, in 1879. A professed pacifist, he took Swiss nationality in 1901 as a protest against increasing German nationalism. In 1905 he published his theory of relativity and obtained his PhD in Zurich before returning to Berlin as director of the Kaiser Wilhelm Physical Institute in 1914. He won the Nobel Prize for Physics in 1921 but his increasingly pacifist views—and the fact that he was a Jew—made his position in Berlin untenable after the rise of Nazism. When Hitler assumed power in 1933 Einstein was touring California and realised that to return to Germany would mean certain death. He decided to stay in the United States and warned President Roosevelt that German scientists were in a position to develop a 'super-weapon'—the atomic bomb.

While this information encouraged Roosevelt to undertake the 'Manhattan Project'—the development of an atomic bomb, which would ultimately be used against Japan—Einstein urged the world to control the development of atomic weapons after World War II. 'This weapon was delivered into the hands of the American and British nations in their roles as trustees of all mankind, and as fighters for peace and liberty,' he stated in New York in 1945, 'The war is won, but the peace is not'.

Bertrand Russell, philosopher, author and mathematician (1872-1970) lost his fellowship at Trinity College and served six months imprisonment in 1918 for his pacifist views. He renounced pacifism in the face of fascist aggression in Europe in 1939 and became a champion of nuclear disarmament at the end of World War II. A Nobel Prize winner in Literature in 1950, Russell corresponded with world leaders and important figures of his time in an effort to bring about greater understanding about the dangers of the unchecked expansion of nuclear weapons.

Working from England, Russell communicated by mail with Albert Einstein, where he was teaching at Princeton, New Jersey. They discussed publishing a document signed by leading scientists of the time. In 1955, Einstein wrote to Russell.

Dear Bertrand Russell,

Thank you for your letter of April 5. I am gladly willing to sign your excellent statement. I also agree with your choice of the prospective signers.

With kind regards,
A. Einstein

A few days later Einstein died aged 76, but he had already sent Russell his final letter confirming his support for their manifesto. It was published in England the July after Einstein's death. It laid the foundations for the modern peace movement and became the credo of the Pugwash Conferences on Science and World Affairs—the Nobel Peace Prize-winning organisation dedicated to eliminating nuclear weapons and war. Russell used the following manifesto as the basis for several BBC broadcasts and lectures.

'In the tragic situation which confronts humanity, we feel that scientists should assemble in conference to appraise the perils that have arisen as a result of the development of weapons of mass destruction, and to discuss a resolution in the spirit of the appended draft.

We are speaking on this occasion, not as members of this or that nation, continent or creed, but as human beings, members of the species man, whose continued existence is in doubt. The world is full of conflicts; and overshadowing all minor conflicts, the titanic struggle between Communism and anti-Communism.

Almost everybody who is not politically conscious has strong feelings about one or more of these issue; but we want you, if you can, to set aside such feelings and consider yourselves only as members of a biological species which has had a remarkable history, and whose disappearance none of us can desire.

We shall try to say no single word which should appeal to one group rather than to another. All, equally, are in peril, and, if the peril is understood, there is hope that we may collectively avert it.

We have to learn to think in a new way. We have to learn to ask ourselves, not what steps can be taken to give military victory to whatever military group we prefer, for there no longer are such steps; the question we have to ask ourselves is: What steps can be taken to prevent a military contest of which the issue must be disastrous to all parties?

The general public, and even many men in positions of authority, have not realized what would be involved in a war with nuclear bombs. The general public still thinks in terms of the obliteration of cities. It is understood that new bombs are more powerful than the old, and that, while one A-bomb could obliterate Hiroshima, one H-bomb could obliterate the largest cities, such as London, New York and Moscow.

No doubt in an H-bomb war great cities would be obliterated. But this is one of the minor disasters that would have to be faced. If everybody in London, New York and Moscow were exterminated, the world might, in the course of a few centuries, recover from the blow. But we now know, especially from the Bikini test, that nuclear bombs can gradually spread destruction over a very much wider area than had been supposed.

It is stated on very good authority that a bomb can now be manufactured which will be 2 500 times as powerful as that which destroyed Hiroshima.

Such a bomb, if exploded near the ground or underwater, sends radioactive particles into the upper air. They sink gradually and reach the surface of the earth in a form of a deadly dust or rain. It was this dust which infected the Japanese fishermen and their catch of fish.

No one knows how widely such lethal radioactive particles might be diffused, but the best authorities are unanimous in saying that a war with H-bombs might quite possibly put an end to the human race. It is feared that if many H-bombs are used there will be universal death— sudden only for a minority, but for the majority a slow torture of disease and disintegration.

Many warnings have been uttered by eminent men of science and by authorities in military strategy. None of them will say that the worst results are certain. What they do say is that these results are possible, and that no one can be sure that they will not be realized.

We have not yet found that the views of experts depend in any way upon their politics or prejudices. They depend only, so far as our researches have revealed, upon the extent of the particular expert's knowledge. We have found that the men who know most are the most gloomy.

'Agreements reached in a time of peace ... would no longer be binding in a time of war.'

Here, then is the problem which we present to you, stark and dreadful, and inescapable: shall we put an end to the human race, or shall mankind renounce war? People will not face this alternative because it is so difficult to abolish war.

The abolition of war will demand distasteful limitations of national sovereignty. But what perhaps impedes understanding of the situation more than anything else, is that the term mankind feels vague and abstract. People scarcely realize in imagination that the danger is to themselves and their children and grandchildren, and not only to their dimly apprehended humanity. They can scarcely bring themselves to grasp that they, individually, and those whom they love are in imminent danger of perishing agonizingly. And so they hope that perhaps war may be allowed to continue provided modern weapons are prohibited.

This hope is illusory. Whatever agreements not to use the H-bombs had been reached in time of peace, they would no longer be considered binding in time of war, and both sides would set to work to manufacture H-bombs as soon as war broke out, for, if one side manufactured H-bombs and the other did not, the side that manufactured them would inevitably be victorious.

BERTRAND RUSSELL

169

Although an agreement to renounce nuclear weapons as part of a general reduction of armaments would not afford an ultimate solution, it would serve certain important purposes.

First: Any agreement between East and West is to the good because it serves to diminish tension. Second: The abolition of thermonuclear weapons, if each side believed that the other had carried it out sincerely, would lessen fear of a sudden attack in the style of Pearl Harbour, which at present keeps both sides in a state of nervous apprehension. We should therefore, welcome such an agreement, though only as a first step.

Most of us are not neutral in feelings, but, as human beings, we have to remember that, if the issues between East and West are to be decided in any manner that can give any possible satisfaction to anybody, whether Communist or anti-Communist, whether Asian or European or American, whether white of black, then these issues must not be decided by war. We should wish this to be understood both in the East and in the West.

There lies before us, if we choose, continual progress in happiness, knowledge and wisdom. Shall we, instead, choose death, because we cannot forget our quarrels? We appeal, as human beings, to human beings: Remember your humanity and forget the rest. If you can do so, the way lies open to a new paradise; if you cannot, there lies before you the risk of universal death.

RESOLUTION

We invite the congress [to be convened], and through it, the scientists of the world and the general public, to subscribe to the following resolution:

In view of the fact that in any future world war, nuclear weapons will certainly be employed, and that such weapons threaten the continued existence of mankind, we urge governments of the world to realize, and to acknowledge publicly that their purposes cannot be furthered by a world war, and we urge them consequently, to find peaceful means for the settlement of all matters of dispute between them.

Professor Max Born (Professor of Theoretical Physics at Berlin, Frankfurt, and Gottingen, and of Natural Philosophy, Edinburgh; Nobel Prize in physics)

Professor P.W. Bridgman (Professor of Physics, Harvard University; Nobel Prize in physics)

Professor Albert Einstein

Professor L. Infeld (Professor of Theoretical Physics, University of Warsaw)

Professor J. F. Joliot-Curie (Professor of Physics, College de France; Nobel Prize in chemistry)

Professor H. J. Muller (Professor of Zoology at the University of Indiana; Nobel Prize in physiology and medicine)

Professor Linus Pauling (Professor of Chemistry, California Institute of Technology; Nobel Prize in chemistry)

Professor J. Rotblat (Professor of Physics, University of London; Medical College of St. Bartholomew's Hospital)

Bertrand Russell

Professor Hideki Yukawa (Professor of Theoretical Physics, Kyoto University; Nobel Prize in physics).’

The Russell-Einstein Manifesto was endorsed by thousands of scientists from many countries. As a direct result of this statement, Bertrand Russell acted as a mediator with President Kennedy on behalf of Nikita Khrushchev during the Cuban Missile Crisis in 1962. Russell passed away in 1972, aged 98, and is regarded as one of the foremost philosophers of the twentieth century.

Half a century after Albert Einstein's death, the ideals which he promoted throughout his life are admired by millions and are gradually being implemented by an ever-increasing number of scientists and politicians.

Nikita Khrushchev
'The Cult of the Individual'

Twentieth Congress of the Communist Party of the Soviet Union, 24 February 1956.

Nikita Kruschchev speaks in 1960.

Nikita Khrushchev (1894-1971) joined the Bolshevik Party in 1918 and by World War II, was serving under Josef Stalin in the Politburo and the Presidium of the Supreme Soviet. Upon Stalin's death in 1953, Khrushchev emerged as the undisputed leader of the Soviet Union. The first secretary of the USSR Communist Party, Khrushchev had Stalin's remains removed from the Kremlin. In 1956, three years after Stalin's death, Khrushchev addressed the Party Congress and denounced the excesses of 'Stalinism', criticising the 'cult of personality' that had corrupted Stalin's terrifying shift from idealist to tyrant.

❝ Comrades!

Quite a lot has been said about the cult of the individual and about its harmful consequences. After Stalin's death the Central Committee began to implement a policy of explaining concisely and consistently that it is impermissible and foreign to the spirit of Marxism-Leninism to elevate one person, to transform him into a superman possessing supernatural characteristics akin to those of a god.

Such a belief about a man, and specifically about Stalin, was cultivated among us for many years.

The objective of the present report is not a thorough evaluation of Stalin's life and activity. Concerning Stalin's merits an entirely sufficient number of books, pamphlets and studies have already been written ... [Khrushchev then reports the positions of Marx, Engels and Lenin in relation to collective leadership, the role of the party and the working class, etc, and introduces the delegates to the documents relating to Lenin's Testament, in which he warns against Stalin, concluding with a reading of a letter from Lenin to Stalin].

When socialism in our country was fundamentally constructed, when the exploiting classes were generally liquidated, when the Soviet social structure had radically changed, when the social basis for political movements and groups hostile to the party had violently contracted, when the ideological opponents of the party had long since been defeated politically—then the repression directed against them began. ... We must assert that, in regard to those persons who in their time had opposed the party line, there were often no sufficiently serious reasons for their physical annihilation. The formula "enemy of the people" was specifically introduced for the purpose of physically annihilating such individuals. ...

Had Leninist principles been observed ... we certainly would not have had such a brutal violation of revolutionary legality and many thousands of people would not have fallen victim to the method of terror. [Khrushchev then recalls the incident of Kamenev and Zinoviev's betrayal of the Revolution in October 1917, and their subsequent reinstatement to the leadership.]

As facts prove, Stalin, using his unlimited power, allowed himself many abuses, acting in the name of the Central Committee, not asking for the opinion of the Committee members nor

'It has happened sometimes that a man goes to Stalin on his invitation as a friend. And, when he sits with Stalin, he does not know where he will be sent next—home or jail'.

even the members of the Politburo, or even informing them ... During Lenin's lifetime, Party Congresses were convened regularly ... It should be sufficient to mention that during all the years of the Great Patriotic War, not a single Central Committee plenum took place ...

A party commission was [recently] charged with investigating what made possible the mass repressions against the majority of the Central Committee members and candidates elected at the Seventeenth Congress ... many party activists who were branded in 1937-38 as "enemies" were actually never enemies, spies, wreckers, etc but were always honest communists ... and often, no longer able to bear barbaric tortures, they charged themselves with all kinds of grave and unlikely crimes.

...of the 139 members and candidates of the party's Central Committee who were elected at the Seventeenth Congress, 98 persons, i.e., 70 per cent, were arrested and shot! [There is consternation in the hall.] What was the composition of the delegates? 80 per cent joined the party during the years of illegality before the Revolution and during the Civil War before 1921. By social origin the basic mass of the delegates were workers (60 per cent of the voting members).

For this reason, it is inconceivable that a congress so composed would have elected a Central Committee a majority of whom would prove to be enemies of the people ... The same fate met not only the Central Committee members but also the majority of the delegates to the Seventeenth Congress. Of 1,966 delegates, 1,108 persons were arrested ... This very fact shows how absurd, wild and contrary to common sense were the charges of counter-revolutionary crimes ... [indignation in the hall].

... repression increased after the congress... after the complete liquidation of the Trotskyites, Zinovievites and Bukharinites, when as a result of that fight the party achieved unity, Stalin ceased to an even greater degree to consider members of the Central Committee or Politburo.

After the criminal murder of S M Kirov, mass repressions and brutal acts of violation of socialist legality began. ... the circumstances surrounding Kirov's murder hide many things which are inexplicable and mysterious ...top functionaries of the NKVD were shot presumably to cover up ...

Mass repressions grew tremendously from the end of 1936 ... the mass repressions at this time were made under the slogan of a fight against the Trotskyites ... but ... Trotskyism was completely disarmed ... it was clear that there was no basis for mass terror in the country. This terror was actually directed not at the remnants of the exploiting classes but against the honest workers. ...

Using Stalin's formulation, namely, that the closer we are to socialism the more enemies we will have ... the number of arrests based on charges of counter-revolutionary crimes grew 10 times between 1936 and 1937. ... Confessions of guilt were gained with the help of cruel and inhuman tortures ... when they retracted their confessions before the military tribunal [no one was told] ...

[Khrushchev cites at length the testimony of Eikhe, a member since 1905, tortured and shot in February 1940, and details the cases other well-known veterans denounced by Stalin, to consternation in the hall. Khrushchev moves on to talk of Stalin's role in World War II.]

... Stalin put forward the thesis that the tragedy which our nation experienced in the first part of the war was the result of the "unexpected" attack of the Germans against the Soviet Union. But, comrades, this is completely untrue. As soon as Hitler came to power in Germany he assigned to himself the task of liquidating Communism. The fascists were saying this openly; they did not hide their plans. ...

Churchill personally warned Stalin [and] ... stressed this repeatedly in his despatches of 18 April and in the following days. However, Stalin took no notice of these warnings ... information of this sort ... was coming from our own military and diplomatic sources ...

[Stalin ordered that] no preparatory defensive work should be undertaken at the borders, that the Germans were not to be given any pretext ... when the fascist armies actually invaded Soviet territory and military operations had begun, Stalin issued the order that the German fire was not to be returned. Why? It was because Stalin, despite evident facts, thought that the war had not yet started ...

'Where were the members of the Politburo? Why did they not assert themselves against the cult of the individual in time? And why is this being done only now?'

Very grievous consequences followed Stalin's annihilation of many military commanders and political workers during 1937-41 because of his suspiciousness and through slanderous accusations ... during this time the cadre of leaders who had gained military experience in Spain and the Far East was almost completely liquidated ... large scale repression against the military cadres led also to undermined military discipline ... after the first severe disaster and defeats at the front, Stalin thought that this was the end. In one of his speeches he said: "All that which Lenin created we have lost forever". After this Stalin for a long time did not direct the military operations and ceased to do anything whatever. ... when he returned to active leadership ... the nervousness and hysteria which Stalin demonstrated, interfering with actual military operations, caused our Army serious damage. ... during the whole Patriotic War, he never visited any section of the front or any liberated city ...

[Laughter begins to break out in the hall from time to time as Khrushchev ridicules Stalin's exaggeration of his role after the war, and he concludes ...]

...All the more monstrous are the acts whose initiator was Stalin .. we refer to the mass deportations from their native places, of whole nations .. not dictated by any military considerations ... the Ukrainians avoided this fate only because there were too many of them and there was no place to deport them [laughter]. [Khrushchev then tells of the 'Leningrad affair' in which eminent military leaders were denounced and shot].

Stalin became even more capricious, irritable and brutal; in particular his suspicion grew. His persecution mania reached unbelievable dimensions ...

NIKITA KHRUSHCHEV

[Khrushchev then delivers a prolonged attack on the role of Beria. He then explains how Stalin personally edited the biographies and histories lauding his role to ensure that his own role was presented in terms of the most extreme glorification, receiving applause as he suggests that Stalin's name be removed from the national anthem, which should praise instead the role of the party, and loud, prolonged applause follows. As Khrushchev turns to the theme of how Stalin elevated himself above Lenin, even in the period of the Revolution, and denounced Stalin for this, he is greeted by repeated bursts of applause].

'Had Leninist principles been observed ... we certainly would not have had such a brutal violation of revolutionary legality and many thousands of people would not have fallen victim to the method of terror.'

...Comrades! If we sharply criticise today the cult of the individual which was so widespread during Stalin's life, and if we speak about so many negative phenomena generated by this cult which is so alien to the spirit of Marxism-Leninism, various persons may ask: How could it be? Stalin headed the party and the country for 30 years and many victories were gained during his lifetime. Can we deny that? ...

The Socialist Revolution was attained by the working class and by the poor peasantry with the partial support of middle-class peasants. It was attained by the people under the leadership of the Bolshevik Party. Lenin's great service consisted in the fact that he created a militant party of the working class, but he was armed with Marxist understanding of the laws of social development and with the science of proletarian victory in the fight with capitalism, and he steeled this party in the crucible of revolutionary struggle of the masses of the people. ... Our historical victories were attained thanks to the organisational work of the party, ...and to the self-sacrificing work of our great nation.

... during the last years of Stalin's life he became a serious obstacle ... During Stalin's leadership our peaceful relations with other nations were often threatened, ... In recent years we managed to free ourselves of the harmful practice of the cult of the individual ...

Some comrades may ask us: Where were the members of the Politburo? Why did they not assert themselves against the cult of the individual in time? And why is this being done only now? ...

Initially many of them backed Stalin actively because Stalin was one of the strongest Marxists and his logic, his strength and his will greatly influenced the cadres and party work. ...

At that time Stalin gained great popularity, sympathy and support. The party had to fight those who attempted to lead the country away from the correct Leninist path; it had to fight Trotskyites, Zinovievites, and Rightists, and Bourgeois Nationalists. This fight was indispensable.

Later, however, Stalin, abusing his power more and more, began to fight eminent party leaders and to use terroristic methods against honest Soviet people. ...

Bulganin once said: "It has happened sometimes that a man goes to Stalin on his invitation as a friend. And, when he sits with Stalin, he does not know where he will be sent next—home or jail".

It is clear that such conditions put every member of the Political Bureau in a very difficult situation ...

... had Stalin remained at the helm for another few months, Comrades Molotov and Mikoyan would probably not have delivered any speeches at this Congress. Stalin had plans to finish off the old members of the Political Bureau. ...

We consider that Stalin was excessively extolled. However, in the past, Stalin doubtless performed great services to the party, to the working class and to the international workers' movement....

Stalin was convinced that [these things he did] were necessary .. He saw this from the position of the interest of the working class, of the interest of the laboring people, of the interests of the victory of Socialism and Communism. We cannot say that these were the deeds of a giddy despot. ... In this lies the whole tragedy!

[Khrushchev then suggests that Stalin's name, and also those of other leaders be removed from towns etc bearing their names, but] this should be done calmly and slowly. ... if we begin to remove the signs everywhere and to change names, people will think that these comrades in whose honour the given enterprises, kolkhozes or cities are named have met some bad fate and that they have also been arrested. ...

We should in all seriousness consider the question of the cult of the individual. We cannot let this matter get out of the party, especially not to the press. It is for this reason that we are considering it here at a closed Congress session. We should know the limits; we should not give ammunition to the enemy; we should not wash our dirty linen before their eyes. I think that the delegates to the Congress will understand and assess properly all these proposals.

We are absolutely certain that our party, armed with the historical resolutions of the Twentieth Congress, will lead the Soviet people along the Leninist path to new successes, to new victories. Long live the victorious banner of our Party—Leninism!'

'Long live the victorious banner of our Party—Leninism!'

Nikita Khrushchev was Soviet Prime Minister from 1958 to 1964 and figured prominently in Cold War rhetoric with two American Presidents, Eisenhower and Kennedy. At times boorish and dramatic in his gestures, he once famously banged his shoe on the podium during a speech to the United Nations General Assembly. Khrushchev was deposed by Brezhnev in 1964, largely over the fallout over the Cuban Missile Crisis, but it was a bloodless transition. Forced into retirement (the only Soviet leader before Mikhail Gorbachev not to die in office) Khrushchev passed away in 1971. Because of his fall from power, he was the only Soviet leader not to be buried in the Kremlin wall.

NIKITA KHRUSHCHEV

Mao Zedong

'Let a Hundred Flowers Blossom'

Address to Supreme State Conference, Beijing, China, 27 February 1957.

An official Chinese newsagency picture of Mao Zedong in 1957.

Mao Zedong (or Tse-tung) was born in Hunan Province in China in 1893. One of the foundation members of the Chinese Communist Party in 1921, Mao worked alongside the Chinese Nationalists, led by Chiang Kai-shek, against Japanese occupation in the north until the civil war in 1927. Mao organised a 'Long March' of his supporters in 1934 to escape Nationalist attacks—a 10 000 km trek from Jiangxi which saw thousands perish—and set up a new base in Yenan. When the Japanese invaded China in 1937, Chiang's Nationalist army retreated to the mountains while Mao's 'People's Liberation Army' fought a guerrilla war against the invaders from village to village. After Japan was defeated in World War II, Mao's army had popular support and captured Beijing in 1949 after defeating the Nationalists in a bitter civil war.

The establishment of the People's Republic of China—the largest Communist state in the world—was perceived as a major threat to the West during the Cold War of the 1950s. China's involvement in the Korean War (1950-53) and the war against French colonial interests in Vietnam—as well as its development of atomic power—only heightened fears of the spread of Communism in South-East Asia. But Mao had internal economic, political and social issues to deal with without worrying about the spread of an ideology, in which he admitted in this 1959 speech, was decidedly 'Chinese' in character and could not be duplicated in other countries.

Mao called for the end of the oppression of China's intellectual community and surprised many by requesting open criticism of his party. Known as the 'Hundred Flowers' campaign, Mao hoped that when the Chinese people were politically re-educated and the majority of peasants had been reorganised into agricultural producer co-operatives, a more tolerant approach towards the expression of artistic and political ideas would actually strengthen the Communist Party's hold on power. A second policy, 'long-term co-existence and mutual supervision' was designed to allow the barest opposition to the CCP from rival democratic parties. In this speech Mao placed the two policies into social and political context.

'Let a hundred flowers blossom, let a hundred schools of thought contend' and 'long-term coexistence and mutual supervision'—how did these slogans come to be put forward? They were put forward in the light of China's specific conditions, in recognition of the continued existence of various kinds of contradictions in socialist society and in response to the country's urgent need to speed up its economic and cultural development. Letting a hundred flow-

MAO ZEDONG

179

ers blossom and a hundred schools of thought contend is the policy for promoting progress in the arts and sciences and a flourishing socialist culture in our land.

Different forms and styles in art should develop freely and different schools in science should contend freely. We think that it is harmful to the growth of art and science if administrative measures are used to impose one particular style of art or school of thought and to ban another. Questions of right and wrong in the arts and science should be settled through free discussion in artistic and scientific circles and through practical work in these fields. They should not be settled in an over-simple manner. A period of trial is often needed to determine whether something is right or wrong. Throughout history at the outset new and correct things often failed to win recognition from the majority of people and had to develop by twists and turns through struggle. Often, correct and good things were first regarded not as fragrant flowers but as poisonous weeds. Copernicus' theory of the solar system and Darwin's theory of evolution were once dismissed as erroneous and had to win out over bitter opposition.

Chinese history offers many similar examples. In a socialist society, the conditions for the growth of the new are radically different from and far superior to those in the old society. Nevertheless, it often happens that new, rising forces are held back and sound ideas stifled. Besides even in the absence of their deliberate suppression, the growth of new things may be hindered simply through lack of discernment. It is therefore necessary to be careful about questions of right and wrong in the arts and sciences, to encourage free discussion and avoid hasty conclusions. We believe that such an attitude will help ensure a relatively smooth development of the arts and sciences.

Marxism, too, has developed through struggle. At the beginning, Marxism was subjected to all kinds of attack and regarded as a poisonous weed. This is still the case in many parts of the world. In the socialist countries, it enjoys a different position. But non-Marxist and, what is more, anti-Marxist ideologies exist even in these countries. In China, although socialist transformation has in the main been completed as regards the system of ownership, and although the large-scale, turbulent class struggles of the masses characteristic of times of revolution have in the main come to an end, there are still remnants of the overthrown landlord and comprador classes, there is still a bourgeoisie, and the remoulding of the petty bourgeoisie has only just started ...

People may ask, since Marxism is accepted as the guiding ideology by the majority of the people in our country, can it be criticized? Certainly it can. Marxism is scientific truth and fears no criticism. If it did, and if it could be overthrown by criticism, it would be worthless. In fact, aren't the idealists criticizing Marxism every day and in every way? And those who harbour bourgeois and petty-bourgeois ideas and do not wish to change—aren't they also criticizing Marxism in every way? Marxists should not be afraid of criticism from any quarter. Quite the contrary, they need to temper and develop themselves and win new positions in the teeth of criticism and in the storm and stress of struggle. Fighting against wrong ideas is like being vaccinated—a man develops greater immunity from disease as a result of vaccination. Plants raised in hothouses are unlikely to be hardy. Carrying out the policy of letting a hundred flowers blossom and a hundred schools of thought contend will not weaken, but strengthen, the leading position of Marxism in the ideological field.

What should our policy be towards non-Marxist ideas? As far as unmistakable counter-revolutionaries and saboteurs of the socialist cause are concerned, the matter is easy, we simply deprive them of their freedom of speech. But incorrect ideas among the people are quite a different matter. Will it do to ban such ideas and deny them any opportunity for expression? Certainly not. It is not only futile but very harmful to use crude methods in dealing with ideological questions among the people, with questions about man's mental world. You may ban the expression of wrong ideas, but the ideas will still be there. On the other hand, if correct ideas are pampered in hothouses and never exposed to the elements and immunized against disease, they will not win out against erroneous ones. Therefore, it is only by employing the method of discussion, criticism and reasoning that we can really foster correct ideas and overcome wrong ones, and that we can really settle issues.

It is inevitable that the bourgeoisie and petty bourgeoisie will give expression to their own ideologies. It is inevitable that they will stubbornly assert themselves on political and ideological questions by every possible means. You cannot expect them to do otherwise. We should not use the method of suppression and prevent them from expressing themselves, but should allow them to do so and at the same time argue with them and direct appropriate criticism at them. Undoubtedly, we must criticize wrong ideas of every description. It certainly would not be right to refrain from criticism, look on while wrong ideas spread unchecked and allow them to dominate the field. Mistakes must be criticized and poisonous weeds fought wherever they crop up. However, such criticism should not be dogmatic, and the metaphysical method should not be used, but instead the effort should be made to apply the dialectical method. What is needed is scientific analysis and convincing argument. Dogmatic criticism settles nothing. We are against poisonous weeds of whatever kind, but we must carefully distinguish between what is really a poisonous weed and what is really a fragrant flower. Together with the masses of the people, we must learn to differentiate carefully between the two and use correct methods to fight the poisonous weeds.

At the same time as we criticize dogmatism, we must direct our attention to criticizing revisionism. Revisionism, or right opportunism, is a bourgeois trend of thought that is even more dangerous than dogmatism. The revisionists, the right opportunists, pay lip-service to Marxism; they too attack "dogmatism". But what they are really attacking is the quintessence of Marxism. They oppose or distort materialism and dialectics, oppose or try to weaken the people's democratic dictatorship and the leading role of the Communist Party, and oppose or try to weaken socialist transformation and socialist construction. Even after the basic victory

'Plants raised in hothouses are unlikely to be hardy. Carrying out the policy of letting a hundred flowers blossom and a hundred schools of thought contend will not weaken, but strengthen, the leading position of Marxism.'

MAO ZEDONG

181

of our socialist revolution, there will still be a number of people in our society who vainly hope to restore the capitalist system and are sure to fight the working class on every front, including the ideological one. And their right-hand men in this struggle are the revisionists.

Literally the two slogans—let a hundred flowers blossom and let a hundred schools of thought contend—have no class character; the proletariat can turn them to account, and so can the bourgeoisie or others. Different classes, strata and social groups each have their own views on what are fragrant flowers and what are poisonous weeds. Then, from the point of view of the masses, what should be the criteria today for distinguishing fragrant flowers from poisonous weeds? In their political activities, how should our people judge whether a person's words and deeds are right or wrong? On the basis of the principles of our Constitution, the will of the overwhelming majority of our people and the common political positions which have been proclaimed on various occasions by our political parties, we consider that, broadly speaking, the criteria should be as follows:

'Words and deeds should unite, and not divide the people.'

1. Words and deeds should help to unite, and not divide, the people of all our nationalities.
2. They should be beneficial, and not harmful, to socialist transformation and socialist construction.
3. They should help to consolidate, and not undermine or weaken, the people's democratic dictatorship.
4. They should help to consolidate, and not undermine or weaken, democratic centralism.
5. They should help to strengthen, and not shake off or weaken, the leadership of the Communist Party.
6. They should be beneficial, and not harmful, to international socialist unity and the unity of the peace-loving people of the world.

Of these six criteria, the most important are the two about the socialist path and the leadership of the Party. These criteria are put forward not to hinder but to foster the free discussion of questions among the people. Those who disapprove these criteria can still state their own views and argue their case. However, so long as the majority of the people have clear-cut criteria to go by, criticism and self-criticism can be conducted along proper lines, and these criteria can be applied to people's words and deeds to determine whether they are right or wrong, whether they are fragrant flowers or poisonous weeds. These are political criteria. Naturally, to judge the validity of scientific theories or assess the aesthetic value of works of art, other relevant criteria are needed. But these six political criteria are applicable to all activities in the arts and sciences. In a socialist country like ours, can there possibly be any useful scientific or artistic activity which runs counter to these political criteria? The views set out above are based on China's specific historical conditions. Conditions vary in different socialist countries and with different Communist Parties. Therefore, we do not maintain that they should or must adopt the Chinese way.'

Originally these policies stagnated because Mao's party officials were uneasy about the effect they would have on the masses. However, when an edited version of Mao's directives was informally published the following spring, the intellectuals grew bolder in their criticism of the Communist Party, especially at university campuses. The democratic United Front parties also openly expressed frustration with China's political system. The movement was abruptly terminated in 1958 because Mao had underestimated the convictions of the intelligentsia. The stinging criticism of the Communist Party brought another purge and many felt it had been a ploy from the beginning to 'ensnare any counter-revolutionary elements' that remained from previous purges earlier in the decade.

The failure of the 'Hundred Flowers' movement provides history with an insight into the contradictory nature of Mao Zedong's leadership. He would preside over two more social policy failures before his death in 1976, aged 83. The 'Great Leap Forward', which sought to modernise China through increased labour productivity, was an economic disaster in the late 1950s and the 'Cultural Revolution', which resulted in the imprisonment and death of thousands of dissidents during the mid 1960s, would provide Mao's considerable political achievements with a bitter postscript.

Charles de Gaulle
'I Have Understood You'

Constantine, Algiers, 3 October 1958.

Charles de Gaulle is welcomed in Mauritania in 1958.

Charles de Gaulle (1890-1970) was the leader of 'Free France' during the Nazi occupation of World War II. General de Gaulle headed a provisional government after the liberation of France in 1944 but resigned two years later disillusioned with the constitution of France's Fourth Republic that placed too much parliamentary power in the hands of unstable post-war political parties. Retiring from public life to write his memoirs, his misgivings about the shortcomings of the Fourth Republic came to fruition with its failures in Indochina (Vietnam) and its poor handling of Algeria's fight for independence in North Africa.

On November 1, 1954 Algerian independence 'maquisards' (guerrillas) attacked French military installations, police posts, communications facilities and public utilities. Moslems were asked to join a national struggle for the restoration of the Algerian state based upon the teachings of the Koran. France's military crackdown left no point for compromise but after four years of civil unrest in Algiers and the dismissal of the French government by Parliament, de Gaulle assumed the position of Premier on June 1 and was granted emergency powers for six months.

De Gaulle immediately flew to Algiers and made his famous 'Je vous ai compris' (I have understood you) speech. In October, he returned to Algiers to reiterate his country's commitment to a peaceful solution to Algerian Independence.

❡ Last Sunday, three and a half million men and women of Algeria, without distinction of community, in complete equality, gave France and myself their vote of confidence. They did this quite simply without any constraint and in spite of the threats that certain fanatics brought to bear against them, their families and their property. This is a fact, as clear as the bright light of day. And this fact is fundamental not only because it mutually and forever pledges, one to the other, Algeria and France, but also because it ties in with what happened that same day in Metropolitan France, in the Overseas Departments, in the Territories of the Community.

The least that can be said of this great demonstration is that the French people proved to themselves and to the entire world their determination for renovation, and that, at the same time, a hundred million men decided to build their future together in Liberty, Equality and Fraternity.

With regard to Algeria, what is the future to which France is calling her? Women and men of Algeria, I have come here to tell you what it is.

What must be achieved is the basic transformation of this country, so brave, so alive, but also so full of difficulties and suffering. This means that it is necessary for the living conditions of each man and woman to improve from day to day. This means that, for the benefit of the inhabitants, the resources of the earth and the ability of the elites must be brought to light and developed. This means that children must be taught. This means that all Algeria must have her share in what modern civilization can and must bring to men in terms of well-being and dignity.

But the loftiest plans call for practical measures. Here are the measures that my Government intends to take in the near future covering the next five years by virtue of the full powers that the new Constitution has just conferred upon it.

During these five years, of the young people in Metropolitan France—yes, I say in Metropolitan France—that enter the service of the State, in the Administration, in the Army, in education and in the public services, at least a tenth of these young people must be recruited from the Arab, the Kabyle and Mozabite communities, and that without prejudice to an increased proportion of Algerians serving in Algeria.

In the course of these five years, salaries and wages in Algeria will be raised to a level comparable to what they are in Metropolitan France.

Before the end of these five years, 250 000 hectares [617 500 acres] of new land will be allotted to Moslem farmers.

Before the end of these five years, the first phase of the plan for the agricultural and industrial development of Algeria will be brought to its conclusion. This phase includes, in particular, the delivery and the distribution of the oil and gas of the Sahara, the setting up, on this soil, of great metallurgical and chemical complexes, the construction of housing for a million people, the corresponding development of health services, of roads, ports, means of communication-in short, the regular employment of 400,000 new workers.

Gradually in the course of these five years, two-thirds of the girls and boys will be enrolled in school and, during the three years after that, complete school enrollment of all Algerian youth will be achieved.

During these five years, the human contact that has been made especially by the French Army-by its career officers, its reserve officers, its fighting men, its young conscripts-will be continued and developed and, in Metropolitan France, the same must be true, in Paris and in our provinces.

What will be the political consequences of this evolution which calls for very extensive and prolonged efforts? I believe it is quite useless to freeze in advance, in words, that which, in any event, is going to take shape, little by little, as it is undertaken. But, in any case, two things are certain as of now: the first concerns the present.

In two months, Algeria will elect her representatives under the same conditions as will Metropolitan France. But at least two thirds of her representatives will have to be Moslem citizens.

The other refers to the future. The future of Algeria will in any event—because that is the nature of things-be built on a double foundation: her personality and her close solidarity with Metropolitan France.

In any case, it is absolutely essential that this fruitful transformation be accomplished. This is necessary for the good of the men of Algeria, for the good of the women, for the good of the children who live here; but it is also necessary for the honor of mankind. It is necessary for the peace of the world. For no one has any interest in the stagnation of a people, except the kind of people, who, to serve their ambitions, gamble on the spirit of revolt and the poverty of others.

This transformation, this immense political, economic, social and cultural task-who could effect this transformation, if not France?

Now it happens that France has the will and the means to do so. It also happens that the vote of the Algerians has just proved that they desire this transformation and that it should be carried out with France.

Therefore, turning toward those who are prolonging a fratricidal conflict, who are organizing lamentable attacks in Metropolitan France, or who are spreading through the chancelleries, through underground dens, by means of the radios and the newspapers of certain foreign capitals-vilifications of France, to those I say: Why kill? We must enable people to live. Why destroy? Our duty is to build. Why hate? We must cooperate.

Stop this absurd fighting and you will at once see a new blossoming of hope over all the land of Algeria. You will see the prisons emptying; you will see the opening up of a future big enough for everybody, and for you yourselves in particular. And then, speaking to those States which are throwing oil on the fire here while their unhappy peoples writhe under dictatorships, I say: Could you do what France is in a position to do here, what only France is capable of doing? Could you people do it? No. Then let France carry on, unless you deliberately decide to envenom the conflict in order to distract attention from your own difficulties. But in the present state of the world, where can these bitter incitements lead if not to a universal cataclysm? Only two paths lie open to the human race today: war or brotherhood. In Algeria as everywhere, France, for her part, has chosen brotherhood.

Long live the Republic! Long live Algeria and long live France!'

> 'Only two paths lie open to the human race today: war or brotherhood. In Algeria as everywhere, France, for her part, has chosen brotherhood.'

De Gaulle and his supporters won a comfortable majority in the November 1958 elections and he was elected President (with 78 per cent of the vote) and inaugurated in January 1959, aged 69. Many in Algeria saw de Gaulle's election as the chance they needed to gain independence but by the middle of the year the French military had regained control.

Feeling betrayed by de Gaulle, there was another insurrection in January 1960 but it was quickly quashed by the French military which remained loyal to their President. However, de Gaulle was losing the support of his generals (there were rumours of a coup in April 1961) and when protestors were killed in a street march in Paris in April, the French President realised that public sentiment had turned in favour of Algerian independence.

On July 1, 1962 some six million voters in Algeria voted in favour of independence in a special referendum. Two days later President de Gaulle announced Algeria an independent country. The total cost was 350 000 Algerians dead (Algerian sources put the figure as high as 1.5 million), 18 000 French military deaths and over 10 000 European civilian casualties in over 42 000 recorded terrorist incidents. The question remains: did de Gaulle proclaim 'I have understood you' for a cynical grab for power or did politics prolong the Algerian war for independence another four years?

Charles de Gaulle was elected to serve a second seven-year term as President in 1965 but resigned in 1969 when an attempted change to the role of the Senate resulted in referendum defeat. He passed away the following year, two weeks before his 80th birthday.

Revolution
1960-1969

Harold MacMillan

'The Wind of Change'

Address to the South African Parliament in Cape Town, 3 February 1960.

Harold MacMillan addresses voters in the 1959 British general election.

Harold MacMillan (1894-1986) was British Prime Minister from 1957 to 1963 at a time when the black independence movement was sweeping the African continent. In 1960 MacMillan visited the African Commonwealth states of Ghana and Nigeria and addressed the South African Parliament. Acknowledging the rights of African nations to rule their own affairs, he stated that it was his government's responsibility to promote the creation of societies that upheld the rights of individuals. This was the first public statement by a British government in this vein and signalled a major shift in attitude not only towards the Commonwealth's colonial past, but towards the apartheid regime in South Africa.

'As I've travelled around the Union I have found everywhere, as I expected, a deep preoccupation with what is happening in the rest of the African continent. I understand and sympathise with your interests in these events and your anxiety about them.

Ever since the break-up of the Roman Empire one of the constant facts of political life in Europe has been the emergence of independent nations. They have come into existence over the centuries in different forms, with different kinds of Government, but all have been inspired by a deep, keen feeling of nationalism, which has grown as the nations have grown.

In the twentieth century, and especially since the end of the war, the processes which gave birth to the nation states of Europe have been repeated all over the world. We have seen the awakening of national consciousness in peoples who have for centuries lived in dependence upon some other power. Fifteen years ago this movement spread through Asia. Many countries there of different races and civilizations pressed their claim to an independent national life. Today the same thing is happening in Africa, and the most striking of all the impressions I have formed is of the strength of this African national consciousness. In different places it takes different forms, but it is happening everywhere. The wind of change is blowing through this continent, and, whether we like it or not, this growth of national consciousness is a political fact. We must all accept it as a fact, and our national policies must take account of it.

'The wind of change is blowing through this continent ...'

Of course, you understand this better than anyone. You are sprung from Europe, the home of nationalism, and here in Africa you have yourselves created a new nation. Indeed, in the history of our times yours will be recorded as the first of the African nationalisms, and this tide of national consciousness which is now rising in Africa is a fact for which you and we and the other nations of the Western World are ultimately responsible. For its causes are to be found in the achievements of Western civilization, in the pushing forward of the frontiers of knowledge, in the applying of science in the service of human needs, in the expanding of food production, in the speeding and multiplying of the means of communication, and perhaps, above all, the spread of education ...

HAROLD MACMILLAN

As I see it the great issue in this second half of the twentieth century is whether the uncommitted peoples of Asia and Africa will swing to the East or to the West. Will they be drawn into the Communist camp? Or will the great experiments in self-government that are now being made in Asia and Africa, especially within the Commonwealth, prove so successful, and by their example so compelling, that the balance will come down in favour of freedom and order and justice?

The struggle is joined, and it is a struggle for the minds of men. What is now on trial is much more than our military strength or our diplomatic and administrative skill. It is our way of life. The uncommitted nations want to see before they choose.

What can we show them to help them choose right? Each of the independent members of the Commonwealth must answer that question for itself. It is a basic principle of our modern Commonwealth that we respect each other's sovereignty in matters of internal policy. At the same time we must recognize that in this shrinking world in which we live today the internal policies of one nation may have effects outside it. We may sometimes be tempted to say to each other, 'Mind your own business,' but in these days I would myself expand the old saying so that it runs: 'Mind your own business, but mind how it affects my business, too.'

Let me be very, frank with you, my friends. What governments and Parliaments in the United Kingdom have done since the war in according independence to India, Pakistan, Ceylon, Malaya and Ghana, and what they will do for Nigeria and other countries now nearing independence, all this, though we take full and sole responsibility for it, we do in the belief that it is the only way to establish the future of the Commonwealth and of the Free World on sound foundations. All this of course is also of deep and close concern to you for nothing we do in this small world can be done in a corner or remain hidden. What we do today in West, Central and East Africa becomes known tomorrow to everyone in the Union, whatever his language, colour or traditions. Let me assure you, in all friendliness, that we are well aware of this and that we have acted and will act with full knowledge of the responsibility we have to all our friends.

Nevertheless I am sure you will agree that in our own areas of responsibility we must each do what we think right. What we think right derives from a long experience both of failure and success in the management of our own affairs. We have tried to learn and apply the lessons of our judgement of right and wrong. Our justice is rooted in the same soil as yours—in Christianity and in the rule of law as the basis of a free society. This experience of our own explains why it has been our aim in the countries for which we have borne responsibility, not only to raise the material standards of living, but also to create a society which respects the rights of individuals, a society in which men are given the opportunity to grow to their full stature—and that must in our view include the opportunity to have an increasing share in political power and responsibility, a society in which individual merit and individual merit alone is the criterion for a man's advancement, whether political or economic ...

The attitude of the United Kingdom towards this problem was clearly expressed by the Foreign Secretary, Mr Selwyn Lloyd, speaking at the United Nations General Assembly on 17 September 1959. These were his words:

"In those territories where different races or tribes live side by side the task is to ensure that all the people may enjoy security and freedom and the chance to contribute as individuals to the progress and well being of these countries. We reject the idea of any inherent superiority of one race over another. Our policy therefore is non-racial. It offers a future in which Africans, Europeans, Asians, the peoples of the Pacific and others with whom we are concerned, will all play their full part as citizens in the countries where they live, and in which feelings of race will be submerged in loyalty to new nations.

'Our justice is rooted in the same soil as yours.'

I have thought you would wish me to state plainly and with full candour the policy for which we in Britain stand. It may well be that in trying to do our duty as we see it we shall sometimes make difficulties for you. If this proves to be so we shall regret it. But I know that even so you would not ask us to flinch from doing our duty.

As a fellow member of the Commonwealth it is our earnest desire to give South Africa our support and encouragement, but I hope you won't mind my saying frankly that there are some aspects of your policies which make it impossible for us to do this without being false to our own deep convictions about the political destinies of free men to which in our own territories we are trying to give effect. I think we ought, as friends, to face together, without seeking to apportion credit or blame, the fact that in the world of today this difference of outlook lies between us ..."

The fact is that in this modern world no country, not even the greatest, can live for itself alone. Nearly two thousand years ago, when the whole of the civilized world was comprised within the confines of the Roman Empire, St Paul proclaimed one of the great truths of history—we are all members one of another. During this twentieth century that eternal truth has taken on a new and exciting significance. It has always been impossible for the individual man to live in isolation from his fellows, in the home, the tribe, the village, or the city. Today it is impossible for nations to live in isolation from one another. What Dr John Donne said of individual men three hundred years ago is true today of my country, your country, and all the countries of the world:

"Any man's death diminishes me, because I am involved in Mankind. And therefore never send to know for whom the bell tolls; it tolls for thee."

All nations now are interdependent one upon another, and this is generally realized throughout the Western World ... Those of us who by grace of the electorate are temporarily in charge of affairs in your country and in mine, we fleeting transient phantoms on the great stage of history, we have no right to sweep aside on this account the friendship that exists between our countries, for that is the legacy of history. It is not ours alone to deal with as we wish. To adapt a famous phrase, it belongs to those who are living, but it also belongs to those who are dead and to those who are yet unborn. We must face the differences, but let us try to see beyond them down the long vista of the future.

I hope—indeed, I am confident—that in another 50 years we shall look back on the differences that exist between us now as matters of historical interest, for as time passes and one

HAROLD MACMILLAN

195

generation yields to another, human problems change and fade. Let us remember these truths. Let us resolve to build, not to destroy, and let us remember always that weakness comes from division, strength from unity.'

The great fear of the British and other Western governments was that newly-independent African nations would align themselves with the Communist East and upset the balance of power during the Cold War. A fortnight after this historic speech, Britain announced a power-sharing agreement with Kenyan nationalists before that country's independence in 1963. By 1961 Nigeria, Somalia, Sierra Leone and Tanzania would also gain their independence.

However, South African Prime Minister Hendrik Verwoerd responded to McMillan's speech by stating that 'justice to all, does not only mean being just to the black man of Africa, but also to the white man of Africa' because it was the white man who 'historically brought civilisation to a bare continent'. On 31 May, 1961—largely in response to domestic civil unrest and the fear of political interference from Britain—the white South African regime pushed through its declaration of independence and created a republic founded on systemic apartheid.

In 1964 several high-profile black nationalists (including Nelson Mandela) were jailed for treason, Prime Minister Verwoerd was assassinated by a mentally disturbed white parliamentary clerk in 1966, and South Africa gradually became the pariah of western democracies during the next three decades.

After the finest moment of his political career, Harold MacMillan resigned his position as Prime Minister because of ill health in 1963 and left parliament the following year. He was made an Earl on his 90th birthday in 1984, two years before his death.

Fidel Castro
'United Nations Address'

United Nations General Assembly, New York, 26 September 1960.

Fidel Castro addresses the United Nations Assembly in 1960.

In 1959 Cuban exile Fidel Castro Ruz invaded his homeland with a band of 80 men trained in guerrilla warfare and overturned the rule of General Fulgencio Batista backed by popular support of his countrymen.

Born in 1926, near Birán, Cuba, Castro graduated from the University of Havana with a law degree in 1950. He intended to stand for parliament but the Cuban government was overthrown in a coup led by General Batista. In 1953 Castro was jailed for 15 years after launching a July 26 attack on Batista's army. 'History will absolve me,' he famously declared at his trial. Castro was released after only two years in a general amnesty. He immediately went into exile and started training a small group of guerrillas near Mexico City.

After invading Cuba in 1956, Castro waged a guerrilla war in the Cuban hills alongside protégé Che Guevara, gathering support from the people as they defeated Batista's army, before capturing Havana in January 1959.

Originally, the United States recognised the new Cuban Government in which Castro had assumed the role of Prime Minister by popular mandate on July 26, 1959. Here was a shining example of true democracy, he said, and quoted Abraham Lincoln: 'a government of the people, by the people, and for the people'. He gestured dramatically toward his audience. 'This,' he said, 'is real democracy'. The Cuban dictator quickly became a vocal critic of US foreign policy. As a committed Marxist, Castro sought to expropriate foreign-owned companies and the United States instigated economic sanctions (especially against the lucrative sugar market) and banned all travel to Cuba. Castro responded by nationalising some $850 million worth of American-owned properties and companies.

In the longest speech in the history of the United Nations, Castro addressed the General Assembly in September 1960 and argued that 'the case of Cuba is the case of all underdeveloped countries'. The Cuban revolutionary leader also used this platform to attack American colonial aggression internationally. In conclusion, Castro publicly stated the revolutionary aims of the Republic of Cuba before the world leadership and made clear his opposition to American colonial interests.

In conclusion, we are going to place our trust in reason and in the decency of all. We wish to sum up our ideas regarding some aspects of these world problems about which there should be no doubt. The problem of Cuba, which we have set forth here, is a part of the problems of the world. Those who attack us today are those who are helping to attack others in other parts of the world.

The United States Government cannot be on the side of the Algerian people, it cannot be on the side of the Algerian people because it is allied to metropolitan France. It cannot be on the side of the Congolese people, because it is allied to Belgium. It cannot be on the side of the Spanish people, because it is allied to Franco. It cannot be on the side of the Puerto Rican people, whose nationhood it has been destroying for fifty years. It cannot be on the side of the Panamanians, who claim the Canal. It cannot support the ascendancy of civil power in Latin America, Germany or Japan. It cannot be on the side of the peasants who want land, because it is allied to the big landowners. It cannot be on the side of the workers who are demanding better living conditions in all parts of the world, because it is allied to the monopolies. It cannot be on the side of the colonies which want their freedom, because it is allied to the colonizers.

> 'The American people need only imagine how uneasy they would feel if the Soviet Union began to establish a ring of atomic bases in Cuba, Mexico, or Canada.'

That is to say, it is for France, for the colonization of Algeria for the colonization of the Congo; it is for the maintenance of its privileges and interests in the Panama Canal, for colonialism through the world. It is for the German militarism and for the resurgence of German militarism. It is for Japanese militarism and for the resurgence of Japanese militarism.

The Government of the United States forgets the millions of Jews murdered in European concentration camps by the Nazis, who are today regaining their influence in the German army. It forgets the Frenchmen who were killed in their heroic struggle against the occupation; it forgets the American soldiers who died on the Siegfried Line, in the Ruhr, on the Rhine, and on the Asian fronts. The United States Government cannot be for the integrity and sovereignty of nations. Why? Because it must curtail the sovereignty of nations in order to keep its military bases, and each base is a dagger thrust into sovereignty; each base is a limitation on sovereignty.

That is why it has to be against the sovereignty of nations, because it must constantly limit sovereignty in order to maintain its policy of encircling the Soviet Union with bases. We believe that these problems are not properly explained to the American people. But the American people need only imagine how uneasy they would feel if the Soviet Union began to establish a ring of atomic bases in Cuba, Mexico, or Canada. The population would not feel secure or calm. World opinion, including American opinion, must be taught to see the other person's point of view.

The underdeveloped peoples should not always be represented as aggressors; revolutionaries should not be presented as aggressors, as enemies of the American people, because we have seen American like Carleton Beals, Waldo Frank, and others, famous and distinguished intellectuals, shed tears at the thought of the mistakes that are being made, at the breach of hospitality towards us; there are many Americans, the most humane, the most progressive, and the most esteemed writers, in whom I see the nobility of this country's early leaders, the Washingtons, the Jeffersons, and the Lincolns. I say this in no spirit of demagogy, but with the sincere admiration that we feel for those who once succeeded in freeing their people from colonial status and who did not fight in order that their country might today be the ally of all the reactionaries, the gangsters, the big landowners, the monopolists, the exploiters, the militarists, the fascists in the world, that is to say, the ally of the most reactionary forces, but rather in order that their country might always be the champion of noble and just ideals.

We know well what will be said about us, today, tomorrow, every day, to deceive the American people. But it does not matter. We are doing our duty by stating our views in this historic Assembly. We proclaim the right of people to freedom, the right of people to nationhood; those who know that nationalism means the desire of the people to regain what is rightly theirs, their wealth, their natural resources, conspire against nationalism.

We are, in short, for all the noble aspirations of all the peoples. That is our position. We are, and always shall be for everything that is just: against colonialism, exploitation, monopolies, militarism, the armaments race, and warmongering. We shall always be against such things. That will be our position.

And to conclude, fulfilling what we regard as our duty, I am going to quote to this Assembly the key part of the Declaration of Havana. As you all know, the Declaration of Havana was the Cuban people's answer to the Declaration of San Jose, Costa Rica. Nor 10, nor 100, nor 100 000, but more than one million Cubans gathered together.

At that Assembly, which was convened as an answer to the Declaration of San Jose, the following principles were proclaimed, in consultation with the people and by acclamation of the people, as the principles of the Cuban Revolution:

'The National General Assembly of the Cuban people condemns large-scale landowning as a source of poverty for the peasant and a backward and inhuman system of agricultural production; it condemns starvation wages and the iniquitous exploitation of human work by illegitimate and privileged interests ...'

"The National General Assembly of the Cuban people condemns large-scale landowning as a source of poverty for the peasant and a backward and inhuman system of agricultural production; it condemns starvation wages and the iniquitous exploitation of human work by illegitimate and privileged interests; it condemns illiteracy, the lack of teachers, of schools, doctor and hospitals; the lack of old-age security in the countries of America; it condemns discrimination against the Negro and the Indian'; it condemns the inequality and the exploitation of women; it condemns political and military oligarchies, which keep our peoples in poverty, prevent their democratic development and the full exercise of their sovereignty; it condemns concessions of the natural resources of our countries as a policy of surrender which betrays the interests of the peoples; it condemns the governments which ignore the demands of their people in order to obey orders from abroad; it condemns the systematic deception of the people by mass communications media which serve the interests of the oligarchies and the policy of imperialist oppression; it condemns the monopoly held by news agencies, which are instruments of monopolist trusts and agents of such interests; it condemns the repressive laws which prevent the workers, the peasants, the students and the intellectuals, the great majorities in each country, from organizing themselves to fight for their social and national rights; it condemns the imperialist monopolies and enterprises which continually plunder our wealth, exploit our workers and peasants, bleed our economies to keep them in a backward state, and subordinate Latin American politics to their designs and interests.

"In short, The National General Assembly of the Cuban People condemns the exploitation of man by man, and the exploitations of underdeveloped countries by imperialists capital.

"Therefore, the National General Assembly of the Cuban People proclaims before America, and proclaims here before the world, the right of the peasants to the land; the right of the workers to the fruits of their labor; the right of the children to education: the right of the sick to medical care and hospitalization; the right of young people to work; the right of students to free vocational training and scientific education; the right of Negroes, and Indians to full human dignity; the right of women to civil, social and political equality; the right of the elderly to security in their old age; the right of intellectuals, artists and scientists to fight through their works for a better world; the right of States to nationalize imperialist monopolies, thus rescuing their national wealth and resources; the right of nations to their full sovereignty; the right of peoples to convert their military fortresses into schools, and to arm their workers— because in this we too have to be arms-conscious, to arm our people in defense against imperialist attacks—their peasants, their students, their intellectuals, Negroes, Indians, women, young people, old people, all the oppressed and exploited, so that they themselves can defend their rights and their destinies."

Some people wanted to know what the policy of the Revolutionary Government of Cuba was. Very well, then, this is our policy.'

'The United States Government cannot be on the side of the Algerian people ... because it is allied to metropolitan France. It cannot be on the side of the Congolese people, because it is allied to Belgium. It cannot be on the side of the Spanish people, because it is allied to Franco.'

Fidel Castro survived an aborted American-backed invasion in the Bay of Pigs in 1961, the Cuban Missile Crisis the following year and the collapse of the Soviet Union in 1991. The revolutionary leader has maintained his dictatorship of Cuba—always an awkward neighbour for the capitalist USA—and at the age of 79 celebrated his 46th year in power in 2005.

FIDEL CASTRO

John F Kennedy

'The Cuban Missile Crisis'

National television broadcast, 22 October 1962.

President Kennedy delivers a televised speech to the nation in October 1962.

John F. Kennedy (1917-63) was regarded as the 'new generation' of US leader—young, charismatic and a powerful communicator. The second son of a former US Ambassador to England, JFK was a Harvard graduate, a war hero, a Democratic Representative (1947) and Senator (1952), whose book, *Profiles in Courage*, won the 1956 Pulitzer Prize for Literature.

It is hard to believe that Kennedy was the underdog to Republican Party candidate, Vice-President Richard Nixon, in the 1960 presidential race. But Kennedy's charisma translated well on television and the medium became an important factor in his election victory when he outpointed the more-experienced Richard Nixon in the first televised series of debates.

Nixon looked decidedly nervous—and untrustworthy—next to the debonair Senator from Massachusetts (interestingly, television viewers thought Kennedy had easily won the debates while radio listeners put Nixon ahead).

On a cold January morning in 1961, John F. Kennedy took the oath of office and became the 35th President of the United States of America. His inauguration speech—with a bold challenge for all Americans and the 'citizens of the world'—signalled the birth of one of the most historic, controversial and mythical periods in American politics. Kennedy's time as president, barely 1000 days, was known as 'Camelot'.

On 16 October 1962, President Kennedy was shown aerial photos taken by an American U-2 spy plane over Cuba—just ninety miles off the coast of Florida—of the Soviet installation of offensive nuclear missiles.

Four days later he summoned the Soviet Minister of Foreign Affairs, Andrei Gromyko, who informed him that the weapons were for defensive purposes only.

The President then met with top military aides—and his brother, Attorney General Robert Kennedy—to discuss America's response. On Sunday October 21, Kennedy and his advisors spent the entire day considering two main military options—an air strike against the bases or a naval blockade of Cuba. The President chose the latter option, which would be referred to by the less provocative term 'quarantine', and forced a stand-off with the Russians.

At 7 pm (EST) on 22 October 1962, President Kennedy informed the American people on national television of the recently discovered Soviet military build-up in Cuba.

❜This Government, as promised, has maintained the closest surveillance of the Soviet Military build-up on the island of Cuba. Within the past week, unmistakable evidence has established the fact that a series of offensive missile sites is now in preparation on that imprisoned island. The purpose of these bases can be none other than to provide a nuclear strike capability against the Western Hemisphere.

Upon receiving the first preliminary hard information of this nature last Tuesday morning at 9 am, I directed that our surveillance be stepped up. And having now confirmed and completed our evaluation of the evidence and our decision on a course of action, this Government feels obliged to report this new crisis to you in fullest detail.

The characteristics of these new missile sites indicate two distinct types of installations. Several of them include medium range ballistic missiles capable of carrying a nuclear warhead for a distance of more than 1 000 nautical miles. Each of these missiles, in short, is capable of striking Washington, DC, the Panama Canal, Cape Canaveral, Mexico City, or any other city in the south-eastern part of the United States, in Central America, or in the Caribbean area.

Additional sites not yet completed appear to be designed for intermediate range ballistic missiles—capable of traveling more than twice as far—and thus capable of striking most of the major cities in the Western Hemisphere, ranging as far north as Hudson Bay, Canada, and as far south as Lima, Peru. In addition, jet bombers, capable of carrying nuclear weapons, are now being uncrated and assembled in Cuba, while the necessary air bases are being prepared.

This urgent transformation of Cuba into an important strategic base—by the presence of these large, long range, and clearly offensive weapons of sudden mass destruction—constitutes an explicit threat to the peace and security of all the Americas, in flagrant and deliberate defiance of the Rio Pact of 1947, the traditions of this Nation and hemisphere, the joint resolution of the 87th Congress, the Charter of the United Nations, and my own public warnings to the Soviets on September 4 and 13. This action also contradicts the repeated assurances of Soviet spokesmen, both publicly and privately delivered, that the arms build-up in Cuba would retain its original defensive character, and that the Soviet Union had no need or desire to station strategic missiles on the territory of any other nation.

The size of this undertaking makes clear that it has been planned for some months. Yet only last month, after I had made clear the distinction between any introduction of ground-to-ground missiles and the existence of defensive antiaircraft missiles, the Soviet Government publicly stated on September 11, and I quote, "the armaments and military equipment sent to Cuba are designed exclusively for defensive purposes," that, and I quote the Soviet Government, "there is no need for the Soviet Government to shift its weapons . . . for a retaliatory blow to any other country, for instance Cuba," and that, and I quote their government, "the Soviet Union has no powerful rockets to carry these nuclear warheads that there is no need to search for sites for them beyond the boundaries of the Soviet Union." That statement was false.

Only last Thursday, as evidence of this rapid offensive build-up was already in my hand, Soviet Foreign Minister Gromyko told me in my office that he was instructed to make it clear once again, as he said his government had already done, that Soviet assistance to Cuba, and I quote, "pursued solely the purpose of contributing to the defense capabilities of Cuba," that, and I quote him, "training by Soviet specialists of Cuban nationals in handling defensive armaments was by no means offensive, and if it were otherwise," Mr. Gromyko went on, "the Soviet Government would never become involved in rendering such assistance." That statement also was false.

Neither the United States of America nor the world community of nations can tolerate deliberate deception and offensive threats on the part of any nation, large or small. We no longer live in a world where only the actual firing of weapons represents a sufficient challenge to a nation's security to constitute maximum peril. Nuclear weapons are so destructive and ballistic missiles are so swift, that any substantially increased possibility of their use or any sudden change in their deployment may well be regarded as a definite threat to peace.

'To the captive people of Cuba ... Now your leaders are no longer Cuban leaders inspired by Cuban ideals. They are puppets and agents of an international conspiracy.'

For many years both the Soviet Union and the United States, recognizing this fact, have deployed strategic nuclear weapons with great care, never upsetting the precarious status quo which insured that these weapons would not be used in the absence of some vital challenge. Our own strategic missiles have never been transferred to the territory of any other nation under a cloak of secrecy and deception; and our history—unlike that of the Soviets since the end of World War II—demonstrates that we have no desire to dominate or conquer any other nation or impose our system upon its people. Nevertheless, American citizens have become adjusted to living daily on the bull's-eye of Soviet missiles located inside the USSR or in submarines.

In that sense, missiles in Cuba add to an already clear and present danger—although it should be noted the nations of Latin America have never previously been subjected to a potential nuclear threat.

But this secret, swift, and extraordinary build-up of Communist missiles—in an area well known to have a special and historical relationship to the United States and the nations of the Western Hemisphere, in violation of Soviet assurances, and in defiance of American and hemispheric policy—this sudden, clandestine decision to station strategic weapons for the first time outside of Soviet soil—is a deliberately provocative and unjustified change in the status quo which cannot be accepted by this country, if our courage and our commitments are ever to be trusted again by either friend or foe.

The 1930's taught us a clear lesson: aggressive conduct, if allowed to go unchecked and unchallenged ultimately leads to war. This nation is opposed to war. We are also true to our word. Our unswerving objective, therefore, must be to prevent the use of these missiles against this or any other country, and to secure their withdrawal or elimination from the Western Hemisphere.

JOHN F KENNEDY

205

Our policy has been one of patience and restraint, as befits a peaceful and powerful nation, which leads a worldwide alliance. We have been determined not to be diverted from our central concerns by mere irritants and fanatics. But now further action is required—and it is under way; and these actions may only be the beginning. We will not prematurely or unnecessarily risk the costs of worldwide nuclear war in which even the fruits of victory would be ashes in our mouth—but neither will we shrink from that risk at any time it must be faced.

Acting, therefore, in the defense of our own security and of the entire Western Hemisphere, and under the authority entrusted to me by the Constitution as endorsed by the resolution of the Congress, I have directed that the following initial steps be taken immediately:

First: To halt this offensive build-up, a strict quarantine on all offensive military equipment under shipment to Cuba is being initiated. All ships of any kind bound for Cuba from whatever nation or port will, if found to contain cargoes of offensive weapons, be turned back. This quarantine will be extended, if needed, to other types of cargo and carriers. We are not at this time, however, denying the necessities of life as the Soviets attempted to do in their Berlin blockade of 1948.

> 'Our goal is not the victory of might, but the vindication of right—not peace at the expense of freedom, but both peace and freedom, here in this hemisphere, and, we hope, around the world.'

Second: I have directed the continued and increased close surveillance of Cuba and its military build-up. The foreign ministers of the OAS, in their communique of October 6, rejected secrecy in such matters in this hemisphere. Should these offensive military preparations continue, thus increasing the threat to the hemisphere, further action will be justified. I have directed the Armed Forces to prepare for any eventualities; and I trust that in the interest of both the Cuban people and the Soviet technicians at the sites, the hazards to all concerned in continuing this threat will be recognized.

Third: It shall be the policy of this Nation to regard any nuclear missile launched from Cuba against any nation in the Western Hemisphere as an attack by the Soviet Union on the United States, requiring a full retaliatory response upon the Soviet Union.

Fourth: As a necessary military precaution, I have reinforced our base at Guantanamo, evacuated today the dependents of our personnel there, and ordered additional military units to be on a standby alert basis.

Fifth: We are calling tonight for an immediate meeting of the Organ of Consultation under the Organization of American States, to consider this threat to hemispheric security and to invoke articles 6 and 8 of the Rio Treaty in support of all necessary action. The United Nations Charter allows for regional security arrangements—and the nations of this hemisphere decided long ago against the military presence of outside powers. Our other allies around the world have also been alerted.

Sixth: Under the Charter of the United Nations, we are asking tonight that an emergency meeting of the Security Council be convoked without delay to take action against this latest

Soviet threat to world peace. Our resolution will call for the prompt dismantling and withdrawal of all offensive weapons in Cuba, under the supervision of U.N. observers, before the quarantine can be lifted.

Seventh and finally: I call upon Chairman Khrushchev to halt and eliminate this clandestine, reckless and provocative threat to world peace and to stable relations between our two nations. I call upon him further to abandon this course of world domination, and to join in an historic effort to end the perilous arms race and to transform the history of man. He has an opportunity now to move the world back from the abyss of destruction—by returning to his government's own words that it had no need to station missiles outside its own territory, and withdrawing these weapons from Cuba—by refraining from any action which will widen or deepen the present crisis—and then by participating in a search for peaceful and permanent solutions.

This Nation is prepared to present its case against the Soviet threat to peace, and our own proposals for a peaceful world, at any time and in any forum—in the OAS, in the United Nations, or in any other meeting that could be useful—without limiting our freedom of action. We have in the past made strenuous efforts to limit the spread of nuclear weapons. We have proposed the elimination of all arms and military bases in a fair and effective disarmament treaty. We are prepared to discuss new proposals for the removal of tensions on both sides—including the possibility of a genuinely independent Cuba, free to determine its own destiny. We have no wish to war with the Soviet Union—for we are a peaceful people who desire to live in peace with all other peoples.

But it is difficult to settle or even discuss these problems in an atmosphere of intimidation. That is why this latest Soviet threat—or any other threat which is made independently or in response to our actions this week—must and will be met with determination. Any hostile move anywhere in the world against the safety and freedom of peoples to whom we are committed—including in particular the brave people of West Berlin—will be met by whatever action is needed.

Finally, I want to say a few words to the captive people of Cuba, to whom this speech is being directly carried by special radio facilities. I speak to you as a friend, as one who knows of your deep attachment to your fatherland, as one who shares your aspirations for liberty and justice for all. And I have watched and the American people have watched with deep sorrow how your nationalist revolution was betrayed—and how your fatherland fell under foreign domination. Now your leaders are no longer Cuban leaders inspired by Cuban ideals. They are puppets and agents of an international conspiracy which has turned Cuba against your friends and neighbors in the Americas—and turned it into the first Latin American country to become a target for nuclear war—the first Latin American country to have these weapons on its soil.

These new weapons are not in your interest. They contribute nothing to your peace and well-being. They can only undermine it. But this country has no wish to cause you to suffer or to impose any system upon you. We know that your lives and land are being used as pawns by those who deny your freedom.

Many times in the past, the Cuban people have risen to throw out tyrants who destroyed their liberty. And I have no doubt that most Cubans today look forward to the time when they will be truly free—free from foreign domination, free to choose their own leaders, free to select their own system, free to own their own land, free to speak and write and worship without fear or degradation. And then shall Cuba be welcomed back to the society of free nations and to the associations of this hemisphere.

My fellow citizens: let no one doubt that this is a difficult and dangerous effort on which we have set out. No one can see precisely what course it will take or what costs or casualties will be incurred. Many months of sacrifice and self-discipline lie ahead -months in which our patience and our will be tested—months in which many threats and denunciations will keep us aware of our dangers. But the greatest danger of all would be to do nothing.

The path we have chosen for the present is full of hazards, as all paths are—but it is the one most consistent with our character and courage as a nation and our commitments around the world. The cost of freedom is always high—and Americans have always paid it. And one path we shall never choose, and that is the path of surrender or submission.

Our goal is not the victory of might, but the vindication of right—not peace at the expense of freedom, but both peace and freedom, here in this hemisphere, and, we hope, around the world. God willing, that goal will be achieved.

Thank you and good night. **'**

The 'Missiles of October' brought the world to the brink of nuclear war, but Kennedy's steel will and unequivocal diplomacy forced the USSR's mighty hand. TheSoviets backed down and removed the missiles.

Although his legislative career during his time as President was not extensive, John Kennedy can be seen as a leader for his time—a man who was able divine the mood of the people, synthesise the major issues of the day and move government policy towards an ideal—especially regarding civil rights.

On Friday, 22 November 1963 JFK was killed by an assassin's bullet as he rode in a motorcade through Dallas, Texas. Later that afternoon, Lee Harvey Oswald was implicated in the President's death when he was arrested in a theatre and charged with the murder of a Dallas policeman (see Lyndon Johnson, 'Let Us Continue', p 215).

Martin Luther King
'I Have a Dream'

Lincoln Memorial, Washington DC, 28 August 1963.

Martin Luther King waves to supporters from the steps of the Lincoln Memorial, before his famous speech.

Atlanta-born Martin Luther King Jnr (1929-68) is rightly regarded by historians as one of the most significant civil rights leaders of the 20th Century—arguably the most significant in the modern history of the United States—and one whose lifetime achievements and lasting impact ranks him alongside that of Mohandas Gandhi.

King graduated from Crozer Theological Seminary in Chester, Pennsylvania in 1953 and was granted his doctorate two years later after completing his dissertation. That same year, he became pastor of the Dexter Avenue Baptist Church in Montgomery, Alabama, at a time when the local black community had a formed a boycott of local bus companies because of the South's strict code of racial segregation. The boycott lasted 382 days, King was arrested and his home was bombed but ultimately, the Supreme Court declared bus segregation unconstitutional and outlawed racial segregation on public transportation.

In August 1963, the Reverend Martin Luther King Jnr led a march to Washington DC to demonstrate the commitment of the American people—of all creeds and religions—to seek equal rights in every facet of American society. King's speech, delivered before hundreds of thousands of followers assembled on the steps of the Lincoln Memorial, is one of the greatest speeches of the twentieth century.

'I am happy to join with you today in what will go down in history as the greatest demonstration for freedom in the history of our nation.

Five score years ago, a great American, in whose symbolic shadow we stand today, signed the Emancipation Proclamation. This momentous decree came as a great beacon light of hope to millions of Negro slaves, who had been seared in the flames of withering injustice. It came as a joyous daybreak to end the long night of their captivity.

'We refuse to believe that the bank of justice is bankrupt.'

But one hundred years later, the Negro still is not free. One hundred years later, the life of the Negro is still sadly crippled by the manacles of segregation and the chains of discrimination. One hundred years later, the Negro lives on a lonely island of poverty in the midst of a vast ocean of material prosperity. One hundred years later, the Negro still languishes in the corners of American society and finds himself an exile in his own land.

So we've come here today to dramatize a shameful condition. In a sense, we've come to our nation's capital to cash a check. When the architects of our Republic wrote the magnificent words of the Constitution and the Declaration of Independence, they were signing a promissory note to which every American was to fall heir. This note was a promise that all men—yes, black men as well as white men—would be guaranteed the unalienable rights of life, liberty, and the pursuit of happiness.

It is obvious today that America has defaulted on this promissory note insofar as her citizens of color are concerned. Instead of honoring this sacred obligation, America has given the Negro people a bad check, a check which has come back marked "insufficient funds." But we refuse to believe that the bank of justice is bankrupt. We refuse to believe that there are insufficient funds in the great vaults of opportunity of this nation. So we've come to cash this check—a check that will give us upon demand the riches of freedom and the security of justice.

We have also come to this hallowed spot to remind America of the fierce urgency of "now." This is no time to engage in the luxury of cooling off or to take the tranquilizing drug of gradualism. Now is the time to make real the promises of democracy. Now is the time to rise from the dark and desolate valley of segregation to the sunlit path of racial justice. Now is the time to lift our nation from the quicksand of racial injustice to the solid rock of brotherhood. Now is the time to make justice a reality for all of God's children.

It would be fatal for the nation to overlook the urgency of the moment. This sweltering summer of the Negro's legitimate discontent will not pass until there is an invigorating autumn of freedom and equality. Nineteen sixty-three is not an end, but a beginning. Those who hope that the Negro needed to blow off steam and will now be content will have a rude awakening if the nation returns to business as usual. There will be neither rest nor tranquillity in America until the Negro is granted his citizenship rights. The whirlwinds of revolt will continue to shake the foundations of our nation until the bright day of justice emerges.

'We will not be satisfied until justice rolls down like waters and righteousness like a mighty stream!'

But that is something that I must say to my people who stand on the warm threshold which leads into the palace of justice. In the process of gaining our rightful place we must not be guilty of wrongful deeds. Let us not seek to satisfy our thirst for freedom by drinking from the cup of bitterness and hatred.

We must forever conduct our struggle on the high plane of dignity and discipline. We must not allow our creative protest to degenerate into physical violence. Again and again we must rise to the majestic heights of meeting physical force with soul force. The marvelous new militancy which has engulfed the Negro community must not lead us to a distrust of all white people, for many of our white brothers, as evidenced by their presence here today, have come to realize that their destiny is tied up with our destiny. And they have come to realize that their freedom is inextricably bound to our freedom. We cannot walk alone.

As we walk, we must make the pledge that we shall always march ahead. We cannot turn back.

There are those who are asking the devotees of civil rights, "When will you be satisfied?" We can never be satisfied as long as the Negro is the victim of the unspeakable horrors of police brutality. We can never be satisfied as long as our bodies, heavy with the fatigue of travel, cannot gain lodging in the motels of the highways and the hotels of the cities. We cannot be satisfied as long as the Negro's basic mobility is from a smaller ghetto to a larger one. We can never be satisfied as long as our children are stripped of their selfhood and robbed of their dignity by signs stating "For Whites Only." We cannot be satisfied as long as a Negro in Mississippi cannot vote and a Negro in New York believes he has nothing for which to vote. No, no, we are not satisfied, and we will not be satisfied until justice rolls down like waters and righteousness like a mighty stream!

I am not unmindful that some of you have come here out of great trials and tribulations. Some of you have come fresh from narrow jail cells. Some of you have come from areas where your quest for freedom left you battered by the storms of persecution and staggered by the winds of police brutality. You have been the veterans of creative suffering. Continue to work with the faith that unearned suffering is redemptive.

Go back to Mississippi, go back to Alabama, go back to South Carolina, go back to Georgia, go back to Louisiana, go back to the slums and ghettos of our Northern cities, knowing that somehow this situation can and will be changed. Let us not wallow in the valley of despair.

'We will be able to join hands and sing in the words of the old Negro spiritual, "Free at last! Free at last! Thank God Almighty, we are free at last!"'

I say to you today, my friends, so even though we face the difficulties of today and tomorrow, I still have a dream. It is a dream deeply rooted in the American dream.

I have a dream that one day this nation will rise up and live out the true meaning of its creed: "We hold these truths to be self-evident; that all men are created equal."

I have a dream that one day on the red hills of Georgia the sons of former slaves and the sons of former slave owners will be able to sit down together at the table of brotherhood.

I have a dream that one day even the state of Mississippi, a state sweltering with the heat of injustice, sweltering with the heat of oppression, will be transformed into an oasis of freedom and justice.

I have a dream that my four little children will one day live in a nation where they will not be judged by the color of their skin but by the content of their character.

I have a dream today!

I have a dream that one day, down in Alabama, with its vicious racists, with its governor having his lips dripping with the words of interposition and nullification, one day right there in Alabama little black boys and black girls will be able to join hands with little white boys and white girls as sisters and brothers ... I have a dream today!

I have a dream that one day every valley shall be exalted, every hill and mountain shall be made low, the rough places will be made plain and the crooked places will be made straight, and the glory of the Lord shall be revealed, and all flesh shall see it together!

This is our hope. This is the faith that I go back to the South with. With this faith, we will be able to hew out of the mountain of despair a stone of hope. With this faith we will be able to transform the jangling discords of our nation into a beautiful symphony of brotherhood.

With this faith we will be able to work together, to pray together, to struggle together, to go to jail together, to stand up for freedom together, knowing that we will be free one day!

This will be the day ... this will be the day when all of God's children will be able to sing with new meaning. "My country 'tis of thee, sweet land of liberty, of thee I sing. Land where my fathers died, land of the Pilgrims' pride, from every mountainside, let freedom ring," and if America is to be a great nation, this must become true.

So let freedom ring! From the prodigious hilltops of New Hampshire, let freedom ring. From the mighty mountains of New York, let freedom ring, from the heightening Alleghenies of Pennsylvania!

Let freedom ring from the snow-capped Rockies of Colorado!

Let freedom ring from the curvaceous slopes of California! But not only that.

Let freedom ring from Stone Mountain of Georgia!

Let freedom ring from Lookout Mountain in Tennessee!

Let freedom ring from every hill and mole hill of Mississippi. From every mountainside, let freedom ring, and when this happens ... when we allow freedom to ring, when we let it ring from every village and every hamlet, from every state and every city, we will be able to speed up that day when all of God's children, black men and white men, Jews and Gentiles, Protestants and Catholics, will be able to join hands and sing in the words of the old Negro spiritual, "Free at last! Free at last! Thank God Almighty, we are free at last!"

Dr Martin Luther King Jnr was named *Time Magazine*'s 'Person of the Year' in 1963 and, a few months later, received the 1964 Nobel Peace Prize—at the time the youngest man to be so honoured. On his return from Norway, King threw himself into a new cause—voter registration in Selma Alabama.

In 1965, President Johnson asked Congress to ratify a tough voting rights bill in his State of the Union speech. When Congress stalled, King and over 500 supporters marched from Selma to Montgomery to register African-Americans to vote. Alabama police attacked the marchers and the violence shown on national television shocked the country. It took government intervention—the 'federalising' of the Alabama National Guard and the addition of another 2000 guards—to allow a second, 3000 strong, march to Montgomery to begin on March 21, 1965. Congress finally passed the bill (known as the Civil Rights Act of 1965 or the Voting Rights Act of 1965) on 5 August 1965.

Dr King went on to battle other issues—domestic poverty, Chicago slums and the war in Vietnam—as well as factions within the equal rights movement in the remaining years of his short life.

In 1968 King was planning another massive march on Washington—'a demonstration of such intensity and size' that Congress would have to finally take notice of the nation's poor—when he was invited to Memphis, Tennessee to support striking sanitation workers. He gave his famous 'I have seen the Promised Land' speech at the Mason Temple in Memphis on the evening of 3 April, 1968.

The following day Martin Luther King Jnr was shot and killed as he stood on the balcony of the black-owned Lorraine Hotel, just off Beale Street. He was talking to Ralph Abernathy and Jesse Jackson when he was struck in the neck and died at the scene soon after.

For a man of peace, Reverend Martin Luther King Jnr died a violent death and his passing caused a wave of destruction in major cities across the United States.

Lyndon B Johnson

'Let Us Continue'

US Congress, Washington DC, 27 November 1963.

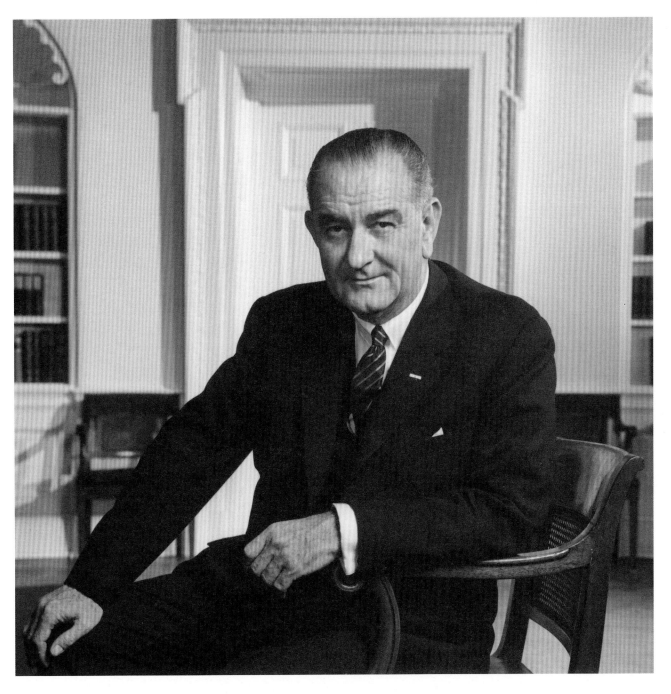

Lyndon B Johnson at The White House in 1963.

On Friday, 22 November 1963 Vice President Lyndon Johnson took the oath of office aboard Air Force One at 2:38pm with the body of the slain president John F Kennedy on board, and in front of JFK's widow Jackie and his own wife, Bird.

Before his unexpected ascension to the presidency, Lyndon Baines Johnson (1908-1973) was a Democratic Representative for ten years before being elected to the US Senate in 1948.

The world stood still on Monday, 25 November 1963 as John F Kennedy was laid to rest. The previous day his alleged assassin Lee Harvey Oswald was himself gunned down by Dallas night-club owner Jack Ruby. The motivations and circumstances surrounding this 'second assassination' raised just as many questions as Kennedy's death. Three days later Lyndon Johnson, the 36th President of the United States, addressed the US Congress. Johnson's words would have to heal a nation … and the entire world.

'Mr. Speaker, Mr. President, Members of the House, Members of the Senate, my fellow Americans:

All I have I would have given gladly not to be standing here today.

The greatest leader of our time has been struck down by the foulest deed of our time. Today, John Fitzgerald Kennedy lives on in the immortal words and works that he left behind. He lives on in the mind and memories of mankind. He lives on in the hearts of his countrymen. No words are sad enough to express our sense of loss. No words are strong enough to express our determination to continue the forward thrust of America that he began.

The dream of conquering the vastness of space, the dream of partnership across the Atlantic—and across the Pacific as well—the dream of a Peace Corps in less developed nations, the dream of education for all of our children, the dream of jobs for all who seek them and need them, the dream of care for our elderly, the dream of an all-out attack on mental illness, and above all, the dream of equal rights for all Americans, whatever their race or color. These and other American dreams have been vitalized by his drive and by his dedication. And now the ideas and the ideals which he so nobly represented must and will be translated into effective action.

Under John Kennedy's leadership, this nation has demonstrated that it has the courage to seek peace, and it has the fortitude to risk war. We have proved that we are a good and reliable friend to those who seek peace and freedom. We have shown that we can also be a formidable foe to those who reject the path of peace and those who seek to impose upon us or our allies the yoke of tyranny. This nation will keep its commitments from South Vietnam to West Berlin. We will be unceasing in the search for peace, resourceful in our pursuit of areas of agreement —

even with those with whom we differ—and generous and loyal to those who join with us in common cause.

In this age when there can be no losers in peace and no victors in war, we must recognize the obligation to match national strength with national restraint. We must be prepared at one and the same time for both the confrontation of power and the limitation of power. We must be ready to defend the national interest and to negotiate the common interest. This is the path that we shall continue to pursue. Those who test our courage will find it strong, and those who seek our friendship will find it honorable. We will demonstrate anew that the strong can be just in the use of strength, and the just can be strong in the defense of justice.

And let all know we will extend no special privilege and impose no persecution. We will carry on the fight against poverty, and misery, and disease, and ignorance, in other lands and in our own. We will serve all the nation, not one section or one sector, or one group, but all Americans.

These are the United States: A united people with a united purpose.

Our American unity does not depend upon unanimity. We have differences; but now, as in the past, we can derive from those differences strength, not weakness, wisdom, not despair. Both as a people and a government, we can unite upon a program, a program which is wise and just, enlightened and constructive.

'All I have I would have given gladly not to be standing here today. The greatest leader of our time has been struck down by the foulest deed of our time.'

For 32 years Capitol Hill has been my home. I have shared many moments of pride with you, pride in the ability of the Congress of the United States to act, to meet any crisis, to distill from our differences strong programs of national action. An assassin's bullet has thrust upon me the awesome burden of the Presidency. I am here today to say I need your help. I cannot bear this burden alone. I need the help of all Americans, and all America.

This nation has experienced a profound shock, and in this critical moment, it is our duty, yours and mine, as the Government of the United States, to do away with uncertainty and doubt and delay, and to show that we are capable of decisive action; that from the brutal loss of our leader we will derive not weakness, but strength; that we can and will act and act now.

From this chamber of representative government, let all the world know and none misunderstand that I rededicate this Government to the unswerving support of the United Nations, to the honorable and determined execution of our commitments to our allies, to the maintenance of military strength second to none, to the defense of the strength and the stability of the dollar, to the expansion of our foreign trade, to the reinforcement of our programs of mutual assistance and cooperation in Asia and Africa, and to our Alliance for Progress in this hemisphere.

On the 20th day of January, in 1961, John F. Kennedy told his countrymen that our national work would not be finished "in the first thousand days, nor in the life of this administration, nor even perhaps in our lifetime on this planet." "But," he said, "let us begin."

Today in this moment of new resolve, I would say to all my fellow Americans, let us continue.

LYNDON B JOHNSON

This is our challenge—not to hesitate, not to pause, not to turn about and linger over this evil moment, but to continue on our course so that we may fulfill the destiny that history has set for us.

Our most immediate tasks are here on this Hill. First, no memorial oration or eulogy could more eloquently honor President Kennedy's memory than the earliest possible passage of the Civil Rights Bill for which he fought so long. We have talked long enough in this country about equal rights. We have talked for a hundred years or more. It is time now to write the next chapter, and to write it in the books of law. I urge you again, as I did in 1957 and again in 1960, to enact a civil rights law so that we can move forward to eliminate from this nation every trace of discrimination and oppression that is based upon race or color. There could be no greater source of strength to this nation both at home and abroad.

And second, no act of ours could more fittingly continue the work of President Kennedy than the early passage of the tax bill for which he fought all this long year. This is a bill designed to increase our national income and Federal revenues, and to provide insurance against recession. That bill, if passed without delay, means more security for those now working, more jobs for those now without them, and more incentive for our economy.

'No memorial oration or eulogy could more eloquently honor President Kennedy's memory than the earliest possible passage of the Civil Rights Bill for which he fought so long.'

In short, this is no time for delay. It is a time for action—strong, forward-looking action on the pending education bills to help bring the light of learning to every home and hamlet in America; strong, forward-looking action on youth employment opportunities; strong, forward-looking action on the pending foreign aid bill, making clear that we are not forfeiting our responsibilities to this hemisphere or to the world, nor erasing Executive flexibility in the conduct of our foreign affairs; and strong, prompt, and forward-looking action on the remaining appropriation bills.

In this new spirit of action, the Congress can expect the full cooperation and support of the executive branch. And, in particular, I pledge that the expenditures of your Government will be administered with the utmost thrift and frugality. I will insist that the Government get a dollar's value for a dollar spent. The Government will set an example of prudence and economy.

This does not mean that we will not meet our unfilled needs or that we will not honor our commitments. We will do both.

As one who has long served in both Houses of the Congress, I firmly believe in the independence and the integrity of the legislative branch. And I promise you that I shall always respect this. It is deep in the marrow of my bones. With equal firmness, I believe in the capacity and I believe in the ability of the Congress, despite the divisions of opinions which characterize our nation, to act—to act wisely, to act vigorously, to act speedily when the need arises.

The need is here. The need is now. I ask your help.

We meet in grief, but let us also meet in renewed dedication and renewed vigor. Let us meet in action, in tolerance, and in mutual understanding.

John Kennedy's death commands what his life conveyed—that America must move forward.

The time has come for Americans of all races and creeds and political beliefs to understand and to respect one another. So let us put an end to the teaching and the preaching of hate and evil and violence. Let us turn away from the fanatics of the far left and the far right, from the apostles of bitterness and bigotry, from those defiant of law, and those who pour venom into our nation's bloodstream.

I profoundly hope that the tragedy and the torment of these terrible days will bind us together in new fellowship, making us one people in our hour of sorrow. So let us here highly resolve that John Fitzgerald Kennedy did not live or die in vain. And on this Thanksgiving eve, as we gather together to ask the Lord's blessing, and give Him our thanks, let us unite in those familiar and cherished words:

America, America, God shed His grace on thee,

And crown thy good, With brotherhood

From sea to shining sea.'

'We meet in grief, but let us also meet in renewed dedication and renewed vigor. Let us meet in action, in tolerance, and in mutual understanding.'

Johnson proved to be both an enigmatic and contradictory President. He was a great domestic reformer who was returned to power with an increased majority in 1964 but a flawed commander-in-chief who escalated the conflict in Vietnam.

The President of the United States pushed Congress to ratify the tough voting rights bill in his State of the Union speech, and the Civil Rights Act of 1965 was finally passed on 5 August that year.

However, any gains Johnson had made on civil issues were brought undone by the escalation of America's commitment to the Vietnam War. In January 1968 the 'Tet' Offensive (launched on the Vietnamese New Year holiday) reiterated North Vietnamese determination to win its civil war at all costs. Just as importantly, uncensored news coverage shown on nightly news programs and in American newspapers reinforced the growing perception that this was not a winnable war. Congressional opposition, media scrutiny and domestic unrest—especially among students—brought President Lyndon Johnson to make the gravest of decisions. In March 1968 Johnson stunned the world with the surprise announcement that he would not seek re-election as president. The Vietnam War had claimed its highest ranking victim.

LYNDON B JOHNSON

Robert F Kennedy

'Announcement of Martin Luther King's Death'

Rally for presidential votes, Indianapolis, Indiana, 4 April 1968.

Robert F Kennedy on the campaign trail in 1968.

Robert Francis Kennedy (1925-68) served on the Select Committee for Improper Activities in the late 1950s—taking on Teamster Union boss Jimmy Hoffa—before being appointed Attorney General during the presidency of his older brother, John. After John Kennedy's death in 1963, Bobby Kennedy left the White House in 1964 and became the Democratic Senator for New York the following year. When President Johnson announced that he would not seek re-election in March 1968, the younger Kennedy stepped up his bid for the Democratic Party nomination and began a hectic schedule of campaigning—largely on an anti-Vietnam war platform.

On 4 April, 1968 Bobby Kennedy arrived by plane into Indianapolis, Indiana, to address a largely black rally to promote 'RFK for President'. On that same day Dr Martin Luther King Jnr had been murdered in Memphis. On his arrival Kennedy asked the rally organiser, 'Do they know about Martin Luther King?' The man responded by saying, 'No. We've left that up to you.' Kennedy asked the crowd to lower their pro-Kennedy placards and then addressed them in this heartfelt, spontaneous speech that evoked the memory of his own slain brother.

'I have bad news for you, for all of our fellow citizens, and people who love peace all over the world, and that is that Martin Luther King was shot and killed tonight.

Martin Luther King dedicated his life to love and to justice for his fellow human beings, and he died because of that effort.

In this difficult day, in this difficult time for the United States, it is perhaps well to ask what kind of a nation we are and what direction we want to move in. For those of you who are black—considering the evidence there evidently is, that there were white people who were responsible—you can be filled with bitterness, with hatred, and a desire for revenge. We can move in that direction as a country, in great polarization—black people amongst black, white people amongst white, filled with hatred toward one another.

Or we can make an effort, as Martin Luther King did, to understand and to comprehend, and to replace that violence, that stain of bloodshed that has spread across our land, with an effort to understand with compassion and love.

For those of you who are black and are tempted to be filled with hatred and distrust at the injustice of such an act, against all white people, I can only say that I feel in my own heart that

'The vast majority of black people in this country want to live together, want to improve the quality of our life, and want justice for all human beings who abide in our land.'

ROBERT F KENNEDY

221

same kind of feeling. I had a member of my family killed, but he was killed by a white man. But we have to make an effort in the United States, we have to make an effort to understand, to go beyond these rather difficult times.

My favorite poet was Aeschylus. He wrote: "In our sleep, pain which cannot forget falls drop by drop upon the heart until, in our own despair, against our will, comes wisdom through the awful grace of God."

'We can make an effort, as Martin Luther King did, to understand and to comprehend, and to replace that violence, that stain of blood shed that has spread across our land, with an effort to understand with compassion and love.'

What we need in the United States is not division; what we need in the United States is not hatred; what we need in the United States is not violence or lawlessness; but love and wisdom, and compassion toward one another, and a feeling of justice toward those who still suffer within our country, whether they be white or they be black.

So I shall ask you tonight to return home, to say a prayer for the family of Martin Luther King, that's true, but more importantly, to say a prayer for our own country, which all of us love—a prayer for understanding and that compassion of which I spoke.

We can do well in this country. We will have difficult times; we've had difficult times in the past; we will have difficult times in the future. It is not the end of violence; it is not the end of lawlessness; it is not the end of disorder.

But the vast majority of white people and the vast majority of black people in this country want to live together, want to improve the quality of our life, and want justice for all human beings who abide in our land.

Let us dedicate ourselves to what the Greeks wrote so many years ago: to tame the savageness of man and make gentle the life of this world.

Let us dedicate ourselves to that, and say a prayer for our country and for our people.'

Ten weeks later, on 4 June 1968, Robert F. Kennedy won the California Primary for the Democratic nomination and pulled away from his closest rivals, Eugene McCarthy and Hubert Humphrey. His short victory speech, delivered at the Ambassador Hotel's Embassy Ballroom just before midnight, constituted his final public appearance:

'I think we can end the divisions within the United States. What I think is quite clear is that we can work together in the last analysis. And that what has been going on with the United States over the period of that last three years, the divisions, the violence, the disenchantment with our society, the divisions—whether it's between blacks and whites, between the poor and the more affluent, or between age groups, or in the war in Vietnam—that we can work together.

We are a great country, an unselfish country and a compassionate country. And I intend to make that my basis for running.'

Kennedy then left the rostrum, behind a curtain, taking a back route to the press room via the hotel kitchen. There, at 12:23 am on the morning of 5 June, Kennedy was shot in the head by Jordanian immigrant Sirhan Sirhan. The 24-year-old assassin was allegedly upset by Kennedy's support of Israel during the Six-Day War the previous year, but as was the case with the death of John Kennedy and Martin Luther King, Sirhan's crime started a conspiracy industry (Sirhan was sentenced to death but this was commuted to life imprisonment). Robert Kennedy was taken to the nearby Good Samaritan Hospital where on the fifth floor, surrounded by family and friends, Kennedy, and his unfulfilled potential, died the following day.

Edward 'Teddy' Kennedy
'Eulogy for Robert F Kennedy'

St. Patrick's Cathedral, New York, 8 June 1968.

Edward Kennedy gives his first press conference after the death of his brother Robert, in August 1968.

Edward Moore 'Teddy' Kennedy was born in 1932, the youngest of four sons and five daughters born to Joseph and Rose Kennedy. After studying at Harvard and the Virginia University Law School, he was admitted to the bar in 1959. Teddy Kennedy was elected Democratic Senator for Massachusetts in 1962—the position vacated by his brother John F. Kennedy when he became President in 1961—at the young age of 30. The youngest Kennedy was an important part of the mythical Kennedy political 'dynasty' but even more pressure was placed on the last of the family line following the assassinations of his brothers in 1963 and 1968. (The Kennedy's oldest brother, Joe Jnr, was killed in World War II while another sister, Kathleen, died in a plane accident).

Senator Teddy Kennedy delivered the eulogy for his brother Bobby at St Patrick's Cathedral, New York, on 8 June 1968. Towards the end of this speech Kennedy's voice strained under the emotion—highlighting the poignancy of the occasion.

'On behalf of Mrs Robert Kennedy, her children and the parents and sisters of Robert Kennedy, I want to express what we feel to those who mourn with us today in this cathedral and around the world. We loved him as a brother and father and son. From his parents, and from his older brothers and sisters—Joe, Kathleen and Jack—he received inspiration which he passed on to all of us. He gave us strength in time of trouble, wisdom in time of uncertainty, and sharing in time of happiness. He was always by our side.

Love is not an easy feeling to put into words. Nor is loyalty, or trust or joy. But he was all of these. He loved life completely and lived it intensely.

A few years back, Robert Kennedy wrote some words about his own father and they expressed the way we in his family feel about him. He said of what his father meant to him:

'Each time a man stands up for an ideal, or acts to improve the lot of others, or strikes out against injustice, he sends forth a tiny ripple of hope.'

"What it really all adds up to is love—not love as it is described with such facility in popular magazines, but the kind of love that is affection and respect, order, encouragement, and support. Our awareness of this was an incalculable source of strength, and because real love is something unselfish and involves sacrifice and giving, we could not help but profit from it.

"Beneath it all, he has tried to engender a social conscience. There were wrongs which needed attention. There were people who were poor and who needed help. And we have a responsibility to them and to this country. Through no virtues and accomplishments of our own, we have been fortunate enough to be born in the United States under the most comfortable conditions. We, therefore, have a responsibility to others who are less well off."

This is what Robert Kennedy was given. What he leaves us is what he said, what he did and what he stood for. A speech he made to the young people of South Africa on their Day of Affirmation in 1966 sums it up best, and I would read it now:

'What it all adds up to is love—not love as it is described in popular magazines, but the kind of love that is affection and respect, order, encouragement and support.'

"There is discrimination in this world, and slavery and slaughter and starvation. Governments repress their people; and millions are trapped in poverty while the nation grows rich; and wealth is lavished on armaments everywhere.

"These are differing evils, but they are common works of man. They reflect the imperfection of human justice, the inadequacy of human compassion, our lack of sensibility toward the sufferings of our fellows.

"But we can perhaps remember—even if only for a time—that those who live with us are our brothers; that they share with us the same short moment of life; that they seek—as we do—nothing but the chance to live out their lives in purpose and happiness, winning what satisfaction and fulfillment they can.

"Surely this bond of common faith, this bond of common goal, can begin to teach us something. Surely, we can learn, at least, to look at those around us as fellow men. And surely we can begin to work a little harder to bind up the wounds among us and to become in our own hearts brothers and countrymen once again.

"Our answer is to rely on youth—not a time of life but a state of mind, a temper of the will, a quality of imagination, a predominance of courage over timidity, of the appetite for adventure over the love of ease. The cruelties and obstacles of this swiftly changing planet will not yield to obsolete dogmas and outworn slogans. They cannot be moved by those who cling to a present that is already dying, who prefer the illusion of security to the excitement and danger that come with even the most peaceful progress. It is a revolutionary world we live in; and this generation, at home and around the world, has had thrust upon it a greater burden of responsibility than any generation that has ever lived.

"Some believe there is nothing one man or one woman can do against the enormous array of the world's ills. Yet many of the world's great movements, of thought and action, have flowed from the work of a single man. A young monk began the Protestant reformation, a young general extended an empire from Macedonia to the borders of the earth, and a young woman reclaimed the territory of France. It was a young Italian explorer who discovered the New World, and the thirty-two-year-old Thomas Jefferson who proclaimed that all men are created equal.

"These men moved the world, and so can we all. Few will have the greatness to bend history itself, but each of us can work to change a small portion of events, and in the total of all those acts will be written the history of this generation. It is from numberless diverse acts of courage and belief that human history is shaped. Each time a man stands up for an ideal, or acts to improve the lot of others, or strikes out against injustice, he sends forth a tiny ripple of hope, and crossing each other from a million different centers of energy and daring, those ripples build a current that can sweep down the mightiest walls of oppression and resistance.

"Few are willing to brave the disapproval of their fellows, the censure of their colleagues, the wrath of their society. Moral courage is a rarer commodity than bravery in battle or great intelligence. Yet it is the one essential, vital quality for those who seek to change a world that yields most painfully to change. And I believe that in this generation those with the courage to enter the moral conflict will find themselves with companions in every corner of the globe.

"For the fortunate among us, there is the temptation to follow the easy and familiar paths of personal ambition and financial success so grandly spread before those who enjoy the privilege of education. But that is not the road history has marked out for us. Like it or not, we live in times of danger and uncertainty. But they are also more open to the creative energy of men than any other time in history. All of us will ultimately be judged, and as the years pass, we will surely judge ourselves on the effort we have contributed to building a new world society and the extent to which our ideals and goals have shaped that effort.

"The future does not belong to those who are content with today, apathetic toward common problems and their fellow man alike, timid and fearful in the face of new ideas and bold projects. Rather it will belong to those who can blend vision, reason and courage in a personal commitment to the ideals and great enterprises of American society.

"Our future may lie beyond our vision, but it is not completely beyond our control. It is the shaping impulse of America that neither fate nor nature nor the irresistible tides of history, but the work of our own hands, matched to reason and principle, that will determine our destiny. There is pride in that, even arrogance, but there is also experience and truth. In any event, it is the only way we can live."

This is the way he lived. My brother need not be idealized, or enlarged in death beyond what he was in life, to be remembered simply as a good and decent man, who saw wrong and tried to right it, saw suffering and tried to heal it, saw war and tried to stop it.

Those of us who loved him and who take him to his rest today, pray that what he was to us and what he wished for others will some day come to pass for all the world. As he said many times, in many parts of this nation, to those he touched and who sought to touch him:

"Some men see things as they are and say why.

I dream things that never were and say why not."'

'As he said many times: "Some men see things as they are and say why not. I dream things that never were and say why not".'

Within a year, Teddy Kennedy's dream of following his slain brothers into the White House disappeared in the murky waters off Chappaquiddick

Island. Kennedy's conduct regarding the death of party secretary Mary Jo Kopechne in a submerged car after a night of partying at Martha's Vineyard did not endear him to the American public. He ultimately ran for President in 1980 but his loss to Jimmy Carter at the Democratic National Convention in New York in August 1980 confirmed what the American public already knew—Teddy Kennedy would never become President. It was the end of the dream of a 'Kennedy dynasty'.

In 1999 Teddy Kennedy—still the Democratic Senator for Massachusetts but promoted by fate from kid brother to family patriarch and eulogiser—was again called upon after his nephew, 38 year-old John Kennedy Jnr, his wife Carolyn and sister-in-law Lauren Bessette, were killed in a light plane crash off the coast of Massachusetts.

Neil Armstrong

'One Small Step'

Live transmission from the Moon, 20 July 1969.

Neil Armstrong photographs Edwin Aldrin as he walks after him on the Moon in 1969.

On May 25 1961, as part of a special message to a joint session of Congress, President John F Kennedy spoke about the challenge of going to the moon before the end of the decade. The USSR had beaten the US in putting a man into space when Yuri Gagarin circled the globe in April 1961, but Kennedy accelerated the 'space race' when he raised the benchmark even higher.

The following year, on 12 September 1962, President Kennedy restated that aim in this speech at Rice University in Houston, Texas:

'We choose to go to the moon. We choose to go to the moon in this decade and do the other things, not because they are easy, but because they are hard, because that goal will serve to organize and measure the best of our energies and skills, because that challenge is one that we are willing to accept, one we are unwilling to postpone, and one which we intend to win, and the others, too.'

Kennedy's words inspired a new generation of scientists to pursue the dream of landing a man on the moon by the end of the decade. On 16 July 1969, Apollo II was launched from the Kennedy Space Centre in Florida with three astronauts on board—Neil Armstrong, Edwin 'Buzz' Aldrin and Michael Collins. Four days later, 240,000 miles away from Earth, the lunar module separated from the command module (with Collins remaining on board) and landed on the Moon in the Sea of Tranquillity.

Armstrong has said that he thought at the time he and Aldrin had only a '50 per cent chance of landing successfully' on the moon. 'After landing, actually having been surprised by the fact that we were able to make a successful touchdown,' Armstrong told Marcia Dunn of the Associated Press in a rare interview, 'I realized I was actually going to have to say something.'

The first words spoken from the surface of the moon were actually 'Okay, engine stop' by Armstrong followed by some technical jargon and then the 'Tranquillity Base' call signal.

But no-one remembers those. On July 20, 1969, at 10:56 pm Eastern Daylight Time, American astronaut Neil Armstrong uttered a brief statement before stepping off the Eagle landing module and onto the surface of the moon. Armstrong had climbed down the module ladder and when he came to the final rung, jumped the rest of the way and landed on a two-foot wide footpad at the base of one of the module's legs. Not yet touching the 'surface' of the moon, Armstrong uttered these famous words as he took another gentle step onto the lunar dust:

'That's one small step for a man, one giant leap for mankind.'

Or that's what Armstrong thought he said. Whether it was the static across space or Armstrong's Ohio drawl that made the 'a' all but inaudible, the word was not picked up by microphones back on the Earth. While most historians reported the quote as 'one small step for man, one giant leap for mankind' (making it seem as though Armstrong was repeating himself with the references to 'man' and 'mankind') all Armstrong would say was that his voice-operated transmitter may not have picked up the missing word.

Neil Armstrong's quiet, understated statement—the shortest speech in this book—is one of the most iconic speeches of the twentieth century.

Before he announced the nation's determination to go to the moon, President Kennedy surmised:

'No man can fully grasp how far and how fast we have come, but condense, if you will, the 50,000 years of man's recorded history in a time span of but a half-century. Stated in these terms, we know very little about the first 40 years, except at the end of them advanced man had learned to use the skins of animals to cover them. Then about 10 years ago, under this standard, man emerged from his caves to construct other kinds of shelter. Only five years ago man learned to write and use a cart with wheels. Christianity began less than two years ago. The printing press came this year, and then less than two months ago, during this whole 50-year span of human history, the steam engine provided a new source of power. Newton explored the meaning of gravity. Last month electric lights and telephones and automobiles and airplanes became available. Only last week did we develop penicillin and television and nuclear power, and now if America's new spacecraft succeeds in reaching Venus, we will have literally reached the stars before midnight tonight.'

John F Kennedy, killed by an assassin's bullet in November 1963, never lived to see his dream of a moon landing fulfilled.

Close to a billion people were listening to Neil Armstrong on Earth as he spoke from the Moon. Aldrin joined him a few minutes later and together they took photographs of the surface, planted a US flag, ran a few scientific tests and spoke with US President Richard M. Nixon. For his part, Nixon had a back-up speech in case things went wrong. Suggested by fellow astronaut Frank Borman, whom NASA had assigned as the White House liaison, the 'moon disaster' speech was written by (later New York Times journalist) Bill Safire but its contents were not revealed until after Nixon's death in 1994.

This brief, unused epitaph was:

'Fate has ordained that the men who went to the moon to explore in peace will stay on the moon to rest in peace.

These brave men, Neil Armstrong and Edwin Aldrin, know that there is no hope for their recovery. But they also know that there is hope for mankind in their sacrifice.

These two men are laying down their lives in mankind's most noble goal: the search for truth and understanding.

They will be mourned by their families and friends; they will be mourned by their nation; they will be mourned by the people of the world; they will be mourned by a Mother earth that dared send two of her sons into the unknown.

In their exploration, they stirred the people of the world to feel as one; in their sacrifice, they bind more tightly the brotherhood of man.

In ancient days, men looked at stars and saw their heroes in the constellations. In modern times, we do much the same, but our heroes are epic men of flesh and blood.

Others will follow, and surely find their way home. Man's search will not be denied. But these men were the first, and they will remain the foremost in our hearts.

For every human being who looks up at the moon in the nights to come will know that there is some corner of another world that is forever mankind.'

Safire then made two important notes:
1. Prior to the President's statement: The President should telephone each of the widows-to-be.
2. After the President's statement, at the point when NASA ends communications with the men: A clergyman should adopt the same procedure as a burial at sea, commending their souls to 'the deepest of the deep,' concluding with the Lord's Prayer.

Thankfully the speech was never used. Armstrong and Aldrin slept on the surface of the moon that night, and at 1:54 pm on 21 July, the Eagle ascended and docked with the Apollo 11 command module and rejoin Collins. They left behind a plaque that read: 'Here men from the planet Earth first set foot on the Moon—July 1969 AD—We came in peace for all mankind.' On July 24, the three men returned to earth and safely splashed down in the Pacific Ocean.

Absolute Power
1970-1979

Shirley Chisolm
'For the Equal Rights Amendment'

US House of Representatives, Washington DC, 10 August 1970.

Shirley Chisholm in 1972.

Shirley Chisolm (1924-2005) was the first African-American woman elected to Congress (1969) and also the first to run for the presidency (1972). A teacher in her native New York whose political career started in 1964 when she was elected to the New York State Assembly in a landslide, Chisolm won the Democratic Party's nomination in 1968 and was elected to Congress. Forthright in her views, she championed causes such as community welfare, veteran affairs, education and federal funding of daycare centres during her early political career.

Chisolm was openly critical of the federal government for failing to make progress on social programs. In August 1970, at a time when the Women's Liberation movement under the auspices of radical feminists such as Gloria Steinem, Germaine Greer and Betty Friedan was starting to gain momentum, Chisholm addressed the US House of Representatives and put forward the case for equal rights for both sexes. Of all the feminist speeches from the 1970s, it was Chisholm's speech that was selected as one of the top 100 speeches of the twentieth century.

'Mr. Speaker, House Joint Resolution 264, before us today, which provides for equality under the law for both men and women, represents one of the most clear-cut opportunities we are likely to have to declare our faith in the principles that shaped our Constitution. It provides a legal basis for attack on the most subtle, most pervasive, and most institutionalized form of prejudice that exists. Discrimination against women, solely on the basis of their sex, is so widespread that it seems to many persons normal, natural and right.

Legal expression of prejudice on the grounds of religious or political belief has become a minor problem in our society. Prejudice on the basis of race is, at least, under systematic attack. There is reason for optimism that it will start to die with the present, older generation. It is time we act to assure full equality of opportunity to those citizens who, although in a majority, suffer the restrictions that are commonly imposed on minorities, to women.

The argument that this amendment will not solve the problem of sex discrimination is not relevant. If the argument were used against a civil rights bill, as it has been used in the past, the prejudice that lies behind it would be embarrassing. Of course laws will not eliminate prejudice from the hearts of human beings. But that is no reason to allow prejudice to continue to be enshrined in our laws—to perpetuate injustice through inaction.

The amendment is necessary to clarify countless ambiguities and inconsistencies in our legal system. For instance, the Constitution guarantees due process of law, in the 5th and 14th amendments. But the applicability of due process of sex distinctions is not clear. Women are excluded from some State colleges and universities. In some States, restrictions are placed on a married woman who engages in an independent business. Women may not be chosen for some juries. Women even receive heavier criminal penalties than men who commit the same crime. What would the legal effects of the equal rights amendment really be? The equal rights amendment would govern only the relationship between the State and its citizens—not relationships between private citizens. The amendment would be largely self-executing, that is, and Federal or State laws in conflict would be ineffective one year after date of ratification without further action by the Congress or State legislatures.

Opponents of the amendment claim its ratification would throw the law into a state of confusion and would result in much litigation to establish its meaning. This objection overlooks the influence of legislative history in determining intent and the recent activities of many groups preparing for legislative changes in this direction.

'Discrimination against women, solely on the basis of their sex, is so widespread that is seems to many persons normal, natural and right.'

State labor laws applying only to women, such as those limiting hours of work and weights to be lifted would become inoperative unless the legislature amended them to apply to men. As of early 1970 most States would have some laws that would be affected. However, changes are being made so rapidly as a result of title VII of the Civil Rights Act of 1964, it is likely that by the time the equal rights amendment would become effective; no conflicting State laws would remain.

In any event, there has for years been great controversy as to the usefulness to women of these State labor laws. There has never been any doubt that they worked a hardship on women who need or want to work overtime and on women who need or want better paying jobs, and there has been no persuasive evidence as to how many women benefit from the archaic policy of the laws. After the Delaware 'hours law' was repealed in 1966, there were no complaints from women to any of the State agencies that might have been approached.

Jury service laws not making women equally liable for jury service would have been revised. The selective service law would have to include women, but women would not be required to serve in the Armed Forces where they are not fitted any more than men are required to serve. Military service, while a great responsibility, is not without benefits, particularly for young men with limited education or training.

Since October 1966, 246 000 young men who did not meet the normal mental or physical requirements have been given opportunities for training and correcting physical problems. This opportunity is not open to their sisters. Only girls who have completed high school and meet high standards on the educational test can volunteer. Ratification of the amendment would not permit application of higher standards to women.

Survivorship benefits would be available to husbands of female workers on the same basis as to wives of male workers. The Social Security Act and the Civil Service and Military Service Retirement Acts are in conflict. Public schools and universities could not be limited to one sex and could not apply different admission standards to men and women. Laws requiring longer prison sentences for women than men would be invalid, and equal opportunities for rehabilitation and vocational training would have to be provided in public correctional institutions. Different ages of majority based on sex would have to be harmonized. Federal, State, and other governmental bodies would be obligated to follow non-discriminatory practices in all aspects of employment, including public school teachers and State university and college faculties.

What would be the economic effects of the equal rights amendment? Direct economic effects would be minor. If any labor laws applying only to women still remained, their amendment or repeal would provide opportunity for women in better-paying jobs in manufacturing. More opportunities in public vocational and graduate schools for women would also tend to open up opportunities in better jobs for women.

Indirect effects could be much greater. The focusing of public attention on the gross legal, economic, and social discrimination against women by hearings and debates in the Federal and State legislatures would result in changes in attitude of parents, educators, and employers that would bring about substantial economic changes in the long run.

Sex prejudice cuts both ways. Men are oppressed by the requirements of the Selective Service Act, by enforced legal guardianship of minors, and by alimony laws. Each sex, I believe, should be liable when necessary to serve and defend this country. Each has a responsibility for the support of children.

There are objections raised to wiping out laws protecting women workers. No one would condone exploitation. But what does sex have to do with it? Working conditions and hours that are harmful to women are harmful to men; wages that are unfair for women are unfair for men. Laws setting employment limitations on the basis of sex are irrational, and the proof of this is their inconsistency from State to State. The physical characteristics of men and women are not fixed, but cover two wide spans that have a great deal of overlap. It is obvious, I think, that a robust woman could be more fit for physical labor than a weak man. The choice of occupation would be determined by individual capabilities, and the rewards for equal work should be equal.

'A robust woman could be more fit for physical labor than a weak man. The choice of occupation would be determined by individual capabilities, and the rewards for equal works should be equal.'

This is what it comes down to: artificial distinctions between persons must be wiped out of the law. Legal discrimination between the sexes is, in almost every instance, founded on outmoded views of society and the pre-scientific beliefs about psychology and physiology. It is time to sweep away these relics of the past and set further generations free of them. Federal agencies and institutions responsible for the enforcement of equal opportunity laws need the authority of a Constitutional amendment. The 1964 Civil Rights Act and the 1963 Equal Pay Act are not enough; they are limited in their coverage—for instance, one excludes teachers, and the other leaves out administrative and professional women. The Equal Employment Opportunity Commission has not proven to be an adequate device, with its power limited to investigation, conciliation, and recommendation to the Justice Department. In its cases involving sexual discrimination, it has failed in more than one-half. The Justice Department has been even less effective. It has intervened in only one case involving discrimination on the basis of sex, and this was on a procedural point. In a second case, in which both sexual and racial discrimination were alleged, the racial bias charge was given far greater weight.

Evidence of discrimination on the basis of sex should hardly have to be cited here. It is in the Labor Department's employment and salary figures for anyone who is still in doubt. Its elimination will involve so many changes in our State and Federal laws that, without the authority and impetus of this proposed amendment, it will perhaps take another 194 years. We cannot be parties to continuing a delay. The time is clearly now to put this House on record for the fullest expression of that equality of opportunity which our founding fathers professed. They professed it, but they did not assure it to their daughters, as they tried to do for their sons.

> 'Women are excluded from some State colleges and universities. In some States, restrictions are placed on a married woman who engages in an independent business. Women may not be chosen for some juries..'

The Constitution they wrote was designed to protect the rights of white, male citizens. As there were no black Founding Fathers, there were no founding mothers—a great pity, on both counts. It is not too late to complete the work they left undone. Today, here, we should start to do so.

In closing I would like to make one point. Social and psychological effects will be initially more important than legal or economic results. As Leo Kanowitz has pointed out:

"Rules of law that treat of the sexes per see inevitably produce far-reaching effects upon social, psychological and economic aspects of male-female relations beyond the limited confines of legislative chambers and courtrooms. As long as organized legal systems, at once the most respected and most feared of social institutions, continue to differentiate sharply, in treatment or in words, between men and women on the basis of irrelevant and artificially created distinctions, the likelihood of men and women coming to regard one another primarily as fellow human beings and only secondarily as representatives of another sex will continue to be remote. When men and women are prevented from recognizing one another's essential humanity by sexual prejudices, nourished by legal as well as social institutions, society as a whole remains less than it could otherwise become."

In 1972 Shirley Chisolm ran as the Democratic candidate for the presidency, stating that someone had to be the 'first', and as an African-American woman, she may as well be the first on both counts. Her 'symbolic' candidacy was under-funded and based upon an unpopular platform in aid of the 'disenfranchised' (including minorities and Vietnam veterans) and she did not win any primaries. She later said that she ran because: 'In this country everybody is supposed to be able to run for president, but that's never really been true. I ran because most people think this country is not ready for a black candidate, not ready for a woman candidate.' She was right; her candidacy took her all the way to the Democratic convention but she was defeated by George McGovern who, in turn, lost in a landslide to Richard Nixon.

Chisolm divorced her first husband, Conrad Chisolm, in 1977 and left Congress in 1982 to care for her ailing second husband, Arthur Hardwick, who died in 1986. She later served as Ambassador to Jamaica during the first Clinton administration and passed away in the first week of January 2005, aged 80.

John Kerry
'Against the War in Vietnam'

House Foreign Relations Committee, Washington DC, 22 April 1971.

John Kerry (centre, back) at a demonstration of Vietnam Veterans Against the War in Washington in 1971.

John F Kerry was the Democratic presidential candidate against George W Bush in 2004. During that campaign, at a time when America was fighting an unpopular war in Iraq, Kerry's Vietnam War experiences became a major issue in his bid to become president. Kerry was both lauded by ex-comrades and publicly vilified by his Republican opponents about his war record. (He accepted the Democratic nomination in July 2004 by stating 'I'm John Kerry … reporting for duty' as he saluted the party faithful.) President George Bush ultimately won the November elections, but the Vietnam veteran pushed Bush to the narrowest margin of primary votes by any sitting president in American history.

Kerry was born on 11 December, 1943 in Colorado, the son of an Army Air Corps test pilot who flew DC-3s and B-29s during World War II. Kerry's father, Richard, was a Foreign Service Officer in the Eisenhower administration. After graduating from Yale University, Kerry—a liberal, well-to-do Catholic with a military heritage—volunteered to serve in Vietnam because he felt it was 'the right thing to do'. Kerry completed two tours of duty and on the latter, volunteered to serve on a patrol boat scouring the Vietnamese river deltas. His leadership and courage under fire earned him a Silver Star, a Bronze Star with Combat V, and three Purple Hearts.

Along with many Vietnam veterans, Kerry's wartime experience led him to speak out against the war. He joined Vietnam Veterans Against the War (VVAW) and was later co-founded Vietnam Veterans of America. In April 1971, the then 27 year-old testified before the House Foreign Relations Committee and openly questioned America's involvement in the civil war in Vietnam.

' I would like to say for the record, and also for the men sitting behind me who are also wearing the uniforms and their medals, that my sitting here is really symbolic. I am not here as John Kerry. I am here as one member of a group of 1,000, which is a small representation of a very much larger group of veterans in this country, and were it possible for all of them to sit at this table, they would be here and have the same kind of testimony. I would simply like to speak in general terms. I apologize if my statement is general because I received notification [only] yesterday that you would hear me, and, I am afraid, because of the injunction I was up most of the night and haven't had a great deal of chance to prepare.

I would like to talk, representing all those veterans, and say that several months ago, in Detroit, we had an investigation at which over 150 honorably discharged, and many very highly decorated, veterans testified to war crimes committed in Southeast Asia. These were not isolated incidents, but crimes committed on a day-to-day basis, with the full awareness of officers at all levels of command. It is impossible to describe to you exactly what did happen in Detroit—the emotions in the room, and the feelings of the men who were reliving their experiences in Vietnam. They relived the absolute horror of what this country, in a sense, made them do.

They told stories that, at times, they had personally raped, cut off ears, cut off heads, taped wires from portable telephones to human genitals and turned up the power, cut off limbs, blown up bodies, randomly shot at civilians, razed villages in fashion reminiscent of Ghengis Khan, shot cattle and dogs for fun, poisoned food stocks, and generally ravaged the countryside of South Vietnam, in addition to the normal ravage of war and the normal and very particular ravaging which is done by the applied bombing power of this country.

'We cannot consider ourselves America's best men when we are ashamed of and hated what we were called on to do in Southeast Asia.'

We call this investigation the Winter Soldier Investigation. The term "winter soldier" is a play on words of Thomas Paine's in 1776, when he spoke of the "sunshine patriots," and "summertime soldiers" who deserted at Valley Forge because the going was rough.

We who have come here to Washington have come here because we feel we have to be winter soldiers now. We could come back to this country, we could be quiet, we could hold our silence, we could not tell what went on in Vietnam, but we feel, because of what threatens this country, not the reds, but the crimes which we are committing that threaten it, that we have to speak out.

I would like to talk to you a little bit about what the result is of the feelings these men carry with them after coming back from Vietnam. The country doesn't know it yet, but it has created a monster, a monster in the form of millions of men who have been taught to deal and to trade in violence, and who are given the chance to die for the biggest nothing in history; men who have returned with a sense of anger and a sense of betrayal which no one has yet grasped.

As a veteran and one who felt this anger, I would like to talk about it. We are angry because we feel we have been used in the worst fashion by the administration of this country.

In 1970, at West Point, Vice President Agnew said, "some glamorize the criminal misfits of society while our best men die in Asian rice paddies to preserve the freedom which most of those misfits abuse," and this was used as a rallying point for our effort in Vietnam.

But for us, as boys in Asia whom the country was supposed to support, his statement is a terrible distortion from which we can only draw a very deep sense of revulsion. Hence the anger of some of the men who are here in Washington today. It is a distortion because we in no way consider ourselves the best men of this country, because those he calls misfits were standing up for us in a way that nobody else in this country dared to, because so many who have died would have returned to this country to join the misfits in their efforts to ask for an immediate withdrawal from South Vietnam, because so many of those best men have returned as quadriplegics and amputees, and they lie forgotten in Veterans' Administration hospitals in this country which fly the flag which so many have chosen as their own personal symbol. And we cannot consider ourselves America's best men when we are ashamed of and hated what we were called on to do in Southeast Asia.

In our opinion, and from our experience, there is nothing in South Vietnam which could happen that realistically threatens the United States of America. And to attempt to justify the loss of one American life in Vietnam, Cambodia, or Laos by linking such loss to the preservation of freedom, which those misfits supposedly abuse, is to us the height of criminal hypocrisy, and it is that kind of hypocrisy which we feel has torn this country apart.

We found that not only was it a civil war, an effort by a people who had for years been seeking their liberation from any colonial influence whatsoever, but, also, we found that the Vietnamese, whom we had enthusiastically molded after our own image, were hard-put to take up the fight against the threat we were supposedly saving them from.

We found most people didn't even know the difference between communism and democracy. They only wanted to work in rice paddies without helicopters strafing them and bombs with napalm burning their villages and tearing their country apart. They wanted everything to do with the war, particularly with this foreign presence of the United States of America, to leave them alone in peace, and they practiced the art of survival by siding with whichever military force was present at a particular time, be it Viet Cong, North Vietnamese or American.

> 'The country doesn't know it yet, but it has created a monster, a monster in the form of millions of men who have been taught to deal and to trade in violence, and who are given the chance to die for the biggest nothing in history.'

We found also that, all too often, American men were dying in those rice paddies for want of support from their allies. We saw first hand how monies from American taxes were used for a corrupt dictatorial regime. We saw that many people in this country had a one-sided idea of who was kept free by the flag, and blacks provided the highest percentage of casualties. We saw Vietnam ravaged equally by American bombs and search-and-destroy missions as well as by Viet Cong terrorism—and yet we listened while this country tried to blame all of the havoc on the Viet Cong.

We rationalized destroying villages in order to save them. We saw America lose her sense of morality as she accepted very coolly a My Lai, and refused to give up the image of American soldiers who hand out chocolate bars and chewing gum.

We learned the meaning of free-fire zones—shooting anything that moves—and we watched while America placed a cheapness on the lives of Orientals.

We watched the United States falsification of body counts, in fact the glorification of body counts. We listened while, month after month, we were told the back of the enemy was about to break. We fought using weapons against "Oriental human beings" with quotation marks around that. We fought using weapons against those people which I do not believe this country would dream of using, were we fighting in the European theater. We watched while men charged up hills because a general said that hill has to be taken, and, after losing one platoon,

JOHN KERRY

245

or two platoons, they marched away to leave the hill for reoccupation by the North Vietnamese. We watched pride allow the most unimportant battles to be blown into extravaganzas, because we couldn't lose, and we couldn't retreat, and because it didn't matter how many American bodies were lost to prove that point, and so there were Hamburger Hills and Khe Sanhs and Hill 81s and Fire Base 6s, and so many others.

Now we are told that the men who fought there must watch quietly while American lives are lost so that we can exercise the incredible arrogance of "Vietnamizing" the Vietnamese.

'When, thirty years from now, our brothers go down the street without a leg, without an arm, or a face, and small boys ask why, we will be able to say "Vietnam" and not mean a filthy obscene memory, but mean instead where America finally turned … '

Each day, to facilitate the process by which the United States washes her hands of Vietnam, someone has to give up his life so that the United States doesn't have to admit something that the entire world already knows, so that we can't say that we have made a mistake. Someone has to die so that President Nixon won't be, and these are his words, "the first President to lose a war."

We are asking Americans to think about that, because how do you ask a man to be the last man to die in Vietnam? How do you ask a man to be the last man to die for a mistake? We are here in Washington to say that the problem of this war is not just a question of war and diplomacy. It is part and parcel of everything that we are trying, as human beings, to communicate to people in this country—the question of racism, which is rampant in the military, and so many other questions, such as the use of weapons: the hypocrisy in our taking umbrage at the Geneva Conventions and using that as justification for a continuation of this war, when we are more guilty than any other body of violations of those Geneva Conventions; in the use of free-fire zones; harassment-interdiction fire, search-and-destroy missions; the bombings; the torture of prisoners; all accepted policy by many units in South Vietnam. That is what we are trying to say. It is part and parcel of everything.

An American Indian friend of mine who lives in the Indian Nation of Alcatraz put it to me very succinctly. He told me how, as a boy on an Indian reservation, he had watched television, and he used to cheer the cowboys when they came in and shot the Indians, and then suddenly one day he stopped in Vietnam and he said, "my God, I am doing to these people the very same thing that was done to my people," and he stopped. And that is what we are trying to say, that we think this thing has to end.

We are here to ask, and we are here to ask vehemently, where are the leaders of our country? Where is the leadership? We're here to ask where are McNamara, Rostow, Bundy, Gilpatrick, and so many others? Where are they now that we, the men they sent off to war, have returned? These are the commanders who have deserted their troops. And there is no more serious crime in the laws of war. The Army says they never leave their wounded. The Marines say they never even leave their dead. These men have left all the casualties and retreated behind a pious shield of public rectitude. They've left the real stuff of their reputations bleaching behind them in the sun in this country....

We wish that a merciful God could wipe away our own memories of that service as easily as this administration has wiped away their memories of us. But all that they have done, and all that they can do by this denial, is to make more clear than ever our own determination to undertake one last mission: to search out and destroy the last vestige of this barbaric war; to pacify our own hearts; to conquer the hate and fear that have driven this country these last ten years and more. And more. And so, when, thirty years from now, our brothers go down the street without a leg, without an arm, or a face, and small boys ask why, we will be able to say "Vietnam" and not mean a desert, not a filthy obscene memory, but mean instead where America finally turned, and where soldiers like us helped it in the turning.'

After delivering this speech, Kerry went to work as a high-profile prosecutor in Middlesex County, Massachusetts. He was elected Lieutenant Governor in 1982 and became a US Senator two years later. In 1988 Senator Kerry chaired the Senate Foreign Relations Subcommittee's investigation into the 'Iran/Contra Affair'. He was serving his fourth term when he announced his candidacy for the Democratic presidential nomination in 2003.

What happened to the earnest young man with the mop of black hair who dared to confront the US military leadership three decades before? Time knocked the edges off the young Vietnam Veteran and the American public ultimately rejected the smoothed-over politician that stood before them in 2004 in favour of four more years of George W Bush.

Richard M Nixon

'Farewell to the Whitehouse'

Washington DC, 9 August 1974.

Richard M Nixon reads his farewell speech to his staff in 1974.

Richard Milhous Nixon (1913-94) enjoyed a spectacular rise to prominence in US politics in the late 1940s and early 1950s. After his return from the political graveyard in 1968, six years later he became the first president in the history of the United States to resign from office.

Elected to the US Congress in 1946 after serving in the Navy during World War II, he had made a name for himself as a fervent 'anti-Communist' on the House Committee on Un-American Activities. In 1950 he was elected to the US Senate and as a high-profile opponent of President Truman's handling of the Korean War, he had enough clout to persuade the Californian delegation to throw their support behind Republican candidate Dwight D. Eisenhower in the 1952 presidential race. Eisenhower rewarded Nixon by choosing him as his running mate.

While the Republicans were holding their National Convention in September 1952 a sensational story appeared in the *New York Post* alleging that a 'secret rich men's trust fund' had kept Nixon in financial style far beyond his congressional salary. There was immediate pressure to remove Nixon from the Republican ticket but in a brilliant tactical move, Nixon appeared on national television in California to 'explain' to the American people his financial situation. Now known as the 'Checkers Speech' because of the reference to a pet dog given to his daughters by a Republican supporter, Richard Nixon turned the performance—part drama, part pathos—into a political triumph.

The Republican Party went on to win the election by a landslide but Nixon could not capitalise on his eight years as vice president and lost the 1960 presidential race to Senator John F. Kennedy. After a failed bid for the governorship of California in 1962 a bitter Nixon told the press, 'You won't have Nixon to kick around any more, gentlemen. This is my last Press Conference.' Almost seven years later to the day, Nixon was elected the 37th President of the United States.

In 1968 Richard Nixon returned from the political scrapheap and the anonymity of corporate life to win the Republican nomination and defeat a decimated Democratic Party to win the presidency. In January 1969 Nixon halted the bombing of North Vietnam but a year later only a token withdrawal of troops had taken place. Under Nixon the Vietnam War entered a new phase when he ordered troops into neighbouring Cambodia to clear out Vietcong training grounds, invaded Laos then resumed the bombing of North Vietnam. By 1972, Dr Henry Kissinger, Nixon's special representative at the Paris Peace talks, declared that peace was 'at hand'. This premature announcement, timed to make maximum impact on that year's presidential race, saw Nixon re-elected in a landslide victory.

Nixon's second term as president was engulfed by 'Watergate'. The scandal grew from a bungled break-in by five burglars who entered the Democratic National Committee offices at the Watergate complex in Washington on the night of 17 June, 1972. Subsequent investigations, most famously by *Washington Post* reporters Carl Bernstein and Bob Woodward, linked the break-in to President Nixon's top aides, who were involved in an extensive cover-up of politically-sanctioned illegal activities. After a two year investigation by the news media, government agencies, the US Senate, the House of Representatives and the US Supreme Court, the extent of the White House cover-up consumed Nixon's Presidency. It gradually became apparent that Nixon would not survive a full impeachment vote in the Congress despite using the prestige and power of the presidency to stonewall the judicial process.

On August 8, 1974, President Richard M. Nixon appeared on television and became the first President in the history of the United States to resign from office. At 11:35 am the following day Nixon's assistant, Alexander Haig Jnr, tended the President's letter of resignation to Secretary of State Henry A. Kissinger in his White House office. Members of Nixon's staff then assembled to farewell the man they had served—in some cases stretching back to Nixon's time as Vice-President in the early 1950s. Nixon then delivered this revealing speech.

❛ I think the record should show that this is one of those spontaneous things that we always arrange whenever the President comes in to speak, and it will be so reported in the press, and we don't mind, because they have to call it as they see it.

But on our part, believe me, it is spontaneous.

You are here to say goodbye to us, and we don't have a good word for it in English—the best is au revoir. We'll see you again.

I just met with the members of the White House staff, you know, those who serve here in the White House day in and day out, and I asked them to do what I ask all of you to do to the extent that you can and, of course, are requested to do so: to serve our next President as you have served me and previous Presidents—because many of you have been here for many years—with devotion and dedication, because this office, great as it is, can only be as great as the men and women who work for and with the President.

This house, for example—I was thinking of it as we walked down this hall, and I was comparing it to some of the great houses of the world that I have been in. This isn't the biggest house. Many, and most, in even smaller countries, are much bigger. This isn't the finest house. Many in Europe, particularly, and in China, Asia, have paintings of great, great value, things that we just don't have here and, probably, will never have until we are 1,000 years old or older.

But this is the best house. It is the best house, because it has something far more important than numbers of people who serve, far more important than numbers of rooms or how big it is, far more important than numbers of magnificent pieces of art.

This house has a great heart, and that heart comes from those who serve. I was rather sorry they didn't come down. We said goodbye to them upstairs. But they are really great. And I recall after so many times I have made speeches, and some of them pretty tough, yet, I always come back, or after a hard day—and my days usually have run rather long—I would always get a lift from them, because I might be a little down but they always smiled.

And so it is with you. I look around here, and I see so many on this staff that, you know, I should have been by your offices and shaken hands, and I would love to have talked to you and found out how to run the world—everybody wants to tell the President what to do, and boy, he needs to be told many times—but I just haven't had the time. But I want you to know that each and every one of you, I know, is indispensable to this Government.

'Sure, we have done some things wrong in this Administration, and the top man always takes the responsibility, and I have never ducked it.'

I am proud of this Cabinet. I am proud of all the members who have served in our Cabinet. I am proud of our sub-Cabinet. I am proud of our White House Staff. As I pointed out last night, sure, we have done some things wrong in this Administration, and the top man always takes the responsibility, and I have never ducked it. But I want to say one thing: We can be proud of it—five and a half years. No man or no woman came into this Administration and left it with more of this world's goods than when he came in. No man or no woman ever profited at the public expense or the public till. That tells something about you.

Mistakes, yes. But for personal gain, never. You did what you believed in. Sometimes right, sometimes wrong. And I only wish that I were a wealthy man—at the present time, I have got to find a way to pay my taxes—and if I were, I would like to recompense you for the sacrifices that all of you have made to serve in government.

But you are getting something in government—and I want you to tell this to your children, and I hope the Nation's children will hear it, too—something in government service that is far more important than money. It is a cause bigger than yourself. It is the cause of making this the greatest nation in the world, the leader of the world, because without our leadership, the world will know nothing but war, possibly starvation or worse, in the years ahead. With our leadership it will know peace, it will know plenty.

We have been generous, and we will be more generous in the future as we are able to. But most important, we must be strong here, strong in our hearts, strong in our souls, strong in our belief, and strong in our willingness to sacrifice, as you have been willing to sacrifice, in a pecuniary way, to serve in government.

There is something else I would like for you to tell your young people. You know, people often come in and say, "What will I tell my kids?" They look at government and say, sort of a rugged life, and they see the mistakes that are made. They get the impression that everybody is here for the purpose of feathering his nest. That is why I made this earlier point—not in this Administration, not one single man or woman.

And I say to them, there are many fine careers. This country needs good farmers, good businessmen, good plumbers, good carpenters.

'As we leave, we leave proud of the people who have stood by us and worked for us and served this country. We want you to be proud of what you have done.'

I remember my old man. I think that they would have called him sort of a little man, common man. He didn't consider himself that way. You know what he was? He was a streetcar motorman first, and then he was a farmer, and then he had a lemon ranch. It was the poorest lemon ranch in California, I can assure you. He sold it before they found oil on it. [Laughter] And then he was a grocer. But he was a great man, because he did his job, and every job counts up to the hilt, regardless of what happens.

Nobody will ever write a book, probably, about my mother. Well, I guess all of you would say this about your mother—my mother was a saint. And I think of her, two boys dying of tuberculosis, nursing four others in order that she could take care of my older brother for three years in Arizona, and seeing each of them die, and when they died, it was like one of her own.

Yes, she will have no books written about her. But she was a saint.

Now, however, we look to the future. I had a little quote in the speech last night from T.R. [Theodore Roosevelt]. As you know, I kind of like to read books. I am not educated, but I do read books—and the T.R. quote was a pretty good one. Here is another one I found as I was reading, my last night in the White House, and this quote is about a young man. He was a young lawyer in New York. He had married a beautiful girl, and they had a lovely daughter, and then suddenly she died, and this is what he wrote. This was in his diary.

He said, "She was beautiful in face and form and lovelier still in spirit. As a flower she grew and as a fair young flower she died. Her life had been always in the sunshine. There had never come to her a single great sorrow. None ever knew her who did not love and revere her for her bright and sunny temper and her saintly unselfishness. Fair, pure and joyous as a maiden, loving, tender and happy as a young wife. When she had just become a mother, when her life seemed to be just begun and when the years seemed so bright before her, then by a strange and terrible fate death came to her. And when my heart's dearest died, the light went from my life forever."

That was T.R. in his twenties. He thought the light had gone from his life forever—but he went on. And he not only became President but, as an ex-President, he served his country, always in the arena, tempestuous, strong, sometimes wrong, sometimes right, but he was a man.

And as I leave, let me say, that is an example I think all of us should remember. We think sometimes when things happen that don't go the right way; we think that when you don't pass the bar exam the first time—I happened to, but I was just lucky; I mean, my writing was so poor the bar examiner said, "We have just got to let the guy through." We think that when someone dear to us dies, we think that when we lose an election, we think that when we suffer a defeat that all is ended. We think, as T.R. said, that the light had left his life forever. Not true.

It is only a beginning, always. The young must know it; the old must know it. It must always sustain us, because the greatness comes not when things go always good for you, but the greatness comes and you are really tested, when you take some knocks, some disappointments, when sadness comes, because only if you have been in the deepest valley can you ever know how magnificent it is to be on the highest mountain.

And so I say to you on this occasion, as we leave, we leave proud of the people who have stood by us and worked for us and served this country. We want you to be proud of what you have done. We want you to continue to serve in government, if that is your wish.

Always give your best, never get discouraged, never be petty; always remember, others may hate you, but those who hate you don't win unless you hate them, and then you destroy yourself.

And so, we leave with high hopes, in good spirit, and with deep humility, and with very much gratefulness in our hearts. I can only say to each and every one of you, we come from many faiths, we pray perhaps to different gods—but really the same God in a sense—but I want to say for each and every one of you, not only will we always remember you, not only will we always be grateful to you but always you will be in our hearts and you will be in our prayers.

Thank you very much.'

Richard Nixon's spontaneous speech exposed a flawed contradiction. Much was made of Nixon's references to his mother and his self-demeaning attitude towards his academic ability but his attempt to explain his behaviour as being 'not for personal gain' did not sit well with those who still remembered the 'Checkers' speech. (By choosing resignation over impeachment, Nixon also kept his presidential pension for the rest of his life.) Unlike Teddy Roosevelt, to whom he alluded in his speech, Nixon did not enjoy a vigorous public life in retirement. Although he re-entered the spotlight under the sponsorship of the Clinton administration—writing books, commenting on political issues and even attending official functions—he remained a national ghost, haunting the public from a time long gone.

Someone once wrote that the only thing history owes us is the truth. History will judge Nixon harshly.

RICHARD M NIXON

253

Gerald Ford
'A Pardon for Richard Nixon'

Radio and television broadcast, Washington DC, 8 September 1974.

Gerald Ford in 1974.

On 9 August 1974 former President Richard Nixon left the White House in disgrace. After escorting the Nixon family to their helicopter, Vice President Gerald R. Ford returned to the White House to take the oath of the office of President, administered by Chief Justice Warren E. Burger.

Gerald Ford was born in Omaha, Nebraska in 1913. After receiving a football scholarship to the University of Michigan, Ford turned his back on a sporting career to study law at Yale. After serving with the navy during World War II, he was elected to Congress as the Republican representative for Grand Rapids in 1948. Ford served eight terms in Congress before becoming House minority leader. When Vice-President Spiro T. Agnew resigned in 1973 after a tax scandal, Ford was the logical replacement—a Republican loyalist who had continually supported Nixon in the House of Representatives—and a candidate acceptable to the Democrat-controlled Congress. What Ford lacked in intelligence he more than made up with personal integrity. When Nixon resigned in August 1974, Ford was left to finish the last two and a half years of the presidential term.

Following the oath, the new President spoke briefly to a huge radio and television audience from the East Room of the White House. 'My fellow Americans', Ford began, 'our long national nightmare is over'.

One month later, Ford announced his decision to grant Nixon a full pardon for any crimes he may have committed while in office. Ford wanted to avoid the public spectacle of Nixon, now a private citizen, being placed on trial and potentially going to jail. But both the decision and its timing were severely criticised. Ford announced the pardon on a Sunday morning—an off-peak time for the Washington media—to minimise the potential public and political backlash.

It didn't work.

'Ladies and gentlemen:

I have come to a decision which I felt I should tell you and all of my fellow American citizens, as soon as I was certain in my own mind and in my own conscience that it is the right thing to do.

I have learned already in this office that the difficult decisions always come to this desk. I must admit that many of them do not look at all the same as the hypothetical questions that I have answered freely and perhaps too fast on previous occasions.

My customary policy is to try and get all the facts and to consider the opinions of my countrymen and to take counsel with my most valued friends. But these seldom agree, and in the

GERALD FORD

255

end, the decision is mine. To procrastinate, to agonize, and to wait for a more favorable turn of events that may never come or more compelling external pressures that may as well be wrong as right, is itself a decision of sorts and a weak and potentially dangerous course for a President to follow.

I have promised to uphold the Constitution, to do what is right as God gives me to see the right, and to do the very best that I can for America.

I have asked your help and your prayers, not only when I became President but many times since. The Constitution is the supreme law of our land and it governs our actions as citizens. Only the laws of God, which govern our consciences, are superior to it.

As we are a nation under God, so I am sworn to uphold our laws with the help of God. And I have sought such guidance and searched my own conscience with special diligence to determine the right thing for me to do with respect to my predecessor in this place, Richard Nixon, and his loyal wife and family.

'My conscience tells me that only I, as President, have the constitutional power to firmly shut and seal this book.'

Theirs is an American tragedy in which we all have played a part. It could go on and on and on, or someone must write the end to it. I have concluded that only I can do that, and if I can, I must.

There are no historic or legal precedents to which I can turn in this matter, none that precisely fit the circumstances of a private citizen who has resigned the Presidency of the United States. But it is common knowledge that serious allegations and accusations hang like a sword over our former President's head, threatening his health as he tries to reshape his life, a great part of which was spent in the service of this country and by the mandate of its people.

After years of bitter controversy and divisive national debate, I have been advised, and I am compelled to conclude that many months and perhaps more years will have to pass before Richard Nixon could obtain a fair trial by jury in any jurisdiction of the United States under governing decisions of the Supreme Court.

I deeply believe in equal justice for all Americans, whatever their station or former station. The law, whether human or divine, is no respecter of persons; but the law is a respecter of reality.

The facts, as I see them, are that a former President of the United States, instead of enjoying equal treatment with any other citizen accused of violating the law, would be cruelly and excessively penalized either in preserving the presumption of his innocence or in obtaining a speedy determination of his guilt in order to repay a legal debt to society.

During this long period of delay and potential litigation, ugly passions would again be aroused. And our people would again be polarized in their opinions. And the credibility of our free institutions of government would again be challenged at home and abroad.

In the end, the courts might well hold that Richard Nixon had been denied due process, and the verdict of history would even be more inconclusive with respect to those charges arising out of the period of his Presidency, of which I am presently aware.

But it is not the ultimate fate of Richard Nixon that most concerns me, though surely it deeply troubles every decent and every compassionate person. My concern is the immediate future of this great country.

In this, I dare not depend upon my personal sympathy as a long-time friend of the former President, nor my professional judgment as a lawyer, and I do not.

As President, my primary concern must always be the greatest good of all the people of the United States whose servant I am. As a man, my first consideration is to be true to my own convictions and my own conscience.

My conscience tells me clearly and certainly that I cannot prolong the bad dreams that continue to reopen a chapter that is closed. My conscience tells me that only I, as President, have the constitutional power to firmly shut and seal this book. My conscience tells me it is my duty, not merely to proclaim domestic tranquility but to use every means that I have to insure it. I do believe that the buck stops here, that I cannot rely upon public opinion polls to tell me what is right. I do believe that right makes might and that if I am wrong, ten angels swearing I was right would make no difference. I do believe, with all my heart and mind and spirit, that I, not as President but as a humble servant of God, will receive justice without mercy if I fail to show mercy.

Finally, I feel that Richard Nixon and his loved ones have suffered enough and will continue to suffer, no matter what I do, no matter what we, as a great and good nation, can do together to make his goal of peace come true.

Now, therefore, I, Gerald R. Ford, President of the United States, pursuant to the pardon power conferred upon me by Article II, Section 2, of the Constitution, have granted and by these presents do grant a full, free, and absolute pardon unto Richard Nixon for all offenses against the United States which he, Richard Nixon, has committed or may have committed or taken part in during the period from July (January) 20, 1969, through August 9, 1974.

In witness whereof, I have hereunto set my hand this eighth day of September, in the year of our Lord nineteen hundred and seventy-four, and of the Independence of the United States of America the one hundred and ninety-ninth.'

> 'The facts, as I see them, are that a former President of the United States, instead of enjoying equal treatment with any other citizen accused of violating the law, would be cruelly and excessively penalized ... '

Gerald Ford's speech further polarised the nation. The decision to pardon the former President caused widespread anger in the press and criticism from those who wanted to see Nixon go on trial and, possibly, to jail. However, among others, the decision evoked sympathy for Nixon. Many still saw Nixon as a victim of political infighting in Washington and considered much of Nixon's behaviour as being 'political', not criminal. It is fair to say however, that although constitutionally permissible (presidential pardons are a particular perk of the office and have been used for political advantage since 1776) Ford's pardon further added to the pain of a country traumatised by the extent of Nixon's deceit.

This one decision, more-so than Ford's mishandling of an economy in deep recession or his apparent public bumbling and awkwardness, cost him any chance of being elected President in his own right in 1976. Ironically, while Richard Nixon would make something of a political 'comeback' before his death in 1994, Gerald Ford was confined to political obscurity after losing the 1976 election to Jimmy Carter.

Gough Whitlam

'Well May We Say, God Save the Queen'

Parliament House Steps, Canberra, Australia, 11 November 1975.

Gough Whitlam leaves Parliament House in Canberra in 11 November 1975.

Edward Gough Whitlam, born in Melbourne on 11 July, 1916, is the only Australian Prime Minister to be dismissed from office. Moving to Sydney at the age of two, Whitlam studied law at Sydney University before joining the Royal Australian Air Force in World War II. In 1945, just before leaving the RAAF, he joined the Labor Party in Sydney. After unsuccessful forays into local and state politics, Whitlam won a seat in federal politics in 1952. He was Deputy Opposition leader to Arthur Calwell from 1960-66 but once he took control of the party, Whitlam swept through the old guard of 'laborites' and established a more democratic style of socialist leadership that appealed to Labor's left-wing and centre-right factions.

In December 1972—on the back of a memorable slogan 'It's Time'—the Labor Party was returned to government after 23 years in opposition. Whitlam's sharp wit and charismatic presence provided many Australians with the hope that the 1970s would be a progressive era after decades of conservative government.

'Maintain your rage and enthusiasm through the campaign for the election now to be held.'

Once in government, Whitlam's initial reforms took Australia by storm—removing race as a criterion for immigration (the 'White Australia' policy was still in unofficial operation), ending conscription, abolishing the British honours system, increasing government support for the arts (and reinvigorating the Australian film industry), reforming health services (and putting contraceptives on the medical benefits list), increasing social and educational opportunities for Aborigines and instituting equal pay for women. He was the first Prime Minister in 24 years to visit China, and he re-opened the Australian Embassey in Peking. Perhaps he moved too quickly.

Despite a booming economy and low inflation when he came to office Australia, like the rest of the world in the mid-1970s, was beset by international economic constraints—especially fuel prices and overseas loans. Whitlam's biggest failing as Prime Minister was that he did not control his ministers, and with a mandate to conduct 'open' government, their economic mismanagement severely embarrassed him and eroded public confidence in his leadership.

Despite this perception, Whitlam was re-elected to a second three-year term in 1974 but with a greatly reduced majority.

The events leading up Whitlam's dismissal have become part of Australian political history. In 1974 Whitlam's Minister for Minerals and Energy, Rex Connor, negotiated a $4 billion loan (incredibly, to be repaid over 20 years) to finance the government's ambitious development projects. Although Whitlam knew of the negotiations, his cabinet did not. When the press reported the story the Federal Opposition, under Liberal leader Malcolm Fraser, went on the attack. Whitlam was then forced to sack his treasurer, Deputy Prime Minister Jim Cairns, who was involved in a messy affair with his Secretary (Juni Morosi) and Rex Connor resigned in October 1975 for misleading the parliament over his negotiations with Pakistani financier Tirath Khemlani.

When Malcolm Fraser used the Liberals' majority in the Senate to block the government's money bills—threatening to bring the country to halt in a bid to force an election in both houses of government—Whitlam had a constitutional crisis on his hands.

One of the quirks of Australia's parliamentary system, which is modelled on Britain's Westminster system, is that the head of state is actually the representative of the ruling monarch of England ... the Governor-General. In 1975, Queen Elizabeth II's representative was Sir John Kerr, the jurist and barrister who had been appointed to the post by his former law colleague, Gough Whitlam.

The Governor-General, in consultation with the Queen, asserted the power to dissolve both houses of parliament—effectively dismissing the elected government of the land—and appoint an interim government of his choosing. This Kerr did on 11 November 1975—a date that had long resonated with the Australian public. It was the date, in 1880, that bushranger Ned Kelly was hanged. It was the date, in 1918, that World War I ended. Now the country had another reason to remember it.

On advice of the Chief Justice of the High Court, Sir John Kerr called Gough Whitlam to Government House at 1:00 pm that afternoon. What Whitlam didn't know was that Liberal leader Malcolm Fraser was waiting in another room, although allegations of collusion between the Governor-General and the Opposition Leader proved unfounded.

Whitlam was dismissed at 1:15 pm, Fraser was commissioned as Prime Minister at 1:30 pm and barely half an hour later the Senate passed the Supply Bill that it had been blocking since October 16. Almost comically, when Fraser announced to the House of Representatives that he was the new Prime Minister and put forward the motion to adjourn the session, the move was defeated by the dismissed former government which still maintained a slender majority in the lower house.

Then, at 3:16 pm, Gough Whitlam sponsored a motion of no-confidence in the new Prime Minister which was passed. Parliament was patently unworkable and the Speaker of the House sought an urgent meeting with the Governor-General but was told that Kerr was not available until 4:45 pm. For the next hour, Australia effectively had no federal government.

At 4:50 pm that afternoon, the Governor-General's secretary, David Smith, went to the steps of Parliament House and read the proclamation dissolving Parliament.

A large, angry crowd mostly made up of Labor supporters had gathered at the base of the original Parliament House steps, with Gough Whitlam standing silently at Smith's shoulder. The proclamation concluded:

'Now therefore, I Sir John Robert Kerr, the Governor General of Australia, do by this my Proclamation dissolve the Senate and the House of Representatives.
Given under my Hand and the Great Seal of Australia on 11 November 1975.
By His Excellency's Command,
Malcolm Fraser
Prime Minister.
God Save the Queen!'

Gough Whitlam immediately addressed the crowd when David Smith finished. His spontaneous speech—a mixture of sarcastic word-play and controlled venom—has since passed into Australian folklore.

❜ Well may we say "God Save the Queen" because nothing will save the Governor-General. The proclamation which you have just heard read by the Governor-General's official secretary was countersigned "Malcolm Fraser" who will undoubtedly go down in Australian history from Remembrance Day, 1975 as "Kerr's cur". They won't silence the outskirts of Parliament House, even if the inside has been silenced for the next few weeks. The Governor-General's proclamation was signed after he already made an appointment to meet the Speaker at a quarter to five. The House of Representatives had requested the Speaker to give the Governor-General its decision that Mr Fraser did not have the confidence of the House and that the Governor-General should call me to form the Government … Maintain your rage and enthusiasm through the campaign for the election now to be held and until polling day.❜

But Whitlam misjudged the mood of the Australian people and the Labor Party lost the 13 December elections by the biggest majority in electoral history. Malcolm Fraser remained Prime Minister until defeated by Bob Hawke in 1983. Although Whitlam and many of Labor's hardcore supporters 'maintained the rage' in the three decades since, Whitlam's relationship towards Malcolm Fraser softened after he left politics in 1977. (Needless to say, Whitlam never again spoke to his former friend, Sir John Kerr, who died in London in 1993.)

The two former Prime Ministers formed something of an 'odd couple' during Australia's Republican debate in the late 1990s, but interestingly, given the opportunity to change the Head of State to an elected or nominated Australian representative, the nation opted to stay part of the British Commonwealth.

Barbara Jordan

'Keynote Address'

Democratic Convention, New York, 12 July 1976.

Barbara Jordan in 1983.

Barbara Jordan (1936-96) was a woman of firsts. After graduating from Texas Southern University in 1956 she attended Boston University Law School. After passing both the Massachusetts and Texas bar examinations Jordan set up her law practice in her parents' kitchen until she saved enough money to move her firm to a black section of Houston.

In 1966 she ran for the Texas Senate and became one of two black candidates elected to the State legislature. However, during the next six years she worked hard to prove that she represented all her constituents and was elected to serve in the 93rd Congress in 1972—the first African-American woman elected to the US House of Representatives from the South.

In 1976 Barbara Jordan was selected to be the keynote speaker at the Democratic National Convention—the first African-American woman to be afforded such an honour by any major political party—and nominated Georgia Governor Jimmy Carter as the Democratic presidential candidate.

Her keynote address came at a time when the United States had lost its confidence in government after the Watergate scandal, the resignation of President Nixon and two years of ineffectual leadership by his successor Gerald Ford.

❝Thank you ladies and gentlemen for a very warm reception.

It was one hundred and forty-four years ago that members of the Democratic Party first met in convention to select a Presidential candidate. Since that time, Democrats have continued to convene once every four years and draft a party platform and nominate a Presidential candidate. And our meeting this week is a continuation of that tradition. But there is something different about tonight. There is something special about tonight. What is different? What is special?

I, Barbara Jordan, am a keynote speaker.

A lot of years passed since 1832, and during that time it would have been most unusual for any national political party to ask that a Barbara Jordan to deliver a keynote address. But tonight here I am. And I feel that notwithstanding the past that my presence here is one additional bit of evidence that the American Dream need not forever be deferred.

Now that I have this grand distinction what in the world am I supposed to say? I could easily spend this time praising the accomplishments of this party and attacking the Republicans— but I don't choose to do that. I could list the many problems which Americans have. I could list the problems which cause people to feel cynical, angry, frustrated: problems which include lack of integrity in government; the feeling that the individual no longer counts; the reality of material and spiritual poverty; the feeling that the grand American experiment is failing or has failed. I could recite these problems, and then I could sit down and offer no solutions. But I don't choose to do that either. The citizens of America expect more. They deserve and they want more than a recital of problems.

We are a people in a quandary about the present. We are a people in search of our future. We are a people in search of a national community. We are a people trying not only to solve the problems of the present, unemployment, inflation, but we are attempting on a larger scale to fulfill the promise of America. We are attempting to fulfill our national purpose, to create and sustain a society in which all of us are equal.

Throughout out history, when people have looked for new ways to solve their problems, and to uphold the principles of this nation, many times they have turned to political parties. They have often turned to the Democratic Party. What is it? What is it about the Democratic Party that makes it the instrument the people use when they search for ways to shape their future? Well I believe the answer to that question lies in our concept of governing. Our concept of governing is derived from our view of people. It is a concept deeply rooted in a set of beliefs firmly etched in the national conscience of all of us.

Now what are these beliefs? First, we believe in equality for all and privileges for none. This is a belief that each American regardless of background has equal standing in the public forum—all of us. Because we believe this idea so firmly, we are an inclusive rather than an exclusive party. Let everybody come! I think it no accident that most of those emigrating to America in the 19th century identified with the Democratic Party.

'A spirit of harmony will survive in America only if each of us remembers that we share a common destiny.'

We are a heterogeneous party made up of Americans of diverse backgrounds. We believe that the people are the source of all governmental power; that the authority of the people is to be extended, not restricted.

This can be accomplished only by providing each citizen with every opportunity to participate in the management of the government.

They must have that, we believe. We believe that the government which represents the authority of all the people, not just one interest group, but all the people, has an obligation to actively seek to remove those obstacles which would block individual achievement—obstacles emanating from race, sex, economic condition. The government must remove them, seek to remove them.

We are a party of innovation. We do not reject our traditions, but we are willing to adapt to changing circumstances, when change we must. We are willing to suffer the discomfort of change in order to achieve a better future. We have a positive vision of the future founded on the belief that the gap between the promise and reality of America can one day be finally closed.

We believe that.

This, my friends, is the bedrock of our concept of governing. This is a part of the reason why Americans have turned to the Democratic Party. These are the foundations upon which a national community can be built. Let's all understand that these guiding principles cannot be discarded for short-term political gains. They represent what this country is all about. They are indigenous to the American idea. And these are principles which are not negotiable.

In other times, I could stand here and give this kind of exposition on the beliefs of the Democratic Party and that would be enough. But today that is not enough. People want more. That is not sufficient reason for the majority of the people of this country to vote Democratic. We have made mistakes. We realize that. In our haste to do all things for all people, we did not foresee the full consequences of our actions. And when the people raised their voices, we didn't hear. But our deafness was only a temporary condition, and not an irreversible condition.

Even as I stand here and admit that we have made mistakes, I still believe that as the people of America sit in judgment on each party, they will recognize that our mistakes were mistakes of the heart. They'll recognize that.

And now we must look to the future. Let us heed the voice of the people and recognize their common sense. If we do not, we not only blaspheme our political heritage, we ignore the common ties that bind all Americans. Many fear the future. Many are distrustful of their leaders, and believe that their voices are never heard. Many seek only to satisfy their private work wants. To satisfy their private interests.

But this is the great danger America faces. That we will cease to be one nation and become instead a collection of interest groups: city against suburb, region against region, individual against individual. Each seeking to satisfy private wants. If that happens, who then will speak for America? Who then will speak for the common good?

This is the question which must be answered in 1976.

Are we to be one people bound together by common spirit, sharing in a common endeavor; or will we become a divided nation? For all of its uncertainty, we cannot flee the future. We must not become the new Puritans and reject our society. We must address and master the future together. It can be done if we restore the belief that we share a sense of national community, that we share a common national endeavor. It can be done.

There is no executive order; there is no law that can require the American people to form a national community. This we must do as individuals, and if we do it as individuals, there is no President of the United States who can veto that decision.

As a first step, we must restore our belief in ourselves. We are a generous people so why can't we be generous with each other? We need to take to heart the words spoken by Thomas Jefferson:

"Let us restore to social intercourse that harmony and affection without which liberty and even life are but dreary things."

A nation is formed by the willingness of each of us to share in the responsibility for upholding the common good. A government is invigorated when each of us is willing to participate in shaping the future of this nation. In this election year we must define the common good and begin again to shape a common future.

Let each person do his or her part. If one citizen is unwilling to participate, all of us are going to suffer. For the American idea, though it is shared by all of us, is realized in each one of us.

BARBARA JORDAN

267

And now, what are those of us who are elected public officials supposed to do? We call ourselves public servants but I'll tell you this: We as public servants must set an example for the rest of the nation. It is hypocritical for the public official to admonish and exhort the people to uphold the common good if we are derelict in upholding the common good. More is required of public officials than slogans and handshakes and press releases. More is required. We must hold ourselves strictly accountable. We must provide the people with a vision of the future.

'We have a positive vision of the future founded on the belief that the gap between the promise and reality of America can one day be finally closed.'

If we promise as public officials, we must deliver. If we as public officials propose, we must produce. If we say to the American people it is time for you to be sacrificial; sacrifice. If the public official says that, we [public officials] must be the first to give. We must be. And again, if we make mistakes, we must be willing to admit them. We have to do that.

What we have to do is strike a balance between the idea that government should do everything and that idea, the belief, that government ought to do nothing. Strike a balance. Let there be no illusions about the difficulty of forming this kind of a national community. It's tough, difficult, not easy. But a spirit of harmony will survive in America only if each of us remembers that we share a common destiny. If each of us remembers when self-interest and bitterness seem to prevail that we share a common destiny.

I have confidence that we can form this kind of national community.

I have confidence that the Democratic Party can lead the way.

I have that confidence.

We cannot improve on the system of government handed down to us by the founders of the Republic. There is no way to improve upon that. But what we can do is to find new ways to implement that system and realize our destiny.

Now, I began this speech by commenting to you on the uniqueness of a Barbara Jordan making a keynote address. Well I am going to close my speech by quoting a Republican President and I ask you that as you listen to these words of Abraham Lincoln, relate them to the concept of a national community in which every last one of us participates:

"As I would not be a slave, so I would not be a master. This expresses my idea of Democracy. Whatever differs from this, to the extent of the difference, is no Democracy."

Thank you.'

Democrat Jimmy Carter was swept to victory in the 1976 presidential election. In 1978 Barbara Jordan left Congress and worked as a Professor at the University of Texas. In 1992 she was again the keynote speaker at the Democratic National Convention where she introduced another successful presidential nominee —Bill Clinton.

One of the most influential women in American domestic politics and a powerful symbol of social change in the latter half of the 20th Century, Barbara Jordan died on 17 January 1996.

In 2001 researchers at the University of Wisconsin-Madison and Texas A & M University—reflecting the opinion of 137 leading scholars of American public address—compiled a list of the 100 greatest American speeches of the 20th Century. Barbara Jordan's 1976 'Keynote Address'—which was placed at number 5—was the highest ranked speech by any American woman.

Anwar el-Sadat

'Peace With Justice'

Address to the Israeli Knesset, Tel Aviv, 20 November 1977.

Anwar el-Sadat in 1977.

Mohammed Anwar el-Sadat (1918-81) was born in the Tala District of Egypt. After the coup that ousted King Farouk in 1952, he succeeded Gamal Abdel Nasser as Egyptian president in 1970. As early as 1971 Sadat had raised the issue of signing a peace agreement with Israel providing that all occupied territories captured during the Six-Day War in 1967 were returned to neighbouring Arab states. During 1972-73 Sadat stated that war was inevitable unless the US forced Israel to accept the United Nations resolution to withdraw from occupied territories.

In 1973-74 Sadat also assumed the role of prime minister—a period in which he presided over Egyptian involvement in the 'Yom Kippur War' against Israel. On the feast of Yom Kippur, 6 October, 1973, the holiest day of the Jewish calendar, Egypt and Syria (backed by nine other Arab states) launched a surprise attack on Israel. The Israeli army recovered brilliantly and Egypt was on the brink of a disastrous defeat when, on 22 October, the United Nations directed all parties to immediately 'terminate all military activity'. With war a diplomatic and military failure, Sadat sought a peaceful end to the conflict by continuing to negotiate with the Israeli government and announced he would be willing to enter into a peace agreement with his country's former enemy.

In an historic move for both Egypt and Israel, Sadat was invited to address the Israeli parliament on 20 November 1977.

'In the name of God, Mr. Speaker of the Knesset, ladies and gentlemen, allow me first to thank deeply the Speaker of the Knesset for affording me this opportunity to address you.

As I begin my address I wish to say, peace and the mercy of God Almighty be upon you and may peace be with us all, God willing. Peace for us all, of the Arab lands and in Israel, as well as in every part of this big world, which is so beset by conflicts, perturbed by its deep contradictions, menaced now and then by destructive wars launched by man to annihilate his fellow men.

Finally, amidst the ruins of what man has built among the remains of the victims of mankind there emerges neither victor nor vanquished. The only vanquished remains always a man, God's most sublime creation. Man, whom God has created, as Gandhi, the apostle of peace puts it, to forge ahead, to mold the way of life and to worship God Almighty.

I come to you today on solid ground to shape a new life and to establish peace. We all love this land, the land of God, we all, Moslems, Christians and Jews, all worship God.

Under God, God's teachings and commandments are: love, sincerity, security and peace.

I do not blame all those who received my decision when I announced it to the entire world before the Egyptian People's Assembly. I do not blame all those who received my decision with surprise and even with amazement—some gripped even by violent surprise. Still others interpreted it as political, to camouflage my intentions of launching a new war.

I would go so far as to tell you that one of my aides at the presidential office contacted me at a late hour following my return home from the People's Assembly and sounded worried as he asked me: "Mr. President, what would be our reaction if Israel actually extended an invitation to you?"

I replied calmly: 'I would accept it immediately. I have declared that I would go to the ends of the earth. I would go to Israel, for I want to put before the people of Israel all the facts."

I can see the faces of all those who were astounded by my decision and had doubts as to the sincerity of the intentions behind the declaration of my decision. No one could have ever conceived that the President of the biggest Arab state, which bears the heaviest burden and the main responsibility pertaining to the cause of war and peace in the Middle East, should declare his readiness to go to the land of the adversary while we were still in a state of war.

We all still bear the consequences of four fierce wars waged within 30 years. All this at the time when the families of the 1973 October war are still mourning under the cruel pain of bereavement of father, son, husband and brother.

As I have already declared, I have not consulted as far as this decision is concerned with any of my colleagues or brothers, the Arab heads of state or the confrontation states.

Most of those who contacted me following the declaration of this decision expressed their objection because of the feeling of utter suspicion and absolute lack of confidence between the Arab states and the Palestine people on the one hand and Israel on the other that still surges in us all.

Many months in which peace could have been brought about have been wasted over differences and fruitless discussions on the procedure of convening the Geneva conference. All have shared suspicion and absolute lack of confidence.

But to be absolutely frank with you, I took this decision after long thought, knowing that it constitutes a great risk, for God Almighty has made it my fate to assume responsibility on behalf of the Egyptian people, to share in the responsibility of the Arab nation, the main duty of which, dictated by responsibility, is to exploit all and every means in a bid to save my Egyptian Arab people and the pan-Arab nation from the horrors of new suffering and destructive wars, the dimensions of which are foreseen only by God Himself.

After long thinking, I was convinced that the obligation of responsibility before God and before the people make it incumbent upon me that I should go to the far corners of the world—even to Jerusalem to address members of the Knesset and acquaint them with all the facts surging in me, then I would let you decide for yourselves.

Following this, may God Almighty determine our fate.

Ladies and gentlemen, there are moments in the lives of nations and peoples when it is incumbent upon those known for their wisdom and clarity of vision to survey the problem, with all its complexities and vain memories, in a bold drive toward new horizons.

Those who like us are shouldering the same responsibilities entrusted to us are the first who should have the courage to make determining decisions that are consonant with the magnitude of the circumstances. We must all rise above all forms of obsolete theories of superiority, and the most important thing is never to forget that infallibility is the prerogative of God alone.

If I said that I wanted to avert from all the Arab people the horrors of shocking and destructive wars I must sincerely declare before you that I have the same feelings and bear the same responsibility toward all and every man on earth, and certainly toward the Israeli people.

Any life that is lost in war is a human life, be it that of an Arab or an Israeli. A wife who becomes a widow is a human being entitled to a happy family life, whether she be an Arab or an Israeli.

Innocent children who are deprived of the care and compassion of their parents are ours. They are ours, be they living on Arab or Israeli land.

They command our full responsibility to afford them a comfortable life today and tomorrow.

For the sake of them all, for the sake of the lives of all our sons and brothers, for the sake of affording our communities the opportunity to work for the progress and happiness of man, feeling secure and with the right to a dignified life, for the generations to come, for a smile on the face of every child born in our land—for all that I have taken my decision to come to you, despite all the hazards, to deliver my address.

'No one could have ever conceived that the President of the biggest Arab state, which bears the heaviest burden and the main responsibility pertaining to the cause of war and peace in the Middle East, should declare his readiness to go to the land of the adversary while we were still in a state of war.'

I have shouldered the prerequisites of the historic responsibility and therefore I declared on February 4, 1971, that I was willing to sign a peace agreement with Israel. This was the first declaration made by a responsible Arab official since the outbreak of the Arab-Israeli conflict. Motivated by all these factors dictated by the responsibilities of leadership on October 16, 1973, before the Egyptian People's Assembly, I called for an international conference to establish permanent peace based on justice. I was not heard.

I was in the position of man pleading for peace or asking for a cease-fire, motivated by the duties of history and leadership, I signed the first disengagement agreement, followed by the second disengagement agreement in Sinai.

Then we proceeded, trying both open and closed doors in a bid to find a certain road leading to a durable and just peace.

We opened our heart to the peoples of the entire world to make them understand our motivations and objectives and actually to convince them of the fact that we are advocates of justice and peacemakers. Motivated by all these factors, I also decided to come to you with an open mind and an open heart and with a conscious determination so that we might establish permanent peace based on justice.

ANWAR EL-SADAT

273

It is so fated that my trip to you, which is a journey of peace, coincided with the Islamic feast the holy Feast of the Sacrifice when Abraham—peace be upon him—forefather of the Arabs and Jews, submitted to God, I say, when God Almighty ordered him not out of weakness, but through a giant spiritual force and by free will to sacrifice his very own son, personified a firm and unshakeable belief in ideals that had for mankind a profound significance.

'Any life that is lost in war is a human life, be it that of an Arab or an Israeli. A wife who becomes a widow is a human being entitled to a happy family life, whether she be an Arab or an Israeli.'

Ladies and gentlemen, let us be frank with each other. Using straightforward words and a clear conception with no ambiguity, let us be frank with each other today while the entire world, both East and West, follows these unparalleled moments which could prove to be a radical turning point in the history of this part of the world if not in the history of the world as a whole.

Let us be frank with each other, let us be frank with each other as we answer this important question:

How can we achieve permanent peace based on justice? Well, I have come to you carrying my clear and frank answer to this big question, so that the people in Israel as well as the entire world may hear it. All those devoted prayers ring in my ears, pleading to God Almighty that this historic meeting may eventually lead to the result aspired to by millions.

Before I proclaim my answer, I wish to assure you that in my clear and frank answer I am availing myself of a number of facts which no one can deny.

The first fact is that no one can build his happiness at the expense of the misery of others.

The second fact: never have I spoken, nor will I ever speak, with two tongues; never have I adopted, nor will I ever adopt, two policies. I never deal with anyone except in one tongue, one policy and with one face.

The third fact: direct confrontation is the nearest and most successful method to reach a clear objective.

The fourth fact: the call for permanent and just peace based on respect for United Nations resolutions has now become the call of the entire world. It has become the expression of the will of the international community, whether in official capitals where policies are made and decisions taken, or at the level of world public opinion, which influences policymaking and decision-taking.

The fifth fact, and this is probably the clearest and most prominent, is that the Arab nation, in its drive for permanent peace based on justice, does not proceed from a position of weakness. On the contrary, it has the power and stability for a sincere will for peace.

The Arab declared intention stems from an awareness prompted by a heritage of civilization, that to avoid an inevitable disaster that will befall us, you and the whole world, there is no alternative to the establishment of permanent peace based on justice, peace that is not swayed by suspicion or jeopardized by ill intentions.

In the light of these facts which I meant to place before you the way I see them, I would also wish to warn you, in all sincerity I warn you, against some thoughts that could cross your minds.

Frankness makes it incumbent upon me to tell you the following:

First, I have not come here for a separate agreement between Egypt and Israel. This is not part of the policy of Egypt. The problem is not that of Egypt and Israel.

An interim peace between Egypt and Israel, or between any Arab confrontation state and Israel, will not bring permanent peace based on justice in the entire region.

Rather, even if peace between all the confrontation states and Israel were achieved in the absence of a just solution of the Palestinian problem, never will there be that durable and just peace upon which the entire world insists.

Second, I have not come to you to seek a partial peace, namely to terminate the state of belligerency at this stage and put off the entire problem to a subsequent stage. This is not the radical solution that would steer us to permanent peace.

Equally, I have not come to you for a third disengagement agreement in Sinai or in Golan or the West Bank. For this would mean that we are merely delaying the ignition of the fuse. It would also mean that we are lacking the courage to face peace, that we are too weak to shoulder the burdens and responsibilities of a durable peace based upon justice.

I have come to you so that together we should build a durable peace based on justice to avoid the shedding of one single drop of blood by both sides. It is for this reason that I have proclaimed my readiness to go to the farthest corner of the earth...

....I repeat with Zachariah: "Love, right and justice." From the holy Koran I quote the following verses: "We believe in God and in what has been revealed to us and what was revealed to Abraham, Ishmael, Isaac, Jacob and the 13 Jewish tribes. And in the books given to Moses and Jesus and the Prophets from their Lord, who made no distinction between them." So we agree, Salam Aleikum—peace be upon you.'

The peace agreement between Egypt and Israel was sponsored by newly-elected US President Jimmy Carter in 1978. Carter invited the Egyptian President and Israeli Prime Minister Menachem Begin to his presidential retreat at Camp David, resulting in the 1978 Camp David Accord. Sadat and Begin were jointly awarded the Nobel Peace Prize for their efforts, but Sadat was severely criticised for his initiative by other Arab leaders and hard-line Muslims from within his own country. On 6 October, 1981 Sadat was attending a military parade when he was fired upon by five gunmen dressed in black ceremonial uniforms who were part of the official parade. The Egyptian president and five other people were killed in the attack. Sadat's successor, former vice-president Hosni Mubarak, pledged to honour all treaties with the Israelis.

Jimmy Carter

'A Crisis of Confidence'

TV broadcast, Washington DC, 15 July 1979.

Jimmy Carter in 1979.

Jimmy Carter seemed to be the perfect solution to America's ailing self-belief after Nixon's Watergate scandal and Gerald Ford's inept presidency. Born in Plains, Georgia in 1924, the quietly-spoken, perennially smiling and deeply religious peanut farmer was swept into power during America's Bicentennial Year on a promise that he would never tell the American public a lie. The amazing thing for many commentators was not that the former Georgia governor won the election—that in itself was a miracle (Carter was unheard of before the primaries)—but that he wanted to run in the first place.

Carter faced an uphill struggle to win public confidence but his presidency was ham-strung from the beginning. Although down-to-earth and unassuming, Carter lacked political astuteness to ask for help when he needed it. Rising inflation, stagnant economic growth, unemployment and rising interest rates—compounded by soaring international fuel prices—saw America gripped by an energy crisis in the late 1970s.

The crisis engulfed the Carter administration, which seemed unable to offer any viable solutions to the economic mess in which America found itself. In July 1979 Carter retired to Camp David for eight days to consider recommendations before delivering the following speech to the American people on the night of Sunday, 15 July.

' Exactly three years ago, on July 15, 1976, I accepted the nomination of my party to run for President of the United States.

I promised you a President who is not isolated from the people, who feels your pain, and who shares your dreams and who draws his strength and his wisdom from you.

During the past three years I've spoken to you on many occasions about national concerns, the energy crisis, reorganizing the Government, our Nation's economy, and issues of war and especially peace. But over those years the subjects of the speeches, the talks, and the press conferences have become increasingly narrow focused more and more on what the isolated world of Washington thinks is important. Gradually, you've heard more and more about what the Government thinks or what the Government should be doing and less and less about our Nation's hopes, our dreams, and our vision of the future.

Ten days ago I had planned to speak to you again about a very important subject—energy. For the fifth time I would have described the urgency of the problem and laid out a series of legislative recommendations to the Congress. But as I was preparing to speak, I began to ask myself the same question that I now know has been troubling many of you. Why have we not been able to get together as a nation to resolve our serious energy problem?

'The threat is nearly invisible in ordinary ways. It is a crisis of confidence. It is a crisis that strikes at the very heart and soul and spirit of our national will. We can see this crisis in the growing doubt about the meaning of our own lives and in the loss of ... purpose for our Nation.'

It's clear that the true problems of our Nation are much deeper—deeper than gasoline lines or energy shortages, deeper even than inflation or recession. And I realize more than ever that as President I need your help. So, I decided to reach out and listen to the voices of America.

I invited to Camp David people from almost every segment of our society—business and labor, teachers and preachers, Governors, mayors, and private citizens. And then I left Camp David to listen to other Americans, men and women like you ... [Carter then outlined a series of comments garnered from the meetings.]

... The threat is nearly invisible in ordinary ways. It is a crisis of confidence. It is a crisis that strikes at the very heart and soul and spirit of our national will. We can see this crisis in the growing doubt about the meaning of our own lives and in the loss of a unity of purpose for our Nation.

The erosion of our confidence in the future is threatening to destroy the social and the political fabric of America.

The confidence that we have always had as a people is not simply some romantic dream or a proverb in a dusty book that we read just on the Fourth of July.

It is the idea which founded our Nation and has guided our development as a people. Confidence in the future has supported everything else—public institutions and private enterprise, our own families, and the very Constitution of the United States. Confidence has defined our course and has served as a link between generations. We've always believed in something called progress. We've always had a faith that the days of our children would be better than our own.

Our people are losing that faith, not only in government itself but in the ability as citizens to serve as the ultimate rulers and shapers of our democracy. As a people we know our past and we are proud of it. Our progress has been part of the living history of America, even the world. We always believed that we were part of a great movement of humanity itself called democracy, involved in the search for freedom, and that belief has always strengthened us in our purpose. But just as we are losing our confidence in the future, we are also beginning to close the door on our past.

In a nation that was proud of hard work, strong families, close-knit communities, and our faith in God, too many of us now tend to worship self- indulgence and consumption. Human identity is no longer defined by what one does, but by what one owns. But we've discovered that owning things and consuming things does not satisfy our longing for meaning. We've learned that piling up material goods cannot fill the emptiness of lives which have no confidence or purpose.

The symptoms of this crisis of the American spirit are all around us. For the first time in the history of our country a majority of our people believe that the next five years will be worse than the past five years. Two-thirds of our people do not even vote. The productivity of American workers is actually dropping, and the willingness of Americans to save for the future has fallen below that of all other people in the Western world.

As you know, there is a growing disrespect for government and for churches and for schools, the news media, and other institutions. This is not a message of happiness or reassurance, but it is the truth and it is a warning.

These changes did not happen overnight. They've come upon us gradually over the last generation, years that were filled with shocks and tragedy.

We were sure that ours was a nation of the ballot, not the bullet, until the murders of John Kennedy and Robert Kennedy and Martin Luther King, Jr. We were taught that our armies were always invincible and our causes were always just, only to suffer the agony of Vietnam. We respected the Presidency as a place of honor until the shock of Watergate.

> 'For the first time in the history of our country a majority of our people believe that the next five years will be worse than the past five years.'

We remember when the phrase "sound as a dollar" was an expression of absolute dependability, until 10 years of inflation began to shrink our dollar and our savings. We believed that our Nation's resources were limitless until 1973, when we had to face a growing dependence on foreign oil.

These wounds are still very deep. They have never been healed. Looking for a way out of this crisis, our people have turned to the Federal Government and found it isolated from the mainstream of our Nation's life. Washington, D.C., has become an island. The gap between our citizens and our Government has never been so wide. The people are looking for honest answers, not easy answers; clear leadership, not false claims and evasiveness and politics as usual.

What you see too often in Washington and elsewhere around the country is a system of government that seems incapable of action. You see a Congress twisted and pulled in every direction by hundreds of well-financed and powerful special interests. You see every extreme position defended to the last vote, almost to the last breath by one unyielding group or another. You often see a balanced and a fair approach that demands sacrifice, a little sacrifice from everyone, abandoned like an orphan without support and without friends.

Often you see paralysis and stagnation and drift. You don't like it, and neither do I. What can we do? [Carter then proposed six points of government intervention to correct the energy problems facing America in the late 1970s.]

… Our Nation must be fair to the poorest among us, so we will increase aid to needy Americans to cope with rising energy prices. We often think of conservation only in terms of sacrifice. In fact, it is the most painless and immediate way of rebuilding our Nation's strength. Every gallon of oil each one of us saves is a new form of production. It gives us more freedom, more confidence, that much more control over our own lives.

JIMMY CARTER

279

So, the solution of our energy crisis can also help us to conquer the crisis of the spirit in our country. It can rekindle our sense of unity, our confidence in the future, and give our Nation and all of us individually a new sense of purpose.

You know we can do it. We have the natural resources. We have more oil in our shale alone than several Saudi Arabias. We have more coal than any nation on Earth. We have the world's highest level of technology. We have the most skilled work force, with innovative genius, and I firmly believe that we have the national will to win this war.

I do not promise you that this struggle for freedom will be easy. I do not promise a quick way out of our Nation's problems, when the truth is that the only way out is an all-out effort. What I do promise you is that I will lead our fight, and I will enforce fairness in our struggle, and I will ensure honesty.

And above all, I will act. We can manage the short-term shortages more effectively and we will, but there are no short-term solutions to our long-range problems. There is simply no way to avoid sacrifice.

Twelve hours from now I will speak again in Kansas City, to expand and to explain further our energy program. Just as the search for solutions to our energy shortages has now led us to a new awareness of our Nation's deeper problems, so our willingness to work for those solutions in energy can strengthen us to attack those deeper problems.

'The solution of our energy crisis can also help us to conquer the crisis of the spirit in our country. It can rekindle our sense of unity, our confidence in the future, and give our nation and all of us individually a new sense of purpose.'

I will continue to travel this country, to hear the people of America. You can help me to develop a national agenda for the 1980s. I will listen and I will act. We will act together. These were the promises I made three years ago, and I intend to keep them.

Little by little we can and we must rebuild our confidence. We can spend until we empty our treasuries, and we may summon all the wonders of science. But we can succeed only if we tap our greatest resources-America's people, America's values, and America's confidence.

I have seen the strength of America in the inexhaustible resources of our people. In the days to come, let us renew that strength in the struggle for an energy secure nation.

In closing, let me say this: I will do my best, but I will not do it alone. Let your voice be heard. Whenever you have a chance, say something good about our country. With God's help and for the sake of our Nation, it is time for us to join hands in America. Let us commit ourselves together to a rebirth of the American spirit ... working together with our common faith we cannot fail.

Thank you and good night.'

It was Jimmy Carter's handling of foreign policy that finally brought about his political downfall. He had several important international victories—handing back control of the Panama Canal, normalising relations with China and sponsoring talks between Egypt and Israel.

But when 52 Americans were taken hostage by Iranian extremists in Teheran on 4 November 1979, his presidency was shaken to its core. Carter's inability to resolve the issue through diplomatic means, and a failed military rescue that resulted in the loss of lives in April 1980, saw him soundly defeated by Republican candidate Ronald Reagan at the end of the year.

Despite his openness and earnestness, Carter had failed to inspire the nation's imagination and restore the confidence it so badly wanted.

However, since his defeat over 25 years ago, Jimmy Carter has continued to grow in statesmanship. Dedicating his public life to humanitarian causes he has been involved an international observer and mediator in many of the world's conflicts—Nicaragua, Panama, Sudan, Ethiopia and North Korea—and remains an important advocate for the rights of the poor and oppressed.

The Big Chill
1980-1989

Indira Gandhi

'True Liberation of Women'

New Delhi, India, 26 March 1980.

Indira Gandhi addresses a meeting in New Delhi in 1979.

The Nehru-Gandhi 'dynasty' in modern Indian politics is as important—and equally tragic—as the Kennedy family in the United
States of America. Indira Gandhi (1917-84) was the daughter of
Jawaharla Nehru, the first Prime Minister of India. After studying at
Oxford she married Feroze Khan in 1942, a Moslem, and converted from
her family's Hindu religion against the wishes of her parents. In order to
facilitate the inter-caste marriage, Mahatma Gandhi 'adopted' Khan (whose
mother's maiden name was the Persian derivative 'Ghandy') but although
the marriage produced two sons (Rajiv and Sanjay) it was not a success.
Indira Gandhi later became president of the Indian Congress Party (1959-
60) and following the death of Lal Shastri, Prime Minister of India in
1966. During the 1970s she struggled to contain national sectarian violence. After her conviction for electoral malpractice in 1975, she declared a
state of emergency that was kept in place for two years. Defeated in 1977
she returned for a second term as Prime Minister in 1980.

In March 1980 she outlined the true liberation of women at the
inauguration of the All-India Women's Conference Building Complex in
New Delhi.

'For several decades the All-India Women's Conference has been the organized voice of the
women of India. I have never been a member of any women's organization but have been interested enough to keep track of their activities and to lend the helping hand whenever I could.

I am glad that at long last the All-India Women's Conference has a home of its own and it is
named after one of the best known and most remarkable women of our times, Sarojini Naidu,
feminine to the core but well able to hold her own in the world of men, whether in letters or
in politics.

To add to the importance of the occasion and to give it a touch of elegance, we have in our
midst His Highness the Aga Khan and Her Highness the Begum Aga Khan. They are friends
of India and have founded or encouraged many projects for
education, health and other aspects of welfare. But for their
timely and generous help, this complex would not have been
ready today. Nor would we have before us the attractive Aga
Khan Hall. We welcome them and wish them well in their work.

I see before me a number of eminent women who have distinguished themselves in various professions—in social work, in
education, in science, in administration, in law and, of course,
in politics. They must all feel gratified to see the completion

'There is no time to lose
and it involves a tremendous
task of educating. We want
to walk together and in step
with all others, but if men
hesitate, should not women
show the way?'

of this building. I have often said that I am not a feminist. Yet, in my concern for the under-privileged, how can I ignore women who, since the beginning of history, have been dominated over and discriminated against in social customs and in laws. How insidious and all-pervasive is this attitude of male' superiority is revealed in the vocabulary of the languages the world over. And this is unquestioningly accepted and acquiesced in by all but a minuscule minority of men and also women. Currently I am reading a book titled World and Women. I learned from it what Mr. Ling White, the President of Mills College in the USA, wrote of the use of masculine generic pronouns. I quote: "The penetration of the habit of language into the minds of little girls as they grow up to be women is more profound than most people, including most women, have realized. For, it implies that personality is really a male attribute and that women are a sub or a human sub-species." The author goes on to say that it is time we looked more carefully where the thoughtless use of stereotypes is taking us. "Man as leader, woman as follower; man as producer, woman as consumer; man as strength, woman as weakness; this is the cosmography that has brought us to man as aggressor and humanity the victim."

'By excluding women, men are depriving themselves of a fuller emancipation or growth for themselves.'

Hence, by excluding women, men are depriving themselves of a fuller emancipation or growth for themselves.

In the West, women's so-called freedom is often equated with imitation of man. Frankly, I feel that is merely an exchange of one kind of bondage for another. To be liberated, woman must feel free to be herself, not in rivalry to man but in the context of her own capacity and her personality. We need women to be more interested, more alive and more active not because they are women but because they do comprise half the human race. Whether they like it or not, they cannot escape their responsibility nor should they be denied its benefits. Indian women are traditionally conservative but they also have the genius of synthesis, to adapt and to absorb. That is what gives them resilience to face suffering and to meet upheavals with a degree of calm, to change constantly and yet remain changeless, which is the quality of India herself.

Today's major concerns are: first, economic and social inequality and injustice between the affluent and developing countries and within countries. Secondly, the anxiety whether human wisdom will prevail over what can only be called a death wish in which the desire to dominate expresses itself in countless ways, the most dangerous being the armament race. And, thirdly, the need to protect this, our only Earth, from human rapacity and exploitation. Only recently have we awakened to the awareness of ancient truths regarding our own utter dependence on the balance of Nature and its resources.

These enormous challenges cannot be met only by some sections, however advanced they may be, while others pull in different directions or watch apathetically. The effort has to be a universal one, conscious and concerted, considering no one too small to contribute. The effort must embrace all nationalities and all classes regardless of religion, caste or sex.

There is no time to lose and it involves a tremendous task of educating. We want to walk together and in step with all others, but if men hesitate, should not women show the way? So, while complimenting the All-India Women's Conference, especially its President, Smt. Lakshmi Raghuramaiah, on their achievements, I dedicate to the nation this building complex of the All-India Women's Conference.'

One of the great ironies of Indira Gandhi's political career was that a predominantly non-Christian country (Hindu/Muslim) would democratically elect a woman as its leader (twice) when some western governments (USA and Australia) have yet to cross that gender barrier. On 31 October 1984 Indira Gandhi was gunned down by her Sikh body guards as she walked through the garden of her New Delhi home to meet with actor Peter Ustinov who was making a documentary about her.

In June that year, Indian troops had stormed the Golden Temple in Amristar in order to end a four-day siege by Sikh militants. (Most commentators saw this as the reason for her murder.) She was succeeded as Prime Minister by her eldest son, Rajiv Gandhi. The elder Gandhi heir was a pilot of India Airlines but his mother sponsored his political career following the death of his younger brother Sanjiv, in 1980.

When general elections were held later that year, Gandhi's Congress Party won with a record majority. In November 1989, Rajiv Gandhi resigned as Premier but suffered a similar fate to his mother when he was assassinated by Tamil separatists in May 1991 while campaigning in Madras.

Margaret Thatcher
'The Falklands War'

Cheltenham, England, 3 July 1982.

Margaret Thatcher in 1982.

The 'Iron Lady' of world politics during the 1980s and Britain's first female Prime Minister was born Margaret Hilda Roberts above a shop in Grantham, Lincolnshire in 1925. An Oxford graduate and research chemist, she married Dennis Thatcher in 1951 before becoming a lawyer. The Conservative Party member for Finchley in 1959, she replaced Edward Heath as Opposition Leader in 1975. In 1979, the Conservative Party was swept to power and Margaret Thatcher duly became Britain's first female Prime Minister.

Under Thatcher's leadership, the Conservative Party privatised national industries and institutions such as education, health care and local government services. Despite presiding over the worst unemployment figures since the Depression, Thatcher's government was re-elected with an increased majority in 1983. The reasons for this were two-fold: the lack of an organised Opposition Party and public support for her after the Falklands War in 1982.

On 2 April, 1982 Argentinean troops invaded the Falkland Islands in the southern Atlantic Ocean. The Falklands, 770 kilometres north-east of Cape Horn, had been a British Crown Colony since 1833 but for many years Argentina had laid claim to the islands (which they called Islas Malvines). As Prime Minister, Margaret Thatcher immediately sent a task force of 30 warships, and some 10 000 troops, to liberate the two larger islands, East and West Falkland.

By 12 April Britain had established a 200-mile exclusion zone around the islands and had recaptured South Georgia, a Falklands dependency to the south-west, by the end of the month. On 1 May the RAF conducted a Vulcan bomber raid on Stanley, the islands' capital, on East Falkland. Many lives were lost on both sides; most notably for Britain on the *HMS Antelope* and *HMS Coventry*, while the *HMS Sheffield* was hit by Exocet missile and the *Atlantic Conveyor* was also sunk. Then, on 28 May, the second battalion of the Parachute Regiment recaptured Goose Green, on the south-west part of East Falkland, and infantry brigades landed at San Carlos, in the north-west corner, three days later.

Although the war had turned in Britain's favour it suffered massive losses on 8 June when the RFA Sir Galahad and RFA Sir Tristram were attacked during the transfer of troops to Fitzroy, south-west of Stanley, and the HMS Fearless was sunk in Choiseul Sound. Within a week, General Mario Menendez, the leader of the Argentinean troops in the Falklands surrendered. The Falklands were recaptured, at a price—255 Britains killed and 777 wounded, 635 Argentineans killed and 1068 wounded.

This speech exemplifies the way Margaret Thatcher used Britain's military success to reverse her polls rating as the 'least popular' Prime Minister of modern times to win the 1983 general election. Thatcher remarked at the time: 'It's exciting to have a real crisis on your hands, when you have spent half your political life dealing with humdrum issues like the environment.'

❝Today we meet in the aftermath of the Falklands Battle. Our country has won a great victory and we are entitled to be proud. This nation had the resolution to do what it knew had to be done—to do what it knew was right.

'For we have learnt something about ourselves—a lesson which we desperately needed to learn. When we started out, there were the waverers and the faint-hearts: the people who thought that Britain could no longer seize the initiative for herself.'

We fought to show that aggression does not pay, and that the robber cannot be allowed to get away with his swag. We fought with the support of so many throughout the world: the Security Council, the Commonwealth, the European Community, and the United States. Yet we also fought alone—for we fought for our own people and for our own sovereign territory.

Now that it is all over, things cannot be the same again, for we have learnt something about ourselves -a lesson which we desperately needed to learn. When we started out, there were the waverers and the faint-hearts: the people who thought that Britain could no longer seize the initiative for herself; the people who thought we could no longer do the great things which we once did; and those who believed that our decline was irreversible—that we could never again be what we were. There were those who would not admit it—even perhaps some here today—people who would have strenuously denied the suggestion but—in their heart of hearts—they too had their secret fears that it was true: that Britain was no longer the nation that had built an Empire and ruled a quarter of the world.

Well, they were wrong. The lesson of the Falklands is that Britain has not changed and that this nation still has those sterling qualities which shine through our history. This generation can match their fathers and grandfathers in ability, in courage, and in resolution. We have not changed. When the demands of war and the dangers to our own people call us to arms—then we British are as we have always been—competent, courageous and resolute.

When called to arms—ah, that's the problem. It took the battle in the South Atlantic for the shipyards to adapt ships way ahead of time; for dockyards to refit merchantmen and cruise liners, to fix helicopter platforms, to convert hospital ships—all faster than was thought possible; it took the demands of war for every stop to be pulled out and every man and woman to do their best.

British people had to be threatened by foreign soldiers and British territory invaded and then—why then—the response was incompar¬able. Yet why does it need a war to bring out our qualities and reassert our pride? Why do we have to be invaded before we throw aside our selfish aims and begin to work together as only we can work, and achieve as only we can achieve?

That really is the challenge we as a nation face today. We have to see that the spirit of the South Atlantic—the real spirit of Britain—is kindled not only by war but can now be fired by peace.

We have the first prerequisite. We know we can do it-we haven't lost the ability. That is the Falklands Factor. We have proved ourselves to ourselves. It is a lesson we must not now forget. Indeed, it is a lesson which we must apply to peace just as we have learnt it in war. The faltering and the self-doubt has given way to achievement and pride. We have the confidence and we must use it.

'But the spirit has stirred and the nation has begun to assert itself. Things are not going to be the same again.'

Just look at the Task Force as an object lesson. Every man had his own task to do and did it superbly. Officers and men, senior NCO and newest recruit—every one realized that his contribution was essential for the success of the whole. All were equally valu¬able—each was differently qualified. By working together, each was able to do more than his best. As a team they raised the average to the level of the best and by each doing his utmost together they achieved the impossible. That's an accurate picture of Britain at war—not yet of Britain at peace. But the spirit has stirred and the nation has begun to assert itself. Things are not going to be the same again.'

In 1987 Margaret Thatcher became the first Prime Minister since the nineteenth century to win three consecutive elections. But Thatcher's autocratic prime ministerial style and her attitude towards the European Community ultimately split her own cabinet and led to her downfall. When Sir Geoffrey Howe, the Leader of the Commons and the last remaining member of her original cabinet in 1979, was publicly critical of her when announcing his resignation in November 1990, Thatcher's days as Prime Minister were numbered. Michael Heseltine was the first to challenge for the leadership of the Conservative Party and when Thatcher could not gather the necessary support to survive the first round of voting, she withdrew from the leadership race. John Major was elected her eventual successor.

Margaret Thatcher was made a life peer of the realm, becoming Lady Thatcher, in 1992.

Pope John Paul II

'Speech to the Polish People'

Czestochowa, Poland, 18 June 1983.

Pope John Paul II meets Lech Walesa in Poland in 1985.

Many historians cite the Pope's 1983 speech to the Polish people as providing the country's millions of oppressed workers with the spirit to stand up to their Communist masters and finally, in 1989, seize back their homeland and proclaim the Republic of Poland.

During World War II, Karol Jozef Wojtyla (1920-2005) was a seminary student in his native Poland, which was also the location of several of the largest Nazi death camps including Auschwitz, Treblinka and Majdanek. Several Jewish friends and neighbours of the young Wojtyla were killed by the Nazis.

Ordained in 1946, he became a professor of moral theology and was named Archbishop of Cracow. Created a Cardinal in 1967, Karol Wojtyla became the first non-Italian Pope in 450 years when he succeeded John Paul I (and took his name) in 1978. An articulate, analytical and popular pontiff, he travelled the world during the first ten years of his papacy which renewed interest in the Catholic Church, especially in Communist countries. In 1981, Pope John Paul II survived an assassination attempt from a Turkish national in St Peters Square in Rome. His health slowly declined in the late 1990s under the ravages of Parkinson's disease.

When the Pope made his third visit to his homeland, in July 1983, and spoke from the battlement of the Jasna Góra monastery in Czestochowa, the Communist government had banned the Polish worker's union Solidarity and enforced martial law. Pope John Paul II gave voice to the 'forgotten people of Eastern Europe'—often using coded words such as 'workers', 'truth' and 'solidarity' (with a small 's' of course)—that drew thunderous applause from the approximately one million pilgrims that had gathered before him. Not surprisingly, many Solidarity banners were present among the crowd.

❝ Our Lady of Jasna Góra is the teacher of true love for all. And this is particularly important for you, dear young people. In you, in fact, is decided that form of love which all of your life will have and, through you human life on Polish soil: the matrimonial, family, social and national form-but also the priestly, religious and missionary one. Every life is determined and evaluated by the interior form of love. Tell me what you love, and I will tell you who you are.

I watch! How beautiful it is that this word is found in the call of Jasna Góra. It possesses a profound evangelical ancestry: Christ says many times: "Watch" (Matt. 26: 41). Perhaps also from the Gospel it passed into the tradition of scouting. In the call of Jasna Góra it is the essential element of the reply that we wish to give to the love by which we are surrounded in the sign of the Sacred Icon.

The response to this love must be precisely the fact that I watch! What does it mean, "I watch"?

It means that I make an effort to be a person with a conscience. I do not stifle this conscience and I do not deform it; I call good and evil by name, and I do not blur them; I develop in myself what is good, and I seek to correct what is evil, by overcoming it in myself. This is a fundamental problem which can never be minimized or put on a secondary level. No! It is everywhere and always a matter of the first importance. Its importance is all the greater in proportion to the increase of circumstances which seem to favour our tolerance of evil and the fact that we easily excuse ourselves from this, especially if adults do so.

'Today when we are fighting for the future form of our social life, remember that this form depends on what people will be like. Therefore: watch!'

My dear friends! It is up to you to put up a firm barrier against immorality, a barrier—I say—to those social vices which I will not here call by name but which you yourselves are perfectly aware of. You must demand this of yourselves, even if others do not demand it of you. Historical experiences tell us how much the immorality of certain periods cost the whole nation. Today when we are fighting for the future form of our social life, remember that this form depends on what people will be like. Therefore: watch!

Christ said to the apostles, during his prayer in Gethsemane:

"Watch and pray that you may not enter into temptation" (Matt. 26: 41).

"I watch" also means: I see another. I do not close in on myself, in a narrow search for my own interests, my own judgements. "I watch" means: love of neighbour; it means: fundamental interhuman solidarity.

Before the Mother of Jasna Góra I wish to give thanks for all the proofs of this solidarity which have been given by my compatriots, including Polish youth, in the difficult period of not many months ago. It would be difficult for me to enumerate here all the forms of this solicitude which surrounded those who were interned, imprisoned, dismissed from work, and also their families. You know this better than I. I received only sporadic news about it.

May this good thing, which appeared in so many places and so many ways, never cease on Polish soil. May there be a constant confirmation of that "I watch" of the call of Jasna Góra, which is a response to the presence of the Mother of Christ in the great family of the Poles.

"I watch" also means: I feel responsible for this great common inheritance whose name is Poland. This name defines us all. This name obliges us all. This name costs us all.

Perhaps at times we envy the French, the Germans or the Americans because their name is not tied to such a historical price and because they are so easily free: while our Polish freedom costs so much.

My dear ones, I will not make a comparative analysis. I will only say that it is what costs that constitutes value. It is not, in fact, possible to be truly free without an honest and profound relationship with values. We do not want a Poland which costs us nothing. We watch, instead, beside all that makes up the authentic inheritance of the generations, seeking to enrich it. A nation, then, is first of all rich in its people. Rich in man. Rich in youth. Rich in every individual who watches in the name of truth: it is truth, in fact, that gives form to love.

My dear young friends! Before our common Mother and the Queen of our hearts, I desire finally to say to you that she knows your sufferings, your difficult youth, your sense of injustice and humiliation, the lack of prospects for the future that is so often felt, perhaps the temptations to flee to some other world.

Even if I am not among you every day, as was the case for many years in the past, nevertheless I carry in my heart a great solicitude. A great, enormous solicitude. A solicitude for you. Precisely because, on you depends tomorrow.

I pray for you every day.

It is good that we are here together at the hour of the call of Jasna Góra. In the midst of the trials of the present time, in the midst of the trial through which your generation is passing, this call of the millennium continues to be a programme.

In it is contained a fundamental way out. Because the way out in whatever dimension—economic, social, political—must happen first in man. Man cannot remain with no way out.

Mother of Jasna Góra, you who have been given to us by Providence for the defence of the Polish nation, accept this evening this call of the Polish youth together with the Polish Pope, and help us to persevere in hope! Amen.'

'Before the Mother of Jasna Góra I wish to give thanks for all the proofs of this solidarity which have been given by my compatriots, including Polish youth, in the difficult period of not many months ago.'

Martial law was lifted in July 1983 in Poland—the month after the Pope John Paul II's visit. But food shortages, controls on civil liberties and limited political representation remained in place during the decade. Then, in April 1989, following a softening in the Communist mood throughout Eastern Europe, Solidarity was legalised and the union was allowed to participate in elections.

Union candidates won an enormous victory and by the end of August, a Solidarity-led coalition government was formed with leader Lech Walesa elected president in December 1990. Rarely during the latter part of the twentieth century had the Catholic Church played such an active role in the downfall of a political system (Bishop Oscar Romero of El Salvador and Cardinal Jaime Sin in the Philippines are notable exceptions).

In March 2000, Pope John Paul II conducted an historic week-long pilgrimage to the Holy Land. Whilst in Jerusalem, the Pope visited Yad Vashem—Israel's main Holocaust memorial—to honour the six million Jews murdered by the Nazis during World War II.

In the Hall of Remembrance, the visibly frail Pontiff laid a wreath and then ceremoniously lit the memorial's eternal flame. Among those present at the emotional ceremony was Israel's Prime Minister, Ehud Barak, and some 50 Holocaust survivors including 13 from the Pope's hometown of Wadowice, Poland.

While Pope John Paul II stopped short of making an official Catholic Church apology many had hoped for (during World War, II Pope Pius XII remained publicly silent to the systematic extermination of Europe's Jewish population, despite the Church's awareness of death camps in Nazi occupied territories.) but the compassion of his speech — more than fifty years after the concentration camps of Europe were liberated — moved many at the ceremony to tears.

Five years later, leading up to Easter 2005, illness robbed Pope John Paul II of his voice and for the first time in the 26 years of his papacy he could not conduct Holy Week mass. He died in Rome on 2 April, aged 84.

Bob Geldof

'Live Aid'

Wembley Stadium, London, 13 July 1985.

Bob Geldorf at Wembley Stadium in July 1985 preparing for the Live Aid concert.

In October 1984 the BBC News carried the story of the developing human tragedy in the African nation of Ethiopia. Three years of continued drought, compounded by two civil wars in the neighbouring countries of Eritrea and Tigre, had left 7 million people in the north of Ethiopia facing starvation. Described as the 'worst catastrophe since World War II', the death of thousands of Ethiopians had gone largely unnoticed by the western world and its leaders. (That year the European Economic Community spent £265 million to destroy its stockpile of 2 million tonnes of vegetables and fruit in order to protect its market). By the time the BBC televised its report, an Ethiopian man, woman or child was dying every 20 minutes.

One of the many people who saw the BBC report, and was immediately appalled by the antipathy shown by his own country, was British musician Bob Geldof. The Irish leader of the English punk band 'The Boomtown Rats' Geldof enjoyed world-wide success with the song 'I Don't Like Mondays' in 1979, but was also an articulate and intelligent commentator on the music scene and world issues

On the 25 November 1984 he hastily assembled a group of top musicians and recorded the song, 'Do They Know It's Christmas?' in time for the lucrative Christmas market. The record, co-written by Geldof and Ultravox frontman Midge Ure and recorded under the 'Band Aid' banner, debuted at No.1 on the music charts and raised £8 million pounds for Ethiopian relief. Similar records around the world, including the Michael Jackson-Lionel Ritchie composition 'We Are the World' which sold a staggering 8 million copies, boosted the relief fund.

Geldof was still not satisfied. A visit to Ethiopia in January 1985 revealed the true scale of the problem. Ethiopia not only lacked food, it also lacked infrastructure—especially the ability to transport grain from its major ports in the east to the drought-stricken north. 'This famine is one of the great shameful things of our time,' said Geldof and, commenting about the price of a vinyl record, added: 'I find it an indictment of us, and a pathetic way of living, that a piece of plastic seven inches across with a hole in the middle is the price of someone's life this year.'

Faced by the reality that he would need a lot more funds, Geldof and the 'Band Aid' group set up a live televised charity concert for 13 July, 1985 to be held back to back on both sides of the Atlantic. The Wembley concert comprised the cream of the English music scene—Status Quo, Dire Straits, Queen, Sting, Phil Collins, David Bowie, Elvis Costello, The Who, Elton John, U2 and Paul McCartney amongst others. The other concert in

Philadelphia had The Beach Boys, Madonna, Neil Young, Bob Dylan, Mick Jagger, Tina Turner, Eric Clapton and, again, Phil Collins who appeared in both venues via the Concorde.

Geldof addressed the packed Wembley crowd and world-wide television audience to open proceedings.

❛Please remember this day for the rest of your lives. It's important.

Remember the day you wanted to help.

Remember the bands and crews who did it. The professionals who made it an extraordinary technological feat.

Remember the dying who were allowed to live.

Remember the day you die, there is someone alive in Africa 'cos one day you watched a pop concert.

Remember your tears and your joy.

Remember the love.

Remember on that day for once in your bloody lives WE WON.

Remember the dying goes on and remember so that as time passes you can tell others "It's possible, I know".

What a day, what a lovely day.❜

The Live Aid concerts and countless other fundraising concerts held all over the world raised £28 million in England with another £29 million donated worldwide. His efforts made a considerable difference to a nation of starving people—and opened the eyes of millions to the indifference of Western governments in caring for Third World Countries. Christened 'Saint Bob' in the media and later 'Sir' Bob Geldof when he was granted an honourary knighthood for his efforts (as an Irish citizen, Geldof was precluded from being awarded a full knighthood), Geldof has not been spared his own personal tragedies.

In 1994 his wife Paula Yates left him for Australian rock star Michael Hutchence (from INXS). The mother of three daughters with Geldof, Yates had another child with Hutchence. When Hutchence committed suicide in Sydney in 1997 and Yates spiralled into drug addiction and suicide in 2000, Geldof gained custody of all four children.

Ronald Reagan
'Tear Down This Wall'

Brandenberg Gate, West Berlin, 12 June 1987.

Ronald Reagan addresses West Berliners in front of the Brandenberg Gate in 1987.

The Berlin Wall was built by the Communists in August 1961 to keep Germans from escaping Communist-dominated East Berlin into Democratic West Berlin. The four-metre concrete wall topped by electrified fences cut a 45-kilometre scar through Berlin and was manned by armed guard posts. For the next three decades the Berlin Wall stood as a stark reminder of the Cold War that existed between the United States and Soviet Union.

Ronald Reagan (1911-2004) was the 40th President of the United States of America. A talented sportsman in his youth, Reagan took a job as a sports announcer in Illinois before moving to Hollywood where he started his film career. Self-depreciatingly describing himself as the 'Errol Flynn of the B movies' the Republican Party groomed him as Californian Governor in 1966. Despite being almost 70 when he ran for the presidency in 1980, the American people were looking for stability after a disillusioned four years under Jimmy Carter, and Reagan was swept to power—the oldest President in the history of the nation.

In March 1981, just six weeks after his inauguration, Reagan barely survived an assassin's bullet. The following year he became the first US President to be invited to speak directly to members of the British Parliament in the Royal Gallery at the Palace of Westminster in London. A master communicator, Reagan outlined his staunch opposition to Communism and encouraged the British to aid the US in the worldwide struggle for freedom. In June 1987, at a time when President Reagan was negotiating with Soviet leader Mikhail Gorbachev to scrap intermediate range nuclear missiles, Reagan travelled to West Berlin and invoking the memory of President John Kennedy's June 1963 visit ('Ich bin ein Berliner!') issued a challenge to his Communist counterpart.

❝ Chancellor Kohl, Governing Mayor Diepgen, ladies and gentlemen:

Twenty-four years ago, President John F Kennedy visited Berlin, speaking to the people of this city and the world at the City Hall. Well, since then two other presidents have come, each in his turn, to Berlin. And today I, myself, make my second visit to your city.

We come to Berlin, we American presidents, because it's our duty to speak, in this place, of freedom. But I must confess, we're drawn here by other things as well: by the feeling of history in this city, more than 500 years older than our own nation; by the beauty of the Grunewald and the Tiergarten; most of all, by your courage and determination. Perhaps the composer Paul Lincke understood something about American presidents. You see, like so many presidents before me, I come here today because wherever I go, whatever I do: Ich hab noch einen Koffer in Berlin. [I still have a suitcase in Berlin.]

Our gathering today is being broadcast throughout Western Europe and North America. I understand that it is being seen and heard as well in the East. To those listening throughout Eastern Europe, a special word: Although I cannot be with you, I address my remarks to you just as surely as to those standing here before me. For I join you, as I join your fellow countrymen in the West, in this firm, this unalterable belief: Es gibt nur ein Berlin. [There is only one Berlin.]

'I noticed words crudely spray-painted upon the wall, perhaps by a young Berliner: "This wall will fall. Beliefs become reality".'

Behind me stands a wall that encircles the free sectors of this city, part of a vast system of barriers that divides the entire continent of Europe. From the Baltic, south, those barriers cut across Germany in a gash of barbed wire, concrete, dog runs, and guard towers. Farther south, there may be no visible, no obvious wall. But there remain armed guards and checkpoints all the same—still a restriction on the right to travel, still an instrument to impose upon ordinary men and women the will of a totalitarian state. Yet it is here in Berlin where the wall emerges most clearly; here, cutting across your city, where the news photo and the television screen have imprinted this brutal division of a continent upon the mind of the world. Standing before the Brandenburg Gate, every man is a German, separated from his fellow men. Every man is a Berliner, forced to look upon a scar.

President von Weizsacker has said, "The German question is open as long as the Brandenburg Gate is closed." Today I say: As long as the gate is closed, as long as this scar of a wall is permitted to stand, it is not the German question alone that remains open, but the question of freedom for all mankind. Yet I do not come here to lament. For I find in Berlin a message of hope, even in the shadow of this wall, a message of triumph.

In this season of spring in 1945, the people of Berlin emerged from their air-raid shelters to find devastation. Thousands of miles away, the people of the United States reached out to help. And in 1947 Secretary of State—as you've been told—George Marshall announced the creation of what would become known as the Marshall Plan. Speaking precisely 40 years ago this month, he said: "Our policy is directed not against any country or doctrine, but against hunger, poverty, desperation, and chaos."

In the Reichstag a few moments ago, I saw a display commemorating this 40th anniversary of the Marshall Plan. I was struck by the sign on a burnt-out, gutted structure that was being rebuilt. I understand that Berliners of my own generation can remember seeing signs like it dotted throughout the western sectors of the city. The sign read simply: "The Marshall Plan is helping here to strengthen the free world." A strong, free world in the West, that dream became real. Japan rose from ruin to become an economic giant. Italy, France, Belgium— virtually every nation in Western Europe saw political and economic rebirth; the European Community was founded.

In West Germany and here in Berlin, there took place an economic miracle, the Wirtschaftswunder. Adenauer, Erhard, Reuter, and other leaders understood the practical importance of liberty—that just as truth can flourish only when the journalist is given freedom of speech, so prosperity can come about only when the farmer and businessman enjoy economic freedom. The German leaders reduced tariffs, expanded free trade, lowered taxes. From 1950 to 1960 alone, the standard of living in West Germany and Berlin doubled.

Where four decades ago there was rubble, today in West Berlin there is the greatest industrial output of any city in Germany—busy office blocks, fine homes and apartments, proud avenues, and the spreading lawns of parkland. Where a city's culture seemed to have been destroyed, today there are two great universities, orchestras and an opera, countless theaters, and museums. Where there was want, today there's abundance—food, clothing, automobiles—the wonderful goods of the Ku'damm. From devastation, from utter ruin, you Berliners have, in freedom, rebuilt a city that once again ranks as one of the greatest on earth. The Soviets may have had other plans. But my friends, there were a few things the Soviets didn't count on—Berliner Herz, Berliner Humor, ja, und Berliner Schnauze. [Berliner heart, Berliner humor, yes, and a Berliner nose.]

In the 1950s, Khrushchev predicted: "We will bury you." But in the West today, we see a free world that has achieved a level of prosperity and well-being unprecedented in all human history. In the Communist world, we see failure, technological backwardness, declining standards of health, even want of the most basic kind--too little food. Even today, the Soviet Union still cannot feed itself. After these four decades, then, there stands before the entire world one great and inescapable conclusion: Freedom leads to prosperity. Freedom replaces the ancient hatreds among the nations with comity and peace. Freedom is the victor.

And now the Soviets themselves may, in a limited way, be coming to understand the importance of freedom. We hear much from Moscow about a new policy of reform and openness. Some political prisoners have been released. Certain foreign news broadcasts are no longer being jammed. Some economic enterprises have been permitted to operate with greater freedom from state control.

Are these the beginnings of profound changes in the Soviet state? Or are they token gestures, intended to raise false hopes in the West, or to strengthen the Soviet system without changing it? We welcome change and openness; for we believe that freedom and security go together, that the advance of human liberty can only strengthen the cause of world peace. There is one sign the Soviets can make that would be unmistakable, that would advance dramatically the cause of freedom and peace.

General Secretary Gorbachev, if you seek peace, if you seek prosperity for the Soviet Union and Eastern Europe, if you seek liberalization: Come here to this gate! Mr. Gorbachev, open this gate! Mr. Gorbachev, tear down this wall!

I understand the fear of war and the pain of division that afflict this continent—and I pledge to you my country's efforts to help overcome these burdens. To be sure, we in the West must resist Soviet expansion. So we must maintain defenses of unassailable strength. Yet we seek peace; so we must strive to reduce arms on both sides.

Beginning 10 years ago, the Soviets challenged the Western alliance with a grave new threat, hundreds of new and more deadly SS-20 nuclear missiles, capable of striking every capital in Europe. The Western alliance responded by committing itself to a counter-deployment unless the Soviets agreed to negotiate a better solution; namely, the elimination of such weapons on both sides. For many months, the Soviets refused to bargain in earnestness. As the alliance, in turn, prepared to go forward with its counter-deployment, there were difficult days—days of protests like those during my 1982 visit to this city—and the Soviets later walked away from the table.

'And I invite Mr. Gorbachev: Let us work to bring the Eastern and Western parts of the city closer together, so that all the inhabitants of all Berlin can enjoy the benefits that come with life in one of the great cities of the world.'

But through it all, the alliance held firm. And I invite those who protested then—I invite those who protest today—to mark this fact: Because we remained strong, the Soviets came back to the table. And because we remained strong, today we have within reach the possibility, not merely of limiting the growth of arms, but of eliminating, for the first time, an entire class of nuclear weapons from the face of the earth.

As I speak, NATO ministers are meeting in Iceland to review the progress of our proposals for eliminating these weapons. At the talks in Geneva, we have also proposed deep cuts in strategic offensive weapons. And the Western allies have likewise made far-reaching proposals to reduce the danger of conventional war and to place a total ban on chemical weapons.

While we pursue these arms reductions, I pledge to you that we will maintain the capacity to deter Soviet aggression at any level at which it might occur. And in cooperation with many of our allies, the United States is pursuing the Strategic Defense Initiative—research to base deterrence not on the threat of offensive retaliation, but on defenses that truly defend; on systems, in short, that will not target populations, but shield them. By these means we seek to increase the safety of Europe and all the world. But we must remember a crucial fact: East and West do not mistrust each other because we are armed; we are armed because we mistrust each other. And our differences are not about weapons but about liberty. When President Kennedy spoke at the City Hall those 24 years ago, freedom was encircled, Berlin was under siege. And today, despite all the pressures upon this city, Berlin stands secure in its liberty. And freedom itself is transforming the globe.

In the Philippines, in South and Central America, democracy has been given a rebirth. Throughout the Pacific, free markets are working miracle after miracle of economic growth. In the industrialized nations, a technological revolution is taking place—a revolution marked by rapid, dramatic advances in computers and telecommunications.

In Europe, only one nation and those it controls refuse to join the community of freedom. Yet in this age of redoubled economic growth, of information and innovation, the Soviet Union faces a choice: It must make fundamental changes, or it will become obsolete.

Today thus represents a moment of hope. We in the West stand ready to cooperate with the East to promote true openness, to break down barriers that separate people, to create a safe, freer world. And surely there is no better place than Berlin, the meeting place of East and West, to make a start. Free people of Berlin: Today, as in the past, the United States stands for the strict observance and full implementation of all parts of the Four Power Agreement of 1971. Let us use this occasion, the 750th anniversary of this city, to usher in a new era, to seek a still fuller, richer life for the Berlin of the future. Together, let us maintain and develop the ties between the Federal Republic and the Western sectors of Berlin, which is permitted by the 1971 agreement.

And I invite Mr. Gorbachev: Let us work to bring the Eastern and Western parts of the city closer together, so that all the inhabitants of all Berlin can enjoy the benefits that come with life in one of the great cities of the world.

To open Berlin still further to all Europe, East and West, let us expand the vital air access to this city, finding ways of making commercial air service to Berlin more convenient, more comfortable, and more economical. We look to the day when West Berlin can become one of the chief aviation hubs in all central Europe.

With our French and British partners, the United States is prepared to help bring international meetings to Berlin. It would be only fitting for Berlin to serve as the site of United Nations meetings, or world conferences on human rights and arms control or other issues that call for international cooperation.

There is no better way to establish hope for the future than to enlighten young minds, and we would be honored to sponsor summer youth exchanges, cultural events, and other programs for young Berliners from the East. Our French and British friends, I'm certain, will do the same. And it's my hope that an authority can be found in East Berlin to sponsor visits from young people of the Western sectors.

One final proposal, one close to my heart: Sport represents a source of enjoyment and ennoblement, and you may have noted that the Republic of Korea—South Korea—has offered to permit certain events of the 1988 Olympics to take place in the North. International sports competitions of all kinds could take place in both parts of this city. And what better way to demonstrate to the world the openness of this city than to offer in some future year to hold the Olympic Games here in Berlin, East and West? In these four decades, as I have said, you Berliners have built a great city. You've done so in spite of threats—the Soviet attempts to impose the East-mark, the blockade. Today the city thrives in spite of the challenges implicit in the very presence of this wall. What keeps you here? Certainly there's a great deal to be said for your fortitude, for your defiant courage. But I believe there's something deeper, something that involves Berlin's whole look and feel and way of life—not mere sentiment. No one could live long in Berlin without being completely disabused of illusions. Something instead, that has seen the difficulties of life in Berlin but chose to accept them, that continues to build this good and proud city in contrast to a surrounding totalitarian presence that refuses to release human

RONALD REAGAN

305

energies or aspirations. Something that speaks with a powerful voice of affirmation, that says yes to this city, yes to the future, yes to freedom. In a word, I would submit that what keeps you in Berlin is love—love both profound and abiding.

Perhaps this gets to the root of the matter, to the most fundamental distinction of all between East and West. The totalitarian world produces backwardness because it does such violence to the spirit, thwarting the human impulse to create, to enjoy, to worship. The totalitarian world finds even symbols of love and of worship an affront. Years ago, before the East Germans began rebuilding their churches, they erected a secular structure: the television tower at Alexander Platz. Virtually ever since, the authorities have been working to correct what they view as the tower's one major flaw, treating the glass sphere at the top with paints and chemicals of every kind. Yet even today when the sun strikes that sphere—that sphere that towers over all Berlin—the light makes the sign of the cross. There in Berlin, like the city itself, symbols of love, symbols of worship, cannot be suppressed.

As I looked out a moment ago from the Reichstag, that embodiment of German unity, I noticed words crudely spray-painted upon the wall, perhaps by a young Berliner: "This wall will fall. Beliefs become reality." Yes, across Europe, this wall will fall. For it cannot withstand faith; it cannot withstand truth. The wall cannot withstand freedom.

And I would like, before I close, to say one word. I have read, and I have been questioned since I've been here about certain demonstrations against my coming. And I would like to say just one thing, and to those who demonstrate so. I wonder if they have ever asked themselves that if they should have the kind of government they apparently seek, no one would ever be able to do what they're doing again.

Thank you and God bless you all. **ʼ**

Ten months after Ronald Reagan left the office of President—on 10 November 1989—the Berlin Wall was torn down as a spontaneous response to East Germany's commitment to social and political reform. The wall which had symbolised the differences between East and West, and had claimed the lives of as many as 75 people during its 28 years of existence, became a gateway to freedom for thousands and hastened the reunification of Germany in October 1990.

Reverend Jimmy Swaggart
'I Have Sinned'

Family Worship Center, Baton Rouge, LA, 21 February 1988.

TV evangelist Jimmy Swaggart preaches to a Flora Blanca Stadium crowd in 1987.

Jimmy Swaggart was born in 1935 in Ferriday, Louisiana, the cousin of rock and roll legend Jerry Lee Lewis. Where as Jerry Lee ('The Killer') used music as his medium to reach millions, his cousin Jimmy became a pioneer in a mass medium that he made his very own—televangelism. By the mid 1980s Swaggart had become the world's richest televangelist with his 'Assemblies of God' ministry earning more than $150 million annually. Each week his 'Jimmy Swaggart Telecast' reached eight million viewers.

In 1986 Swaggart publicly 'defrocked' fellow Assemblies of God minister Marvin Gorman for having an extra-marital affair with one of his parishioners. When rival PTL ministry leaders Jimmy and Tammy Bakker were exposed as corrupt hypocrites, Swaggart called them a 'cancer in the body of Christ' on national television. But Swaggart's own words would come back to condemn him and lead to his infamous on-camera confession in February, 1988.

It was Marvin Gorman who laid the trap for Swaggart: hiring a private detective to take photos of his former colleague looking at pornography and having sex with prostitutes. When Gorman confronted the Church leadership with his evidence, Swaggart confessed to everything—even having a lifelong addiction to pornography! Defrocked for one year and vilified in the country's mainstream media, Swaggart turned in a bravura performance as he tearfully confessed to his television congregation of his undisclosed 'sin'.

'Everything that I will attempt to say to you this morning will be from my heart. I will not speak from a prepared script. Knowing the consequences of what I will say and that much of it will be taken around the world, as it should be, I am positive that all that I want to say I will not be able to articulate as I would desire. But I would pray that you will somehow feel the anguish, the pain, and the love of my heart. I have always—every single time that I have stood before a congregation and a television camera—I have met and faced the issues head-on. I have never sidestepped or skirted unpleasantries. I have tried to be like a man and to preach this gospel exactly as I have seen it without fear or reservation or compromise. I can do no less this morning.

I do not plan in any way to whitewash my sin. I do not call it a mistake, a mendacity; I call it sin. I would much rather, if possible—and in my estimation it would not be possible—to make it worse than less than it actually is. I have no one but myself to blame. I do not lay the fault or the blame of the charge at anyone else's feet. For no one is to blame but Jimmy Swaggart. I take the responsibility. I take the blame. I take the fault.

Many times I have addressed the media in a very stern manner, and I have chastised them for what I thought and believed was error in their reporting or their investigation even. This time I do not. I commend them. I feel that the media, both in print and by television, radio, have been fair and objective and even compassionate. Ted Koppel on "Nightline," I feel, did everything within his power, in going the second, third, fourth, fifth, tenth mile to make doubly certain that what he reported was at least as fair and as honest as he, the spokesman for this world-famed news program, could make it. And I thank him for his objectivity, his kindness, and his fairness.

> 'I have sinned against you and I have brought disgrace and humiliation and embarrassment upon you. I beg your forgiveness.'

And I also want to express appreciation to the entire media everywhere, but especially here in Baton Rouge—Channels 9, 2, and 33, the newspapers, the radio stations. They've been hard, but they have been fair. They have been objective and at times, I believe, they have even been compassionate—even my old nemesis, John Camp, that we have disagreed with very strongly. And I love you, John. And in spite of our differences, I think you are one of the finest investigative reporters in the world—and I mean that.

I want to address myself as best as I know how to those that I have wronged, that I have sinned against. First of all, my wife, Frances—God never gave a man a better helpmate and companion to stand beside him. And as far as this gospel has been taken through the airwaves to the great cities of the world and covered this globe, it would never have been done were it not for her strength, her courage, her consecration to her Redeemer, the Lord Jesus Christ. I have sinned against you. And I beg your forgiveness.

God said to David 3,000 years ago, you have done this thing in secret, but I will do what I do openly before all of Israel. My sin was done in secret, and God has said to me, "I will do what I do before the whole world." Blessed be the name of the Lord.

God could never give a man, a father, a minister of the gospel, a finer son than he has given me and his mother—Donnie and my beautiful and lovely daughter-in-law, Debbie. Donnie has stood with me. I have relied upon him. And in these trying days, his mother and myself, we do not know what we would have done without his strength, his courage, and his utter devotion to the Lord Jesus Christ. Donnie and Debbie, I have sinned against you and I beg you to forgive me.

To the Assemblies of God, which helped bring the gospel to my little beleaguered town when my family was lost without Jesus—this movement and fellowship that ... has been more instrumental in taking this gospel through the ... night of darkness to the far-flung hundreds of millions than maybe in the effort in annals of human history. Its leadership has been compassionate and kind and considerate and long-suffering toward me without exception, but never for one moment condoning sin, both on the national level and this esteemed district level. But to its thousands and thousands of pastors that are godly, that uphold the standard of righteousness, its evangelists that are heralds and criers of redemption, its missionaries on the front lines

... holding back the path of hell—I have sinned against you and I have brought disgrace and humiliation and embarrassment upon you. I beg your forgiveness.

This church [Family Worship Center], this ministry, this Bible college [Jimmy Swaggart Bible College], these professors, this choir, these musicians, these singers that have stood with me on a thousand crusade platforms around the world, that have labored unstintedly [sic] and tirelessly to lift up that great name of Jesus Christ, to tell the weary that He is rest, and the sin-cursed that he, Jesus, is victory, my associates—and no evangelist ever had a greater group of men and women, given by the hand of God—have stood with me unstintedly [sic], unflaggingly. I have sinned against you. I have brought shame and embarrassment to you. I beg your forgiveness.

To my fellow television ministers and evangelists, you that are already bearing an almost unbearable load, to continue to say and tell the great story of Jesus' love, I have made your load heavier and I have hurt you. Please forgive me for sinning against you.

And to the hundreds of millions that I have stood before in over a hundred countries of the world, and I've looked into the cameras and so many of you with a heart of loneliness, needing help, have reached out to the minister of the gospel as a beacon of light. You that are nameless—most I will never be able to see except by faith. I have sinned against you. I beg you to forgive me.

And most of all, to my Lord and my Savior, my Redeemer, the One whom I have served and I love and I worship. I bow at His feet, who has saved me and washed me and cleansed me. I have sinned against You, my Lord. And I would ask that Your precious blood would wash and cleanse every stain, until it is in the seas of God's forgetfulness, never to be remembered against me anymore.

I say unto you that watch me today, through His mercy, His grace and His love, the sin of which I speak is not a present sin; it is a past sin. I know that so many would ask why, why? I have asked myself that 10,000 times through 10,000 tears. Maybe Jimmy Swaggart has tried to live his entire life as though he were not human. And I have thought that with the Lord, knowing He is omnipotent and omniscient, that there was nothing I could not do—and I emphasize with His help and guidance. And I think this is the reason (in my limited knowledge) that I did not find the victory I sought because I did not seek the help of my brothers and my sisters in the Lord. I have had to come to the realization that this gospel is flawless even though it is ministered at times by flawed men. If I had sought the help of those that loved me, with their added strength, I look back now and know that victory would have been mine. They have given me strength along with the compassion of our Savior in these last few days that I have needed for a long, long time.

Many ask, as I close, this: will the ministry continue? Yes, the ministry will continue. Under the guidance, leadership and directives (as best we know how and can) of the Louisiana District of the Assemblies of God, we will continue to take this gospel of Jesus Christ all over the world. I step out of this pulpit at the moment for an indeterminate period of time and we will leave that in the hands of the Lord. The Bible college of these young men and young ladies whom I have tried to set a standard for and have miserably failed, its most esteemed president,

Ray Tresk—I, too, beg you, the future pastors, evangelists and missionaries, to forgive me. But this Bible college will continue.

I close this today with the words of another man that lived 3,000 years ago—and I started to say who committed sin that was worse than mine, but I take that back. And if the Holy Spirit will allow me to borrow His words, I will review that which is as real now as when it was penned in Jerusalem:

"Have mercy upon me, O God. According to thy loving kindness; according unto the multitude of thy tender mercies, blot out my transgressions. Wash me thoroughly from mine iniquity, and cleanse me from my sin. For I acknowledge my transgressions; and my sin is ever before me. Against thee, thee only, have I sinned and done this evil in thy sight, that thou mightest be justified when thou speakest, and be clear when thou judgest. Behold, I was shapen in iniquity; and in sin did my mother conceive me. Behold, thou desireth truth in the inward parts; and in the hidden parts thou shalt make me to know wisdom. Purge me with hyssop, and I shall be clean; wash me, and I shall be whiter than snow. Make me to hear joy and gladness; that the bones which thou hast broken my rejoice. Hide thy face from my sins, and blot out all mine iniquities. Create in me a clean heart, O God; and renew a right spirit within me. Cast me not away from thy presence; and take not thy holy spirit from me. Restore unto me the joy of thy salvation; and uphold me with thy free spirit. Then will I teach transgressors thy ways; and sinners shall be converted unto thee. Deliver me from blood guiltiness, O God, thou God of my salvation: and my tongue shall sing aloud of thy righteousness. O Lord, open thou my lips; and my mouth shall shew forth thy praise. For thou desireth not sacrifice; else would I give it; thou delightest not in a broken spirit; a broken and a contrite heart, O God, thou wilt not despise. Do good in thy good pleasure unto Zion; build thou the walls of Jerusalem. Then shalt thou be pleased with the sacrifices of righteousness, with burnt offering and with whole burnt offering; then shall they offer bullocks upon thine altar." [Psalm 51]

Thank you. Thank you and God bless you.'

The Assemblies of God ministry never recovered from Jimmy Swaggart's disclosure and by 1991 the Church had lost 80 per cent of its audience and was $4.5 million in debt. For Swaggart's part, he kept on preaching but was forced to deny allegations that he had an extra-marital affair with a woman who later sold her story to Penthouse magazine. Just when things couldn't get any tackier he was arrested in Indio, California with a prostitute in his car. A decade later he was still preaching—denouncing the Prophet Muhammad and the country's homosexual community amongst other things—but was anybody listening?

Somehow, televangelists would never be credible again.

Jesse Jackson
'Keep Hope Alive'

Atlanta, Georgia, 19 July, 1988

Jesse Jackson addresses a rally in 1988.

The first African American presidential candidate in US history to be a major political force, Jesse Louis Jackson was born in 1941 in Greenville, South Carolina, the son of a 17-year-old, unmarried high school student. When his mother married Charles Jackson, Jesse took his stepfather's surname and later won a football scholarship to the University of Illinois. Jackson returned to the South during his first year of University and transferred to North Carolina Agricultural and Technical College and received a BA in Sociology. He then accepted a Rockefeller grant to attend the Chicago Theological Seminary where he planned to train as a Baptist minister. There Jackson became involved in the Civil Rights movement and although he was later ordained a minister, he left CTS in 1966 without finishing his course work.

Jackson joined Martin Luther King Jnr and the Southern Christian Leadership Conference in 1965 and was directly involved in the 'Chicago Freedom' movement the following year. In April 1968 Jackson was with King in Alabama when the Civil Rights leader was assassinated. He later resigned from the SCLC to found his own organisation, People United to Save Humanity (PUSH) in 1971.

Jackson's bold ambition, and his alleged misrepresentation of his role in the Civil Rights movement, put him offside with many black leaders but he continually proved himself to be an articulate and charismatic speaker on such as issues as education, welfare support and political representation.

In 1984 Jackson launched his first campaign for the Democratic presidential nomination and performed well in several southern states including Alabama, Georgia, Louisiana and Florida, but not enough to secure the nomination. Four years later his political campaign was better co-ordinated and his 'Rainbow Coalition' attracted widespread support from urban blacks, feminists and other minorities.

Although Michael Dukakis was the party's eventual choice as presidential nominee, Jackson's 19 July speech saw him accept the nomination for Vice-President:

❛I'm often asked, "Jesse, why do you take on these tough issues? They're not very ... political. We can't win that way."

If an issue is morally right, it will eventually be political. It may be political and never be right. Fannie Lou Hamer didn't have the most votes in Atlantic City, but her principles have outlasted every delegate who voted to lock her out. Rosa Parks did not have the most votes, but she was morally right. Dr King didn't have the most votes about the Vietnam War, but he

'And then, for our children, young America, hold your head high now. We can win. We must not lose you to drugs and violence, premature pregnancy, suicide, cynicism, pessimism and despair. We can win.'

was morally right. If we're principled first, our politics will fall in place.

"Jesse, why did you take these big bold initiatives?" A poem by an unknown author went something like this: We mastered the air, we've conquered the sea, and annihilated distance and prolonged life, we were not wise enough to live on this earth without war and without hate.

As for Jesse Jackson, I'm tired of sailing my little boat, far inside the harbor bar. I want to go out where the big ships float, out on the deep where the great ones are. And should my frail craft prove too slight, the waves that sweep those billows o'er, I'd rather go down in a stirring fight than drown to death in the sheltered shore. We've got to go out, my friends, where the big boats are.

And then, for our children, young America, hold your head high now. We can win. We must not lose you to drugs and violence, premature pregnancy, suicide, cynicism, pessimism and despair. We can win.

Wherever you are tonight, I challenge you to hope and to dream. Don't submerge your dreams. Exercise above all else, even on drugs, dream of the day you're drug-free. Even in the gutter, dream of the day that you'll be upon your feet again. You must never stop dreaming. Face reality, yes. But don't stop with the way things are; dream of things as they ought to be. Dream. Face pain, but love, hope, faith, and dreams will help you rise above the pain.

Use hope and imagination as weapons of survival and progress, but you keep on dreaming, young America. Dream of peace. Peace is rational and reasonable. War is irrational in this age and unwinnable.

Dream of teachers who teach for life and not for living. Dream of doctors who are concerned more about public health than private wealth. Dream of lawyers more concerned about justice than a judgeship. Dream of preachers who are concerned more about prophecy than profiteering. Dream on the high road of sound values. And in America, as we go forth to September, October and November and then beyond, America must never surrender to a high moral challenge.

Do not surrender to drugs. The best drug policy is a no first use. Don't surrender with needles and cynicism. Let's have no first use on the one hand, or clinics on the other. Never surrender, young America.

Go forward. America must never surrender to malnutrition. We can feed the hungry and clothe the naked. We must never surrender. We must go forward. We must never surrender to illiteracy. Invest in our children. Never surrender; and go forward.

We must never surrender to inequality. Women cannot compromise ERA [the Equal Rights Amendment] or comparable worth. Women are making 60 cents on the dollar to what a man makes. Women cannot buy milk cheaper. Women deserve to get paid for the work that you do.

It's right and it's fair. Don't surrender, my friends. Those who have AIDS tonight, you deserve our compassion. Even with AIDS you must not surrender in your wheelchairs. I see you sitting here tonight in those wheelchairs. I've starved with you. I've reached out to you across our nation. Don't you give up. I know it's tough sometimes. People look down on you. It took you a little more effort to get here tonight.

And no one should look down on you, but sometimes mean people do. The only justification we have for looking down on someone is that we're going to stop and pick them up. But even in your wheelchairs, don't you give up. We cannot forget fifty years ago when our backs were against the wall, [Franklin D.] Roosevelt was in a wheelchair. I would rather have Roosevelt in a wheelchair than Reagan and [George] Bush on a horse. Don't you surrender and don't give up.

Don't surrender and don't give up. Why can I challenge you this way? "Jesse Jackson, you don't understand my situation. You be on television. You don't understand. I see you with the big people. You don't understand my situation." I understand. You're seeing me on TV but you don't know the me that makes me, me. They wonder why does Jesse run, because they see me running for the White House. They don't see the house I'm running from.

I have a story. I wasn't always on television. Writers were not always outside my door. When I was born late one afternoon, October 8th, in Greenville, SC, no writers asked my mother her name. Nobody chose to write down her address. My mama was not supposed to make it. And I was not supposed to make it. You see, I was born to a teenage mother who was born to a teenage mother.

I understand. I know abandonment and people being mean to you, and saying you're nothing and nobody, and can never be anything. I understand. Jesse Jackson is my third name. I'm adopted. When I had no name, my grandmother gave me her name. My name was Jesse Burns until I was twelve. So I wouldn't have a blank space, she gave me a name to hold me over. I understand when nobody knows your name. I understand when you have no name. I understand.

I wasn't born in the hospital—Mama didn't have insurance. I was born in the bed at the house. I really do understand. Born in a three-room house, bathroom in the backyard, slop jar by the bed, no hot and cold running water. I understand. Wallpaper used for decoration—No. For a windbreaker. I understand. I'm a working person's person, that's why I understand you whether you're black or white.

I understand work. I was not born with a silver spoon in my mouth. I had a shovel programmed for my hand. My mother, a working woman. So many days she went to work with runs in her stockings. She knew better, but she wore runs in her stockings so that my brother and I could have matching socks and not be laughed at at school.

I understand. At three o'clock on Thanksgiving Day we couldn't eat turkey because mama was preparing someone else's turkey at three o'clock. We had to play football to entertain ourselves and then around six o'clock she would get off the Alta Vista bus when we would bring up the

'I wasn't born in the hospital [but] in a three-room house, bathroom in the backyard, slop jar by the bed, no hot and cold running water. I understand.'

leftovers and eat our turkey—leftovers, the carcass, the cranberries around eight o'clock at night. I really do understand.

'Hold your head high, stick your chest out. You can make it.'

Every one of these funny labels they put on you, those of you who are watching this broadcast tonight in the projects, on the corners, I understand. Call you outcast, low down, you can't make it, you're nothing, you're from nobody, subclass, underclass—when you see Jesse Jackson, when my name goes in nomination, your name goes in nomination.

I was born in the slum, but the slum was not born in me. And it wasn't born in you, and you can make it. Wherever you are tonight you can make it. Hold your head high, stick your chest out. You can make it. It gets dark sometimes, but the morning comes. Don't you surrender. Suffering breeds character. Character breeds faith. In the end faith will not disappoint.

You must not surrender. You may or may not get there, but just know that you're qualified and you hold on and hold out. We must never surrender. America will get better and better. Keep hope alive. Keep hope alive. Keep hope alive. On tomorrow night and beyond, keep hope alive. I love you very much. I love you very much.'

The 1988 Presidential race was won by Republican candidate George Bush and Jackson moved from Chicago to Washington DC where he was elected the District of Columbia's 'statehood senator'—a position created to press for the district's statehood. During the 1980s and 1990s Jackson often acted as international peace negotiator and although there were some important successes, he drew criticism for embracing the PLO, Fidel Castro and the Marxist Sandinista government of Nicaragua (his description of New York as 'Hymie Town' was another error of judgment). In 2000 he finally graduated from the Chicago Theological Seminary.

Ryan White

'I Have AIDS'

Testimony before the President's Commission on AIDS, Washington DC, 1988.

Ryan White handles the press in 1988.

In the early 1980s, cases of a retrovirus that infected the cells of the human immune system were first diagnosed in the United States and Europe (although it was later thought the disease had its origins in Africa). Human Immunodeficiency Virus, which was researched by scientists on both sides of the Atlantic, was not officially named until 1986. Although it was known that HIV was the underlying cause of AIDS (Acquired Immune Deficiency Syndrome) the causes, methods of transmission and suitable treatment was originally the source of much controversy. Originally viewed as a disease that only affected the homosexual community, it soon became clear that HIV/AIDS was indiscriminate in choosing its victims and was transferable through penetrative sexual contact, blood transfusion, the sharing of contaminated needles and between mother and infant during pregnancy, childbirth and breast-feeding.

Kokomo, Indiana schoolboy Ryan White contacted HIV/AIDS in 1984 when he was given a blood transfusion during an operation to remove part of his lung. A haemophiliac since birth, the 13-year-old was unknowingly susceptible to contracting the disease and was given only six months to live. However, despite the fact that he was determined to live his life as normally as possible, Ryan White and his family came up against systematic discrimination and small-town prejudice.

His school tried to keep him from attending and after several legal battles, the White family settled with the school to use separate restrooms and disposable servery materials in the cafeteria. Even then, the discrimination did not stop; ignorance and misunderstanding about Ryan's condition led the White family to move from Kokomo, Indiana to Cicero, Indiana.

In 1988, as the world gradually began to understand the causes and effects—especially the social effects—of contracting HIV/AIDS, Ryan White addressed the President's Commission on AIDS, Washington DC. White's story did more to combat AIDS-related discrimination and shamed the Reagan government to become more proactive in its research funding and education programs than any other person.

❛Thank You, Commissioners:

My name is Ryan White. I am sixteen years old. I have haemophilia, and I have AIDS.

When I was three days old, the doctors told my parents I was a severe haemophiliac, meaning my blood does not clot. Lucky for me, there was a product just approved by the Food and Drug Administration. It was called Factor VIII, which contains the clotting agent found in blood.

While I was growing up, I had many bleeds or haemorrhages in my joints which make it very painful. Twice a week I would receive injections or IVs of Factor VIII which clotted the blood and then broke it down. A bleed occurs from a broken blood vessel or vein. The blood then had nowhere to go so it would swell up in a joint. You could compare it to trying to pour a quart of milk into a pint-sized container of milk.

The first five to six years of my life were spent in and out of the hospital. All in all I led a pretty normal life. Most recently my battle has been against AIDS and the discrimination surrounding it. On December 17, 1984, I had surgery to remove two inches of my left lung due to pneumonia. After two hours of surgery the doctors told my mother I had AIDS. I contracted AIDS through my Factor VIII which is made from blood. When I came out of surgery, I was on a respirator and had a tube in my left lung. I spent Christmas and the next thirty days in the hospital. A lot of my time was spent searching, thinking and planning my life.

I came face to face with death at thirteen years old. I was diagnosed with AIDS: a killer. Doctors told me I'm not contagious. Given six months to live, and being the fighter that I am, I set high goals for myself. It was my decision to live a normal life, go to school, be with my friends, and enjoying day to day activities. It was not going to be easy.

The school I was going to said they had no guidelines for a person with AIDS. The school board, my teachers, and my principal voted to keep me out of the classroom even after the guidelines were set by the I.S.B.H., for fear of someone getting AIDS from me by casual contact. Rumors of sneezing, kissing, tears, sweat, and saliva spreading AIDS caused people to panic.

We began a series of court battles for nine months, while I was attending classes by telephone. Eventually, I won the right to attend school, but the prejudice was still there. Listening to medical facts was not enough. People wanted one hundred percent guarantees. There are no one hundred percent guarantees in life, but concessions were made by Mom and me to help ease the fear. We decided to meet them halfway:

- Separate restrooms
- No gym
- Separate drinking fountains
- Disposable eating utensils and trays

Even though we knew AIDS was not spread through casual contact. Nevertheless, parents of twenty students started their own school. They were still not convinced. Because of the lack of education on AIDS, discrimination, fear, panic, and lies surrounded me:

'I was labelled a troublemaker, my mom an unfit mother, and I was not welcome anywhere. People would get up and leave so they would not have to sit anywhere near me. Even at church, people would not shake my hand.'

RYAN WHITE

319

- I became the target of Ryan White jokes
- Lies about me biting people
- Spitting on vegetables and cookies
- Urinating on bathroom walls
- Some restaurants threw away my dishes
- My school locker was vandalized inside and folders were marked FAG and other obscenities.

'AIDS can destroy a family if you let it, but luckily for my sister and me, Mom taught us to keep going. Don't give up, be proud of who you are, and never feel sorry for yourself.'

I was labelled a troublemaker, my mom an unfit mother, and I was not welcome anywhere. People would get up and leave so they would not have to sit anywhere near me. Even at church, people would not shake my hand.

This brought on the news media, TV crews, interviews, and numerous public appearances. I became known as the AIDS boy. I received thousands of letters of support from all around the world, all because I wanted to go to school. Mayor Koch, of New York, was the first public figure to give me support. Entertainers, athletes, and stars started giving me support. I met some of the greatest like Elton John, Greg Louganis, Max Headroom, Alyssa Milano (my teen idol), Lyndon King (Los Angeles Raiders), and Charlie Sheen. All of these plus many more became my friends, but I had very few friends at school. How could these people in the public eye not be afraid of me, but my whole town was?

It was difficult, at times, to handle; but I tried to ignore the injustice, because I knew the people were wrong. My family and I held no hatred for those people because we realized they were victims of their own ignorance. We had great faith that with patience, understanding, and education, that my family and I could be helpful in changing their minds and attitudes around. Financial hardships were rough on us, even though Mom had a good job at G.M. The more I was sick, the more work she had to miss. Bills became impossible to pay. My sister, Andrea, was a championship roller skater who had to sacrifice too. There was no money for her lessons and travel. AIDS can destroy a family if you let it, but luckily for my sister and me, Mom taught us to keep going. Don't give up, be proud of who you are, and never feel sorry for yourself.

After two and a half years of declining health, two attacks of pneumocystis, shingles, a rare form of whooping cough, and liver problems, I faced fighting chills, fevers, coughing, tiredness, and vomiting. I was very ill and being tutored at home. The desire to move into a bigger house, to avoid living AIDS daily, and a dream to be accepted by a community and school, became possible and a reality with a movie about my life, *The Ryan White Story*.

My life is better now. At the end of the school year (1986-87), my family and I decided to move to Cicero, Indiana. We did a lot of hoping and praying that the community would welcome us, and they did. For the first time in three years, we feel we have a home, a supportive school, and lots of friends. The communities of Cicero, Atlanta, Arcadia, and Noblesville,

Indiana, are now what we call "home." I'm feeling great. I am a normal happy teenager again. I have a learner's permit. I attend sports functions and dances. My studies are important to me. I made the honor role just recently, with 2 As and 2 Bs. I'm just one of the kids, and all because the students at Hamilton Heights High School listened to the facts, educated their parents and themselves, and believed in me.

I believe in myself as I look forward to graduating from Hamilton Heights High School in 1991.

Hamilton Heights High School is proof that AIDS education in schools works.'

'I believe in myself as I look forward to graduating from Hamilton Heights High School in 1991. Hamilton Heights High School is proof that AIDS education in schools works.'

Ryan White's story focused national and international attention on HIV/AIDS. Congress later passed the $1.8 billion Ryan White Comprehensive AIDS Resources Emergency (CARE) Act that sought to address the unmet health needs of people living with HIV by funding primary health care and support services. Ryan White passed away from the effects of his disease on April 8 1990, aged 18, but his short life made an extraordinary impact.

The Dawn of
Enlightenment
1990-1999

Mikhail Gorbachev

'Dissolving the Soviet Union'

Televised address, 25 December 1991.

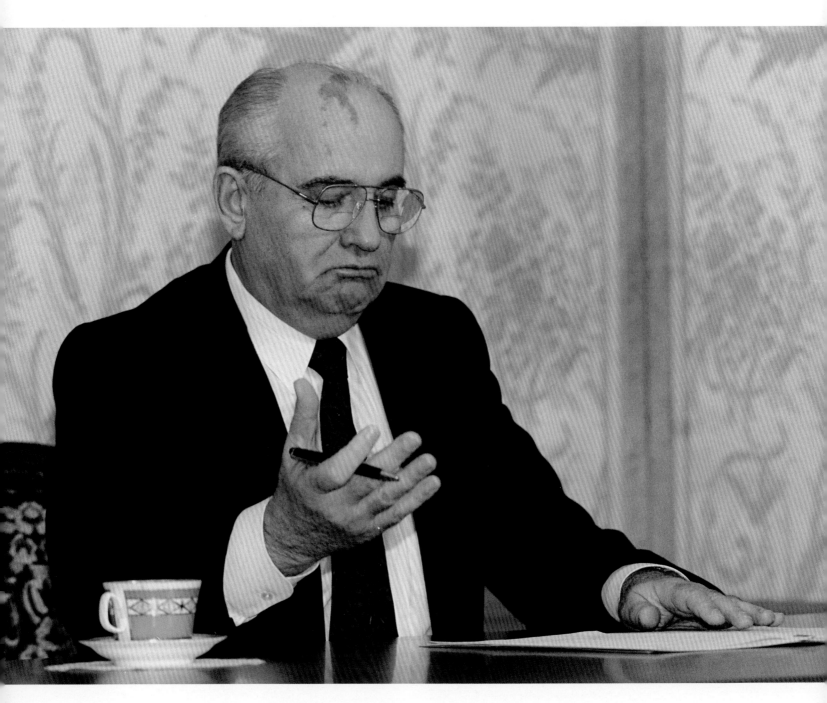

Mikhail Gorbachev reads his resignation statement in 1991.

Mikhail Sergeyevich Gorbachev was born in Privolyne, Russia in 1931. A member of the Communist Party since 1952, he rose through the ranks of the Party Central Committee and upon the death of Konstantin Chernenko in 1985, became party general secretary of the Central Committee. In the 1980s Gorbachev undertook two wide-reaching programs—openness (glasnost) and reconstruction (perestroika)—to modernise the Soviet Union and its failing economy. In 1988 he became chairman of the Presidium of the Supreme Soviet and two years later was named the first—and last—executive president of the USSR.

Paradoxically, Gorbachev's reforms brought about the end of the Communist regime that he sought to maintain. Gorbachev's reforms created greater domestic freedoms, reduced military spending and promoted a healthier relationship with the West. In 1989 Soviet troops withdrew from Afghanistan, the Communist Party voted to end 'one party rule' and Soviet republics threatened to leave the Union to govern themselves.

One of the most powerful undertakings Gorbachev was involved in was to publicly 'reinstate' the reputations of thousands of citizens jailed and executed under the Stalin regime in the 1930s and 1940s. This had a strong effect on the nation's consciousness and how the country viewed itself nationally.

In August 1991 Gorbachev survived an attempted coup in Moscow—rescued by newly elected Russian Federative President Boris Yelstsin who organised the seizure of government buildings in Moscow and then banned the Communist Party. This shift in the political and social mood of the country led to the establishment of the Commonwealth of Independent States.

On (Western Christendom's) Christmas Day, 1991, Mikhail Gorbachev resigned as president of the Union of Soviet Socialist Republics. This was the final act in an ironically peaceful dissolution of a communist (socialist) nation that had been borne in so much bloodshed and maintained by fear and oppression since the October Revolution in 1917.

❡ Dear compatriots, fellow citizens, as a result of the newly formed situation, creation of the Commonwealth of Independent States, I cease my activities in the post of the USSR president. I am taking this decision out of considerations based on principle. I have firmly stood for independence, self-rule of nations, for the sovereignty of the republics, but at the same time for preservation of the union state, the unity of the country.

Events went a different way. The policy prevailed of dismembering this country and disuniting the state, with which I cannot agree. And after the Alma-Ata meeting and the decisions

MIKHAIL GORBACHEV

325

taken there, my position on this matter has not changed. Besides, I am convinced that decisions of such scale should have been taken on the basis of a popular expression of will.

Yet, I will continue to do everything in my power so that agreements signed there should lead to real accord in the society, (and) facilitate the escape from the crisis and the reform process. Addressing you for the last time in the capacity of president of the USSR, I consider it necessary to express my evaluation of the road we have travelled since 1985, especially as there are a lot of contradictory, superficial and subjective judgments on that matter.

> 'The society was suffocating … doomed to serve ideology and bear the terrible burden of the arms race. We could not go on living like that. Everything had to be changed radically.'

Fate had it that when I found myself at the head of the state it was already clear that all was not well in the country. There is plenty of everything: land, oil and gas, other natural riches, and God gave us lots of intelligence and talent, yet we lived much worse than developed countries and keep falling behind them more and more.

The reason could already be seen: The society was suffocating in the vice of the command-bureaucratic system, doomed to serve ideology and bear the terrible burden of the arms race. It had reached the limit of its possibilities. All attempts at partial reform, and there had been many, had suffered defeat, one after another. The country was losing perspective. We could not go on living like that. Everything had to be changed radically.

The process of renovating the country and radical changes in the world turned out to be far more complicated than could be expected. However, what has been done ought to be given its due. This society acquired freedom, liberated itself politically and spiritually, and this is the foremost achievement which we have not yet understood completely, because we have not learned to use freedom.

However, work of historic significance has been accomplished. The totalitarian system which deprived the country of an opportunity to become successful and prosperous long ago has been eliminated. A breakthrough has been achieved on the way to democratic changes. Free elections, freedom of the press, religious freedoms, representative organs of power, a multiparty (system) became a reality; human rights are recognized as the supreme principle.

The movement to a diverse economy has started, equality of all forms of property is becoming established, people who work on the land are coming to life again in the framework of land reform, farmers have appeared, millions of acres of land are being given over to people who live in the countryside and in towns.

Economic freedom of the producer has been legalized, and entrepreneurship, shareholding, privatization are gaining momentum. In turning the economy toward a market, it is important to remember that all this is done for the sake of the individual. At this difficult time, all should be done for his social protection, especially for senior citizens and children.

We live in a new world. The Cold War has ended, the arms race has stopped, as has the insane militarization which mutilated our economy, public psyche and morals. The threat of a world war has been removed. Once again I want to stress that on my part everything was done during the transition period to preserve reliable control of the nuclear weapons.

We opened ourselves to the world, gave up interference into other people's affairs, the use of troops beyond the borders of the country, and trust, solidarity and respect came in response.

The nations and peoples of this country gained real freedom to choose the way of their self-determination. The search for a democratic reformation of the multinational state brought us to the threshold of concluding a new Union Treaty. All these changes demanded immense strain. They were carried out with sharp struggle, with growing resistance from the old, the obsolete forces.

The old system collapsed before the new one had time to begin working, and the crisis in the society became even more acute.

'Economic freedom of the producer has been legalized, and entrepreneurship, shareholding, privatization are gaining momentum.'

The August coup brought the general crisis to its ultimate limit. The most damaging thing about this crisis is the break-up of the statehood. And today I am worried by our people's loss of the citizenship of a great country. The consequences may turn out to be very hard for everyone.

I am leaving my post with apprehension, but also with hope, with faith in you, your wisdom and force of spirit. We are the heirs of a great civilization, and its rebirth into a new, modern and dignified life now depends on one and all.

Some mistakes could surely have been avoided, many things could have been done better, but I am convinced that sooner or later our common efforts will bear fruit, our nations will live in a prosperous and democratic society.

I wish all the best to all of you.'

The following day the Russian government took over the offices of the former USSR. Gorbachev was now politically dead—the former leader of a system of government that no longer existed. Slow to call for democratic elections, he had failed to see the threat from hardline communists within his own party and underestimated the power of the truth to erode the credibility—from both outside and within the Soviet Union—of a discredited regime.

MIKHAIL GORBACHEV

Paul Keating
'Redfern Speech'

Redfern Park, Sydney, 10 December 1992.

Paul Keating in 1993.

In a volatile career in which he was never afraid to use a sharp-tongue to make his political point, Paul Keating deposed long-serving Australian Prime Minister Bob Hawke in December 1991 after spending eight years as his deputy. Keating's tenure as Australian Prime Minister (1991-96) was marked by his determination to put Australia's trade future in the Asian-Pacific region, the need for Aboriginal reconciliation and the creation of an Australian republic (Keating once earned the ire of the British press when he placed his hand on Queen Elizabeth II's back during a Royal tour).

During Keating's first year as Prime Minsiter, the 'Mabo decision' in the High Court decreed that the notion of 'terra nullius' (literally, 'nobody's land'), that had underpinned the British colonialists ownership of Australia, was invalid.

Eddie Koiki Mabo (1936-1992) was a Torres Strait Islander who had lived on Murray Island off the coast of North Queensland. Although regulated by the Queensland government, in Mabo's mind the island had always belonged to his ancestors who had passed it down to him. Although Eddie Mabo died of cancer in January 1992, his ten-year challenge in the courts and battle for formal recognition that the indigenous people of the continent indeed held 'native title' of the land, was ratified by the High Court five months later.

Prime Minister Paul Keating went to Redfern Park in Sydney on 10 December 1992, the centre of Sydney's Aboriginal community and the site of the first piece of land formally handed back to the Aboriginals by Labor Prime Minister Gough Whitlam. There he gave the speech which was the Australian launch of the International Year for the World's Indigenous People.

‘Ladies and gentlemen,

I am very pleased to be here today at the launch of Australia's celebration of the 1993 International Year of the World's Indigenous People.

It will be a year of great significance for Australia.

It comes at a time when we have committed ourselves to succeeding in the test which so far we have always failed.

Because, in truth, we cannot confidently say that we have succeeded as we would like to have succeeded if we have not managed to extend opportunity and care, dignity and hope to the indigenous people of Australia—the Aboriginal and Torres Strait Island people.

This is a fundamental test of our social goals and our national will: our ability to say to ourselves and the rest of the world that Australia is a first rate social democracy, that we are what

PAUL KEATING

329

we should be—truly the land of the fair go and the better chance. There is no more basic test of how seriously we mean these things.

It is a test of our self-knowledge. Of how well we know the land we live in. How well we know our history. How well we recognise the fact that, complex as our contemporary identity is, it cannot be separated from Aboriginal Australia. How well we know what Aboriginal Australians know about Australia.

Redfern is a good place to contemplate these things.

'We smashed the traditional way of life. We brought the disasters. The alcohol. We committed the murders. We took the children from their mothers. It was our ignorance and our prejudice.'

Just a mile or two from the place where the first European settlers landed, in too many ways it tells us that their failure to bring much more than devastation and demoralisation to Aboriginal Australia continues to be our failure.

More I think than most Australians recognise, the plight of Aboriginal Australians affects us all. In Redfern it might be tempting to think that the reality Aboriginal Australians face is somehow contained here, and that the rest of us are insulated from it. But of course, while all the dilemmas may exist here, they are far from contained. We know the same dilemmas and more are faced all over Australia.

This is perhaps the point of this Year of the World's Indigenous People: to bring the dispossessed out of the shadows, to recognise that they are part of us, and that we cannot give indigenous Australians up without giving up many of our own most deeply held values, much of our own identity—and our own humanity.

Nowhere in the world, I would venture, is the message more stark than in Australia.

We simply cannot sweep injustice aside. Even if our own conscience allowed us to, I am sure, that in due course, the world and the people of our region would not. There should be no mistake about this—our success in resolving these issues will have a significant bearing on our standing in the world.

However intractable the problems may seem, we cannot resign ourselves to failure—any more than we can hide behind the contemporary version of Social Darwinism which says that to reach back for the poor and dispossessed is to risk being dragged down.

That seems to me not only morally indefensible, but bad history.

We non-Aboriginal Australians should perhaps remind ourselves that Australia once reached out for us. Didn't Australia provide opportunity and care for the dispossessed Irish? The poor of Britain? The refugees from war and famine and persecution in the countries of Europe and Asia? Isn't it reasonable to say that if we can build a prosperous and remarkably harmonious multicultural society in Australia, surely we can find just solutions to the problems which beset the first Australians—the people to whom the most injustice has been done.

And, as I say, the starting point might be to recognise that the problem starts with us non-Aboriginal Australians.

It begins, I think, with the act of recognition. Recognition that it was we who did the dispossessing. We took the traditional lands and smashed the traditional way of life. We brought the disasters. The alcohol. We committed the murders. We took the children from their mothers. We practised discrimination and exclusion. It was our ignorance and our prejudice. And our failure to imagine these things being done to us. With some noble exceptions, we failed to make the most basic human response and enter into their hearts and minds. We failed to ask—how would I feel if this were done to me?

As a consequence, we failed to see that what we were doing degraded all of us.

If we needed a reminder of this, we received it this year. The Report of the Royal Commission into Aboriginal Deaths in Custody showed with devastating clarity that the past lives on in inequality, racism and injustice in the prejudice and ignorance of non-Aboriginal Australians, and in the demoralisation and desperation, the fractured identity, of so many Aborigines and Torres Strait Islanders.

For all this, I do not believe that the Report should fill us with guilt. Down the years, there has been no shortage of guilt, but it has not produced the responses we need. Guilt is not a very constructive emotion.

I think what we need to do is open our hearts a bit.

All of us.

Perhaps when we recognise what we have in common we will see the things which must be done—the practical things.

There is something of this in the creation of the Council for Aboriginal Reconciliation. The council's mission is to forge a new partnership built on justice and equity and an appreciation of the heritage of Australia's indigenous people. In the abstract those terms are meaningless. We have to give meaning to 'justice' and 'equity'—and, as I have said several times this year, we will only give them meaning when we commit ourselves to achieving concrete results.

If we improve the living conditions in one town, they will improve in another. And another. If we raise the standard of health by 20 per cent one year, it will be raised more the next. If we open one door others will follow.

When we see improvement, when we see more dignity, more confidence, more happiness—we will know we are going to win. We need these practical building blocks of change.

The Mabo judgment should be seen as one of these. By doing away with the bizarre conceit that this continent had no owners prior to the settlement of Europeans, Mabo establishes a fundamental truth and lays the basis for justice. It will be much easier to work from that basis than has ever been the case in the past.

For this reason alone we should ignore the isolated outbreaks of hysteria and hostility of the past few months. Mabo is an historic decision—we can make it an historic turning point, the basis of a new relationship between indigenous and non-Aboriginal Australians.

The message should be that there is nothing to fear or to lose in the recognition of historical truth, or the extension of social justice, or the deepening of Australian social democracy to include indigenous Australians.

PAUL KEATING

There is everything to gain.

Even the unhappy past speaks for this. Where Aboriginal Australians have been included in the life of Australia they have made remarkable contributions. Economic contributions, particularly in the pastoral and agricultural industry. They are there in the frontier and exploration history of Australia. They are there in sport to an extraordinary degree. In literature and art and music.

In all these things they have shaped our knowledge of this continent and of ourselves. They have shaped our identity. They are there in the Australian legend. We should never forget—they helped build this nation. And if we have a sense of justice, as well as common sense, we will forge a new partnership.

As I said, it might help us if we non-Aboriginal Australians imagined ourselves dispossessed of land we have lived on for 50 000 years —and then imagined ourselves told that it had never been ours.

'Surely we can find just solutions to the problems which beset the first Australians—the people to whom the most injustice has been done. The starting point might be to recognise that the problem starts with us non-Aboriginal Australians.'

Imagine if ours was the oldest culture in the world and we were told that it was worthless. Imagine if we had resisted this settlement, suffered and died in the defence of our land, and then were told in history books that we had given up without a fight. Imagine if non-Aboriginal Australians had served their country in peace and war and were then ignored in history books. Imagine if our feats on sporting fields had inspired admiration and patriotism and yet did nothing to diminish prejudice. Imagine if our spiritual life was denied and ridiculed.

Imagine if we had suffered the injustice and then were blamed for it.

It seems to me that if we can imagine the injustice then we can imagine its opposite. And we can have justice.

I say that for two reasons: I say it because I believe that the great things about Australian social democracy reflect a fundamental belief in justice. And I say it because in so many other areas we have proved our capacity over the years to go on extending the realism of participating, opportunity and care.

Just as Australian living in the relatively narrow and insular Australia of the 1960s imagined a culturally diverse, worldly and open Australia, and in a generation turned the idea into reality, so we can turn the goals of reconciliation into reality.

There are very good signs that the process has begun. The creation of the Reconciliation Council is evidence itself. The establishment of the ATSIC —the Aboriginal and Torres Strait Islander Commission—is also evidence. The Council is the product of imagination and goodwill. ATSIC emerges from the vision of indigenous self-determination and self-management. The vision has already become the reality of almost 800 elected Aboriginal Regional Councillors and Commissioners determining priorities and developing their own programs.

All over Australia, Aboriginal and Torres Strait Islander communities are taking charge of their own lives. And assistance with the problems which chronically beset them is at last being made available in ways developed by the communities themselves. If these things offer hope, so does the fact that this generation of Australians is better informed about Aboriginal culture and achievement, and about the injustice that has been done, than any generation before.

We are beginning to more generally appreciate the depth and the diversity of Aboriginal and Torres Strait Islander cultures. From their music and art and dance we are beginning to recognise how much richer our national life and identity will be for the participation of Aboriginals and Torres Strait Islanders. We are beginning to learn what the indigenous people have known for many thousands of years—how to live with our physical environment.

Ever so gradually we are learning how to see Australia through Aboriginal eyes, beginning to recognise the wisdom contained in their epic story.

I think we are beginning to see how much we owe the indigenous Australians and how much we have lost by living so apart.

I said we non-indigenous Australians should try to imagine the Aboriginal view.

It can't be too hard. Someone imagined this event today, and it is now a marvellous reality and a great reason for hope.

There is one thing today we cannot imagine. We cannot imagine that the descendants of people whose genius and resilience maintained a culture here through 50 000 years or more, through cataclysmic changes to the climate and environment, and who then survived two centuries of dispossession and abuse, will be denied their place in the modern Australian nation.

We cannot imagine that.

We cannot imagine that we will fail.

And with the spirit that is here today I am confident that we won't.

I am confident that we will succeed in this decade.

Thank you.'

Queen Elizabeth II
'Annus Horribilis'

The Guildhall, London, 24 November 1992.

Queen Elizabeth II speaks at a State Dinner in 1991.

Queen Elizabeth II of England, the eldest daughter of King George VI, was born in 1926. Elizabeth was proclaimed Queen of England upon the death of her father on 6 February 1952 and crowned the following year, on 2 June 1953, in Westminster Abbey.

The 27-year-old monarch had already married Philip Mountbatten (her fourth cousin and Prince of Greece) in 1947 and had two of her four children—Charles (in 1948), Anne (1950), Andrew (1960), and Edward (1964). Hugely popular with her post-war Commonwealth subjects, she nevertheless oversaw the decline of the British Empire as India, Pakistan, Burma (Myanmar), Malaysia, Pacific Island, West Indian and African colonies successfully sought independence.

As Elizabeth and Philip's children grew to adulthood the public behaviour of the 'royals' and their spouses exposed those human foibles common to the rest of society—jealousy, pettiness and infidelity.

Anne, the Princess Royal, divorced her husband Mark Phillips; Prince Andrew separated from his wife Sarah Ferguson, and the marriage of the British heir, Prince Charles, and his immensely popular and beautiful wife, Diana, Princess of Wales, publicly disintegrated.

On 20 November, 1992, the Queen's primary residence, Windsor Castle, was severely damaged by fire. Rather than provoking a wave of sympathy, news that the Royal Family would not have to pay for the restoration—the British taxpayer would foot the bill—drew stinging criticism.

Celebrating the fortieth year of her reign in 1992, many started to question the need for a monarchy which lived in great pomp and spectacle but paid not a shilling in tax. When Queen Elizabeth appeared at a City of London luncheon, she delivered a speech that permeated the façade of her position and touched the hearts of her subjects.

'Nineteen ninety-two is not a year I shall look back on with undiluted pleasure. In the words of one of my more sympathetic correspondents, it has turned out to be an 'Annus Horribilis'.

I suspect that I am not alone in thinking it so. Indeed, I suspect that there are very few people or institutions unaffected by these last months of worldwide turmoil and uncertainty. This generosity and wholehearted kindness of the Corporation of the City to Prince Philip and me would be welcome at any time, but at this particular moment, in the aftermath of Friday's tragic fire at Windsor, it is especially so. And, after this last weekend, we appreciate all the more what has been set before us today. Years of experience, however, have made us a bit more canny than the lady, less well-versed than us in the splendours of City hospitality, who, when she was offered a balloon glass for her brandy, asked for "only half a glass, please". It is possible to have too much of a good thing. A well-meaning Bishop was obviously doing his best when he told Queen Victoria, "Ma'am, we cannot pray too often, nor too fervently, for the Royal Family." The Queen's reply was, "Too fervently, no; too often, yes."

I, like Queen Victoria, have always been a believer in that old maxim "moderation in all things". I sometimes wonder how future generations will judge the events of this tumultuous year. I dare say that history will take a slightly more moderate view than that of some contemporary commentators. Distance is well known to lend enchantment, even to the less attractive views. After all, it has the inestimable advantage of hindsight. But it can also lend an extra dimension to judgement, giving it a leavening of moderation and compassion—even of wisdom—that is sometimes lacking in the reactions of those whose task it is in life to offer instant opinions on all things great and small.

'Nineteen ninety two is not a year I shall look back on with undiluted pleasure ... it has turned out to be an 'Annus Horribilis.'

No section of the community has all the virtues; neither does any have all the vices. I am quite sure that most people try to do their jobs as best they can, even if the result is not always entirely successful. He who has never failed to reach perfection has a right to be the harshest critic. There can be no doubt, of course, that criticism is good for people and institutions that are part of public life.

No institution—City, Monarchy, whatever—should expect to be free from the scrutiny of those who give it their loyalty and support, not to mention those who don't. But we are all part of the same fabric of our national society and that scrutiny, by one part of another, can be just as effective if it is made with a touch of gentleness, good humour and understanding. This sort of questioning can also act, and it should do so, as an effective engine for change.

The City is a good example of the way the process of change can he incorporated into the stability and continuity of a great institution. I particularly admire, my Lord Mayor, the way in which the City has adapted to what the Prayer Book calls "the changes and chances of this mortal life." You have set an example of how it is possible to remain effective and dynamic without losing those indefinable qualities, style and character. We only have to look around this great hall to see the truth of that.

Forty years is quite a long time. I am glad to have had the chance to witness, and to take part in, many, dramatic changes in life in this country. But I am glad to say that the magnificent standard of hospitality, given on so many occasions to the Sovereign by the Lord Mayor of London has not changed at all. It is an outward symbol of one other unchanging factor which I value above all—the loyalty given to me and my family by so many people in this country, and the Commonwealth, throughout my reign.

You, my Lord Mayor and all those whose prayers—fervent, I hope, but not too frequent—have sustained me through all these years, are friends indeed. Prince Philip and I give you all, wherever you may be, our most humble thanks.'

Although 'Annus Horribilis' was a light-hearted reference to John Dryden's 1666 poem Annus Mirabilis (The Year of Wonders), Queen Elizabeth was asking for understanding from her subjects. She accepted the public criticism but reiterated her commitment to serve her people—a constant theme that she often returned to during her long reign. But the public had spoken and she had listened.

In the following weeks it was announced that the Queen would pay tax, that the restoration of Windsor Castle (which would cost over £36 million) would be funded by public ticket sales to view Buckingham Palace and that the 'fairy-tale' marriage between the Prince of Wales and his wife was indeed over.

However, criticism of an aloof and out-of-touch monarch would hound her throughout the 1990s, rising to a deafening crescendo with the funeral arrangements for her former daughter-in-law Diana in 1997.

Despite these concerns, Queen Elizabeth has never considered stepping down in favour of her son Charles. Approaching her 80th birthday, she continues to 'do her duty'.

'There can be no doubt, of course, that criticism is good for people and institutions that are part of public life. No institution—City, Monarchy, whatever—should expect to be free from the scrutiny of those who give it their loyalty and support, not to mention those who don't.'

Nelson Mandela
'Release from Prison'

Address to a rally upon release from prison at Cape Town, 11 February 1990.

Nelson Mandela walks from Victor Verster Prison in 1990.

Nelson Mandela fought against the brutal apartheid regime of South Africa and became the national and international symbol of the struggle for black South Africa's self-determination.

He was born Rolihlahla Dalibhunga Mandela, the son of a Thembu tribal chieftain on 18 July 1918 in a small village in the Transkei province in South Africa. Given the English name 'Nelson' by a schoolteacher, Mandela was raised by the acting regent of the Thembu people after the death of his father in 1927. Mandela later attended Fort Hare University, became a lawyer in Johannesburg and joined the African National Congress (ANC) in 1944. With friends Oliver Tambo and Walter Sisulu, Mandela formed the Youth League of the ANC when he felt the ANC leadership was too conservative. The same year he married his first wife, Evelyn Mase, the mother of his first three children.

For the next 20 years Mandela was involved in a campaign of non-violent defiance against the South African government's apartheid policies. In 1952 he was arrested for violating the Suppression of Communism Act (which was intended to crush any mass movement against apartheid) and banned from attending meetings for the next two years. In 1955 the 'Freedom Charter' adopted at the Congress of the People called for equal rights for blacks and equal share of the country's wealth with whites.

The following year, Nelson Mandela, along with 155 other political activists, was accused of attempting to overthrow the South African government by violent means. Charged with high treason, the charges were dropped against Mandela after a four-year trial. During this time, Mandela divorced his first wife and married Winnie Madikizela in 1958.

On 21 March, 1960 South African police opened fire on unarmed anti-apartheid protestors in Sharpeville, killing 69 civilians—most of whom were shot in the back as they ran away from the police. The government declared a State of Emergency and banned the ANC and other opposition minority groups. Nelson Mandela responded to the banning of the ANC by forming the underground Umkhonto we Sizwe ('Spear of the Nation' or 'MK') movement whose policy was to target and destroy government utilities and symbols of apartheid—but not people. In 1961 Mandela 'illegally' escaped the country and studied guerrilla warfare in Africa and Europe. Returning from overseas after a year on the run, Mandela was arrested by South African security police and sentenced to five years jail on Robben Island. In 1964 the government brought further charges including sabotage, high treason and conspiracy to overthrow the government against him.

Although Nelson Mandela and the other accused escaped execution they were sentenced to life imprisonment. At Robben Island Prison, Mandela was confined to a small cell without a bed or plumbing and was forced to do hard labour in a quarry. He could write and receive a letter every six months and was allowed to meet with a visitor for thirty minutes once every year. In the late 1960s his mother and eldest son were killed in separate car accidents but Mandela was not allowed to attend either funeral. But even when confined to prison, Mandela led a protest of civil disobedience at Robben Island that effectively forced the South African government to improve prison conditions.

During the 1970s and 1980s Mandela became the symbolic leader of an international movement (led by exiled colleague Oliver Tambo) to end apartheid in South Africa. In the last nine years of his sentence, after contracting tuberculosis, Mandela was moved to Pollsmoor Prison where he effectively lived under house arrest whilst the Botha government negotiated with him. In 1989 F W de Klerk became South African president and bowing to political, social and economic pressures, immediately instigated a program to end apartheid. International sanctions had cost the country $4 billion between 1988 and 1990 and de Klerk knew that the apartheid goal of congregating blacks into separate homelands was impossible to maintain. The South African president lifted the ban on the ANC, suspended executions and released most of the prisoners from the Rivonia Trial in 1964.

Finally, in February 1990, de Klerk ordered Mandela's release. Nelson delivered this speech to acknowledge the litany of people who had been involved in the struggle to end apartheid.

Friends, comrades and fellow South Africans.

I greet you all in the name of peace, democracy and freedom for all.

I stand here before you not as a prophet but as a humble servant of you, the people. Your tireless and heroic sacrifices have made it possible for me to be here today. I therefore place the remaining years of my life in your hands.

On this day of my release, I extend my sincere and warmest gratitude to the millions of my compatriots and those in every corner of the globe who have campaigned tirelessly for my release.

I send special greetings to the people of Cape Town, this city which has been my home for three decades. Your mass marches and other forms of struggle have served as a constant source of strength to all political prisoners.

I salute the African National Congress. It has fulfilled our every expectation in its role as leader of the great march to freedom. I salute our President, Comrade Oliver Tambo, for leading the ANC even under the most difficult circumstances.

I salute the rank and file members of the ANC. You have sacrificed life and limb in the pursuit of the noble cause of our struggle.

I salute combatants of Umkhonto we Sizwe, like Solomon Mahlangu and Ashley Kriel who have paid the ultimate price for the freedom of all South Africans.

I salute the South African Communist Party for its sterling contribution to the struggle for democracy. You have survived 40 years of unrelenting persecution. The memory of great communists like Moses Kotane, Yusuf Dadoo, Bram Fischer and Moses Mabhida will be cherished for generations to come.

I salute General Secretary Joe Slovo, one of our finest patriots. We are heartened by the fact that the alliance between ourselves and the Party remains as strong as it always was.

I salute the United Democratic Front, the National Education Crisis Committee, the South African Youth Congress, the Transvaal and Natal Indian Congresses and COSATU and the many other formations of the Mass Democratic Movement.

'Today the majority of South Africans, black and white, recognise that apartheid has no future. It has to be ended by our own decisive mass action in order to build peace and security.'

I also salute the Black Sash and the National Union of South African Students. We note with pride that you have acted as the conscience of white South Africa. Even during the darkest days in the history of our struggle you held the flag of liberty high. The large-scale mass mobilisation of the past few years is one of the key factors which led to the opening of the final chapter of our struggle.

I extend my greetings to the working class of our country. Your organised strength is the pride of our movement. You remain the most dependable force in the struggle to end exploitation and oppression.

I pay tribute to the many religious communities who carried the campaign for justice forward when the organisations for our people were silenced.

I greet the traditional leaders of our country—many of you continue to walk in the footsteps of great heroes like Hintsa and Sekhukune.

I pay tribute to the endless heroism of youth, you, the young lions. You, the young lions, have energised our entire struggle. I pay tribute to the mothers and wives and sisters of our nation. You are the rock-hard foundation of our struggle. Apartheid has inflicted more pain on you than on anyone else.

On this occasion, we thank the world community for their great contribution to the anti-apartheid struggle. Without your support our struggle would not have reached this advanced stage. The sacrifice of the frontline states will be remembered by South Africans forever.

My salutations would be incomplete without expressing my deep appreciation for the strength given to me during my long and lonely years in prison by my beloved wife and family. I am convinced that your pain and suffering was far greater than my own.

NELSON MANDELA

341

Before I go any further I wish to make the point that I intend making only a few preliminary comments at this stage. I will make a more complete statement only after I have had the opportunity to consult with my comrades.

'I have fought against white domination and I have fought against black domination. I have cherished the ideal of a democratic and free society in which all persons live together.'

Today the majority of South Africans, black and white, recognise that apartheid has no future. It has to be ended by our own decisive mass action in order to build peace and security. The mass campaign of defiance and other actions of our organisation and people can only culminate in the establishment of democracy. The destruction caused by apartheid on our sub-continent is incalculable. The fabric of family life of millions of my people has been shattered. Millions are homeless and unemployed. Our economy lies in ruins and our people are embroiled in political strife. Our resort to the armed struggle in 1960 with the formation of the military wing of the ANC, Umkhonto we Sizwe, was a purely defensive action against the violence of apartheid. The factors which necessitated the armed struggle still exist today. We have no option but to continue. We express the hope that a climate conducive to a negotiated settlement will be created soon so that there may no longer be the need for the armed struggle. I am a loyal and disciplined member of the African National Congress. I am therefore in full agreement with all of its objectives, strategies and tactics. The need to unite the people of our country is as important a task now as it always has been. No individual leader is able to take on this enormous task on his own. It is our task as leaders to place our views before our organisation and to allow the democratic structures to decide. On the question of democratic practice, I feel duty bound to make the point that a leader of the movement is a person who has been democratically elected at a national conference. This is a principle which must be upheld without any exceptions.

Today, I wish to report to you that my talks with the government have been aimed at normalising the political situation in the country. We have not as yet begun discussing the basic demands of the struggle. I wish to stress that I myself have at no time entered into negotiations about the future of our country except to insist on a meeting between the ANC and the government. Mr. De Klerk has gone further than any other Nationalist president in taking real steps to normalise the situation. However, there are further steps as outlined in the Harare Declaration that have to be met before negotiations on the basic demands of our people can begin. I reiterate our call for—inter alia—the immediate ending of the State of Emergency and the freeing of all, and not only some, political prisoners. Only such a normalised situation, which allows for free political activity, can allow us to consult our people in order to obtain a mandate. The people need to be consulted on who will negotiate and on the content of such negotiations. Negotiations cannot take place above the heads or behind the backs of our people. It is our belief that the future of our country can only be determined by a body which is democratically elected on a non-racial basis. Negotiations on the dismantling of apartheid will have to address the overwhelming demand of our people for a democratic, non-racial and unitary South Africa. There must be an end to white monopoly on political power and a fundamental restructuring of our political and economic systems to ensure that the inequalities of apartheid are addressed and our society thoroughly democratised.

It must be added that Mr. De Klerk himself is a man of integrity who is acutely aware of the dangers of a public figure not honouring his undertakings. But as an organisation we base our policy and strategy on the harsh reality we are faced with. And this reality is that we are still suffering under the policy of the Nationalist government.

Our struggle has reached a decisive moment. We call on our people to seize this moment so that the process towards democracy is rapid and uninterrupted. We have waited too long for our freedom. We can no longer wait. Now is the time to intensify the struggle on all fronts. To relax our efforts now would be a mistake which generations to come will not be able to forgive. The sight of freedom looming on the horizon should encourage us to redouble our efforts.

It is only through disciplined mass action that our victory can be assured. We call on our white compatriots to join us in the shaping of a new South Africa. The freedom movement is a political home for you too. We call on the international community to continue the campaign to isolate the apartheid regime. To lift sanctions now would be to run the risk of aborting the process towards the complete eradication of apartheid.

Our march to freedom is irreversible. We must not allow fear to stand in our way. Universal suffrage on a common voters' role in a united democratic and non-racial South Africa is the only way to peace and racial harmony.

In conclusion I wish to quote my own words during my trial in 1964. They are true today as they were then:

"I have fought against white domination and I have fought against black domination. I have cherished the ideal of a democratic and free society in which all persons live together in harmony and with equal opportunities. It is an ideal which I hope to live for and to achieve. But if needs be, it is an ideal for which I am prepared to die."

After his release from prison in 1990, Nelson Mandela led the ANC in its negotiations with the minority National Party government to bring an end to apartheid, the armed struggle in the Natal province and to establish a multiracial government. But the battle was not won without bloodshed. The ANC adopted a policy of a 'rolling mass action' of protests and strikes to show the government that people supported an end to violence. In September 1992 Mandela and de Klerk signed the 'Record of Understanding' which promised to investigate the role of the police in propagating violence and established an elected constitutional assembly to develop a new South African constitution. The following year Mandela and the South African President were jointly awarded the Nobel Peace Prize for their efforts.

Nelson Mandela's achievement in leading his country to freedom did not come without personal sacrifice—even after his release. In 1992 he separated from his wife Winnie after she was convicted of kidnapping and being an accessory to assault by men acting as her bodyguards in the murder of 13-year-old Stompie Seipei. Mandela married Graca Machel, the widow of the former president of Mozambique, in 1998, a year before he retired to private life.

In 1994 the ANC won 252 of the 400 seats in the country's first free elections with Nelson Mandela elected South African President on 10 May 1994. At age 76, the 'walk to freedom' had taken an entire lifetime.

Earl Spencer

'Eulogy for Diana, Princess of Wales'

Westminster Abbey, London, 9 September 1997.

Earl Spencer (centre) walks behind the funeral cortege to Westminster Abbey with members of the Royal Family.

The tragic death of Princess Diana in a car accident in Paris in 1997 created an unprecedented outpouring of emotion in England and around the world.

Lady Diana Frances Spencer was born in Norfolk, England on 1 July, 1961, the third child of Earl Spencer and his first wife. On 29 July, 1981, shortly after her 20th birthday and in a frenzied atmosphere of world-wide media scrutiny, Diana married Charles, the Prince of Wales and heir to the British throne. Diana bore two sons, Princes William (b.1982) and Henry 'Harry' (b.1984) and threw her considerable position and newfound celebrity behind several charitable causes—notably children, the homeless, AIDS sufferers and a Red Cross campaign to ban land mines world-wide.

But her marriage to Prince Charles was doomed—a mismatch from the start—and the pair grew increasingly alienated before announcing their separation in 1992 and eventual divorce four years later. Diana kept her title, the Princess of Wales, and continued her charitable works. But her public comments on the failings of her marriage and her relationship with the Royal Family only increased media interest in her personal life. Hounded by Europe's voracious 'paparazzi' she was killed in a car accident on the night of 31 August, 1997, along with boyfriend Dodi Fayed, as their driver sped away from a media pack in Paris.

Diana's tragic death shocked the Royal Family into making a formal announcement of regret, which the Queen delivered at 6:00pm from Buckingham Palace on Friday, 5 September. Four days later, Diana's coffin was borne in procession from Kensington Palace to Westminster Abbey with her brother, Earl Spencer, Prince William, Prince Harry, The Prince of Wales and The Duke of Edinburgh walking behind.

At the funeral at Westminster Abbey, her brother—the ninth Earl Spencer—delivered a moving eulogy.

'I stand before you today, the representative of a family in grief, in a country in mourning, before a world in shock.

We are all united, not only in our desire to pay our respects to Diana, but rather in our need to do so, because such was her extraordinary appeal that the tens of millions of people taking part in this service all over the world via television and radio who never actually met her feel that they too lost someone close to them in the early hours of Sunday morning.

It is a more remarkable tribute to Diana then I can ever hope to offer to her today.

Diana was the very essence of compassion, of duty, of style, of beauty.

All over the world she was the symbol of selfless humanity. A standard bearer for the rights of the truly downtrodden. A very British girl who transcended nationality. Someone with a natural nobility who was classless and who proved in the last year that she needed no royal title to continue to generate her particular brand of magic.

Today is our chance to say 'thank you' for the way you brightened our lives, even though God granted you but half a life. We will all feel cheated always that you were taken from us so young and yet we must learn to be grateful that you came at all.

Only now you are gone do we truly appreciate what we are without, and we want you to know that life without you is very, very difficult.

We have all despaired for our loss over the past week and only the strength of the message you gave us through your years of giving has afforded us the strength to move forward.

There is a temptation to rush, to canonize your memory. There is no need to do so. You stand tall enough as a human being of unique qualities, and do not need to be seen as a saint.

'Diana was the very essence of compassion, of duty, of style, of beauty.'

Indeed, to sanctify your memory would be to miss out on the very core of your being—your wonderfully mischievous sense of humour with a laugh that bent you double, your joy for life transmitted wherever you took your smile and the sparkle in those unforgettable eyes, your boundless energy which you could barely contain.

But your greatest gift was your intuition and it was a gift you used wisely. This is what under pinned all your other wonderful attributes.

And if we look to analyse what it was about you that had such a wide appeal we find it in your instinctive feel for what was really important in all our lives.

Without your God-given sensitivity, we would be immersed in greater ignorance at the anguish of AIDS and HIV sufferers, the plight of the homeless, the isolation of lepers, the random destruction of land mines.

Diana explained to me once that it was her innermost feelings of suffering that made it possible for her to connect with her constituency of the rejected.

And here we come to another truth about her. For all the status, the glamour, the applause, Diana remained throughout a very insecure person at heart, almost childlike in her desire to do good for others so she could release herself from deep feelings of unworthiness of which her eating disorders were merely a symptom.

The world sensed this part of her character and cherished her vulnerability.

The last time I saw Diana was on July 1st, her birthday, in London when typically she was not taking time to celebrate her special day with friends but was guest of honour at a fundraising charity evening. She sparkled, of course.

But I would rather cherish the days I spent with her in March when she came to visit me and my children at our home in South Africa. I am proud of the fact that, apart from when she was on public display meeting President Mandela, we managed to contrive to stop the ever-present paparazzi from getting a single picture of her. That meant a lot to her.

EARL SPENCER

These are days I will always treasure. It was as if we were transported back to our childhood when we spent such an enormous amount of time together as the two youngest in the family.

Fundamentally she hadn't changed at all from the big sister who mothered me as a baby, fought with me at school, who endured those long journeys between our parents' home with me at weekends.

'Of all the ironies about Diana, perhaps the greatest was this: a girl given the name of the ancient goddess of hunting was, in the end, the most hunted person of the modern age.'

It is a tribute to her level-headedness and strength that despite the most bizarre life after her childhood, she remained intact, true to herself.

There is no doubt she was looking for a new direction in her life at this time.

She talked endlessly of getting away from England, mainly because of the treatment that she received at the hands of the newspapers.

I don't think she ever understood why her genuinely good intentions were sneered at by the media, why there appeared to be a permanent quest on their behalf to bring her down. It is baffling.

My own and only explanation is that genuine goodness is threatening to those at the opposite end of the moral spectrum.

It is a point to remember that of all the ironies about Diana, perhaps the greatest was this: a girl given the name of the ancient goddess of hunting was, in the end, the most hunted person of the modern age.

She would want us today to pledge ourselves to protecting her beloved boys, William and Harry, from a similar fate, and I do this here, Diana, on your behalf.

We will not allow them to suffer the anguish that used regularly to drive you to tearful despair. And beyond that, on behalf of your mother and sisters, I pledge that we, your blood family, will do all we can to continue the imaginative and loving way in which you were steering these two exceptional young men so that their souls are not simply immersed by duty and tradition but can sing openly as you planned.

We fully respect the heritage into which they have both been born and will always respect and encourage them in their royal role. But we, like you, recognize the need for them to experience as many different aspects of life as possible to arm them spiritually and emotionally for the years ahead. I know you would have expected nothing less from us.

William and Harry, we all care desperately for you today. We are all chewed up with sadness at the loss of a woman who wasn't even our mother. How great your suffering is we cannot even imagine.

I would like to end by thanking God for the small mercies he has shown us at this dreadful time, for taking Diana at her most beautiful and radiant and when she had joy in her private life.

Above all, we give thanks for the life of a woman I'm so proud to be able to call my sister the unique, the complex, the extraordinary and irreplaceable Diana whose beauty, both internal and external, will never be extinguished from our minds.'

As Earl Spencer spoke, a spontaneous wave of applause from the thousands of mourners outside the Abbey swept over the congregation inside. While many applauded his condemnation of the role the media played in his sister's death and agreed with his stinging criticism of the conditions that had allowed Diana's life to be so publicly exposed, just as many thought the eulogy ungracious to the Royal Family.

That afternoon Diana's body was interred on the Spencer family home, Althorp, in Northamptonshire on a landscaped island known as 'The Oval'. Diana, the 'Princess of Hearts', was finally at rest away from the prying eyes of the public.

Bill Clinton

'The Sorrow I Feel Is Genuine'

White House, Washington DC, 11 September, 1998

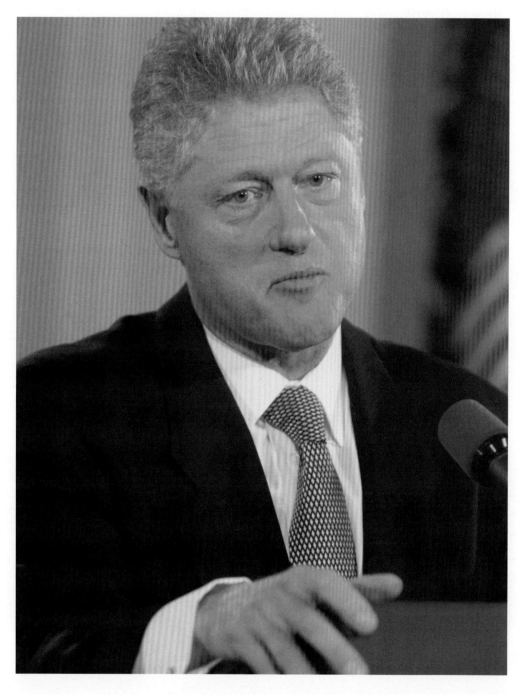

President Bill Clinton in 1998.

The charismatic US President Bill Clinton was born William Jefferson Blythe III in Hope, Arkansas, in 1946. Taking his stepfather's name, Clinton suffered a troubled childhood but following a chance meeting with President John F. Kennedy in 1962, he knew that he wanted a career in politics. A Rhodes Scholar, Clinton overcame electoral defeat (as Arkansas Attorney-General) to become the country's youngest governor, at age 33, in 1980. In the 1992 presidential race the 'New Democrat's' charm and sincerity made him a viable alternative to the staid, conservative incumbent, George Bush Senior and despite the exposure of a 'discreet' relationship with Gennifer Flowers, the public took a liking to the Southern governor and his articulate, equally ambitious wife, Hillary Rodham.

Bill Clinton's first term as president (1993-1997) saw the Republican Party seize control of the House of Representatives for only the third time since the end of World War II. Clinton was in danger of becoming a 'lame-duck' President but he had the unique ability to reinvent himself and to slip out of the tightest political situations (earning the nickname 'Slick Willy'). In 1997 he made a phoenix-like comeback in the polls to win a second term as president.

Clinton made many political enemies when he undertook a government shutdown in November 1995. When Paula Jones sued the President for sexual harassment over alleged incidents during his time as Arkansas governor, independent council Kenneth Starr unearthed evidence of a cover-up of a sexual relationship between Clinton and White House intern Monica Lewinsky in 1995. Both parties originally lied about the affair, with Clinton famously declaring in a televised statement, 'I did not have sexual relations with that woman.'

The media scandal effectively brought Clinton's presidency to a standstill in 1998 before he came to his senses in August and admitted to the affair. 'This has gone on too long, cost too much and hurt too many innocent people,' Clinton told the American people in a four-minute, personal 'confession' on 17 August 1998.

The following month, Bill Clinton and his wife hosted the annual White House breakfast for Washington's clergy. There a contrite US President apologised for his actions.

Thank you very much, ladies and gentlemen. Welcome to the White House and to this day to which Hillary and the Vice President and I look forward to so much every year.

This is always an important day for our country, for the reasons that the Vice President said. It is an unusual and, I think, unusually important day today. I may not be quite as easy with my words today as I have been in years past, and I was up rather late last night thinking about and praying about what I ought to say today. And rather unusual for me, I actually tried to write it down. So if you will forgive me, I will do my best to say what it is I want to say to you … and I may have to take my glasses out to read my own writing. [Clinton then put on his glasses and read from hand-written notes.]

First, I want to say to all of you that, as you might imagine, I have been on quite a journey these last few weeks to get to the end of this, to the rock-bottom truth of where I am and where we all are.

I agree with those who have said that in my first statement after I testified I was not contrite enough. I don't think there is a fancy way to say that I have sinned.

'I am grateful for those who have stood by me and who say that in this case and many others, the bounds of privacy have been excessively and unwisely invaded. That may be. Nevertheless, in this case, it may be a blessing, because I still sinned.'

It is important to me that everybody who has been hurt know that the sorrow I feel is genuine: First and most important, my family; also my friends, my staff, my Cabinet, Monica Lewinsky and her family, and the American people. I have asked all for their forgiveness.

But I believe that to be forgiven, more than sorrow is required-at least two more things. First, genuine repentance—a determination to change and to repair breaches of my own making. I have repented. Second, what my Bible calls a "broken spirit"; an understanding that I must have God's help to be the person that I want to be; a willingness to give the very forgiveness I seek; a renunciation of the pride and the anger which cloud judgment, lead people to excuse and compare and to blame and complain.

Now, what does all this mean for me and for us? First, I will instruct my lawyers to mount a vigorous defense, using all available appropriate arguments. But legal language must not obscure the fact that I have done wrong. Second, I will continue on the path of repentance, seeking pastoral support and that of other caring people so that they can hold me accountable for my own commitment.

Third, I will intensify my efforts to lead our country and the world toward peace and freedom, prosperity and harmony, in the hope that with a broken spirit and a still strong heart I can be used for greater good, for we have many blessings and many challenges and so much work to do.

In this, I ask for your prayers and for your help in healing our nation. And though I cannot move beyond or forget this—indeed, I must always keep it as a caution light in my life—it is very important that our nation move forward.

I am very grateful for the many, many people—clergy and ordinary citizens alike—who have written me with wise counsel. I am profoundly grateful for the support of so many Americans who somehow through it all seem to still know that I care about them a great deal, that I care about their problems and their dreams. I am grateful for those who have stood by me and who say that in this case and many others, the bounds of privacy have been excessively and unwisely invaded. That may be. Nevertheless, in this case, it may be a blessing, because I still sinned. And if my repentance is genuine and sustained, and if I can maintain both a broken spirit and a strong heart, then good can come of this for our country as well as for me and my family. [Applause.]

The children of this country can learn in a profound way that integrity is important and selfishness is wrong, but God can change us and make us strong at the broken places. I want to embody those lessons for the children of this country—for that little boy in Florida who came up to me and said that he wanted to grow up and be President and to be just like me. I want the parents of all the children in America to be able to say that to their children.

A couple of days ago when I was in Florida a Jewish friend of mine gave me this liturgy book called Gates of Repentance. And there was this incredible passage from the Yom Kippur liturgy. I would like to read it to you:

"Now is the time for turning. The leaves are beginning to turn from green to red to orange. The birds are beginning to turn and are heading once more toward the south. The animals are beginning to turn to storing their food for the winter. For leaves, birds and animals, turning comes instinctively. But for us, turning does not come so easily. It takes an act of will for us to make a turn. It means breaking old habits. It means admitting that we have been wrong, and this is never easy. It means losing face. It means starting all over again. And this is always painful. It means saying I am sorry. It means recognizing that we have the ability to change. These things are terribly hard to do. But unless we turn, we will be trapped forever in yesterday's ways. Lord help us to turn, from callousness to sensitivity, from hostility to love, from pettiness to purpose, from envy to contentment, from carelessness to discipline, from fear to faith. Turn us around, O Lord, and bring us back toward you. Revive our lives as at the beginning, and turn us toward each other, Lord, for in isolation there is no life."

I thank my friend for that. I thank you for being here. I ask you to share my prayer that God will search me and know my heart, try me and know my anxious thoughts, see if there is any hurtfulness in me, and lead me toward the life everlasting. I ask that God give me a clean heart, let me walk by faith and not sight.

I ask once again to be able to love my neighbour—all my neighbors—as myself, to be an instrument of God's peace; to let the words of my mouth and the meditations of my heart and, in the end, the work of my hands, be pleasing.

This is what I wanted to say to you today.

Thank you. God bless you.**"**

President Bill Clinton was impeached by the House of Representatives but escaped conviction in the Senate in February 1999. It was as if the American public disapproved of his behaviour but did not want him removed from office. Clinton always wanted to be remembered as an 'above average', if not a great, president. Although he was capable of important things—not least the continued economic growth at home or internationally, the forced back-down by Serbian leader Slobodan Milosevic to avoid a ground war with American forces in Kosovo in June 1999—Clinton's credibility as a leader was overshadowed by the 'Lewinsky Affair'.

Tony Blair
'Address to the Irish Parliament'

Irish Parliament, Dublin, 26 November 1998.

Prime Minister Tony Blair in 1998.

Tony Blair is the longest serving Labour Prime Minister in British history. On Thursday, 26 November 1998 Tony Blair also made history when he became the first British Prime Minister to address the Irish Parliament.

Tony Charles Lynton Blair was born in Edinburgh on 6 May 1953, the son of a barrister and lecturer. After spending most of his childhood in Durham, Blair returned to Edinburgh with his family at the age of 14 before studying law at Oxford and becoming a barrister. He stood unsuccessfully as a Labour Party candidate in a bi-election before winning the seat of Sedgefield in the 1983 General Election at age 30. Blair served in the Shadow Ministry for the next decade until the sudden death of Labour Party leader John Smith in 1994 saw him gain widespread support to take on the role. The new leader set about modernising the Labour Party, coining the term 'New Labour', and led the Party to a landslide victory in 1997 after 18 years in opposition.

Blair's government immediately implemented a program of constitutional change—reducing the number of hereditary peers in the House of Lords to just 92, offering referendums on home rule to Scotland and Wales before taking on the most divisive and violent issue in Britain during the twentieth century—relations with Ireland. Southern Ireland had won its independence from England in the early 1920s, but with the province of Northern Ireland annexed to Britain, decades of violence and animosity between the two nations had followed.

In this speech Blair recalled his own Irish heritage and extended hope for heartfelt reconciliation by declaring an end to more than 800 years of enmity between England and Ireland.

❝Members of the Dail and Seanad, after all the long and torn history of our two peoples, standing here as the first British prime minister ever to address the joint Houses of the Oireachtas, I feel profoundly both the history in this event, and I feel profoundly the enormity of the honour that you are bestowing upon me. From the bottom of my heart, go raibh mile maith agaibh.

Ireland, as you may know, is in my blood. My mother was born in the flat above her grandmother's hardware shop on the main street of Ballyshannon in Donegal. She lived there as a child, started school there and only moved when her father died; her mother remarried and they crossed the water to Glasgow.

We spent virtually every childhood summer holiday up to when the troubles really took hold in Ireland, usually at Rossnowlagh, the Sands House Hotel, I think it was. And we would travel in the beautiful countryside of Donegal. It was there in the seas off the Irish coast that I learned to swim, there that my father took me to my first pub, a remote little house in the country, for a Guinness, a taste I've never forgotten and which it is always a pleasure to repeat.

Even now, in my constituency of Sedgefield, which at one time had 30 pits or more, all now gone, virtually every community remembers that its roots lie in Irish migration to the mines of Britain.

So like it or not, we, the British and the Irish, are irredeemably linked.

We experienced and absorbed the same waves of invasions: Celts, Vikings, Normans—all left their distinctive mark on our countries. Over a thousand years ago, the monastic traditions formed the basis for both our cultures. Sadly, the power games of medieval monarchs and feudal chiefs sowed the seeds of later trouble.

Yet it has always been simplistic to portray our differences as simply Irish versus English—or British. There were, after all, many in Britain too who suffered greatly at the hands of powerful absentee landlords, who were persecuted for their religion, or who were for centuries disenfranchised. And each generation in Britain has benefited, as ours does, from the contribution of Irishmen and women.

Today the links between our parliaments are continued by the British-Irish Parliamentary Body, and last month 60 of our MPs set up a new all-party "Irish in Britain Parliamentary Group."

Irish parliamentarians have made a major contribution to our shared parliamentary history. Let me single out just two:

- Daniel O'Connell, who fought against injustice to extend a franchise restricted by religious prejudice;
- Charles Stewart Parnell, whose statue stands today in the House of Commons and whose political skills and commitment to social justice made such an impact in that House.

So much shared history, so much shared pain.

And now the shared hope of a new beginning.

The peace process is at a difficult juncture. Progress is being made, but slowly. There is an impasse over the establishment of the executive; there is an impasse over decommissioning. But I have been optimistic the whole way through. And I am optimistic now. Let us not underestimate how far we have come; and let us agree that we have come too far to go back now.

Politics is replacing violence as the way people do business. The Good Friday Agreement, overwhelmingly endorsed by the people on both sides of the Border, holds out the prospect of a peaceful long-term future for Northern Ireland, and the whole island of Ireland.

The Northern Ireland Bill provides for the new Assembly and Executive, the North-South Ministerial Council, and the British-Irish Council. It incorporates the principle of consent into British constitutional law and repeals the Government of Ireland Act of 1920. It establishes a

Human Rights Commission with the power to support individual cases. We will have an Equality Commission to police a new duty on all public bodies in Northern Ireland to promote equality of opportunity. We have set up the Patten Commission to review policing. We are scaling down the military presence. Prisoners are being released.

'Let us not underestimate how far we have come; and let us agree that we have come too far to go back now.'

None of this is easy. I get many letters from the victims of violence asking why we are freeing terrorist prisoners. It is a tough question but my answer is clear: the agreement would never have come about if we had not tackled the issue of prisoners. That agreement heralds the prospect of an end to violence and a peaceful future for Northern Ireland. Our duty is to carry it out. That is a duty I feel more strongly than ever, having seen for myself the horror of Omagh. This was not the first such atrocity. But with all of my being, I will it to be the last. I will never forget the meeting I had, with Bill Clinton, with survivors, and with relatives of those who died. Their suffering and their courage was an inspiration. They will never forget their loved ones. Nor must we. We owe it to them above all to build a lasting peace, when we have the best opportunity in a generation to do so.

The Taoiseach's personal contribution has been immense. I pay tribute to his tireless dedication. I value his friendship. I also salute the courage of our predecessors, Deputy Albert Reynolds, Deputy John Bruton and John Major; and I also salute Deputy Dick Spring, whose role in this process goes back a long way.

Like us, you are living up to your side of the bargain too. You have voted to end the territorial claim over Northern Ireland, essential to the agreement.

It is time now for all the parties to live up to all their commitments. Time for North/South bodies to be established to start a new era of co-operation between you and Northern Ireland— I hope agreement on these is now close. Time to set up the institutions of the new government. Time for the gun and the threat of the gun to be taken out of politics once and for all; for decommissioning to start.

I am not asking anyone to surrender. I am asking everyone to declare the victory of peace.

In Belfast or Dublin, people say the same thing: make the agreement work.

It is never far from my mind. My sense of urgency and mission comes from the children in Northern Ireland. I reflect on those who have been victims of violence, whose lives are scarred and twisted through the random wickedness of a terrorist act, on those who grow up in fear, those whose parents and loved ones have died.

And I reflect on those, who though untouched directly by violence, are nonetheless victims - - victims of mistrust and misunderstanding who through lack of a political settlement miss the chance of new friendships, new horizons, because of the isolation from others that the sectarian way of life brings.

I reflect on the sheer waste of children taught to hate when I believe passionately children should be taught to think.

Don't believe anyone who says the British people don't care about the peace process. People in my country care deeply about it, are willing it to work. And in our two countries, it is not just the politicians who have a role to play.

No one should ignore the injustices of the past, or the lessons of history. But too often between us, one person's history has been another person's myth.

We need not be prisoners of our history. My generation in Britain sees Ireland differently today and probably the same generation here feels differently about Britain.

We can understand the emotions generated by Northern Ireland's troubles, but we cannot really believe, as we approach the 21st century, there is not a better way forward to the future than murder, terrorism and sectarian hatred.

We see a changed Republic of Ireland today:

- a modern, open economy;
- after the long years of emigration, people beginning to come back for the quality of life you now offer;
- a country part of Europe's mainstream, having made the most of European structural funds but no longer reliant on them;
- some of the best business brains in the business world;
- leaders in popular culture, U2, the Corrs, Boyzone, B-Witched;
- a country that had the courage to elect its first woman president and liked it so much, you did it again; and the politics of Northern Ireland would be better for a few more women in prominent positions too.

And you see, I hope, a Britain emerging from its post-Empire malaise, modernizing, becoming as confident of its future as it once was of its past.

The programme of the new Labour government: driving up standards in education; welfare reform; monetary and fiscal stability as the foundation of a modern economy; massive investment in our public services tied to the challenge of modernization; a huge programme of constitutional change; a new positive attitude to Europe—it is a program of national renewal as ambitious as any undertaken in any western democracy in recent times.

It is precisely the dramatic changes in both countries that allow us to see the possibilities of change in our relationship with each other.

It will require vision, but no more than the vision that has transformed Ireland. It will require imagination, but no more than that shown by the British people in the last two years. The old ways are changing between London and Dublin. And this can spur the change and healing in Northern Ireland too. The old notions of unionist supremacy and of narrow nationalism are gradually having their fingers prised from their grip on the future.

Different traditions have to understand each other. Just as we must understand your yearning for a united Ireland, so too must you understand what the best of unionism is about. They

TONY BLAIR

359

are good and decent people, just like you. They want to remain part of the UK—and I have made it clear that I value that wish. They feel threatened. Threatened by the terrorism with which they have had to live for so long. Threatened, until the Good Friday Agreement, that they would be forced into a united Ireland against the will of the people of Northern Ireland.

Yet they realize now that a framework in which consent is guaranteed is also one in which basic rights of equality and justice are guaranteed, and that those who wish a united Ireland are free to make that claim, provided it is democratically expressed, just as those who believe in the Union can make their claim.

It is all about belonging. The wish of unionists to belong to the UK. The wish of nationalists to belong to Ireland. Both traditions are reasonable. There are no absolutes. The beginning of understanding is to realize that.

My point is very simple. Those urges to belong, divergent as they are, can live together more easily if we, Britain and the Irish Republic, can live closer together too.

Down through the centuries, Ireland and Britain have inflicted too much pain, each on the other. But now, the UK and Ireland as two modern countries, we can try to put our histories behind us, try to forgive and forget those age-old enmities.

We have both grown up now. A new generation is in power in each country.

We now have a real opportunity to put our relations on a completely new footing, not least through working together in Europe. I know that is what our peoples want and I believe we can deliver it.

Our ties are already rich and diverse:

- the UK is the largest market for Irish goods. And you are our fifth most important market in the world;
- in trade unions, professional bodies and the voluntary sector, our people work together to help their communities; in culture, sport and academic life there is an enormous crossover. Our theatres are full of Irish plays. Our television is full of Irish actors and presenters. Your national football team has a few English accents too;
- above all, at the personal level, millions of Irish people live and work in Britain, and hundreds of thousands of us visit you every year.

As ties strengthen, so the past can be put behind us. Nowhere was this better illustrated than at the remarkable ceremony at Messines earlier this month. Representatives of nationalists and unionists travelled together to Flanders to remember shared suffering. Our army bands played together. Our heads of state stood together. With our other European neighbours, such a ceremony would be commonplace. For us it was a first. It shows how far we have come. But it also shows we still have far to go.

The relationships across these islands are also changing in a significant way.

The Taoiseach has spoken of the exciting new relationships that will unfold as the people of

Scotland and Wales, as well as Northern Ireland, express their wishes through their own parliaments and assemblies. The new British Irish Council must reflect and explore these opportunities. We have much to gain by co-operating better across these islands in areas like transport, education, the fight against illegal drugs.

But I want our co-operation to be wider and more fundamental still—above all in Europe.

It is 25 years since we both joined what was then the EEC. We have had different approaches to agriculture, to monetary union, to defence. But increasingly we share a common agenda and common objectives:

- completion of the Single Market and structural economic reform;
- better conditions for growth and jobs in Europe;
- successful enlargement;
- a united and coherent foreign policy voice for Europe;
- a more effective fight against crime, drugs, illegal immigration and environmental damage;
- flexible, open and accountable European institutions.

We must work to make the single currency a success. Unlike Ireland, we are not joining in the first wave. But we have made clear that we are prepared to join later if the economic benefits are clear and unambiguous. For my government, there is no political or constitutional barrier to joining. There is no resistance to full-hearted European co-operation wherever this brings added value to us all.

Enlargement will increasingly test our political and economic imaginations, as we struggle with policy reform and future financing. The international financial system must be reformed. We must learn to apply real political will and harness our skills and resources far more effectively to solve regional problems—notably in the Balkans and the Middle East. Above all, Europe must restate its vision for today's world, so that our people understand why it is so important. This means defining the priorities where common European action makes obvious sense and can make a real difference, like economic co-ordination, foreign and security policy, the environment, crime and drugs. It also means distinguishing them from areas where countries or regions can best continue to make policy themselves, to suit local circumstances, while still learning from each other—for example, tax, education, health, welfare.

That is why I want to forge new bonds with Dublin. Together we can have a stronger voice in Europe and work to shape its future in a way which suits all our people. It is said there was a time when Irish diplomats in Europe spoke French in meetings to ensure they were clearly distinguished from us. I hope those days are long behind us. We can accomplish much more when our voices speak in harmony.

'I do not believe Northern Ireland can or should any longer define the relationship between us. Our common interests, what we can achieve together, go much, much wider than that.'

TONY BLAIR

361

Our ministers and officials are increasingly consulting and coordinating systematically. We can do more. I believe we can transform our links if both sides are indeed ready to make the effort. For our part, we are.

This must also involve a dramatic new effort in bilateral relations, above all to bring our young generations together. We need new youth and school exchanges, contact through the new University for Industry, better cultural programs in both directions. We need to work much more closely to fight organized crime and drugs. We can do much more to enrich each other's experience in areas like health care and welfare.

None of this threatens our separate identities. Co-operation does not mean losing distinctiveness.

What the Taoiseach and I seek is a new dimension to our relationships—a real partnership between governments and peoples, which will engage our societies at every level.

We have therefore agreed to launch a new intensive process. The Taoiseach and I will meet again next spring in London, with key ministerial colleagues, to give this the necessary impetus and agenda, and will thereafter meet at least once a year to review progress. This will be part of the work of the new Intergovernmental Conference. The objective is threefold:

- first, revitalized and modernized bilateral relations where we can finally put the burden of history behind us;
- second, a habit of close consultation on European issues, marked by a step-change in contacts at every level, particularly in key areas such as agriculture, justice and home affairs, employment and foreign and security policy;
- third, working together on international issues more widely, for example UN peacekeeping, to which both our countries have been important contributors, arms proliferation and the Middle East.

What I welcome above all is that, after keeping us apart for so long, Northern Ireland is now helping to bring us closer together. But I do not believe Northern Ireland can or should any longer define the relationship between us. Our common interests, what we can achieve together, go much, much wider than that.

Our two countries can look to the future with confidence in our separate ways. But we will be stronger and more prosperous working together.

That is my ambition. I know it is shared by the Taoiseach. I believe it is an ambition shared by both our nations. The 21st century awaits us. Let us confront its challenge with confidence, and together give our children the future they deserve.'

Elie Wiesel
'The Perils of Indifference'

East Room, White House, Washington DC, 12 April 1999.

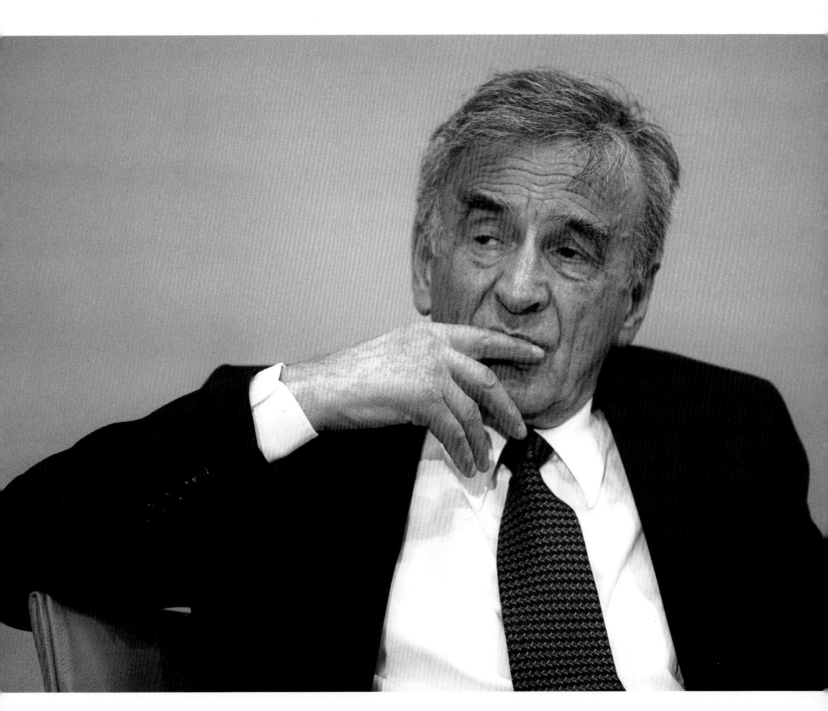

Elie Wiesel at the Universal Academy of Culture in Paris in 2001.

An impassioned insight into the causes and nature of the Holocaust during World War II came from a scholar born in Sighet, Transylvania (now part of Romania). Eliezer Wiesel was born on 30 September 1928 in a small village, his life revolving around 'family, religious study, community and God'.

In the summer of 1944, 15-year-old Elie Wiesel, along with his father, mother and sisters, was deported by the Nazis to the Auschwitz death camp in occupied Poland. Wiesel and his father were selected for slave labour and were set to work at the nearby Buna rubber factory. Daily life was a constant struggle against overwhelming despair—starvation rations, brutal discipline and, as Wiesel later wrote, the memory of children whose bodies were 'turned into wreaths of smoke beneath a silent blue sky'.

Wiesel and his father were hurriedly evacuated from Auschwitz by a forced march to Gleiwitz in January 1945 as the Russian Army drew near, and then to Buchenwald via an open train car. There, his father, mother, and a younger sister eventually died but Elie Wiesel was liberated by American troops in April 1945. After the war, he moved to Paris and became a journalist. Originally vowing to remain silent on his Holocaust experiences, he was encouraged to write about them by French Nobel laureate Francois Mauriac. Since then, Wiesel has written over 40 books including *Night,* which was first published in 1960. Settling in New York and becoming an American citizen, he has been Andrew Mellon Professor in the Humanities at Boston University since 1976 and has received numerous awards and honours including the 1986 Nobel Peace Prize and the Presidential Medal of Freedom.

The Founding Chair of the United States Holocaust Memorial, Elie Wiesel was invited to participate in a series of Millennium Lectures hosted by President Bill Clinton and First Lady Hillary Rodham Clinton at the White House leading up to the year 2000. Here, in his speech in the East Room of the White House, Wiesel reiterated his belief that 'to remain silent and indifferent is the greatest sin of all'

'Mr President, Mrs Clinton, members of Congress, Ambassador Holbrooke, Excellencies, friends.

Fifty-four years ago to the day, a young Jewish boy from a small town in the Carpathian Mountains woke up, not far from Goethe's beloved Weimar, in a place of eternal infamy called Buchenwald. He was finally free, but there was no joy in his heart. He thought there never would be again.

Liberated a day earlier by American soldiers, he remembers their rage at what they saw. And even if he lives to be a very old man, he will always be grateful to them for that rage, and also for their compassion. Though he did not understand their language, their eyes told him what he needed to know—that they, too, would remember, and bear witness.

And now, I stand before you, Mr. President—Commander-in-Chief of the army that freed me, and tens of thousands of others—and I am filled with a profound and abiding gratitude to the American people.

Gratitude is a word that I cherish. Gratitude is what defines the humanity of the human being. And I am grateful to you, Hillary—or Mrs. Clinton—for what you said, and for what you are doing for children in the world, for the homeless, for the victims of injustice, the victims of destiny and society. And I thank all of you for being here.

We are on the threshold of a new century, a new millennium. What will the legacy of this vanishing century be? How will it be remembered in the new millennium? Surely it will be judged, and judged severely, in both moral and metaphysical terms. These failures have cast a dark shadow over humanity: two World Wars, countless civil wars, the senseless chain of assassinations—Gandhi, the Kennedys, Martin Luther King, Sadat, Rabin—bloodbaths in Cambodia and Nigeria, India and Pakistan, Ireland and Rwanda, Eritrea and Ethiopia, Sarajevo and Kosovo; the inhumanity in the gulag and the tragedy of Hiroshima. And, on a different level, of course, Auschwitz and Treblinka. So much violence, so much indifference.

What is indifference? Etymologically, the word means "no difference." A strange and unnatural state in which the lines blur between light and darkness, dusk and dawn, crime and punishment, cruelty and compassion, good and evil.

What are its courses and inescapable consequences? Is it a philosophy? Is there a philosophy of indifference conceivable? Can one possibly view indifference as a virtue? Is it necessary at times to practice it simply to keep one's sanity, live normally, enjoy a fine meal and a glass of wine, as the world around us experiences harrowing upheavals?

Of course, indifference can be tempting—more than that, seductive. It is so much easier to look away from victims. It is so much easier to avoid such rude interruptions to our work, our dreams, our hopes. It is, after all, awkward, troublesome, to be involved in another person's pain and despair. Yet, for the person who is indifferent, his or her neighbor are of no consequence. And, therefore, their lives are meaningless. Their hidden or even visible anguish is of no interest. Indifference reduces the other to an abstraction.

Over there, behind the black gates of Auschwitz, the most tragic of all prisoners were the "Muselmanner," as they were called. Wrapped in their torn blankets, they would sit or lie on the ground, staring vacantly into space, unaware of who or where they were, strangers to their surroundings. They no longer felt pain, hunger, thirst. They feared nothing. They felt nothing. They were dead and did not know it.

> 'Of course, indifference can be tempting—more than that, seductive. It is so much easier to look away from victims.'

ELIE WIESEL

365

Rooted in our tradition, some of us felt that to be abandoned by humanity then was not the ultimate. We felt that to be abandoned by God was worse than to be punished by Him. Better an unjust God than an indifferent one. For us to be ignored by God was a harsher punishment than to be a victim of His anger. Man can live far from God—not outside God. God is wherever we are. Even in suffering? Even in suffering.

In a way, to be indifferent to that suffering is what makes the human being inhuman. Indifference, after all, is more dangerous than anger and hatred. Anger can at times be creative. One writes a great poem, a great symphony, one does something special for the sake of humanity because one is angry at the injustice that one witnesses. But indifference is never creative. Even hatred at times may elicit a response. You fight it. You denounce it. You disarm it. Indifference elicits no response. Indifference is not a response.

Indifference is not a beginning, it is an end. And, therefore, indifference is always the friend of the enemy, for it benefits the aggressor—never his victim, whose pain is magnified when he or she feels forgotten. The political prisoner in his cell, the hungry children, the homeless refugees—not to respond to their plight, not to relieve their solitude by offering them a spark of hope is to exile them from human memory. And in denying their humanity we betray our own.

'Indifference is always the friend of the enemy, for it benefits the aggressor.'

Indifference, then, is not only a sin, it is a punishment. And this is one of the most important lessons of this outgoing century's wide-ranging experiments in good and evil.

In the place that I come from, society was composed of three simple categories: the killers, the victims, and the bystanders. During the darkest of times, inside the ghettoes and death camps—and I'm glad that Mrs. Clinton mentioned that we are now commemorating that event, that period, that we are now in the Days of Remembrance—but then, we felt abandoned, forgotten. All of us did.

And our only miserable consolation was that we believed that Auschwitz and Treblinka were closely guarded secrets; that the leaders of the free world did not know what was going on behind those black gates and barbed wire; that they had no knowledge of the war against the Jews that Hitler's armies and their accomplices waged as part of the war against the Allies.

If they knew, we thought, surely those leaders would have moved heaven and earth to intervene. They would have spoken out with great outrage and conviction. They would have bombed the railways leading to Birkenau, just the railways, just once.

And now we knew, we learned, we discovered that the Pentagon knew, the State Department knew. And the illustrious occupant of the White House then, who was a great leader—and I say it with some anguish and pain, because, today is exactly 54 years marking his death—Franklin Delano Roosevelt died on April the 12th, 1945, so he is very much present to me and to us.

No doubt, he was a great leader. He mobilized the American people and the world, going into battle, bringing hundreds and thousands of valiant and brave soldiers in America to fight fascism, to fight dictatorship, to fight Hitler. And so many of the young people fell in battle. And, nevertheless, his image in Jewish history—I must say it—his image in Jewish history is flawed.

The depressing tale of the *St. Louis* is a case in point. Sixty years ago, its human cargo—maybe 1,000 Jews—was turned back to Nazi Germany. And that happened after the Kristallnacht, after the first state sponsored pogrom, with hundreds of Jewish shops destroyed, synagogues burned, thousands of people put in concentration camps. And that ship, which was already on the shores of the United States, was sent back.

I don't understand. Roosevelt was a good man, with a heart. He understood those who needed help. Why didn't he allow these refugees to disembark? A thousand people—in America, a great country, the greatest democracy, the most generous of all new nations in modern history. What happened? I don't understand. Why the indifference, on the highest level, to the suffering of the victims?

But then, there were human beings who were sensitive to our tragedy. Those non-Jews, those Christians, that we called the "Righteous Gentiles," whose selfless acts of heroism saved the honor of their faith. Why were they so few? Why was there a greater effort to save SS murderers after the war than to save their victims during the war?

Why did some of America's largest corporations continue to do business with Hitler's Germany until 1942? It has been suggested, and it was documented, that the Wehrmacht could not have conducted its invasion of France without oil obtained from American sources. How is one to explain their indifference?

'Have we really learned from our experiences? Are we less insensitive to the plight of victims of ethnic cleansing and other forms of injustices in places near and far?'

And yet, my friends, good things have also happened in this traumatic century: the defeat of Nazism, the collapse of communism, the rebirth of Israel on its ancestral soil, the demise of apartheid, Israel's peace treaty with Egypt, the peace accord in Ireland. And let us remember the meeting, filled with drama and emotion, between Rabin and Arafat that you, Mr. President, convened in this very place. I was here and I will never forget it.

And then, of course, the joint decision of the United States and NATO to intervene in Kosovo and save those victims, those refugees, those who were uprooted by a man whom I believe that because of his crimes, should be charged with crimes against humanity. But this time, the world was not silent. This time, we do respond. This time, we intervene.

Does it mean that we have learned from the past? Does it mean that society has changed? Has the human being become less indifferent and more human? Have we really learned from our experiences? Are we less insensitive to the plight of victims of ethnic cleansing and other forms of injustices in places near and far? Is today's justified intervention in Kosovo, led by you, Mr. President, a lasting warning that never again will the deportation, the terrorization of children and their parents be allowed anywhere in the world? Will it discourage other dictators in other lands to do the same?

ELIE WIESEL

What about the children? Oh, we see them on television, we read about them in the papers, and we do so with a broken heart. Their fate is always the most tragic, inevitably. When adults wage war, children perish. We see their faces, their eyes. Do we hear their pleas? Do we feel their pain, their agony? Every minute one of them dies of disease, violence, famine. Some of them— so many of them—could be saved.

And so, once again, I think of the young Jewish boy from the Carpathian Mountains. He has accompanied the old man I have become throughout these years of quest and struggle. And together we walk towards the new millennium, carried by profound fear and extraordinary hope.'

When introduced by Hillary Clinton, the First Lady stated, 'It was more than a year ago that I asked Elie if he would be willing to participate in these Millennium Lectures ... I never could have imagined that when the time finally came for him to stand in this spot and to reflect on the past century and the future to come, that we would be seeing children in Kosovo crowded into trains, separated from families, separated from their homes, robbed of their childhoods, their memories, their humanity.'

She could just as easily have commented that those who refuse to heed the lessons of history are condemned to repeat it.

The New Millennium
2000-

George W Bush

'A Great People Has Been Moved'

Washington, DC, 11 September 2001.

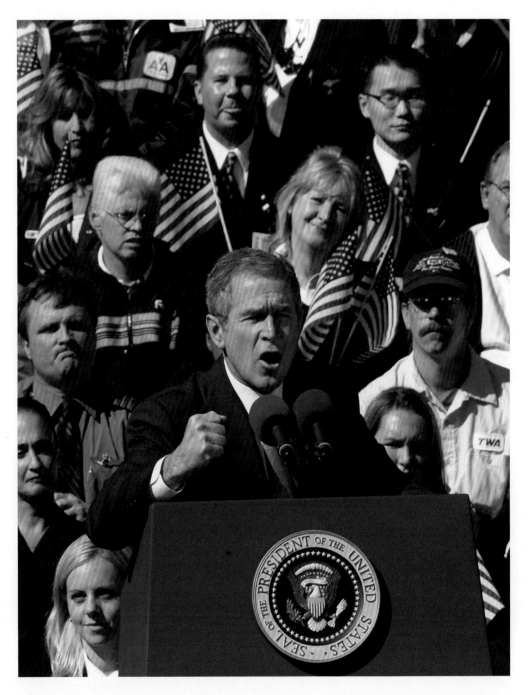

President Bush speaks to airline workers about increased aviation security in September 2001.

The ramifications of the jumbo attacks in New York and Washington on September 11 2001 changed global politics and the position of the United States within it. This speech, given on the night of the attack by US President George W Bush, marked the beginning of America and its allies' 'war on terror' at the start of the new millennium.

George Walker Bush was born in New Haven, Connecticut on 6 July, 1946, the oldest son of George and Barbara Bush. The Bush family grew up in Midland and Houston, Texas, with George W. attending Yale University (his father George H. Bush's alma mater) and earned an MBA from Harvard Business School. When Bush ran for the presidency in 2000 much was made of his wild youth, his national guard service during the Vietnam War and his shift to sobriety after his marriage in 1976. The millions he made from the oil industry and his stake in the Texas Rangers baseball franchise – all while his father was President of the United States – also raised concerns but it didn't stop him from being electable in his own right.

In 1978 Bush tried to follow his father into the House of Representatives but was defeated by his Democratic rival, Kent Hance. In 1994, after his father had been voted out of the White House, George W. was elected governor of Texas and went onto become the first Texas governor to be elected to a second four-year term.

In 2001 George W (nicknamed 'Dubya' by a sceptical press) became the 42nd President of the United States after one of the closest and most controversial elections in American history. Bush defeated former Democratic Vice-President Al Gore by a mere five electoral votes (despite Gore securing 500 000 more primary votes). The outcome was ultimately decided in Florida, where Bush's younger brother Jeb was the governor, but it was a result contested by the Gore camp until mid-December 2000.

In his first year as president, Bush faced the biggest test of any world leader in a generation. On Tuesday, September 11, 2001, two fully-fuelled jumbo jets—American Airlines Flight 11 carrying 92 people and United Airlines Flight 175 carrying 65 people—departed Boston for Los Angeles. Both jets were commandeered by terrorists operating from inside the United States to fly to New York City and were crashed into the twin towers of the World Trade Centre at 8:46 am and 9:02 am respectively. The impact and subsequent fire caused both 110-story towers to collapse, killing 2792 people, including hundreds of New York rescue workers—police, fire and ambulance personnel—as well as people employed in the two towers.

United Airlines Flight 93, departing Newark for San Francisco, and American Airlines Flight 77, which left Dulles (Virginia) for Los Angeles, were also hijacked by two other teams of hijackers. Flight 77, with 64 people on board, was diverted to Washington, D.C., and then crashed into the Pentagon—killing another 125 military personnel inside the building. Flight 93, with 44 people on board, had also been redirected toward Washington—its target unclear—but passengers were alerted by loved ones on cell phones and overpowered the terrorists and crashed the plane into a field in Pennsylvania.

President Bush was visiting a primary school in Sarasota, Florida when he was informed of the attacks. He made a brief statement at 9:15am before leaving Florida and remaining in the air until midday, when he landed in Barksdale Air Force Base in Louisiana. That evening he returned to the White House and addressed the American people.

Good evening.

Today, our fellow citizens, our way of life, our very freedom came under attack in a series of deliberate and deadly terrorist acts. The victims were in airplanes or in their offices: secretaries, business men and women, military and federal workers, moms and dads, friends and neighbors. Thousands of lives were suddenly ended by evil, despicable acts of terror. The pictures of airplanes flying into buildings, fires burning, huge structures collapsing have filled us with disbelief, terrible sadness, and a quiet, unyielding anger. These acts of mass murder were intended to frighten our nation into chaos and retreat. But they have failed. Our country is strong.

A great people has been moved to defend a great nation. Terrorist attacks can shake the foundations of our biggest buildings, but they cannot touch the foundation of America. These acts shatter steel, but they cannot dent the steel of American resolve. America was targeted for attack because we're the brightest beacon for freedom and opportunity in the world. And no one will keep that light from shining. Today, our nation saw evil—the very worst of human nature—and we responded with the best of America. With the daring of our rescue workers, with the caring for strangers and neighbors who came to give blood and help in any way they could.

Immediately following the first attack, I implemented our government's emergency response plans. Our military is powerful, and it's prepared. Our emergency teams are working in New York city and Washington D.C. to help with local rescue efforts. Our first priority is to get help to those who have been injured, and to take every precaution to protect our citizens at home and around the world from further attacks. The functions of our government continue without interruption. Federal agencies in Washington which had to be evacuated today are reopening for essential personnel tonight and will be open for business tomorrow. Our financial institutions remain strong, and the American economy will be open for business as well.

The search is underway for those who were behind these evil acts. I have directed the full resources of our intelligence and law enforcement communities to find those responsible and to bring them to justice. We will make no distinction between the terrorists who committed these acts and those who harbor them.

I appreciate so very much the members of Congress who have joined me in strongly condemning these attacks. And on behalf of the American people, I thank the many world leaders who have called to offer their condolences and assistance. America and our friends and allies join with all those who want peace and security in the world, and we stand together to win the war against terrorism.

Tonight, I ask for your prayers for all those who grieve, for the children whose worlds have been shattered, for all whose sense of safety and security has been threatened. And I pray they will be comforted by a Power greater than any of us, spoken through the ages in Psalm 23:

"Even though I walk through the valley of the shadow of death, I fear no evil for you are with me."

This is a day when all Americans from every walk of life unite in our resolve for justice and peace. America has stood down enemies before, and we will do so this time. None of us will ever forget this day, yet we go forward to defend freedom and all that is good and just in our world.

Thank you. Good night. And God bless America.'

'A great people has been moved to defend a great nation. Terrorist attacks can shake the foundations of our biggest buildings, but they cannot touch the foundation of America.'

History now shows that the United States of America responded to the attack with all its military might. Afghanistan was 'liberated' from Taliban rule in 2002 and Iraq was invaded on a false premise (in search of 'weapons of mass destruction') against the wishes of the United Nations in 2003. The world would never be the same again.

GEORGE W. BUSH

375

Arundhati Roy

'Peace and the New Corporate Liberation Theology'

Sydney Peace Prize, Australia, 3 November 2004.

Arundhati Roy speaks at a Mumbai Resistance rally against the World Trade Organisation in January 2004.

Indian novelist and peace activist Arundhati Roy was born in 1961 to a Hindu father and Christian mother. At the age of 16 she moved to Delhi where she lived a subsistence lifestyle selling empty bottles out of a tin hut. Roy later studied architecture at university and married her first husband, also an architect, before turning to writing. She married her second husband, filmmaker Pradeep Kishen, in 1984 and wrote several screenplays. In 1997 she won the prestigious Booker Prize for her semi-autobiographical novel *The God of Small Things*. A noted peace activist, Roy criticised India's nuclear weapons program, America's invasion of Afghanistan and was convicted (she was sentenced to a single day's 'symbolic' imprisonment and fined) for contempt of court because of her demonstrations against the Narmada Dam Project.

In May 2004, Arundhati Roy was awarded the Sydney Peace Prize. Her acceptance speech delivered the following November—a stinging critique of the Bush administration's decision to invade Iraq without United Nations authority—provides a thoughtful antidote to post-9/11 war rhetoric.

❢ Today, it is not merely justice itself, but the idea of justice that is under attack. The assault on vulnerable, fragile sections of society is at once so complete, so cruel and so clever—all encompassing and yet specifically targeted, blatantly brutal and yet unbelievably insidious—that its sheer audacity has eroded our definition of justice. It has forced us to lower our sights, and curtail our expectations. Even among the well-intentioned, the expansive, magnificent concept of justice is gradually being substituted with the reduced, far more fragile discourse of 'human rights'.

If you think about it, this is an alarming shift of paradigm. The difference is that notions of equality, of parity have been pried loose and eased out of the equation. It's a process of attrition. Almost unconsciously, we begin to think of justice for the rich and human rights for the poor. Justice for the corporate world, human rights for its victims. Justice for Americans, human rights for Afghans and Iraqis. Justice for the Indian upper castes, human rights for Dalits and Adivasis (if that.) Justice for white Australians, human rights for Aboriginals and immigrants (most times, not even that.)

It is becoming more than clear that violating human rights is an inherent and necessary part of the process of implementing a coercive and unjust political and economic structure on the world. Without the violation of human rights on an enormous scale, the neo-liberal project would remain in the dreamy realm of policy. But increasingly Human Rights violations are being portrayed as the unfortunate, almost accidental fallout of an otherwise acceptable political and economic system. As though they're a small problem that can be mopped up with a little extra attention from some NGOs. This is why in areas of heightened conflict—in Kashmir and in Iraq for example—Human Rights Professionals are regarded with a degree of suspicion. Many resistance movements in poor countries which are fighting huge injustice and questioning the underlying principles of what constitutes "liberation" and "development", view Human Rights NGOs as modern day missionaries who've come to take the ugly edge off Imperialism. To defuse political anger and to maintain the status quo.

It has been only a few weeks since a majority of Australians voted to re-elect Prime Minister John Howard who, among other things, led Australia to participate in the illegal invasion and occupation of Iraq. The invasion of Iraq will surely go down in history as one of the most cowardly wars ever fought. It was a war in which a band of rich nations, armed with enough nuclear weapons to destroy the world several times over, rounded on a poor nation, falsely accused it of having nuclear weapons, used the United Nations to force it to disarm, then invaded it, occupied it and are now in the process of selling it.

'It is becoming more than clear that violating human rights is an inherent and necessary part of the process of implementing a coercive and unjust political and economic structure on the world.'

I speak of Iraq, not because everybody is talking about it, (sadly at the cost of leaving other horrors in other places to unfurl in the dark), but because it is a sign of things to come. Iraq marks the beginning of a new cycle. It offers us an opportunity to watch the Corporate-Military cabal that has come to be known as 'Empire' at work. In the new Iraq the gloves are off.

As the battle to control the world's resources intensifies, economic colonialism through formal military aggression is staging a comeback. Iraq is the logical culmination of the process of corporate globalization in which neo-colonialism and neo-liberalism have fused. If we can find it in ourselves to peep behind the curtain of blood, we would glimpse the pitiless transactions taking place backstage. But first, briefly, the stage itself.

In 1991 US President George Bush senior mounted Operation Desert Storm. Tens of thousands of Iraqis were killed in the war. Iraq's fields were bombed with more than 300 tonnes of depleted uranium, causing a fourfold increase in cancer among children. For more than 13 years, twenty four million Iraqi people have lived in a war zone and been denied food and medicine and clean water. In the frenzy around the US elections, let's remember that the levels of cruelty did not fluctuate whether the Democrats or the Republicans were in the White House. Half a million Iraqi children died because of the regime of economic sanctions in the run up to Operation Shock and Awe. Until recently, while there was a careful record of how many US soldiers had lost their lives, we had no idea of how many Iraqis had been killed. US General Tommy Franks said "We don't do body counts" (meaning Iraqi body counts). He could have added "We don't do the Geneva Convention either." A new, detailed study, fast-tracked by *The Lancet* medical journal and extensively peer reviewed, estimates that 100 000 Iraqis have lost their lives since the 2003 invasion. That's one hundred halls full of people—like this one. That's one hundred halls full of friends, parents, siblings, colleagues, lovers…like you. The difference is that there aren't many children here today …let's not forget Iraq's children. Technically that bloodbath is called precision bombing. In ordinary language, it's called butchering.

Most of this is common knowledge now. Those who support the invasion and vote for the invaders cannot take refuge in ignorance. They must truly believe that this epic brutality is right and just or, at the very least, acceptable because it's in their interest.

So the 'civilized' 'modern' world—built painstakingly on a legacy of genocide, slavery and colonialism—now controls most of the world's oil. And most of the world's weapons, most of the world's money, and most of the world's media. The embedded, corporate media in which the doctrine of Free Speech has been substituted by the doctrine of Free If You Agree Speech.

The UN's Chief Weapons Inspector Hans Blix said he found no evidence of nuclear weapons in Iraq. Every scrap of evidence produced by the US and British governments was found to be false—whether it was reports of Saddam Hussein buying uranium from Niger, or the report produced by British Intelligence which was discovered to have been plagiarized from an old student dissertation. And yet, in the prelude to the war, day after day the most 'respectable' newspapers and TV channels in the U.S., headlined the 'evidence' of Iraq's arsenal of weapons of nuclear weapons. It now turns out that the source of the manufactured 'evidence' of Iraq's arsenal of nuclear weapons was Ahmed Chalabi who, (like General Suharto of Indonesia, General Pinochet of Chile, the Shah of Iran, the Taliban and of course, Saddam Hussein himself)—was bankrolled with millions of dollars from the good old CIA.

And so, a country was bombed into oblivion. It's true there have been some murmurs of apology. Sorry 'bout that folks, but we have really have to move on. Fresh rumours are coming in about nuclear weapons in Iran and Syria. And guess who is reporting on these fresh rumours? The same reporters who ran the bogus 'scoops' on Iraq. The seriously embedded A Team.

The head of Britain's BBC had to step down and one man committed suicide because a BBC reporter accused the Blair administration of 'sexing up' intelligence reports about Iraq's WMD programme. But the head of Britain retains his job even though his government did much more than 'sex up' intelligence reports. It is responsible for the illegal invasion of a country and the mass murder of its people.

Visitors to Australia like myself, are expected to answer the following question when they fill in the visa form: Have you ever committed or been involved in the commission of war crimes or crimes against humanity or human rights? Would George Bush and Tony Blair get visas to Australia? Under the tenets of International Law they must surely qualify as war criminals.

However, to imagine that the world would change if they were removed from office is naive. The tragedy is that their political rivals have no real dispute with their policies. The fire and brimstone of the US election campaign was about who would make a better 'Commander-in-Chief' and a more effective manager of the American Empire. Democracy no longer offers voters real choice. Only specious choice.

Even though no weapons of mass destruction have been found in Iraq—stunning new evidence has revealed that Saddam Hussein was planning a weapons programme. (Like I was planning to win an Olympic Gold in synchronized swimming.) Thank goodness for the doctrine of pre-emptive strike. God knows what other evil thoughts he harbored—sending Tampax in the mail to American senators, or releasing female rabbits in burqas into the London underground. No doubt all will be revealed in the free and fair trial of Saddam Hussein ....that's coming up soon in the New Iraq.

All except the chapter in which we would learn of how the U.S. and Britain plied him with money and material assistance at the time he was carrying out murderous attacks on Iraqi Kurds and Shias. All except the chapter in which we would learn that a 12,000 page report submitted by the Saddam Hussein government to the UN, was censored by the United States because it lists twenty-four US corporations that participated in Iraq's pre-Gulf War nuclear and conventional weapons programme. (They include Bechtel, DuPont, Eastman Kodak, Hewlett Packard, International Computer Systems and Unisys.)

So Iraq has been 'liberated.' Its people have been subjugated and its markets have been 'freed'. That's the anthem of neo-liberalism. Free the markets. Screw the people.

The US government has privatized and sold entire sectors of Iraq's economy. Economic policies and tax laws have been re-written. Foreign companies can now buy 100% of Iraqi firms and expatriate the profits. This is an outright violation of international laws that govern an occupying force, and is among the main reasons for the stealthy, hurried charade in which power was 'handed over' to an 'interim Iraqi government'. Once handing over of Iraq to the Multi-nationals is complete, a mild dose of genuine democracy won't do any harm. In fact it might be good PR for the Corporate version of Liberation Theology, otherwise known as New Democracy…

In New Iraq, privatization has broken new ground. The US Army is increasingly recruiting private mercenaries to help in the occupation. The advantage with mercenaries is that when they're killed they're not included in the US soldiers' body count. It helps to manage public opinion, which is particularly important in an election year. Prisons have been privatized. Torture has been privatized. We have seen what that leads to. Other attractions in New Iraq include newspapers being shut down. Television stations bombed. Reporters killed. US soldiers have opened fire on crowds of unarmed protestors killing scores of people. The only kind of resistance that has managed to survive is as crazed and brutal as the occupation itself. Is there space for a secular, democratic, feminist, non-violent resistance in Iraq? There isn't really.

That is why it falls to those of us living outside Iraq to create that mass-based, secular and non-violent resistance to the US occupation. If we fail to do that, then we run the risk of allowing the idea of resistance to be hijacked and conflated with terrorism and that will be a pity because they are not the same thing.

So what does peace mean in this savage, corporatized, militarized world? What does it mean in a world where an entrenched system of appropriation has created a situation in which poor countries which have been plundered by colonizing regimes for centuries are steeped in debt to the very same countries that plundered them, and have to repay that debt at the rate of 382 billion dollars a year? What does peace mean in a world in which the combined wealth of the world's 587 billionaires exceeds the combined gross domestic product of the world's 135 poorest countries? Or when rich countries that pay farm subsidies of a billion dollars a day, try and force poor countries to drop their subsidies? What does peace mean to people in occupied Iraq, Palestine, Kashmir, Tibet and Chechnya? Or to the Aboriginal people of Australia? Or the Ogoni of Nigeria? Or the Kurds in Turkey? Or the Dalits and Adivasis of India? What does peace mean to non-Muslims in Islamic countries, or to women in Iran, Saudi Arabia and Afghanistan? What does it mean to the millions who are being uprooted from their lands by dams and development projects? What does peace mean to the poor who are being actively robbed of their resources and for whom everyday life is a grim battle for water, shelter, survival and, above all, some semblance of dignity? For them, peace is war.

> 'So the 'civilized' 'modern' world—built painstakingly on a legacy of genocide, slavery and colonialism—now controls most of the world's oil. And most of the world's weapons, most of the world's money, and most of the world's media.'

We know very well who benefits from war in the age of Empire. But we must also ask ourselves honestly who benefits from peace in the age of Empire? War mongering is criminal. But talking of peace without talking of justice could easily become advocacy for a kind of capitulation. And talking of justice without unmasking the institutions and the systems that perpetrate injustice, is beyond hypocritical.

It's easy to blame the poor for being poor. It's easy to believe that the world is being caught up in an escalating spiral of terrorism and war. That's what allows the American President to say "You're either with us or with the terrorists." But we know that that's a spurious choice. We know that terrorism is only the privatization of war. That terrorists are the free marketers of war. They believe that the legitimate use of violence is not the sole prerogative of the State.

It is mendacious to make moral distinction between the unspeakable brutality of terrorism and the indiscriminate carnage of war and occupation. Both kinds of violence are unacceptable. We cannot support one and condemn the other.

The real tragedy is that most people in the world are trapped between the horror of a putative peace and the terror of war. Those are the two sheer cliffs we're hemmed in by. The question is: How do we climb out of this crevasse?

For those who are materially well-off, but morally uncomfortable, the first question you must ask yourself is do you really want to climb out of it? How far are you prepared to go? Has the crevasse become too comfortable?

If you really want to climb out, there's good news and bad news.

The good news is that the advance party began the climb some time ago. They're already halfway up. Thousands of activists across the world have been hard at work preparing footholds and securing the ropes to make it easier for the rest of us. There isn't only one path up. There are hundreds of ways of doing it. There are hundreds of battles being fought around the world that need your skills, your minds, your resources. No battle is irrelevant. No victory is too small.

ARUNDHATI ROY

The bad news is that colorful demonstrations, weekend marches and annual trips to the World Social Forum are not enough. There have to be targeted acts of real civil disobedience with real consequences. Maybe we can't flip a switch and conjure up a revolution. But there are several things we could do. For example, you could make a list of those corporations who have profited from the invasion of Iraq and have offices here in Australia. You could name them, boycott them, occupy their offices and force them out of business. If it can happen in Bolivia, it can happen in India. It can happen in Australia. Why not?

> 'The bad news is that colorful demonstrations, weekend marches and annual trips to the World Social Forum are not enough. There have to be targeted acts of real civil disobedience with real consequences.'

That's only a small suggestion. But remember that if the struggle were to resort to violence, it will lose vision, beauty and imagination. Most dangerous of all, it will marginalize and eventually victimize women. And a political struggle that does not have women at the heart of it, above it, below it and within it is no struggle at all.

The point is that the battle must be joined. As the wonderful American historian Howard Zinn put it: "You can't be neutral on a moving train".'

Sources

Print

Andrews, James and David Zarefsky, (1989), *American Voices*, Longman, White Plains, NY.

Berkman, Alexander, *Anarchism on Trial: Speeches of Alexander Berkman and Emma Goldman Before the United States District Court in the City of New York*, July, 1917,' New York, Mother Earth Publishing Association.

Ferrell, Robert H. 1980, *Off the Record: The Private Papers of Harry S. Truman*, New York, Harper and Row.

Graham, John, 1970, *Great American Speeches*, 1898-1963, Text Studies, New York: Meredith Corporation.

Lenin, VI, *Collected Works*, Volume 28.

'Live Aid' CD (2004) Warner Vision Australia.

MacArthur, Brian, *The Penguin Book of Twentieth Century Speeches* (1999), Penguin, London.

McPherson, James M. ed. (2000), *To the Best of My Ability: The American Presidents*, Dorling Kindersley, New York

'Public Papers of the Presidents of the United States', Washington, D. C. Government Printing Office, various.

Stalin, J, 'From the Pamphlet Collection', J. Stalin, *Speeches Delivered at Meetings of Voters of the Stalin Electoral District*, Foreign Languages Publishing House, Moscow, 1950.

Tojo, *Washington Post*, 30 November, 1941.

Electronic

www.amercianrhetoric.com.

www.anc.org.za

Fidel Castro, by Robert E. Quirk (1993) www.fiu.edu

Castro Speech Data Base (www.lanic.utexas)

Chase Smith, US Senate Website, www.senate.gov.

Chamberlain, www.lib.byu.edu, www.mtholyoke.edu, www.historyplace.com.

Churchill, W, www.raf.mod.uk, www.espeeches.com.

Darrow, Clarence, www.federalobserver.com

Edward VIII, www.thamesweb.co.uk.

Einstein and Russell, www.ppu.org.uk, www.velapanthi.com, www.ppu.org.uk

www.ex.ac.uk

 www.elf.net/bjordan

www.ford.utexas.edu

Ghandi, www.mkgandhi.org.

Gehrig, Lou, www.nationalpastime.com and www.baseballhalloffame.org.

www.theremnant.com

www.historyplace.com

Adolf Hitler: An Apolitical Historical Website (www.adolfhitler.ws/lib/speeches)

www.ibiblio.org

www.international.activism.uts.edu.au

Krushchev, www.sovietrevolution.net

www.librarylink.org.ph

Lindbergh, Charles, www.charleslindbergh.com

An Early Spring: Mao Tse-tung, the Chinese Intellectuals and the Hundreds Flowers Campaign by John M. Jackson (2004) www.filebox.vt.edu

McArthur, www.hundredpercenter.com

McCarthy, Joe, www.mnstate.edu

McMillan, www.africanhistory.about.com, www.africanhistory.about.com

Golda Meir, www.localvoter.com/speech.

Nixon, www.nixonfoundation.org

Pearse, Padriac, www.easter1916.net/oration.htm.

Patton, www.famousquotes.me.uk, worldatwar.net, www.pattonhq.com.

www.pbs.org

www.rainbowpush.org

www.reaganfoundation.org

Australian Federal Parliament, opening, www.chr.org.au, www.peo.gov.au/resources/federation.htm.

Roosevelt, www.historyplace.com.

Ryan White, www.ryanwhite.com

www.spacerace.com

www.spaceguy.com

Terrell, Mary Church, www.gos.sbc.edu.

www.thinkingpeace.com

www.tungate.com

www.usconstitution.com

Von Galen, www.geocities.com, www.oldion.com.

Whitlam, www.pandora.nla.gov.au, transcript of ATN Channel 7 news report, 11 November 1975.

Wilson, Woodrow, www.historyplace.com/speeches.

www.worldhistory.com

Women's Library: Women's Internet Information Network (www.undelete.org/library).

First published in Australia in 2005 by
New Holland Publishers (Australia) Pty Ltd
Sydney • Auckland • London • Cape Town

14 Aquatic Drive Frenchs Forest NSW 2086 Australia
218 Lake Road Northcote Auckland New Zealand
86 Edgware Road London W2 2EA United Kingdom
80 McKenzie Street Cape Town 8001 South Africa

National Library of Australia Cataloguing-in-Publication Data:

Whiticker, Alan.
Speeches that shaped the modern world.

Bibliography.
ISBN 1 74110 309 6.

1. Speeches, addresses, etc. I. Title.

808.85

Publisher: Fiona Schultz
Project Editor: Lliane Clarke
Designer: Karl Roper
Production Manager: Linda Bottari
Printer: SNP/Leefung

10 9 8 7 6 5 4 3 2 1